Nikolay Gavrilovich Chernyshevsky

What's To Be Done?

A Romance

Nikolay Gavrilovich Chernyshevsky

What's To Be Done?
A Romance

ISBN/EAN: 9783337007287

Printed in Europe, USA, Canada, Australia, Japan

Cover: Foto ©Thomas Meinert / pixelio.de

More available books at **www.hansebooks.com**

BY
N. G. TCHERNYCHEWSKY.

TRANSLATED BY
BENJ. R. TUCKER.

BOSTON:
BENJ. R. TUCKER, PUBLISHER.
1886.

TRANSLATOR'S PREFACE.

This romance, the last work and only novel from Tchernychewsky's pen, originally appeared in 1863 in a St. Petersburg magazine, the author writing it at that time in a St. Petersburg dungeon, where he was confined for twenty-two months prior to being sent into exile in Siberia by the cruel Czar who has since paid the penalty of this crime and many others. This martyr-hero of the modern Revolution still languishes in a remote corner of that cheerless country, his health ruined and — if report be true — his mind shattered by his long solitude and enforced abstention from literary and revolutionary work. The present Czar, true son of his father, persistently refuses to mitigate his sentence, despite the petition for Tchernychewsky's freedom sent not long ago to Alexander III. by the literary celebrities of the world gathered in international congress at Vienna.

The Russian Nihilists regard the present work as a faithful portraiture of themselves and their movement, and as such they contrast it with the celebrated "Fathers and Sons" of Tourguéneff, which they consider rather as a caricature. The fundamental idea of Tchernychewsky's work is that woman is a human being and not an animal created for man's benefit, and its chief purpose is to show the superiority of free unions between men and women over the indissoluble marriage sanctioned by Church and State. It may almost be considered a continuation of the great Herzen's novel, "Who Is To Blame?" written fifteen years before on the same subject. If the reader should find the work singular in form and sometimes obscure, he must remember that it was written under the eye of an autocrat, who punished with terrific severity any one who wrote against "the doctrines of the Orthodox Church, its traditions and ceremonies, or the truths and dogmas of Christian faith in general," against "the inviolability of the Supreme Autocratic Power or the respect due to the Imperial Family," anything contrary to "the fundamental regulations of the State," or anything tending to "shock good morals and propriety."

As a work of art "What's To Be Done?" speaks for itself. Nevertheless, the words of a European writer regarding it may not be amiss. "In the author's view the object of art is not to embellish and idealize nature, but to reproduce her interesting phases; and poetry — verse, the drama, the novel — should explain nature in reproducing her; the poet must pronounce sentence. He must represent human beings as they really are, and not incarnate in them an abstract principle, good or bad; that is why in this romance men indisputably good have faults, as reality shows them to us, while bad people possess at the same time some good qualities, as is almost always the case in real life."

Tyranny knows no better use for such an author than to exile him. But Liberty can still utilize his work. Tyranny, torture Truth's heralds as it may, cannot kill Truth itself, — nay, can only add to its vitality. Tchernychewsky is in isolation, but his glad tidings to the poor and the oppressed are spreading among the peoples of the earth, and now in this translation for the first time find their way across the ocean to enlighten our New World.

B. R. T.

WHAT'S TO BE DONE?

An Imbecile.

On the morning of the eleventh of July, 1856, the *attachés* of one of the principal hotels in St. Petersburg, situated near the Moscow railway station, became greatly perplexed and even somewhat alarmed. The night before, after eight o'clock, a traveller had arrived, carrying a valise, who, after having given up his passport that it might be taken to the police to be viséed, had ordered a cutlet and some tea, and then, pleading fatigue and need of sleep as a pretext, had asked that he might be disturbed no further, notifying them at the same time to awaken him without fail at exactly eight o'clock in the morning, as he had pressing business.

As soon as he was alone, he had locked his door. For a while was heard the noise of the knife, fork, and tea-service; then all became silent again: the man doubtless had gone to sleep.

In the morning, at eight o'clock, the waiter did not fail to knock at the newcomer's door.

But the new-comer did not respond. The waiter knocked louder, and louder yet. Still the new-comer did not respond: he probably was very tired. The waiter waited a quarter of an hour, then began again to knock and call, but with no better success. Then he went to consult the other waiters and the butler.

"May not something have happened to the traveller?"

"We must burst open the door," he concluded.

"No," said another, "the door can be burst open only in presence of the police."

They decided to try once more, and with greater energy, to awaken the obstinate traveller, and, in case they should not succeed, to send for the police.

Which they had to do. While waiting for the police, they looked at each other anxiously, saying: "What can have happened?"

Towards ten o'clock the commissioner of police arrived; he began by knocking at the door himself, and then ordered the waiters to knock a last time. The same success.

"There is nothing left but to burst open the door," said the official; "do so, my friends."

The door yielded; they entered; the room was empty.

"Look under the bed," said the official. At the same time, approaching the table, he saw a sheet of paper, unfolded, upon which were written these words:

"I leave at eleven o'clock in the evening and shall not return. I shall be heard on the Liteing Bridge between two and three o'clock in the morning. Suspect no one."

"Ah! the thing is clear now! at first we did not understand," said the official.

"What do you mean, Ivan Afanacievitch?" asked the butler.

"Give me some tea, and I will tell you."

The story of the commissioner of police was for a long time the subject of conversations and discussions; as for the adventure itself, this was it: At half-past two in the morning, the night being extremely dark, something like a flash was seen on the Liteing Bridge, and at the same time a pistol shot was heard. The guardians of the bridge and the few people who were passing ran to the spot, but found nobody.

"It is not a murder; some one has blown his brains out," they said; and some of the more generous offered to search the river. Hooks were brought and even a fisherman's net; but they pulled from the water only a few pieces of wood. Of the body no trace, and besides the night was very dark, and much time had elapsed: the body had had time to drift out to sea.

"Go search yonder!" said a group of carpers, who maintained that there was no body and that some drunkard or practical joker had simply fired a shot and fled; "perhaps he has even mingled with the crowd, now so anxious, and is laughing at the alarm which he has caused." These carpers were evidently *progressives*. But the majority, *conservative*, as it always is when it reasons prudently, held to the first explanation.

"A practical joker? Go to! Some one has really blown his brains out."

Being less numerous, the progressives were conquered. But the conquerors split at the very moment of victory.

He had blown his brains out, certainly, but why?

"He was drunk," said some.

"He had dissipated his fortune," thought others.

"Simply an imbecile!" observed somebody.

Upon this word *imbecile*, all agreed, even those who disputed suicide.

In short, whether it was a drunkard or a spendthrift who had blown his brains out or a practical joker who had made a pretence of killing himself (in the latter case the joke was a stupid one), he was an imbecile.

There ended the night's adventure. At the hotel was found the proof that it was no piece of nonsense, but a real suicide.

This conclusion satisfied the conservatives especially; for, said they, it proves that we are right. If it had been only a practical joker, we might have hesitated between the terms imbecile and insolent. But to blow one's brains out on a bridge! On a bridge, I ask you? Does one blow his brains out on a bridge? Why on a bridge? It would be stupid to do it on a bridge. Indisputably, then, he was an imbecile.

"Precisely," objected the progressives; "does one blow his brains out on a bridge?" And they in their turn disputed the reality of the suicide.

But that same evening the hotel *attachés*, being summoned to the police bureau to examine a cap pierced by a ball, which had been taken from the water, identified it as the actual cap worn by the traveller of the night before.

There had been a suicide, then, and the spirit of negation and progress was once more conquered.

Yes, it was really an imbecile; but suddenly a new thought struck them: to blow one's brains out on a bridge, — why, it is most adroit! In that way one avoids long suffering in case of a simple wound. *He* calculated wisely; he was prudent.

Now the mystification was complete. Imbecile and prudent!

First Consequence of the Imbecile Act.

The same day, towards eleven o'clock in the morning, in a little country-house on the island of Kamennoy,* a young woman sat sewing and humming a singularly bold French song:

>Sous nos guenilles, nous sommes
>>De courageux travailleurs;
>>Nous voulons pour tous les hommes
>>Science et destins meilleurs.
>>Etudions, travaillons,
>>La force est à qui saura;
>>Etudions, travaillons,
>>L'abondance nous viendra!
>>Ah! ça ira! ça ira! ça ira!
>>Le peuple en ce jour répète:
>>Ah! ça ira! ça ira! ça ira!
>>Qui vivra verra!
>
>Et qui de notre ignorance
>>Souffre donc? N'est-ce pas nous?
>>Qu'elle vienne, la science
>>Qui nous affranchira tous!
>>Nous plions sous la douleur;
>>Mais, par la fraternité.
>>Nous hâterons le bonheur
>>De toute l'humanité.
>>Ah! ça ira! &c.
>
>Faisons l'union féconde
>>Du travail et du savoir;
>>Pour être heureux, en ce monde,
>>S'entr'aimer est un devoir.
>>Instruisons-nous, aimons-nous,
>>Nous sommes frères et sœurs;
>>Travaillons chacun pour tous;
>>Devenons toujours meilleurs.
>>Ah! ça ira! &c.

---

* An island in the vicinity of St. Petersburg, full of country houses, where citizens of St. Petersburg go to spend their summers.

> Oui, pour vaincre la misère,
> Instruisons-nous, travaillons ;
> Un paradis de la terre,
> En nous aimant, nous ferons.
> Travaillons, aimons, chantons,
> Tous les vrais biens nous aurons ;
> Un jour vient où nous serons
> Tous heureux, instruits, et bons.
> Ah! ça ira! ça ira! ça ira!
> Le peuple en ce jour répète :
> Ah! ça ira! ça ira! ça ira!
> Qui vivra verra!
> Donc vivons!
> Ça bien vite ira!
> Ça viendra!
> Nous tous le verrons!

The melody of this audacious song was gay; there were two or three sad notes in it, but they were concealed beneath the general character of the motive; they entirely disappeared in the refrain and in the last complet. But such was the condition of the mind of the songstress that these two or three sad notes sounded above the others in her song. She saw this herself, started, and tried to sustain the gay notes longer and glide over the others. Vain efforts! her thought dominated her in spite of herself, and the sad notes always prevailed over the others.

It was easy to see that the young woman was trying to repress the sadness which had taken possession of her, and when, from time to time, she succeeded and the song then took its joyous pace, her work doubled in rapidity; she seemed, moreover, to be an excellent seamstress. At this moment the maid, a young and pretty person, entered.

"See, Macha,"* the young lady said to her, "how well I sew! I have almost finished the ruffles which I am embroidering to wear at your wedding."

"Oh! there is less work in them than in those which you desired me to embroider."

"I readily believe it! Should not the bride be more beautifully adorned than her guests?"

"I have brought you a letter, Véra Pavlovna."

Véra Pavlovna took the letter with an air of perplexity which depicted itself in her face. The envelope bore the city stamp.

"He is then at Moscow!" she whispered, and she hastily broke open the letter and turned pale.

---

* Macha is the diminutive of Maria.

"It is not possible!...... I did not read it right....... The letter does not say that!" she cried, letting her arms fall by her sides.

Again she began to read. This time her eyes fixed themselves on the fatal paper, and those beautiful clear eyes became dimmer and dimmer. She let the letter fall upon her work-table, and, hiding her head in her hands, she burst into sobs.

"What have I done? What have I done?" she cried, despairingly. "What have I done?"

"Vérotchka!" * suddenly exclaimed a young man, hurrying into the room; "Vérotchka! What has happened to you? And why these tears?"

"Read!"... She handed him the letter. Véra Pavlovna sobbed no longer, but remained motionless as if nailed to her seat, and scarcely breathing.

The young man took the letter; he grew pale, his hands trembled, and his eyes remained fixed for a long time upon the text, though it was brief. This letter was thus framed:

"I disturbed your tranquillity: I quit the scene. Do not pity me. I love you both so much that I am quite content in my resolution. Adieu."

Absorbed for a moment in his sadness, the young man then approached the young woman, who still was motionless and in a seeming lethargy, and, taking her hand:

"Vérotchka!"...

But the young woman uttered a cry of terror, and, rising, as if moved by an electric force, she convulsively repulsed the young man, separating herself from him.

"Back! Do not touch me! You are covered with blood! Leave me!"

She continued to recoil, making gestures of terror and waving her arms in space as if to repel an object of fear. Suddenly she staggered and sank into an arm-chair, her head in her hands.

"It is also on me, his blood! on me especially! You are not guilty.... it is I, I alone! What have I done? What have I done?"

And her sobs redoubled.

"Vérotchka," said the young man, timidly; "Vérotchka, my beloved!"

"No, leave me," she answered, with a trembling voice, as soon as she could get breath. "Do not speak to me! In a moment you will find me calmer; leave me."

He went into his study, and sat down again at the writing-table where a quarter of an hour before he had been so calm and happy. He took up his pen, and, after the article which he had begun, he permitted himself to write: "It is in such moments that one must retain self-possession. I have will, and it will all pass over, it will all pass over. But will she bear it? Oh! it is horrible! Happiness is lost!"

---

* Vérotchka is the diminutive of **Véra**.

"Shall we talk together now, beloved?" said an altered voice, which tried to appear firm.

"We must separate," continued Véra Pavlovna, "we must separate! I have decided upon it. It is frightful; but it would be more frightful still to continue to live in each other's sight. Am I not his murderer? Have I not killed him for you?"

"But, Vérotchka, it is not your fault."

"Do not try to justify me, unless you wish me to hate you. I am guilty. Pardon me, my beloved, for taking a resolution so painful to you. To me also it is painful, but is the only one that we can take. You will soon recognize it yourself. So be it, then! I wish first to fly from this city, which would remind me too vividly of the past. The sale of my effects will afford me some resources. I will go to Tver, to Nijni,* I know not where, and it matters little. I will seek a chance to give singing-lessons; being in a great city, I shall probably find one; or else I will become a governess. I can always earn what is necessary. But in case I should be unable to get enough, I will appeal to you. I count then on you; and let that prove to you that you are ever dear to me. And now we must say farewell . . . . farewell forever! Go away directly; I shall be better alone; and tomorrow you can come back, for I shall be here no longer. I go to Moscow; there I will find out what city is best adapted to my purpose. I forbid your presence at the depot at the time of my departure. Farewell, then, my beloved; give me your hand that I may press it a last time before we separate forever."

He desired to embrace her; but she thrust him back forcibly, saying:

"No! that would be an outrage upon him. Give me your hand; do you feel with what force I press it? But adieu!"

He kept her hand in his till she withdrew it, he not daring to resist.

"Enough! Go! Adieu!"

And after having encircled him with a look of ineffable tenderness, she retired with a firm step and without turning back her head.

He went about, dazed, like a drunken man, unable to find his hat, though he held it in his hand without knowing it; at last, however, he took his overcoat from the hall and started off. But he had not yet reached the gateway when he heard footsteps behind him. Doubtless it was Macha. Had *she* vanished? He turned around; it was—— Véra Pavlovna, who threw herself into his arms and said, embracing him with ardor:

"I could not resist, dear friend; and now farewell forever!"

She ran rapidly away, threw herself upon her bed, and burst into tears.

* Nijni Novgorod.

PREFACE.

Love is the subject of this novel; a young woman is its principal character.

"So far good, even though the novel should be bad," says the feminine reader; and she is right.

But the masculine reader does not praise so readily, thought in man being more intense and more developed than in woman. He says (what probably the feminine reader also thinks without considering it proper to say so, which excuses me from discussing the point with her),— the masculine reader says: "I know perfectly well that the man who is said to have blown his brains out is all right."

I attack him on this phrase *I know*, and say to him: "You *do not know it*, since it has not been told you. You know nothing, not even that by the way in which I have begun my novel I have made you my dupe. For have you not failed to perceive it?"

Know, then, that my first pages prove that I have a very poor opinion of the public. I have employed the ordinary trick of romancers. I have begun with dramatic scenes, taken from the middle or the end of my story, and have taken care to confuse and obscure them.

Public, you are good-natured, very good-natured, and consequently you are neither quick to see nor difficult to please. One may be sure that you will not see from the first pages whether a novel is worthy of being read. Your scent is not keen, and to aid you in deciding two things are necessary: the name of the author and such a style of writing as will produce an effect.

This is the first novel that I offer you, and you have not yet made up your mind whether or not I have talent and art (and yet this talent and art you grant liberally to so many authors!) My name does not yet attract you. I am obliged, therefore, to decoy you. Do not consider it a crime; for it is your own ingenuousness that compels me to stoop to this triviality. But now that I hold you in my hands, I can continue my story as I think proper,— that is, without subterfuge. There will be no more mystery; you will be able to foresee twenty pages in advance the climax of each situation, and I will even tell you that all will end gaily amid wine and song.

I do not desire to aid in spoiling you, kind public, you whose head is already so full of nonsense. How much useless trouble the confusion of your perceptions causes you! Truly, you are painful to look at; and yet I cannot help deriding you, the prejudices with which your head is crammed render you so base and wicked!

I am even angry with you, because you are so wicked towards men, of whom you nevertheless are a part. Why are you so wicked towards yourself? It is for your own good that I preach to you; for I desire to be useful to you, and am seeking the way. In the meantime you cry out:

"Who, then, is this insolent author, who addresses me in such a tone?"

Who am I? An author without talent who has not even a complete command of his own language. But it matters little. Read at any rate, kind public; truth is a good thing which compensates even for an author's faults. This reading will be useful to you, and you will experience no deception, since I have warned you that you will find in my romance neither talent nor art, only the truth.

For the rest, my kind public, however you may love to read between the lines, I prefer to tell you all. Because I have confessed that I have no shadow of talent and that my romance will lack in the telling, do not conclude that I am inferior to the story-tellers whom you accept and that this book is beneath their writings. That is not the purpose of my explanation. I merely mean that my story is very weak, so far as execution is concerned, in comparison with the works produced by real talent. But, as for the celebrated works of your favorite authors, you may, even in point of execution, put it on their level; you may even place it above them; for there is more art here than in the works aforesaid, you may be sure. And now, public, thank me! And since you love so well to bend the knee before him who disdains you, salute me!

Happily, scattered through your throngs, there exist, O public, persons, more and more numerous, whom I esteem. If I have just been impudent, it was because I spoke only to the vast majority of you. Before the persons to whom I have just referred, on the contrary, I shall be modest and even timid. Only, with them, long explanations are useless; I know in advance that we shall get along together. Men of research and justice, intelligence and goodness, it is but yesterday that you arose among us; and already your number is great and ever greater. If you were the whole public, I should not need to write; if you did not exist, I could not write. But you are a part of the public, without yet being the whole public; and that is why it is possible, that is why it is necessary, for me to write.

CHAPTER FIRST.

The Life of Véra Pavlovna with her Parents.

I.

The education of Véra Pavlovna was very ordinary, and there was nothing peculiar in her life until she made the acquaintance of Lopoukhoff, the medical student.

Véra Pavlovna grew up in a fine house, situated on the Rue Gorokhovaïa, between the Rue Sadovaïa and the Sémenovsky Bridge. This house is now duly labelled with a number, but in 1852, when numbers were not in use to designate the houses of any given street, it bore this inscription : —

House of Ivan Zakharovitch Storechnikoff, present Councillor of State.

So said the inscription, although Ivan Zakharovitch Storechnikoff died in 1837. After that, according to the legal title-deeds, the owner of the house was his son, Mikhaïl Ivanytch. But the tenants knew that Mikhaïl Ivanytch was only the son of the mistress, and that the mistress of the house was Anna Petrovna.

The house was what it still is, large, with two carriage-ways, four flights of steps from the street, and three interior court-yards.

Then (as is still the case today) the mistress of the house and her son lived on the first and naturally the principal floor. Anna Petrovna has remained a beautiful lady, and Mikhaïl Ivanytch is to-day, as he was in 1852, an elegant and handsome officer. Who lives now in the dirtiest of the innumerable flats of the first court, fifth door on the right? I do not know. But in 1852 it was inhabited by the steward of the house, Pavel Konstantinytch Rosalsky, a robust and fine-looking man. His wife, Maria Alexevna, a slender person, tall and possessed of a strong constitution, his young and beautiful daughter (Véra Pavlovna), and his son Fédia, nine years old, made up the family.

Besides his position of steward, Pavel Konstantinytch was employed as chief deputy in I know not which ministerial bureau. As an employee he had no perquisites; his perquisites as steward were very moderate; for Pavel Konstantinytch, as he said to himself, had a conscience, which he valued at least as highly as the benevolence of the proprietor. In short, the worthy steward had amassed in fourteen years about ten thousand roubles, of which but three thousand had come from the proprietor's pocket. The rest was derived from a little business peculiarly his own: Pavel Konstantinytch combined with his other functions that of a pawn-broker. Maria Alexevna also had her little capital: almost five thousand roubles, she told the gossips, but really much more. She had begun fifteen years before by the sale of a fur-lined pelisse, a poor lot of furniture, and an old coat left her by her brother, a deceased government employee.

These brought her one hundred and fifty roubles, which she lost no time in lending on security. Much bolder than her husband, she braved risks for the sake of greater gains. More than once she had been caught. One day a sharper pawned to her for five roubles a stolen passport, and Maria Alexevna not only lost the five roubles, but had to pay fifteen to get out of the scrape. Another time a swindler, in consideration of a loan of twenty roubles, left with her a gold watch, the proceeds of a murder followed by robbery, and Maria Alexevna had to pay heavily this time to get clear. But if she suffered losses which her more prudent husband had no occasion to fear, on the other hand she saw her profits rolling up more rapidly.

To make money she would stop at nothing.

One day — Véra Pavlovna was still small and her mother did not mistrust her ears — a somewhat strange event occurred. Vérotchka, indeed, would not have understood it, had not the cook, beaten by Maria Alexevna, been eager to explain to the little girl, in a very intelligible fashion, the matter in question.

Matroena was often beaten for indulging the passion of love, — notwithstanding which she always had a black eye given her really by her lover.

Maria Alexevna passed over this black eye because cooks of that character work for less money. Having said this, we come to the story.

A lady as beautiful as she was richly dressed stopped for some time at the house of Maria Alexevna.

This lady received the visits of a very fine-looking gentleman, who often gave bonbons to Vérotchka and even made her a present of two illustrated books. The engravings in one of these books represented animals and cities; as for the other, Maria Alexevna took it away from her daughter as soon as the visitor had gone, and the only time when Vérotchka saw the engravings was on that same day when he showed them to her.

While the lady remained, an unusual tranquillity prevailed in the apartments of the pawn-brokers; Maria Alexevna neglected the closet (of which she always carried the key) in which the decanter of brandy was kept; she whipped neither Matroena nor Vérotchka, and even ceased her continual vociferations. But one night the little girl was awakened and frightened by the cries of the tenant and by a great stir and uproar going on in the house. In the morning, nevertheless, Maria Alexevna, in better humor than ever, opened the famous closet and said between two draughts of brandy:

"Thank God! all has gone well." Then she called Matroena, and instead of abusing or beating her, as was generally the case when she had been drinking, she offered her a glass of brandy, saying:

"Go on! Drink! You too worked well."

After which she went to embrace her daughter and lie down. As for the tenant, she cried no more, did not even leave her room, and was not slow in taking her departure.

Two days after she had gone a captain of police, accompanied by two of his officers, came and roundly abused Maria Alexevna, who, it must be allowed, took no pains on her part, as the phrase goes, to keep her tongue in her pocket. Over and over again she repeated:

"I do not know what you mean. If you wish to find out, you will see by the books of the establishment that the woman who was here is named Savastianoff, one of my acquaintances, engaged in business at Pskow. And that is all."

After having redoubled his abuse, the captain of police finally went away.

That is what Vérotchka saw at the age of eight.

At the age of nine she received an explanation of the affair from Matroena. For the rest, there had been but one case of the kind in the house. Sometimes other adventures of a different sort, but not very numerous.

One day, as Vérotchka, then a girl of ten years, was accompanying her mother as usual to the old clothes shop, at the corner of the Rue Gorokhovaïa and the Rue Sadovaïa she was struck a blow on the neck, dealt her doubtless to make her heed this observation of her mother:

"Instead of sauntering, why do you not cross yourself as you go by the church? Do you not see that all respectable people do so?"

At twelve Vérotchka was sent to boarding-school, and received in addition lessons in piano-playing from a teacher who, though a great drunkard, was a worthy man and an excellent pianist, but, on account of his drunkenness, had to content himself with a very moderate reward for his services.

At fourteen Vérotchka did the sewing for the whole family, which, to be sure, was not a large one.

When she was fifteen, such remarks as this were daily addressed to her:

"Go wash your face cleaner! It is as black as a gypsy's. But you will wash it in vain; you have the face of a scarecrow; you are like nobody else."

The little girl, much mortified at her dark complexion, gradually came to consider herself very homely.

Nevertheless, her mother, who formerly covered her with nothing but rags, began to dress her up. When Vérotchka in fine array followed her mother to church, she said sadly to herself:

"Why this finery? For a gypsy's complexion like mine a dress of serge is as good as a dress of silk. This luxury would become others better. It must be very nice to be pretty! How I should like to be pretty!"

When she was sixteen, Vérotchka stopped taking music lessons, and became a piano-teacher herself in a boarding-school. In a short time Maria Alexevna found her other lessons.

Soon Vérotchka's mother stopped calling her gypsy and scare-crow; she dressed her even with greater care, and Matroena (this was a third Matroena, who, like her predecessors, always had a black eye and sometimes a swollen cheek), Matroena told Vérotchka that the chief of her father's bureau desired to ask her hand in marriage, and that this chief was a grave man, wearing a cross upon his neck.

In fact, the employees of the ministry had noticed the advances of the chief of the department towards his subordinate. And this chief said to one of his colleagues that he intended to marry and that the dowry was of little consequence, provided the woman was beautiful; he added that Pavel Konstantinytch was an excellent official.

What would have happened no one knows; but, while the chief of the department was in this frame of mind, an important event occurred:

The son of the mistress appeared at the steward's to say that his mother desired Pavel Konstantinytch to bring her several samples of wall paper, as she wished to newly furnish her apartments. Orders of this nature were generally transmitted by the major-domo. The intention was evident, and would have been to people of less experience than Vérotchka's parents. Moreover, the son of the proprietor remained more than half an hour to take tea.

The next day Maria Alexevna gave her daughter a bracelet which had not been redeemed and ordered new dresses for her. Vérotchka much admired both the bracelet and the dresses, and was given further occasion to rejoice by her mother's purchase for her at last of some glossy boots of admirable elegance. These toilet expenses were not lost, for Mikhail Ivanytch came every day to the steward's and found — it goes without saying — in Vérotchka's conversation a peculiar charm, which — and this too goes without saying — was not displeasing to the steward and his wife. At least the latter gave her daughter long instructions, which it is useless to detail.

"Dress yourself, Vérotchka," she said to her one evening, on rising from the table; "I have prepared a surprise for you. We are going to the opera, and I have taken a box in the second tier, where there are none but generals. All this is for you, little stupid. For it I do not hesitate to spend my last copecks and your father on his side scatters his substance in foolish expenditures for your sake. To the governess, to the boarding-school, to the piano-teacher, what a sum we have paid! You know nothing of all that, ingrate that you are! You have neither soul nor sensibilities."

Maria Alexevna said nothing further; for she no longer abused her daughter, and, since the reports about the chief of the department, had even ceased to beat her.

So they went to the opera. After the first act the son of the mistress came in, followed by two friends, one of whom, dressed as a civilian, was very thin and very polite, while the other, a soldier, inclined to stoutness and had simple manners. Mikhaïl Ivanytch, I say, came into the box occupied by Vérotchka and her parents.

Without further ceremony, after the customary salutations, they sat down and began to converse in low tones in French, Mikhaïl Ivanytch and the civilian especially; the soldier talked little.

Maria Alexevna lent an attentive ear and tried to catch the conversation; but her knowledge of French was limited. However, she knew the meaning of certain words which perpetually recurred in the conversation: *beautiful, charming, love, happiness.*

Beautiful! Charming! Maria Alexevna has long heard those adjectives applied to her daughter. *Love!* She clearly sees that Mikhaïl Ivanytch is madly in love. Where there is *love* there is *happiness.* It is complete; but when will he speak of marriage?

"You are very ungrateful, Vérotchka," said Maria Alexevna in a low voice to her daughter; "why do you turn away your head? They certainly pay you enough attention, little stupid! Tell me the French for *engaged* and *marriage.* Have they said those words?"

"No, mamma."

"Perhaps you are not telling me the truth? Take care!"

"No; no such words have passed their lips. . . . Let us go; I can stay here no longer!"

"Go! What do you say, wretch?" muttered Maria Alexevna, into whose eyes the blood shot.

"Yes, let us go! Do with me what you will; but I stay here no longer. Later I will tell you why. Mamma," continued the young girl, in a loud voice, "I have too severe a headache; I can remain no longer. Let us go, I beg of you."

And at the same time Vérotchka rose.

"It is nothing," said Maria Alexevna, severely; "promenade in the corridor a little while with Mikhaïl Ivanytch, and it will pass away."

"Mamma, I feel very ill; come quickly, I beg of you."

The young people hastened to open the door and offered their arms to Vérotchka, who had the impoliteness to refuse. They placed the ladies in the carriage. Meanwhile Maria Alexevna looked upon the valets with an air which seemed to say: "See, rabble, how eager these fine gentlemen are in their attentions, and that one there will be my son-in-law, and soon I too shall have at my bidding wretches like you." Then mentally addressing her daughter:

"Must you be obstinate, stupid that you are! But I will put you on your good behavior. . . . Stay, stay, my future son-in-law is speaking to her; he arranges her in the carriage. Listen: *health, visit, permit* (he is asking her permission to call and inquire after her health.)" Without becoming any the less angry, Maria Alexevna took into consideration the words she had just heard.

"What did he say on leaving you?" she asked, as soon as the carriage had started.

"He told me that tomorrow morning he would come to our house to ask after my health."

"You are not lying? He really said tomorrow?"

Vérotchka said nothing.

"You have escaped finely," resumed her mother, who could not refrain from pulling her hair; "but once only and narrowly enough. I will not beat you," she continued, "but be gay tomorrow! Sleep tonight, stupid, and above all do not take it into your head to weep; for if tomorrow morning you are pale, if your eyes are red, beware! I shall be pitiless; your pretty face will be gone; but I shall have asserted myself!"

"I long since ceased to weep, as you well know."

"That's right! But talk with him a little more."

"I will try tomorrow."

"That's right! It is time to become reasonable. Fear God and have a little pity for your mother, boldface that you are!"

After a silence of ten minutes:

"Vérotchka, do not be angry with me; it is through love for you and for your good that I torment you. Children are so dear to their mothers. I carried you for nine months in my womb. I ask of you only gratitude and obedience. Do as I tell you, and tomorrow he will propose."

"You are mistaken, mamma; he does not dream of it. If you knew of what they talked!"

"I know it. If he does not think of marriage, I know of what he thinks. But he does not know the people with whom he has to deal. We will reduce him to servile obedience, and, if necessary, I will carry him to the altar in a sack, or I will drag him there by the hair, and still he will be content. But a truce to babbling! I have already said too much to you; young girls should not know so much. It is the business of their mothers. The daughters have only to obey. Tomorrow you will speak to him."

"Yes."

"And you, Pavel Konstantinytch, of what are you thinking with your chilly air? You tell her also, in the name of your paternal authority, that you order her to obey her mother in everything."

"Maria Alexevna, you are a wise woman; but the affair is difficult, and even dangerous. Can you carry it through?"

"Imbecile! That is very appropriate now! And before Vérotchka, too! The proverb is quite right: *do not stir up ordure if you fear its stench.* It is not your advice that I ask; only this: should a daughter obey her mother?"

"Certainly! Certainly! Maria Alexevna, that is just."

"Well, do you order her as a father?"

"Vérotchka, obey in all things your mother, who is a wise woman, an experienced woman. She will not teach you to do evil. This obedience I enjoin upon you as a father."

On stepping from the carriage Vérotchka said to her mother:

"It is well; I will talk with him tomorrow. But I am very tired, and I need rest."

"Yes, go to bed. I will not disturb you. Sleep well; you need to for tomorrow."

In order to keep her promise Maria Alexevna entered the house without making a disturbance. How much that cost her! How much it cost her also to see Vérotchka enter her room directly without stopping to take tea!

"Vérotchka, come here!" she said to her, pleasantly.

The young girl obeyed.

"Bow your little head; I wish to bless you. There! May God bless you, Vérotchka, as I bless you!"

Three times in succession she blessed her daughter, after which she offered her her hand to kiss.

"No, mamma. I long ago told you that I will not kiss your hand. Let me go now, for I really feel very ill."

The eyes of Maria Alexevna blazed with hatred, but she again restrained herself, and gently said:

"Go! Rest yourself!"

Vérotchka spent much time in undressing.

While taking off her dress and putting it in the closet, while taking off her bracelets and ear-rings, each of those simple operations was followed by a long reverie. It was some time before she discovered that she was very tired, and that she had sunk into an arm-chair, being unable to stand erect before the mirror. At last she perceived it, and made haste to get into bed.

She had scarcely lain down when her mother entered, carrying on a tray a large cup of tea and a number of biscuits.

"Come, eat, Vérotchka, it will do you good. You see that your mother does not forget you. I said to myself: Why has my daughter gone to bed without her tea? And I desired to bring it to you myself; help yourself, dear child."

This kind and gentle voice which Vérotchka had never heard surprised her very much, till, looking at her mother, she saw her cheeks inflamed and her eyes disordered.

"Eat!" continued Maria Alexevna; "when you have finished, I will go for more."

The tea and cream which she had brought aroused Vérotchka's appetite, and, raising herself on her elbow, she began to drink.

"Tea is really good when it is fresh and strong, with plenty of sugar and cream. When I get rich, I shall always drink it so; it is not like warmed-over, half-sweetened tea, which is so unpalatable. Thank you, mamma."

"Do not go to sleep; I am going to get you another cup. Drink," she continued, as she came back bearing an excellent cup of tea; "drink, my child; I wish to stay with you longer."

Accordingly she sat down, and, after a moment's silence, she began to talk in a somewhat confused voice, now slowly, now rapidly.

"Vérotchka, you just said 'Thank you' to me; it is a long time since those words escaped your lips. You think me wicked; well, yes, I am wicked! Can one help it?

"But, dear me! how weak I am! Three punches in succession — at my age! And then you vexed me; that is why I am weak.

"My life has been a very hard one, my daughter! I do not want you to live one like it. You shall live in luxury. How many torments I have endured! Oh, yes! how many torments!

"You do not remember the life that we lived before your father got his stewardship. We lived very poorly; I was virtuous then, Vérotchka. But now I am no longer so, and I will not burden my soul with a new sin by falsely telling you that I am still virtuous. I have not been for a long time, Vérotchka; you are educated, I am not; but I know all that is written in your books, and I know that it is written there that no one should be treated as I have been. They reproach me for not being virtuous, too! and your father the first, the imbecile!

"My little Nadinka was born; he was not her father. Well, what of it! What harm did that do him?

"Was it I who received the position of chief deputy?

"And was it not his fault as much as mine, and more?

"They took my child to put it with the foundlings, and I know not what became of her. Now I hardly care whether she is still living; but then I suffered much. I became wicked, and then all began to go well. I made your father chief deputy, I made him steward, and at last we were where we could live well. Now, how have I succeeded in doing that? By becoming dishonest; for it is written in your books, I know, Vérotchka, that none but rascals make any figure in the world. Is it not true?

"Now your fool of a father has money, thanks to me. And I too have money! Perhaps more than he. It was I who made it all!

"Your fool of a father has come to esteem me, and I have made him walk straight. When I was virtuous, he ill-treated me without reason, and just because I was good. I had to become wicked.

"It is written in your books that we should be good; but can one in the present arrangement of things? For it is necessary to live. Why do they not make society anew, and in accordance with the beautiful order which exists only in your books? It would be better, I know, but the people are so stupid! What can be done with such people? Let us live, then, according to the old order. The old order, your books say, is built on robbery and falsehood. The new order not existing, we must live according to the old. Steal and lie, my daughter; it is through love of you . . . that I speak . . . and . . ."

The voice of Maria Alexevna was extinguished in a loud snore.

II.

Maria Alexevna, while she knew what had happened at the theatre, did not however know the sequel. While she was snoring on a chair, Storechnikoff, his two friends, and the officer's French mistress were finishing supper in one of the most fashionable restaurants.

"M'sieur Storechnik!" — Storechnikoff beamed, this being the third time that the young Frenchwoman had addressed him since the beginning of the supper.— "M'sieur Storechnik! let me call you so, it sounds better and is easier to pronounce; you did not tell me that I was to be the only lady in your society. I hoped to meet Adèle here; I should have been pleased, for I see her so rarely!"

"Adèle, unfortunately, has fallen out with me."

The officer started as if to speak; then, changing his mind, kept silent. It was the civilian who said:

"Do not believe him, Mademoiselle Julie. He is afraid to tell you the truth and confess that he has abandoned this Frenchwoman for a Russian."

"I do not clearly understand why we came here either," muttered the officer.

"But," replied Julie, "why not, Serge, since Jean invited us? I am very glad to make the acquaintance of M. Storechnik, though he has very bad taste, I admit. I should have nothing to say, M. Storechnik, if you had abandoned Adèle for the beautiful Georgian whom you visited in her box, but to exchange a Frenchwoman for a Russian! I can fancy her pale cheeks, — no, I beg pardon, that is not exactly the word; blood with cream in it, as you call it, — that is, a dish which only you Esquimaux are able to relish. Jean, hand me the cigar-ash tray to pass to M. Storechnik that he may humble his guilty head beneath the ashes."

"You have just said so many foolish things, Julie, that you are the one to humble your guilty head beneath the ashes. She whom you call Georgian is precisely the Russian in question." Thus spoke the officer.

"You are laughing at me."

"Not at all; she is a pure-blooded Russian."

"It is impossible."

"You are wrong in supposing, my dear Julie, that our country has but one type of beauty. Have you not brunettes and blondes in France? As for us, we are a mixture of tribes including blondes like the Finns ("Finns! that is it! that is it!" exclaimed the Frenchwoman) and brunettes darker than the Italians, the Tartars, and the Mongolians ("The Mongolians! very good!" again exclaimed the Frenchwoman). These different types are mingled, and our blondes whom you so hate are but a local type, very numerous, but not exclusive."

"That is astonishing! But she is splendid! Why does she not become an actress? But mind, gentlemen, I speak only of what I have seen; there is still an important question to be settled, — her foot? Has not your great poet Karassin said that in all Russia there could not be found five pairs of dainty little feet?"

"Julie, it was not Karassin who said that. Karassin, whom you would do better to call Kuramzine, is neither a Russian nor a poet; he is a Tartar historian. It was Pouchkine who spoke of the little feet. That poet's verses, very popular in his day, have lost a little of their value. As for the Esquimaux, they live in America, and our savages who drink stags' blood are called Samoyèdes."

"I thank you, Serge; Karamzine historian. Pouchkine: . . . I know. The Esquimaux in America, the Russians Samoyèdes . . . Samoyèdes, that name sounds well, Sa-mo-yèdes. I shall remember, gentlemen, and will make Serge repeat it all to me when we get home. These things are useful to know in a conversation. Besides, I have a passion for knowledge; I was born to be a Staël. But that is another affair. Let us come back to the question, — her foot?"

"If you will allow me to call upon you to-morrow, M'elle Julie, I shall have the honor to bring you her shoe."

"I hope so; I will try it on; that excites my curiosity."

Storechnikoff was enchanted. And how could he help it? Hitherto he had been the follower of Jean, who had been the follower of Serge, who had been the follower of Julie, one of the most elegant of the Frenchwomen in Serge's society. It was a great honor that they did him.

"The foot is satisfactory," said Jean; "I, as a positive man, am interested in that which is more essential; I looked at her neck."

"Her neck is very beautiful," answered Storechnikoff, flattered at the praises bestowed upon the object of his choice, and he added, to flatter Julie:

"Yes, ravishing! And I say it, though it be a sacrilege in this presence to praise the neck of another woman."

"Ha! Ha! Ha! He thinks to pay me a compliment! I am neither a hypocrite nor a liar, M. Storechnik; I do not praise myself, nor do I suffer others to praise me where I am unworthy. I have plenty of other charms left, thank God! But my neck! . . . Jean, tell him what it is. Give me your hand, M. Storechnik, and feel here, and there. You see that I wear a false neck, as I wear a dress, a petticoat, a chemise. Not that it pleases me; I do not like such hypocrisies; but it is admitted in society: a woman who has led the life that I have led — M. Storechnik, I am now an anchorite in comparison with what I have been — such a woman cannot preserve the beauty of her throat."

And Julie burst into tears, crying:

"O my youth! O my purity! O God! was it for so much infamy that I was born?"

"You lie, gentlemen," she cried, rising suddenly from her seat and striking her hand upon the table; "you slander this young girl; you are vile! She is not his mistress; I saw it all. He wishes to buy her of her mother. I saw her turn her back upon him, quivering with indignation. Your conduct is abominable! She is a pure and noble girl!"

"Yes," said Jean, languidly stretching himself. "My dear Storechnikoff, you must prove your words. You describe very well what you have not seen. What matters it, after all, whether it be a week before or a week after. For you will not be disenchanted, and the reality will surpass your imagination. I surveyed her; you will be content."

Storechnikoff held back no longer:

"Pardon, Mademoiselle Julie, you are mistaken in your conclusions; she is really my mistress. It was a cloud caused by jealousy. She had taken offence because during the first act I had remained in Mademoiselle Mathilde's box. That was all."

"You are lying, my dear," said Jean, yawning.

"No, truly!"

"Prove it! I am positive, and do not believe without proofs."

"What proof can I give you?"

"You yield already! What proof? This, for instance. Tomorrow we will take supper here again together. Mademoiselle Julie shall bring Serge, I will bring my little Berthe, and you shall bring the beauty in question. If you bring her, I lose, and will pay for the supper; if you do not bring her, we will banish you in shame from our circle."

While speaking Jean had rung, and a waiter had come.

"Simon," he said to him, "prepare a supper tomorrow for six persons. A supper such as we had here at the time of my marriage to Berthe. Do you remember it, before Christmas? In the same room."

"Ah, sir, could one forget such a supper? You shall have it."

"Abominable people!" resumed Julie; "do you not see that he will set some trap for her? I have been plunged in all the filth of Paris, and I never met three men like these! In what society must I live? for what crime do I deserve such ignominy?"

And falling on her knees:

"My God! I was only a poor and weak woman! I endured hunger and cold in Paris. But the cold was so intense, the temptations so irresistible. I wished to live; I wished to love! Was that, then, so great a crime that you punish me thus severely? Lift me from this mire! My old life in Paris! Rather that than live among such people!"

She rose suddenly and ran to the officer:

"Serge, are you like these people? No, you are better."

"*Better*," echoed the officer, phlegmatically.

"Is this not abominable?"

"Abominable! Julie."

"And you say nothing! You let them go on? You become an accomplice!"

"Come and sit on my knee, my girl." And he began to caress her until she grew calm:

"Come, now, you are a brave little woman; I adore you at such times. Why will you not marry me? I have asked you so often."

"Marriage! Yoke! Appearances! No, never! I have already forbidden you to talk to me of such nonsense. Do not vex me. But, my beloved Serge, defend her. He fears you; save her!"

"Be calm, Julie! What would you have me do? If it is not he, it will be another; it comes to the same thing. Do you not see that Jean, too, already dreams of capturing her? And people of his sort, you know, are to be found by thousands. One cannot defend her against everybody, especially when the mother desires to put her daughter into the market. As well might one butt his head against the wall, as the Russian proverb says. We are a wise people, Julie: see how calm my life is, because I know how to bow to fate."

"That is not the way of wisdom. I, a Frenchwoman, struggle; I may succumb, but I struggle. I, for my part, will not tolerate this infamy! Do you know who this young girl is and where she lives?"

"Perfectly well."

"Well, let us go to her home; I will warn her."

"To her home! And past midnight! Let us rather go to bed. *Au revoir*, Jean; *au revoir*, Storeshnikoff. You will not look for me at your supper tomorrow. Julie is incensed, and this affair does not please me either. *Au revoir.*"

"That Frenchwoman is a devil unchained," said Jean, yawning, when the officer and his mistress had gone. "She is very piquant; but she is getting stout already. Very agreeable to the eye is a beautiful woman in anger! All the same, I would not have lived with her four years, like Serge. Four years! Not even a quarter of an hour! But, at any rate, this little caprice shall not lose us our supper. Instead of them I will bring Paul and Mathilde. Now it is time to separate. I am going to see Berthe a moment, and then to the little Lotchen's, who is veritably charming."

III.

"It is well, Véra; your eyes are not red; hereafter you will be tractable, will you not?"

Vérotchka made a gesture of impatience.

"Come! come!" continued the mother, "do not get impatient; I am silent. Last night I fell asleep in your room; perhaps I said too much: but you see, I was drunk, so do not believe anything I told you. Believe none of it, do you understand?" she repeated, threateningly.

The young girl had concluded the night before that, beneath her wild beast's aspect, her mother had preserved some human feelings, and her hatred for her had changed into pity; suddenly she saw the wild beast reappear, and felt the hatred returning; but at least the pity remained.

"Dress yourself," resumed Maria Alexevna, "he will probably come soon." After a careful survey of her daughter's toilet, she added:

"If you behave yourself well, I will give you those beautiful emerald earrings left with me as security for one hundred and fifty roubles. That is to say, they are worth two hundred and fifty roubles, and cost over four hundred. Act accordingly, then!"

Storechnikoff had pondered as to the method of winning his wager and keeping his word, and for a long time sought in vain. But at last, while walking home from the restaurant, he had hit upon it, and it was with a tranquil mind that he entered the steward's apartments. Having inquired first as to the health of Véra Pavlovna, who answered him with a brief "I am well," Storechnikoff said that youth and health should be made the most of, and proposed to Véra Pavlovna and her mother to take a sleigh-ride that very evening in the fine frosty weather. Maria Alexevna consented; adding that she would make haste to prepare a breakfast of meat and coffee, Vérotchka meanwhile to sing something.

"Sing us something, Vérotchka," she said, in a tone that suffered no reply.

The Life of Véra Pavlovna with her Parents.

Vérotchka sang " Troïka," * which describes, as we know, a girl of charming beauty all eyes to see an officer pass.

" Well, now, that's not so bad," murmured the old woman from the adjoining room. " When she likes, this Verka† can be very agreeable at least."

Soon Vérotchka stopped singing and began to talk with Storechnikoff, but in French.

" Imbecile that I am ! " thought the old woman ; " to think that I should have forgotten to tell her to speak Russian ! But she talks in a low voice, she smiles ; it's going well ! it's going well ! Why does he make such big eyes ? It is easy to see that he is an imbecile, and that is what we are after. Good ! she extends her hand to him. Is she not agreeable, this Verka ? "

This is what Vérotchka said to Storechnikoff:

" I must speak severely to you, sir; last evening at the theatre you told your friends that I was your mistress. I will not tell you that this lie was cowardly ; for, if you had understood the whole import of your words, I do not think that you would have uttered them. But I warn you that if, at the theatre or in the street, you ever approach me, I will give you a blow. I know that my mother will kill me with ill-treatment [it was here that Vérotchka smiled], but what does that matter, since life is so little to me ? This evening you will receive from my mother a note informing you that I am indisposed and unable to join you in the sleigh-ride."

He looked at her with big eyes, as Maria Alexevna had observed.

She resumed :

" I address you, sir, as a man of honor not yet utterly depraved. If I am right, I pray you to cease your attentions, and I, for my part, will pardon your calumny. If you accept, give me your hand."

He shook her hand without knowing what he did.

" Thank you," she added ; " and now go. You can give as a pretext the necessity for ordering the horses."

He stood as one stupefied, while she began once more to sing " Troïka."

If connoisseurs had heard Vérotchka, they would have been astonished at the extraordinary feeling which she put into her song; in her, feeling surely dominated art.

Meanwhile Maria Alexevna was coming, followed by her cook carrying the breakfast and coffee on a tray. But Storechnikoff, pretending that he had orders to give concerning the preparation of the horses, withdrew toward the door instead of approaching, and, before the steward's wife could protest, the young man went out.

---

* A song by Nekrassoff.
† Verka is an ill-natured diminutive of Véra.

Maria Alexevna, pale with rage and fists lifted in the air, rushed into the parlor, crying:

"What have you done, wench? Wait for me!"

Vérotchka had hurried into her room. Thither the mother ran like a hurricane; but the door was locked. Beside herself, she tried to break down the door, and struck it heavy blows.

"If you break down the door," cried the young girl, "I will break the windows and call for help; in any case, I warn you that you shall not take me alive."

The calm and decided tone with which these words were uttered did not fail to make an impression on the mother, who contented herself with shouting and made no more attacks on the door.

As soon as she could make herself heard, Vérotchka said to her:

"I used to detest you, but since last night I have pitied you. You have suffered, and that has made you wicked. If you wish it, we will talk together pleasantly, as we have never talked together before."

These words did not go straight to the heart of Maria Alexevna, but her tired nerves demanded rest: she asked herself if, after all, it were not better to enter into negotiations. She will no longer obey, and yet she must be married to that fool of a Michka.* And then, one cannot tell exactly what has happened; they shook hands. . . . . . . no, one cannot tell. She was still hesitating between stratagem and ferocity, when a ring of the bell interrupted her reflections; it was Serge and Julie.

IV.

"Serge, does her mother speak French?" had been Julie's first word on waking.

"I know nothing about it. What! have you still that idea?"

"Still. But I do not believe she speaks French: you shall be my interpreter."

Had Véra's mother been Cardinal Mezzofanti,† Serge would have consented to go to her with Julie To follow Julie everywhere, as the confidant always follows the heroines of Corneille, had become his destiny, and we must add that he did not complain of it.

But Julie had waked late and had stopped at four or five stores on the way, so that Storechnikoff had time to explain himself and Maria Alexevna to rage and calm down again before their arrival.

"What horrible stairs! I never saw anything like them in Paris. And, by the way, what shall be our excuse for calling?"

"No matter what; the mother is a usurer; we will pawn your brooch. No, I

---

* Michka is an ill-natured diminutive of Mikhail.
† Who spoke sixty languages, it is said.

have a better idea; the daughter gives piano lessons. We will say that you have a niece, etc."

At the sight of Serge's beautiful uniform and Julie's dazzling toilette Matroena blushed for the first time in her life; she had never seen such fine people. No less were the enthusiasm and awe of Maria Alexevna when Matroena announced Colonel X. and his wife.

And his wife!

The scandals which Maria Alexevna started or heard of concerned nobody higher in station than counsellors. Consequently she did not suspect that Serge's marriage might be only one of those so-called *Parisian* marriages, in which legality goes for nothing. Besides, Serge was brilliant; he explained to her that he was fortunate in having met them at the theatre, that his wife had a niece, etc., and that, his wife not speaking Russian, he had come to act as an interpreter.

"Oh yes! I may thank heaven; my daughter is a very talented musician, and were she to be appreciated in a house like yours I should be extremely happy; only, she is not very well; I do not know whether she can leave her room."

Maria Alexevna spoke purposely in a very loud voice in order that Vérotchka might hear and understand that an armistice was proposed. At the same time she devoured her callers with her eyes.

"Vérotchka, can you come, my dear?"

Why should she not go out? Her mother certainly would not dare to make a scene in public. So she opened her door; but at sight of Serge she blushed with shame and anger. This would have been noticed even by poor eyes, and Julie's eyes were very good; therefore, without indirection, she explained herself:

"My dear child, you are astonished and indignant at seeing here the man before whom last night you were so shamefully outraged. But though he be thoughtless, my husband at least is not wicked; he is better than the scamps who surround him. Forgive him for love of me; I have come with good intentions. This niece is but a pretext; but your mother must think it genuine. Play something, no matter what, provided it be very short, and then we will retire to your room to talk."

Is this the Julie known to all the rakes of the aristocracy, and whose jokes have often caused even the libidinous to blush? One would say, rather, a princess whose ear has never been soiled.

Vérotchka went to the piano; Julie sat near her, and Serge busied himself in sounding Maria Alexevna in order to ascertain the situation regarding Storechnikoff. A few minutes later Julie stopped Vérotchka, and, taking her around the waist, led her to her room. Serge explained that his wife wished to talk a little longer with Vérotchka in order to know her character, etc. Then he led the conversation back to Storechnikoff. All this might be charming; but Maria

Alexevna, who was by no means innocent, began to cast suspicious looks about her. Meanwhile Julie went straight to the matter in hand.

"My dear child, your mother is certainly a very bad woman, but in order that I may know how to speak to you, tell me why you were taken to the theatre last evening. I know already from my husband; but I wish to get your view of the matter."

Vérotchka needed no urging, and, when she had finished, Julie cried:

"Yes, I may tell you all!"

And in the most fitting and chaste language she told her of the wager of the night before. To which Vérotchka answered by informing her of the invitation to a sleigh-ride.

"Did he intend to deceive your mother? Or were they in conspiracy?"

"Oh!" quickly cried Vérotchka, "my mother does not go as far as that."

"I shall know presently. Stay here; there you would be in the way."

Julie went back to the parlor.

"Serge," she said, "he has already invited this woman and her daughter to a sleigh-ride this evening. Tell her about the supper."

"Your daughter pleases my wife; it remains but to fix the price, and we shall be agreed. Let us come back to our mutual acquaintance, Storechnikoff. You praise him highly. Do you know what he says of his relations with your daughter? Do you know his object in inviting us into your box?"

Maria Alexevna's eyes flashed.

"I do not retail scandal, and seldom listen to it," she said, with restrained anger; "and besides," she added, while striving to appear humble, "the chatter of young people is of little consequence."

"Possibly! But what do you say to this?" And he told the story of the previous night's wager.

"Ah! the rascal, the wretch, the ruffian! That is why he desired to take us out of the city, — to get rid of me and dishonor my daughter."

Maria Alexevna continued a long time in this strain; then she thanked the colonel; she had seen clearly that the lessons sought were but a feint; she had suspected them of desiring to take Storechnikoff away from her; she had misjudged them; and humbly asked their pardon.

Julie, having heard all, hastened back to Vérotchka, and told her that her mother was not guilty, that she was full of indignation against the impostor, but that her thirst for lucre would soon lead her to look for a new suitor, which would at once subject Vérotchka to new annoyances. Then she asked her if she had relatives in St. Petersburg, and, being answered in the negative, Julie said further:

"That is a pity. Have you a lover?"

Vérotchka opened her eyes wide.

"Forgive me, forgive me! That is understood. But then you are without protection? What's to be done? But wait, I am not what you think me; I am not his wife, but his mistress; I cannot ask you to my house, I am not married; all St. Petersburg knows me. Your reputation would be lost; it is enough already that I should have come here; to come a second time would be to ruin you. But I must see you once more, and still again perhaps,—that is, if you have confidence in me? Yes? Good! At what hour shall you be free to-morrow?"

"At noon."

Noon was a little early for Julie; nevertheless she will arrange to be called and will meet Vérotchka by the side of the Gastinoï Dvor,* opposite the Nevsky.† There no one knows Julie.

"What a good idea!" continued the Frenchwoman. "Now give me some paper, that I may write to M. Storechnikoff."

The note which she wrote read as follows:

"Monsieur, you are probably very much disturbed by your position. If you wish me to aid you, call on me this evening at seven o'clock.

"Now, adieu.
"J. LETELLIER."

But instead of taking the hand which she extended, Vérotchka threw herself upon her neck and wept as she kissed her. Julie, also much moved, likewise could not restrain her tears, and with an outburst of extreme tenderness she kissed the young girl several times, while making a thousand protests of affection.

"Dear child," she said at last, "you cannot understand my present feelings. For the first time in many years pure lips have touched mine. O my child, if you knew! . . . Never give a kiss without love! Choose death before such a calamity!"

V.

Storechnikoff's plan was not so black as Maria Alexevna had imagined, she having no reason to disbelieve in evil; but it was none the less infamous. They were to start off in a sleigh and get belated in the evening; the ladies soon becoming cold and hungry, Storechnikoff was to offer them some tea; in the mother's cup he was to put a little opium; then, taking advantage of the young girl's anxiety and fright, he was to conduct her to the supper-room, and the wager was won. What would happen then chance was to decide; perhaps Vérotchka, dazed and not clearly understanding, would remain a moment; if, on

---

* The Palais Royal of St. Petersburg.
† That is, the Perspective Nevsky, the finest street in St. Petersburg.

the contrary, she only entered and at once went out again, he would assert that it was the first time she had been out alone, and the wager would be won just the same. Finally he was to offer money to Maria Alexevna. . . . Yes, it was well planned. But now. . . . He cursed his presumption, and wished himself under the earth.

It was in this frame of mind that he received Julie's letter; it was like a sovereign elixir to a sick man, a ray of light in utter darkness, firm ground under the feet of one sinking. Storechnikoff rose at a bound to the most sanguine hope.

"She will save me, this generous woman. She is so intelligent that she can invent something imperative. O noble Julie!"

At ten minutes before seven, he stood at her door.

"Madame is waiting for you; please come in."

Julie received him without rising. What majesty in her mien! What severity in her look!

"I am very glad to see you; be seated," she said to him in answer to his respectful salutation.

Not a muscle of his face moved; Storechnikoff was about to receive a stern reprimand. What matter, provided she would save him?

"Monsieur Storechnikoff," began Julie, in a cold, slow voice, "you know my opinion of the affair which occasions our interview; it is useless to recall the details. I have seen the person in question, and I know the proposition that you made to her this morning. Therefore I know all, and am very glad to be relieved from questioning you. Your position is clear, to you and to me. ("God!" thought Storechnikoff, "I would rather be upbraided by far!") You can escape only through me. If you have any reply to make, I am waiting. . . . You do not reply? You believe, then, that I alone can come to your aid. I will tell you what I can do, and, if you deem it satisfactory, I will submit my conditions."

Storechnikoff having given sign of assent, she resumed:

"I have prepared here a letter for Jean, in which I tell him that, since the scene of last night, I have changed my mind, and that I will join in the supper, but not this evening, being engaged elsewhere; so I beg him to induce you to postpone the supper. I will make him understand that, having won your wager, it will be hard for you to put off your triumph. Does this letter suit you?"

"Perfectly."

"But I will send the letter only on two conditions. You can refuse to accept them, and in that case I will burn the letter.

"These two conditions," she continued, in a slow voice which tortured Storechnikoff, — "these two conditions are as follows:

"First, you shall stop persecuting this young person.

"Second, you shall never speak her name again in your conversations."

"Is that all?"

"Yes."

A ray of joy illuminated Storechnikoff's countenance. "Only that," he thought. "It was hardly worth while to frighten me so. God knows how ready I was to grant it."

But Julie continued with the same solemnity and deliberation:

"The first is necessary for her, the second for her also, but still more for you; I will postpone the supper from week to week until it has been forgotten. And you must see that it will not be forgotten unless you speak the name of this young person no more."

Then, in the same tone, she went into the details of carrying out the plan. "Jean will receive the letter in season. I have found out that he is to dine at Bertha's. He will go to your house after smoking his cigar. We will send the letter, then. Do you wish to read it? Here is the envelope. I will ring . . . Pauline, you will take this letter. We have not seen each other today, Monsieur Storechnikoff and I. Do you understand?"

At last the letter is sent; Storechnikoff breathes more freely, and is quite overjoyed at his deliverance.

But Julie has not yet done.

"In a quarter of an hour you must be at home in order that Jean may find you there; you have a moment left, and I wish to take advantage of it to say a few words more. You will follow my advice, or not, as you please; but you will reflect upon it.

"I will not speak of the duties of an honest man toward a young girl whose reputation he has compromised. I know our worldly youth too well to think it useful to examine that side of the question at any length. Your marriage with this young person would seem to me a good thing for you. I will explain myself with my usual frankness and though some of the things that I am going to say may wound you. If I go too far, a word from you will stop me short. Listen, then:

"You have a weak character, and, if you fall into the hands of a bad woman, you will be duped, deceived, and tortured into the bargain. *She* is good, and has a noble heart; in spite of her plebeian birth and poverty, she will aid you singularly in your career.

"Introduced into the world by you, she will shine and wield an influence there. The advantages which such a situation procure for a husband are easy to see. Besides these external advantages, there are others more intimate and precious still. You need a peaceful home and even a little watchful care. All this she can give you. I speak in all seriousness; my observations of this morning tell me that she is perfection. Think of what I have said to you.

"If she accepts, which I very much doubt, I shall consider the acceptance a great piece of good fortune for you.

"I keep you no longer; it is time for you to go."

VI.

Vérotchka was at least tranquil for the time being; her mother could not in fairness be angry with her for having escaped a trap so basely laid; consequently she was left free enough the next day to enable her to go to the Gastinoï Dvor without hindrance.

"It is very cold here, and I do not like the cold. But wait here a moment," said Julie, on arriving. She entered a store, where she bought a very thick veil.

"Put that on! Now you may come with me without being recognized. Pauline is very discreet; yet I do not wish her to see you, so jealous am I of your reputation; and, above all, do not lift your veil while we are together."

Julie was dressed in her servant's cloak and hat, and her face was hidden beneath a thick veil. First they were obliged to warm themselves; after which, being questioned by Julie, Vérotchka gave her the latest details.

"Good, my dear child; now be sure that he asks your hand in marriage Men like him become madly amorous when their gallantries are received unfavorably. Do you know that you have dealt with him like an experienced coquette? Coquetry — I do not mean the affected and false imitation of this method of acting — coquetry is nothing but a high degree of wit and tact applied to the relations between man and woman. Thus it is that innocent young girls act like experienced coquettes without knowing it; all that they need is wit. Perhaps, too, my arguments will have some influence on him. But the principal thing is your firmness; however that may be, he is almost sure to make you a proposition of marriage, and I advise you to accept him."

"You! who told me yesterday that it was better to die than to give a kiss without love."

"My dear child, I said that in a moment of exaltation; it is right, but it is poetry, and life is made up of very prosaic interests."

"No! I will never marry him; he fills me with horror! I will never stoop to that! I would rather die, throw myself out of the window, ask alms! Yes, rather death than a man so debased!"

Julie, without being disconcerted, began to explain the advantages of the marriage which she had planned:

"You would be delivered from your mother's persecutions; you would run no more risk of being sold. As for him, he is rather stupid, but he is not such a wretch. A husband of that sort is what an intelligent woman like you needs; you would rule the household."

Then she told her in a lively way of the actresses and singers who, far from being made submissive to men through love, subjugate them, on the contrary.

"That is a fine position for a woman! and finer yet when she joins to such independence and power a legality of ties which commands the respect of society;

that is, when she is married, and loved and admired by her husband, as the actress is by the lover whom she has subjugated."

The conversation grew more and more animated. Julie said much, and Vérotchka replied:

"You call me whimsical, and you ask me how I look upon life. I wish neither to dominate nor be dominated; I wish neither to dissimulate nor deceive; nor do I wish to exert myself to acquire that which I am told is necessary, but of which I do not feel the need. I do not desire wealth; why should I seek it? The world does not attract me; to shine in society is of little moment to me; why should I make efforts in that direction?

"Not only would I not sacrifice myself for those things of which the world boasts so loudly, but I would not even sacrifice one of my caprices. I wish to be independent and live in my own fashion. What I need I feel that I have the strength to earn; what I do not need I do not desire. You say that I am young, inexperienced, and that I shall change with time; that remains to be seen. For the present I have no concern with the wealth and splendor of the world.

"You will ask me what I desire. I do not know. If I need to be in love, I do not know it. Did I know, yesterday morning, that I was going to love you? that my heart was going to be taken possession of by friendship a few hours later? Certainly not. No more can I know how I shall feel toward a man when I shall be in love with him. What I do know is that I wish to be free; that I do not wish to be under obligations to any one, dependent on any one; I wish to act after my own fancy; let others do the same. I respect the liberty of others, as I wish them to respect mine."

Julie listened, moved and thoughtful, and several times she blushed.

"Oh! my dear child, how thoroughly right you are!" she cried, in a broken voice. "Ah! if I were not so depraved! They call me an immoral woman, my body has been polluted, I have suffered so much, — but that is not what I consider my depravity. My depravity consists in being habituated to luxury and idleness; in not being able to live without others . . . .

"Unfortunate that I am! I deprave you, poor child, and without intending it. Forgive me, and forget all that I have said. You are right in despising the world; it is vile and even more worthless than I.

"Wherever idleness is, there is vice and abomination; wherever luxury is there also is vice and abomination. Adieu! Go quickly!"

VII.

Storechnikoff remained plunged in this thought, cherished more and more: *If indeed I should marry her.* Under these circumstances there happened to him what happens, not only to inconstant men like him, but also to men of firmer character. The history of peoples is full of similar cases: see the pages of Hume, Gibbon, Ranke, Thierry. Men drag themselves along in a beaten track simply because they have been told to do so; but tell them in a very loud voice to take another road, and, though they will not hear you at first, they will soon throw themselves into the new path with the same spirit. Storechnikoff had been told that, with a great fortune, a young man has only to choose among the poor the beauty whom he desires for a mistress, and that is why he had thought of making a mistress of Vérotchka. Now a new word had been thrown into his head: *Marriage!* And he pondered over this question: *Shall I marry her?* as before he had pondered over the other: *Shall I make her my mistress?*

That is the common trait by which Storechnikoff represented in his person, in a satisfactory manner, nine-tenths of his fellow-citizens of the world. Historians and psychologists tell us that in each special fact the common fact is *individualized* by local, temporary, individual elements, and that these particular elements are precisely those of most importance. Let us examine, then, our particular case. The main feature had been pointed out by Julie (as if she had taken it from Russian novels, which all speak of it): resistance excites desire. Storechnikoff had become accustomed to dream of the *possession* of Vérotchka. Like Julie I call things by their names, as, moreover, almost all of us do in current conversation. For some time his imagination had represented Vérotchka in poses each more voluptuous than its predecessor; these pictures had inflamed his mind, and, when he believed himself on the point of their realization, Vérotchka had blown upon his dream, and all had vanished. But if he could not have her as a mistress, he could have her as a wife: and what matters it which after all, provided his gross sensuality be satisfied, provided his wildest erotic dreams be realized? O human degradation! to *possess!* Who dares possess a human being? One may possess a pair of slippers, a dressing-gown. But what do I say? Each of us, men, *possesses* some one of you, our sisters! Are you, then, our sisters? You are our servants. There are, I know, some women who subjugate some men; but what of that? Many valets rule their masters, but that does not prevent valets from being valets.

These amorous images had developed in Storechnikoff's mind after the interview at the theatre; he had found her a hundred times more beautiful than at first he deemed her, and his polluted imagination was excited.

It is with beauty as with wit, as with all qualities; men value it by the judgment of general opinion. Every one sees that a beautiful face is beautiful, but how beautiful is it? It is at this point that the data of current opinion become necessary to classification. As long as Vérotchka sat in the galleries or in the back rows of the pit, she was not noticed; but when she appeared in one of the boxes of the second tier, several glasses were levelled at her; and how many were the expressions of admiration heard by Storechnikoff when he returned to the lobby after escorting her to the carriage!

"Serge," said Storechnikoff, " is a man of very fine taste! And Julie? how about her? But . . . when one has only to lay his hand on such a marvel, he does not ask himself by what title he shall *possess* her."

His ambition was aroused as well as his desires. Julie's phrase, " I doubt very much whether she accepts you," excited him still more. "What! she will not accept me, with such a uniform and such a house! I will prove to you, Frenchwoman, that she will accept me; yes, she shall accept me!"

There was still another influence that tended to inflame Storechnikoff's passion: his mother would certainly oppose the marriage, and in this she represented the opinion of society. Now, heretofore Storechnikoff had feared his mother; but evidently this dependence was a burden to him. And the thought, " I do not fear her, I have a character of my own," was very well calculated to flatter the ambition of a man as devoid of character as he.

He was also urged on by the desire to advance a little in his career through the influence of his wife.

And to all this it must be added that Storechnikoff could not present himself before Vérotchka in his former *rôle*, and he desired so much to see her!

In short, he dreamed of the marriage more and more every day, and a week afterwards, on Sunday, while Maria Alexevna, after attending mass, was considering how she could best coax him back, he presented himself and formulated his request. Vérotchka remaining in her room, he had to address himself to Maria Alexevna, who answered that for her part the marriage would be a great honor, but that as an affectionate mother she wished to consult her daughter, and that he might return the next morning to get his answer.

"What an excellent daughter we have!" said Maria Alexevna to her husband a moment later. "How well she knew how to take him! And I who, not knowing how to reëntice him, thought that all was to begin over again! I even thought it a hopeless affair. But she, my Verka, did not spoil matters; she conducted them with perfect strategy. Good girl!"

"It is thus that the Lord inspires children," said Pavel Konstantinytch.

He rarely played a part in the family life. But Maria Alexevna was a strict observer of traditions, and in a case like this, of conveying to her daughter the proposition that had been made, she hastened to give her husband the *rôle* of honor which by right belongs to the head of the family and the master.

Pavel Konstantinytch and Maria Alexevna installed themselves upon the divan, the only place solemn enough for such a purpose, and sent Matroena to ask Mademoiselle to be good enough to come to them.

"Véra," began Pavel Konstantinytch, "Mikhail Ivanytch does us a great honor: he asks your hand. We have answered him that, as affectionate parents, we did not wish to coerce you, but that for our part we were pleased with his suit. Like the obedient and wise daughter that we have always found you to be, trust to our experience; we have never dared to ask of God such a suitor. Do you accept him, Véra?"

"No," said Vérotchka.

"What do I hear, Véra?" cried Pavel Konstantinytch (the thing was so clear that he could fall into a rage without asking his wife's advice).

"Are you mad or an idiot? Just dare to repeat what you said, detestable rag that you are!" cried Maria Alexevna, beside herself and her fists raised over her daughter.

"Calm yourself, Mamma," said Vérotchka, rising also. "If you touch me, I will leave the house; if you shut me up, I will throw myself out of the window. I knew how you would receive my refusal, and have considered well all that I have to do. Seat yourself, and be tranquil, or I go."

Maria Alexevna sat down again. "What stupidity!" she thought; "we did not lock the outer door. It takes but a second to push the bolt back. This mad creature will go, as she says, and no one will stop her."

"I will not be his wife," repeated the young girl, "and without my consent the marriage cannot take place."

"Véra, you are mad," insisted the mother with a stifled voice.

"Is it possible? What shall we say to him tomorrow?" added the father.

"It is not your fault; it is I who refuse."

The scene lasted nearly two hours. Maria Alexevna, furious, cried, and twenty times raised her tightly clenched fists; but at each outbreak Vérotchka said:

"Do not rise, or I go."

Thus they disputed without coming to any conclusion, when the entrance of Matroena to ask if it was time to serve dinner — the cake having been in the oven too long already — put an end to it all.

"Reflect until evening, Véra, there is yet time; reconsider your determination; it would be unspeakable foolishness."

Then Maria Alexevna said something in Matroena's ear.

"Mamma, you are trying to set some trap for me, to take the key from my chamber door, or something of that sort. Do nothing of the kind: it would be worse."

Again Maria Alexevna yielded.

"Do not do it," she said, addressing the cook. "This jade is a wild beast. Oh! if it were not that he wants her for her face, I would tear it to pieces. But if I touch her, she is capable of self-mutilation. Oh, wretch! Oh, serpent! If I could!"

They dined without saying a word. After dinner Vérotchka went back to her room. Pavel Konstantinytch lay down, according to his habit, to sleep a little; but he did not succeed, for hardly had he begun to doze when Matroena informed him that the servant of the mistress of the house had come to ask him to call upon her instantly.

Matroena trembled like a leaf.

Why?

VIII.

And why should she not tremble? Had she not, without loss of time, told the wife of the mistress's cook of the suit of Mikhail Ivanytch? The latter had complained to the second waiting-maid of the secrets that were kept from her. The second servant had protested her innocence: if she had known anything, she would have said so; she had no secrets, she told everything. The cook's wife then made apologies; but the second servant ran straight to the first servant and told her the great news.

"Is it possible?" cried the latter. "As I did not know it, then Madame does not; he has concealed his course from his mother." And she ran to warn Anna Petrovna.

See what a fuss Matroena had caused.

"O my wicked tongue!" said she, angrily. "Fine things are going to happen to me now! Maria Alexevna will make inquiries."

But the affair took such a turn that Maria Alexevna forgot to look for the origin of the indiscretion.

Anna Petrovna sighed and groaned; twice she fainted before her first waiting-maid. That showed that she was deeply afflicted. She sent in search of her son.

He came.

"Can what I have heard, Michel, be true?" she said to him in French in a voice at once broken and furious.

"What have you heard, Mamma?"

"That you have made a proposition of marriage to that . . . . . to that . . . to that . . . . . to the daughter of our steward."

"It is true, Mamma."

"Without asking your mother's advice?"

"I intended to wait, before asking your consent, until I had received hers."

"You ought to know, it seems to me, that it is easier to obtain her consent than mine."

"Mamma, it is now allowable to first ask the consent of the young girl and then speak to the parents."

"That is allowable, for you? Perhaps for you it is also allowable that sons of good family should marry a . . . . . one knows not what, and that mothers should give their consent!"

"Mamma, she is not a *one knows not what*; when you know her, you will approve my choice."

"When I know her! I shall never know her! Approve your choice! I forbid you to think of it any longer! I forbid you, do you understand?"

"Mamma, this parental absolutism is now somewhat out of date; I am not a little boy, to be led by the end of the nose. I know what I am about."

"Ah!" cried Anna Petrovna, closing her eyes.

Though to Maria Alexevna, Julie, and Vérotchka, Mikhaïl Ivanytch seemed stupid and irresolute, it was because they were women of mind and character; but here, so far as mind was concerned, the weapons were equal, and if, in point of character, the balance was in favor of the mother, the son had quite another advantage. Hitherto he had feared his mother from habit; but he had as good a memory as hers. They both knew that he, Mikhaïl Ivanytch, was the real proprietor of the establishment. This explains why Anna Petrovna, instead of coming straight to the decisive words, *I forbid you*, availed herself of expedients and prolonged the conversation. But Mikhaïl Ivanytch had already gone so far that he could not recoil.

"I assure you, Mamma, that you could not have a better daughter."

"Monster! Assassin of your mother!"

"Mamma, let us talk in cold blood. Sooner or later I must marry; now, a married man has more expenses than a bachelor. I could, if I chose, marry such a woman that all the revenues of the house would hardly be enough for us. If, on the contrary, I marry this girl, you will have a dutiful daughter, and you can live with us as in the past."

"Be silent, monster! Leave me!"

"Mamma, do not get angry, I beg of you; it is not my fault."

"You marry a plebeian, a servant, and it is not your fault!"

"Now, Mamma, I leave you without further solicitation, for I cannot suffer her to be thus characterized in my presence."

"Go, assassin!"

Anna Petrovna fainted, and Michel went away, quite content at having come off so well in this first skirmish, which in affairs of this sort is the most important.

When her son had gone, Anna Petrovna hastened to come out of her fainting fit. The situation was serious; her son was escaping her. In reply to "I forbid you," he had explained that the house belonged to him. After calming herself a little, she called her servant and confided her sorrow to her; the latter, who shared the contempt of her mistress for the steward's daughter, advised her to bring her influence to bear upon the parents. And that is why Anna Petrovna had just sent for her steward.

"Hitherto I have been very well satisfied with you, Pavel Konstantinytch, but intrigues, in which, I hope, you have no part, may set us seriously at variance."

"Your excellency, it is none of my doing, God is my witness."

"I already know that Michel was paying court to your daughter. I did not prevent it, for a young man needs distraction. I am indulgent toward the follies of youth. But I will not allow the degradation of my family. How did your daughter come to entertain such hopes?"

"Your excellency, she has never entertained them. She is a respectful girl; we have brought her up in obedience."

"What do you mean by that?"

"She will never dare to thwart your will."

Anna Petrovna could not believe her ears. Was it possible? She could, then, relieve herself so easily!

"Listen to my will. I cannot consent to so strange, I should say so unfitting, a marriage."

"We feel that, your excellency, and Vérotchka feels it too. These are her own words: 'I dare not, for fear of offending her excellency.'"

"How did all this happen?"

"It happened in this wise, your excellency: Mikhail Ivanytch condescended to express his intentions to my wife, and my wife told him that she could not give him a reply before tomorrow morning. Now, my wife and I intended to speak to you first. But we did not dare to disturb your excellency at so late an hour. After the departure of Mikhail Ivanytch, we said as much to Vérotchka, who answered that she was of our opinion and that the thing was not to be thought of."

"Your daughter is, then, a prudent and honest girl?"

"Why, certainly, your excellency, she is a dutiful daughter!"

"I am very glad that we can remain friends. I wish to reward you instantly. The large room on the second floor, facing on the street and now occupied by the tailor, will soon be vacant?"

"In three days, your excellency."

"Take it yourself, and you may spend up to a hundred roubles to put it in good order. Further, I add two hundred and forty roubles a year to your salary."

"Deign to let me kiss your hand, your excellency."

"Pshaw, pshaw! Tatiana!" The servant came running in.

"Bring me my blue velvet cloak. I make your wife a present of it. It cost one hundred and fifty roubles [it really cost only seventy-five], and I have worn it only twice [she had worn it more than twenty times]. This is for your daughter [Anna Petrovna handed the steward a small watch such as ladies carry] ; I paid three hundred roubles for it [she paid one hundred and twenty]. You see, I know how to reward, and I shall always remember you, always! Do not forget that I am indulgent toward the foibles of the young."

When the steward had gone, Anna Petrovna again called Tatiana.

"Ask Mikhaïl Ivanytch to come and talk with me. . . . . But no, I will go myself instead." She feared that the ambassadress would tell her son's servant, and the servant her son, what had happened. She wished to have the pleasure of crushing her son's spirit with this unexpected news. She found Mikhaïl Ivanytch lying down and twirling his moustache, not without some inward satisfaction.

"What brings her here? I have no preventive of fainting fits," thought he, on seeing his mother enter. But he saw in her countenance an expression of disdainful triumph.

She took a seat and said:

"Sit up, Mikhaïl Ivanytch, and we will talk."

She looked at him a long time, with a smile upon her lips. At last she said slowly:

"I am very happy, Mikhaïl Ivanytch: guess at what."

"I do not know what to think, Mamma; your look is so strange."

"You will see that it is not strange at all; look closely and you will divine, perhaps."

A prolonged silence followed this fresh thrust of sarcasm. The son lost himself in conjectures; the mother delighted in her triumph.

"You cannot guess; I will tell you. It is very simple and very natural; if you had had a particle of elevated feeling, you would have guessed. Your mistress,"—in the previous conversation Anna Petrovna had manœuvred; now it was no longer necessary, the enemy being disarmed,—"your mistress,—do not reply, Mikhaïl Ivanytch, you have loudly asserted on all sides yourself that she is your mistress,—your mistress, this creature of base extraction, base education, base conduct, this even contemptible creature" . . . .

"Mamma, my ear cannot tolerate such expressions applied to a young girl who is to be my wife."

"I would not have used them if I had had any idea that she could be your wife. I did so with the view of explaining to you that that will not occur and of telling you at the same time why it will not occur. Let me finish, then. Afterwards you can reproach me, if you like, for the expressions which I have used, supposing that you still believe them out of place. But meantime let me finish. I wish to say to you that your mistress, this creature without name or education, devoid of sentiment, has herself comprehended the utter impropriety of your designs. Is not that enough to cover you with shame?"

The Life of Véra Pavlovna with her Parents.

"What? What do you say? Finish!"

"You do not let me. I meant to say that even this creature — do you understand? even this creature! — comprehended and appreciated my feelings, and, after learning from her mother that you had made a proposition for her hand, she sent her father to tell me that she would never rise against my will and would not dishonor our family with her degraded name."

"Mamma, you deceive me."

"Fortunately for you and for me, I tell only the exact truth. She says that" . . . . .

But Mikhaïl Ivanytch was no longer in the room; he was putting on his cloak to go out.

"Hold him, Pietre, hold him!" cried Anna Petrovna.

Pietre opened his eyes wide at hearing so extraordinary an order. Meanwhile Mikhaïl Ivanytch rapidly descended the staircase.

IX.

"Well?" said Maria Alexevna, when her husband reëntered.

"All goes well, all goes well, little mother! She knew already, and said to me: 'How dare you?' and I told her; 'We do not dare, your excellency, and Vérotchka has already refused him.'"

"What? What? You were stupid enough to say that, ass that you are?"

"Maria Alexevna" . . . .

"Ass! Rascal! You have killed me, murdered me, you old stupid! There's one for you! [the husband received a blow.] And there's another! [the husband received a blow on the other cheek]. Wait. I will teach you, you old imbecile!" And she seized him by the hair and pulled him into the room. The lesson lasted sufficiently long, for Storechnikoff, reaching the room after the long pauses of his mother and the information which she gave him between them, found Maria Alexevna still actively engaged in her work of education.

"Why did you not close the door, you imbecile? A pretty state we are found in! Are you not ashamed, you old he-goat?" That was all that Maria Alexevna found to say.

"Where is Véra Pavlovna? I wish to see her directly. Is it true that she refuses me?" said Storechnikoff.

The circumstances were so embarrassing that Maria Alexevna could do nothing but desist. Precisely like Napoleon after the battle of Waterloo, when he believed himself lost through the incapacity of Marshal Grouchy, though really the fault was his own, so Maria Alexevna believed her husband the author of the evil. Napoleon, too, struggled with tenacity, did marvels, and ended only with these words: "I abdicate; do what you will."

"Is it true that you refuse me, Véra Pavlovna?"

"I leave it to you, could I do otherwise than refuse you?"

"Véra Pavlovna, I have outraged you in a cowardly manner; I am guilty; but your refusal kills me." And again he began his supplications.

Vérotchka listened for some minutes; then, to end the painful interview, she said:

"Mikhail Ivanytch, your entreaties are useless. You will never get my consent."

"At least grant me one favor. You still feel very keenly how deeply I outraged you. Do not give me a reply to-day; let me have time to become worthy of your pardon! I seem to you despicable, but wait a little: I wish to become better and more worthy; aid me, do not repel me, grant me time. I will obey you in all things! Perhaps at last you will find me worthy of pardon."

"I pity you; I see the sincerity of your love [it is not love, Vérotchka; it is a mixture of something low with something painful; one may be very unhappy and deeply mortified by a woman's refusal without really loving her; love is quite another thing,—but Vérotchka is still ignorant regarding these things, and she is moved],—you wish me to postpone my answer; so be it, then! But I warn you that the postponement will end in nothing; I shall never give you any other reply than that which I have given you to-day."

"I will become worthy of another answer; you save me!"

He seized her hand and kissed it rapturously.

Maria Alexevna entered the room, and in her enthusiasm blessed her dear children without the traditional formalities,—that is, without Pavel Konstantinytch; then she called her husband to bless them once more with proper solemnity. But Storechnikoff dampened her enthusiasm by explaining to her that Véra Pavlovna, though she had not consented, at least had not definitely refused, and that she had postponed her answer.

This was not altogether glorious, but after all, compared with the situation of a moment before, it was a step taken.

Consequently Storechnikoff went back to his house with an air of triumph, and Anna Petrovna had no resource left but fainting.

Maria Alexevna did not know exactly what to think of Vérotchka, who talked and seemed to act exactly against her mother's intentions, and who, after all, surmounted difficulties before which Maria Alexevna herself was powerless. Judging from the progress of affairs, it was clear that Vérotchka's wishes were the same as her mother's; only her plan of action was better laid and, above all, more effective. Yet, if this were the case, why did she not say to her mother: "Mamma, we have the same end in view; be tranquil." Was she so out of sorts with her mother that she wished to have nothing to do with her? This postponement, it was clear to Maria Alexevna, simply signified that her daughter wished to excite Storechnikoff's love and make it strong enough to break down the resistance of Anna Petrovna.

"She is certainly even shrewder than I," concluded Maria Alexevna after much reflection. But all that she saw and heard tended to prove the contrary.

"What, then, would have to be done," said she to herself, "if Véra really should not wish to be Storechnikoff's wife? She is so wild a beast that one does not know how to subdue her. Yes, it is altogether probable that this conceited creature does not wish Storechnikoff for a husband; in fact, it is indisputable."

For Maria Alexevna had too much common sense to be long deceived by artificial suppositions representing Vérotchka as an intriguer.

"All the same, one knows not what may happen, for the devil only knows what she has in her head; but, if she should marry Storechnikoff, she would control both son and mother. There is nothing to do, then, but wait. This spirited girl may come to a decision after a while, ... and we may aid her to it, but prudently, be it understood."

For the moment, at any rate, the only course was to wait, and so Maria Alexevna waited.

It was, moreover, very pleasant, this thought, which her common sense would not let her accept, that Vérotchka knew how to manœuvre in order to bring about her marriage; and everything except the young girl's words and actions supported this idea.

The suitor was as gentle as a lamb. His mother struggled for three weeks; then the son got the upper hand from the fact that he was the proprietor, and Anna Petrovna began to grow docile; she expressed a desire to make Vérotchka's acquaintance. The latter did not go to see her. Maria Alexevna thought at first that, in Vérotchka's place, she would have acted more wisely by going; but after a little reflection she saw that it was better not to go. "Oh! she is a shrewd rogue!"

A fortnight later Anna Petrovna came to the steward's herself, her pretext being to see if the new room was well arranged. Her manner was cold and her amiability biting; after enduring two or three of her caustic sentences, Vérotchka went to her room. While her daughter remained, Maria Alexevna did not think she was pursuing the best course; she thought that sarcasm should have been answered with sarcasm; but when Vérotchka withdrew, Maria Alexevna instantly concluded: "Yes, it was better to withdraw; leave her to her son, let him be the one to reprimand her; that is the best way."

Two weeks afterwards Anna Petrovna came again, this time without putting forward any pretext; she simply said that she had come to make a call; and nothing sarcastic did she say in Vérotchka's presence.

Such was the situation. The suitor made presents to Vérotchka through Maria Alexevna, and these presents very certainly remained in the latter's hands, as did Anna Petrovna's watch, always excepting the gifts of little value, which Maria Alexevna faithfully delivered to her daughter as articles which had been deposited with her and not redeemed; for it was necessary that the suitor should see some of these articles on his sweetheart. And, indeed, he did see them, and was convinced that Vérotchka was disposed to consent; otherwise she would not have accepted his gifts; but why, then, was she so slow about it? Perhaps she was waiting until Anna Petrovna should be thoroughly softened; this thought was whispered in his ear by Maria Alexevna. And he continued to break in his mother, as he would a saddle-horse, an occupation which was not without charm for him. Thus Vérotchka was left at rest, and everything was done to please her. This watch-dog kindness was repugnant to her; she tried to be with her mother as little as possible. The mother, on the other hand, no longer dared to enter her daughter's room, and when Vérotchka stayed there a large portion of the day, she was entirely undisturbed. Sometimes she allowed Mikhaïl Ivanytch to come and talk with her.

Then he was as obedient as a grandchild. She commanded him to read and he read with much zeal, as if he was preparing for an examination; he did not reap much profit from his reading, but nevertheless he reaped a little; she tried to aid him by conversation; conversation was much more intelligible to him than books, and thus he made some progress, slow, very slow, but real. He began by treating his mother a little better than before: instead of breaking her in like a saddle-horse, he preferred to hold her by the bridle.

Thus things went on for two or three months. All was quiet, but only because of a truce agreed upon, with the tempest liable to break forth again any day. Vérotchka viewed the future with a shrinking heart: some day or other would not Mikhaïl Ivanytch or Maria Alexevna press her to a decision? For their impatience would not put up long with this state of things.

Here I might have invented a tragic climax; in reality there was none. I might have put everything into confusion to allure the reader. But, a friend of truth and an enemy of subterfuge, I warn my readers in advance that there will be no tragic climax and that the clouds will roll away without lightning or thunder or tempest.

CHAPTER SECOND.
The First Love and Legal Marriage.
I.

We know how in former times such situations were brought to an issue: an amiable young girl was in a worthless family; and they imposed upon her a lover, disagreeable and brutal, whom she did not love. But constant association with his betrothed improved the wooer somewhat; he became an ordinary man, neither agreeable nor disagreeable; his obedience and gentleness were exemplary. After becoming accustomed to having him near her, always in a humble attitude, and after saying to herself that she was very unhappy in her family, and that this husband would be an improvement, she decided to take him.

She had to overcome a great deal of repugnance when she first learned what it was to give one's self without love; but, after all, the husband was not a bad man, and in the long run one gets accustomed to everything; she became an ordinarily good woman, — that is, a person who, intrinsically good, had reconciled herself to triviality and accommodated herself to a vegetative life. That is what became of young girls formerly.

It was almost the same with young men, who themselves became as comfortable inhabitants of this world as stupidity, selfishness, and triviality could desire. That is why so few really human men were to be found; of these the harvest was so small that the ears were not within speaking distance of each other.*

Now, one cannot live alone all his life without consuming himself by his own force; truly human men wasted away and were submerged in material life.

In our day it is no longer the same; the number of these human beings grows continually, and from year to year the increase is perceptible. As a result they become acquainted with each other, and their number increases further on this account.

In time they will be the majority. In time, even, they will be the totality; then all will be well in the world.

Vérotchka in her individual life knew how to realize this ideal; and that is why (with her permission) I tell her story.

She, as I happen to know is one of the first women whose life was thus ordered; now, beginnings are interesting to history. The first swallow is the dearest to dwellers in the North.

* An old Russian saying.

Let us return to Véra Pavlovna. The time came for preparing Vérotchka's little brother for college. Pavel Konstantinytch inquired among his colleagues to find a tutor whose prices were low; they recommended a medical student named Lopoukhoff.

Lopoukhoff came five or six times to give lessons to his new pupil before he met Vérotchka. He stayed with Fédia at one end of the apartments, while she remained in her room at the other end. But as the examinations at the Medico-Surgical Academy were approaching and he had to study in the morning, he came to give his lessons in the evening. This time, on his arrival, he found the whole family at tea: the father and mother, Fédia, and an unknown person,—a young girl of large and beautiful figure, bronzed complexion, black hair, and black eyes.

Her hair was beautiful and thick; her eyes were beautiful, very beautiful indeed, and quite of a southern type, as if she came from Little Russia. One would have said even a Caucasian type rather; an admirable countenance, which had no fault beyond indicating an extreme coldness,—which is not a southern trait.

She seemed beaming with health; the redness of her cheeks was wholesome; there would be no need of so many doctors, were there many such constitutions as hers.

When she enters society, she will make an impression. But what is that to me? Such were Lopoukhoff's reflections as he looked at her.

She, too, threw her eyes upon the teacher who had just entered. The student was no longer a youth; he was a man of a little above the average height, with hair of a deep chestnut color, regular and even handsome features, the whole relieved by a proud and fearless bearing. " He is not bad, and ought to be good; but he must be too serious." She did not add in her thought: "But what is that to me?" and for the very simple reason that it had not occurred to her that he could interest her. Besides, Fédia had said so much to her of his teacher that she could no longer bear him spoken of without impatience.

" He is very good, my dear sister; only he is not a talker. And I told him, my dear sister, that you were a beauty in our house, and he answered: 'How does that concern me?' And I, my dear sister, replied: 'Why, everybody loves beauties,' and he said in return: 'All imbeciles love them,' and I said: 'And do you not love them, too?' And he answered me: 'I have not the time.' And I said to him, my dear sister: ' So you do not wish to make Vérotchka's acquaintance?' 'I have many acquaintances without her,' he answered me."

Such was Fédia's account. And it was not the only one; he told others of the same sort, such as this:

" I told him to-day, my dear sister, that everybody looks at you when you pass, and he replied: · So much the better.' I said to him: 'And do you not wish to see her?' He answered: 'There is time enough for that.'"

Or like this other:

"I told him, my dear sister, what pretty little hands you have, and he answered me: 'You are bound to babble, so be it; but have you no other subjects more interesting?'"

Willy nilly, the teacher had learned from Fédia all that he could tell him on the subject of "his dear sister;" he always stopped the little fellow whenever he began to babble about family affairs; but how prevent a child of nine years from telling you everything, especially if he loves you more than he fears you. At the fifth word you may succeed in interrupting him, but it is already too late: children begin without preface, directly, at the essential; and among the bits of information of all sorts upon family affairs, the teacher had heard such things as these:

"My sister has a wealthy suitor! But Mamma says that he is very stupid." "Mamma also pays court to the suitor; she says that my sister has trapped him very adroitly." "Mamma says: 'I am shrewd, but Vérotchka is even shrewder than I!' Mamma says also: 'We will show his mother the door.'" And so on. It was natural that, hearing such things about each other, the young people should not feel any desire to become more intimately acquainted.

We know, moreover, that this reserve was natural on Vérotchka's side; the degree of her intellectual development did not permit her to attempt to *conquer this unsociable savage*, to *subdue this bear*. Further, for the time being she had something else to think of; she was content to be left tranquil; she was like a bruised and weary traveller, or like an invalid who has stretched himself out to rest and does not dare to make a movement for fear of reviving his pains. Finally, it was not in accordance with her character to search for new acquaintances, especially among the young.

It was easy to see why Vérotchka should think thus. But what was he really? According to Fédia, a savage with head full of books and anatomical preparations, — all the things which make up the principal intellectual enjoyment of a good student of medicine. Or had Fédia slandered him?

II.

No, Fédia had not slandered him; Lopoukhoff was actually a student with *head full of books*, and what books? The bibliographical researches of Maria Alexevna will tell us that in due time. Lopoukhoff's head was also full of anatomical preparations, for he dreamed of a professorship. But, just as the information communicated by Fédia to Lopoukhoff concerning Vérotchka has given an imperfect knowledge of the young girl, there is reason to believe that the information imparted by the pupil as to his teacher needs to be completed.

In regard to his pecuniary situation Lopoukhoff belonged to that small minority of day students not maintained by the crown, who suffer, nevertheless, neither from hunger nor cold. How and whereby do the great majority of these students live? God knows, of course; to men it is a mystery. But it is not agreeable to think so much about people who die of hunger; therefore we will only indicate the period during which Lopoukhoff found himself also in this embarrassing situation, and which lasted three years.

Before he entered the Academy of Medicine he was well supported by his father, a small *bourgeois* of Riazan, who lived well enough for his station: that is, his family had *stchi** on Sundays and meat and tea every day.

To maintain his son in college, starting at the age of fifteen, was difficult for the elder Lopoukhoff; his son had to aid him by giving lessons. If it was difficult in a provincial college, it was much more so in the St. Petersburg Academy of Medicine.

Lopoukhoff received, nevertheless, during the first two years, thirty-five roubles per year, and he earned almost as much more as a copyist in one of the quarters of the district of Wyborg without being an office-holder.

If he suffered still, it was his own fault.

He had been offered maintenance by the crown; but then had gotten into I know not what quarrel, which cost him a tolerably stern reprimand and a complete abandonment. In his third year his affairs began to take a better turn: the deputy head clerk of the police office offered him a chance to give lessons, and to these he added others, which for two years had given him at least the necessaries of life.

He and his friend Kirsanoff, a student like him, a laborer like him, occupied two adjacent rooms.

The two friends had early become accustomed to depending only on themselves; and in general they acted so much in concert that one meeting them separately would have taken them for men of the same character. But when one saw them together, it then became plain that, although both were very serious and very sincere, Lopoukhoff was a little more reserved, and his companion a little more open. For the present only Lopoukhoff is before us; Kirsanoff will appear much later.

All that may be said of Lopoukhoff can be repeated of Kirsanoff.

At the present stage of our story Lopoukhoff was absorbed by this thought: How to arrange his life after ending his studies? It was time to think about that: there were but a few months left. Their projects differed little.

Lopoukhoff felt sure of being received as a doctor in one of the military hospitals of St. Petersburg (that is considered a great piece of good fortune) and of obtaining a chair in the Academy of Medicine.

---

* A soup peculiar to Russia.

As for being simply a practitioner, he did not dream of it.

It is a very curious trait, this resolution of the medical students of these last ten years not to engage in practice. Even the best disdained this precious resource of the exercise of their art, which alone would have assured their existence, or accepted it only provisionally, being always ready to abandon medicine, as soon as possible, for some auxiliary science, like physiology, chemistry, or something similar. Moreover, each of them knew that by practice he could have made a reputation at the age of thirty, assured himself a more than comfortable existence at the age of thirty-five, and attained wealth at forty-five.

But our young people reason otherwise. To them the medical art is in its infancy, and they busy themselves less with the art of attending the sick than with gathering scientific materials for future physicians. They busy themselves less with the practice of their art than with the progress of beloved science.

They cry out against medicine, and to it devote all their powers; for it they renounce wealth and even comfort, and stay in the hospitals to make observations interesting to science; they cut up frogs; they dissect hundreds of bodies every year, and, as soon as possible, fit themselves out with chemical laboratories.

Of their own poverty they think little. Only when their families are in straitened circumstances do they practice, and then just enough to afford them necessary aid without abandoning science; that is, they practice on a very small scale, and attend only such people as are really sick and as they can treat effectively in the present deplorable state of science, — not very profitable patients as a general thing. It was precisely to this class of students that Lopoukhoff and Kirsanoff belonged. As we know, they were to finish their studies in the current year, and were preparing to be examined for their degrees; they were at work upon their theses. For that purpose they had exterminated an enormous quantity of frogs.

Both had chosen the nervous system as a specialty. Properly speaking, they worked together, mutually aiding each other. Each registered in the materials of his thesis the facts observed by both and relating to the question under consideration.

But for the present we are to speak of Lopoukhoff only.

At the time when he went without tea and often without boots, he gave himself up to some excesses in the matter of drinking.

Such a situation is very favorable to these excesses: to say nothing of the fact that one is then more disposed to them, one is influenced by the further fact that it is cheaper to drink than to eat or dress, and Lopoukhoff's excesses had no other causes. Now he led a life of exemplary sobriety and strictness.

Likewise he had had many gallant adventures. Once, for example, he became enamored of a dancing girl. What should he do? He reflected, reflected again,

and for a long time reflected, and at last went to find the beauty at her house.
"What do you want?" he was asked. "I am sent by Count X with a letter."

His student's costume was easily mistaken by the servant for that of an officer's amanuensis or attendant.

"Give me the letter. Will you wait for a reply?"

"Such was the Count's order."

The servant came back, and said to him with an astonished air:

"I am ordered to ask you to come in."

"Ah! is it you?" said the dancing girl; "you, my ardent applauder! I often hear your voice, even from my dressing room. How many times have you been taken to the police station for your excess of zeal in my honor?"

"Twice."

"That is not often. And why are you here?"

"To see you."

"Exactly; and what then?"

"I don't know."

"Well, I know what I want; I want some breakfast. See, the table is laid. Sit you down, too."

Another plate was brought. She laughed at him, and he could not help following her example. But he was young, good-looking, and had an air of intelligence; his bearing was original; so many advantages conquered the dancing girl, who for him was very willing to add another to her list of adventures.

A fortnight later she said to him:

"Now are you going?"

"I was already desirous of doing so, but I did not dare."

"Well, then, we part friends?"

Once more they embraced each other, and separated in content.

But that was three years ago, and it was already two years since Lopoukhoff had entirely given up adventures of that sort

Except his comrades, and two or three professors who foresaw in him a true man of science, he saw no one outside the families where he gave lessons. And among them with what reserve! He avoided familiarity as he would the fire, and was very dry and cold with all the members of these families, his pupils of course excepted.

III.

Thus, then, Lopoukhoff entered the room where he found at the tea-table a company of which Vérotchka was one.

"Take a seat at the table, please," said Maria Alexevna; "Matroena, another cup."

"If it is for me, I do not care for anything, thank you."

" Matrœna, we do not want the cup. (What a well-brought-up young man!) Why do you not take something? It would not hurt you."

He looked at Maria Alexevna; but at the same moment, as if intentionally, his eyes fell on Vérotchka, and indeed perhaps it was intentional. Perhaps even he noticed that she made a motion, which in Vérotchka meant: Could he have seen me blush?

" Thank you, I take tea only at home," he answered.

At bottom he was not such a barbarian; he entered and bowed with ease.

" This girl's morality may be doubtful," thought Lopoukhoff, " but she certainly blushed at her mother's lack of good-breeding."

Fédia finished his tea and went out with his tutor to take his lesson.

The chief result of this first interview was that Maria Alexevna formed a favorable opinion of the young man, seeing that her sugar-bowl probably would not suffer much by the change of lessons from morning to evening.

Two days later Lopoukhoff again found the family at tea and again refused a cup, a resolution which drove the last trace of anxiety from Maria Alexevna's mind. But this time he saw at the table a new personage, an officer, in whose presence Maria Alexevna was very humble.

" Ah! this is the suitor!" thought he.

The suitor, in accordance with the custom of his station and house, deemed it necessary, not simply to look at the student, but to examine him from head to foot with that slow and disdainful look which is permitted in people of high society.

But he was embarrassed in his inspection by the fixed and penetrating gaze of the young tutor. Wholly disconcerted, he hastened to say:

" The medical profession is a difficult one, is it not, Monsieur Lopoukhoff?"

" Very difficult, sir." And Lopoukhoff continued to look the officer in the eye.

Storechnikoff, for some inexplicable reason, placed his hand on the second and third buttons from the top of his tunic, which meant that he was so confused that he knew no other way out of his embarrassment than to finish his cup of tea as quickly as possible in order to ask Maria Alexevna for another.

" You wear, if I mistake not, the uniform of the S—— regiment?"

" Yes, I serve in that regiment."

" How long since?"

" Nine years."

" Did you enter the service in that same regiment?"

" The same."

" Have you a company?"

" Not yet. (But he is putting me through an examination as if I were under orders)."

"Do you hope to get a company soon?"

"Not so very soon."

Lopoukhoff thought that enough for once, and left the suitor alone, after having looked him again in the eye.

"'Tis curious," thought Vérotchka; "'tis curious; yes, 'tis curious!"

This *'tis curious* meant: "He behaves as Serge would behave, who once came here with the good Julie. Then he is not such a barbarian. But why does he talk so strangely of young girls? Why does he dare to say that none but imbeciles love them? And .... why, when they speak to him of me, does he say: 'That does not interest me.'"

"Vérotchka, will you go to the piano? Mikhaïl Ivanytch and I will take pleasure in listening to you," said Maria Alexevna, after Vérotchka had put her second cup back upon the table.

"Very well."

"I beg you to sing us something, Véra Pavlovna," added Mikhaïl Ivanytch, gently.

"Very well."

"This *very well* means: 'I will do it in order to be in peace,'" thought Lopoukhoff.

He had been there five minutes, and, without looking at her, he knew that she had not cast a single glance at her suitor except when obliged to answer him. Moreover, this look was like those which she gave her father and mother, — cold and not at all loving. Things were not entirely as Fédia had described them. "For the rest," said Lopoukhoff to himself, "probably the young girl is really proud and cold; she wishes to enter fashionable society to rule and shine there; she is displeased at not finding for that purpose a suitor more agreeable to her; but, while despising the suitor, she accepts his hand, because there is no other way for her to go where she wants to go. Nevertheless she is interesting."

"Fédia, make haste to finish your tea," said the mother.

"Do not hurry him, Maria Alexevna; I would like to listen a little while, if Véra Pavlovna will permit."

Vérotchka took the first book of music which fell under her hand, without even looking to see what it was, opened it at hazard, and began to play mechanically. Although she played thus mechanically and just to get rid as soon as possible of the attention of which she was the object, she executed the piece with singular art and perfect measure; before finishing she even put a little animation into her playing. As she rose, the officer said:

"But you promised to sing us something, Véra Pavlovna; if I dared, I would ask you to sing a motive from 'Rigoletto.'" That winter *la donna è mobile* was very popular.

" Very well," said Vérotchka, and she sang *la donna è mobile*, after which she rose and went to her room.

" No, she is not a cold and insensible young girl. She is interesting."

" Perfect! was it not?" said Mikhaïl Ivanytch to the student, simply and without any look of disdain; (" it is better not to be on a bad footing with spirited fellows who question you so coolly. Talk amicably with him. Why not address him without pretension, that he may not take offence?")

" Perfect!" answered Lopoukhoff.

" Are you versed in music?"

" Hm! Well enough."

" Are you a musician yourself?"

" In a small way."

A happy idea entered the head of Maria Alexevna, who was listening to the conversation.

" On what instrument do you play, Dmitry Serguéitch?" she asked.

" I play the piano."

" Might we ask you to favor us?"

" Certainly."

He played a piece, and sufficiently well. After the lesson Maria Alexevna approached him, told him that they were to have a little company the following evening in honor of her daughter's birthday, and asked him to be good enough to come.

" There are never very many at such companies," thought he; " they lack young people, and that is why I am invited; all the same, I will go, if only to see the young girl a little more closely. There is something in her, or out of her, that is interesting."

" I thank you," he answered, " I will be there."

But the student was mistaken as to the motive of this invitation: Maria Alexevna had an object much more important than he imagined.

Reader, you certainly know in advance that at this company an explanation will take place between Lopoukhoff and Vérotchka, and they will form an affection for each other.

IV.

It had been Maria Alexevna's desire to give a grand party on the evening of Vérotchka's birthday, but Vérotchka begged her to invite nobody; one wished to make a public show of the suitor; to the other such a show would have been distressing. It was agreed finally to give a small party and invite only a few intimate friends. They invited the colleagues of Pavel Konstantinytch (at least those of them whose grade and position were the highest), two friends of

Maria Alexevna, and the three young girls with whom Vérotchka was most intimate.

Running his eyes over the assembled guests, Lopoukhoff saw that young people were not lacking. By the side of each lady was a young man, an aspirant for the title of suitor or perhaps an actual suitor. Lopoukhoff, then, had not been invited in order to get one dancer more. For what reason, then? After a little reflection, he remembered that the invitation had been preceded by a test of his skill with the piano. Perhaps he had been invited to save the expense of a pianist.

"I will upset your plan, Maria Alexevna," thought he; so approaching Pavel Konstantinytch, he said:

"Is it not time, Pavel Konstantinytch, to make up a game of cards; see how weary the old people are getting!"

"Of how many points?"

"As you prefer."

A game was forthwith made up, in which Lopoukhoff joined.

The Academy in the district of Wyborg is an institution in which card-playing is a classic. In any of the rooms occupied by the crown students it is no rare thing to see thirty-six hours' continuous playing. It must be allowed that, although the sums which change hands over the cloth are much smaller than those staked in English club-rooms, the players are much more skilful. At the time when Lopoukhoff was short of money, he played a great deal.

"Ladies, how shall we arrange ourselves?" said some one. "*Tour à tour* is good, but then there will be seven of us, and either one dancer will be lacking, or a lady for the quadrille."

When the first game was over, one young lady, bolder than the others, came to the student and said:

"Monsieur Lopoukhoff, are you going to dance?"

"On one condition," said he, rising to salute her.

"What is it?"

"That I may dance the first quadrille with you."

"Alas! I am engaged; I am yours for the second."

Lopoukhoff bowed again profoundly. Two of the dancers played *tour à tour*. He danced the third quadrille with Vérotchka.

He studied the young girl, and became thoroughly convinced that he had done wrong in believing her a heartless girl, marrying for selfish purposes a man whom she despised.

Yet he was in the presence of a very ordinary young girl who danced and laughed with zest. Yes, to Vérotchka's shame it must be said that as yet she was only a young person fond of dancing. She had insisted that no party should be given, but, the party having been made,—a small party, without the public show which would have been repugnant to her,—she had forgotten her chagrin. Therefore, though Lopoukhoff was now more favorably disposed toward her, he did not exactly understand why, and sought to explain to himself the strange being before him.

"Monsieur Lopoukhoff, I should never have expected to see you dance."

"Why? Is it, then, so difficult to dance?"

"As a general thing, certainly not; for you evidently it is."

"Why is it difficult for me?"

"Because I know your secret, yours and Fédia's; you disdain women."

"Fédia has not a very clear idea of my secret: I do not disdain women, but I avoid them; and do you know why? I have a sweetheart extremely jealous, who, in order to make me avoid them, has told me their secret."

"You have a sweetheart?"

"Yes."

"I should hardly have expected that! Still a student and already engaged! Is she pretty? Do you love her?"

"Yes, she is a beauty, and I love her much."

"Is she a brunette or a blonde?"

"I cannot tell you. That is a secret."

"If it is a secret, keep it. But what is this secret of the women, which she has betrayed to you, and which makes you shun their society?"

"She had noticed that I do not like to be in low spirits; now, since she told me their secret, I cannot see a woman without being cast down; that is why I shun women."

"You cannot see a woman without being cast down! I see you are not a master of the art of gallantry."

"What would you have me say? Is not a feeling of pity calculated to cast one down?"

"Are we, then, so much to be pitied?"

"Certainly. You are a woman: do you wish me to tell you the deepest desire of your soul?"

"Tell it, tell it!"

"It is this: 'How I wish I were a man!' I never met a woman who had not that desire planted deep within her. How could it be otherwise? There are the facts of life, bruising and crushing woman every hour because she is woman. Consequently, she only has to come to a struggle with life to have occasion to cry out: *Poor beings that we are, what a misfortune that we are women!* or else: *With man it is not the same as with woman*, or, very simply: 'Ah, why am I not a man!'"

Vérotchka smiled: "It is true; every woman may be heard saying that."

"See, then, how far women are to be pitied, since, if the profoundest desire of each of them were to be realized, there would not remain a single woman in the world."

"It seems to be so," said Vérotchka.

"In the same way, there would not remain a single poor person, if the profoundest desire of each poor person were to be realized. Women, therefore, are to be pitied as much as the poor, since they have similar desires; now, who can feel pleasure at the sight of the poor? It is quite as disagreeable to me to see women, now that I have learned their secret from my jealous sweetheart, who told me on the very day of our engagement. Till then I had been very fond of the society of women; but since I have been cured of it. My sweetheart cured me."

"She is a good and wise girl, your sweetheart; yes, the rest of us poor women are beings worthy of pity. But who, then, is your sweetheart, of whom you speak so enigmatically?"

"That is a secret which Fédia will not reveal to you. Do you know that I share absolutely the desire of the poor,—that there may be no more poverty, and that a time may come, be it nearer or farther, when it will be abolished and when we shall know how to organize a system of justice which will not admit the existence of poor people?"

"No more poor people! And I too have that desire. How can it be realized? Tell me. My thought has given me no information on this subject."

"For my part I do not know; only my sweetheart can tell you that. I can only assure you that she is powerful, more powerful than all the world beside, and that she desires justice. But let us come back to the starting-point. Though I share the hopes of the poor concerning the abolition of poverty, I cannot share the desire of women, which is not capable of realization, for I cannot admit that which cannot be realized. But I have another desire: I would like women to be bound in ties of friendship with my sweetheart, who is concerned about them also, as she is concerned about many things, I might say, about all things. If women cultivated her acquaintance, I should no longer have to pity them, and their desire: 'Ah, why am I not a man!' would lose its justification. For, knowing her, women would not have a destiny worse than that of men."

"Monsieur Lopoukhoff! another quadrille! I desire it absolutely!"

"I am content." And the student pressed the young girl's hand, but in a manner as calm and serious as if Vérotchka had been his comrade or he her friend. "Which, then?" he added.

"The last."

"Good."

Maria Alexevna strolled around them several times during this quadrille. What idea would she have formed of their conversation, if she had heard it? We who have heard it from end to end will declare frankly that such a conversation is a very strange one to occur during a quadrille.

Finally came the last quadrille.

"So far we have talked only of myself," began Lopoukhoff, "but that is not at all agreeable on my part. Now I wish to be agreeable; let us talk about you, Véra Pavlovna. Do you know that I had a still worse opinion of you than you had of me? But now .... well, we wi 1 postpone that. Only there is one question I should like to put to you. When is your marriage to take place?"

"Never!"

'I have been certain of it for the last three hours, ever since I left the game to dance with you. But why is he treated as your affianced?"

"Why is he treated as my affianced? Why? The first reason I cannot tell you, for it would give me pain. But I can tell you the second: I pity him. He loves me so dearly. You will say that I ought to tell him frankly what I think of our projected marriage; but when I do that, he answers: 'Oh! do not say so! That kills me; do not say so!'"

"The first reason, which you cannot tell me, I know; it is that your family relations are horrible."

"For the present they are endurable; no one torments me; they wait, and almost always leave me alone."

"But that cannot last long. Soon they will press you. And then?"

"Do not be troubled. I have thought of that and have decided. Then I will not stay here. I will be an actress. It is a very desirable career. Independence! Independence!"

"And applause."

"Yes, that gives pleasure too. But the principal thing is independence. One does as she likes, one lives as she likes, without asking the advice of any one, without feeling the need of any one. That is how I should like to live!"

"Good, very good! Now I have a request to make of you,—that you will allow me to gather information which will aid you t an entrance."

"Thank you," said Vérotchka, pressing his hand. "Do so as quickly as possible. I so much wish to free myself from this humiliating and frightful situation. I said, indeed: 'I am tranquil, my situation is endurable;' but no, it is not so. Do I not see what they are doing with my name? Do I not know what those who are here think of me? An intriguer, schemer, greedy for wealth, she wishes to get into high society and shine there; her husband will be under her feet, she will turn him about at pleasure and deceive him. Yes, I know all that, and I wish to live so no longer, I wish it no longer!" Suddenly she became thoughtful, and added: "Do not laugh at what I am going to say: I pity him much, for he loves me so dearly!"

"He loves you? Does he look at you, as I do, for instance? Tell me."

"You look at me in a frank and simple way. No, your look does not offend me."

"See, Véra Pavlovna, it is because..... But never mind..... And does he look at you in that way?"

Vérotchka blushed and said nothing.

"That means that he does not love you. That is not love, Véra Pavlovna."

"But".... Vérotchka did not dare to finish.

"You intended to say: 'But what is it, then, if it is not love?' What is it? What you will. But that it is not love you will say yourself. Whom do you like best? I do not refer now to love, but friendship."

"Really? No one. Ah, yes, I did happen to meet not long ago a very strange woman. She talked to me very disparagingly of herself, and forbade me to continue in her society; we saw each other for a special purpose, and she told me that, when I should have no hope left but in death, I might apply to her, but not otherwise. That woman I love much."

"Would you like to have her do something for you which would be disagreeable or injurious to her?"

Vérotchka smiled. "Of course not."

"No. Well, suppose it were necessary, absolutely necessary to you that she should do something for you, and she should say to you: 'If I do that, I shall be very miserable myself.' Would you renew your request? Would you insist?"

"I would die first."

"And you say that he loves you. Love! Such love is only a sentiment, not a passion. What distinguishes a passion from a simple sentiment? Intensity. Then, if a simple friendship makes you prefer to die rather than owe your life to troubles brought upon your friend,—if a simple friendship speaks thus, what, then, would passion say, which is a thousand times stronger? It would say: Rather die than owe happiness to the sorrow of the one I love! Rather die than cause her the slightest trouble or embarrass her in any way! A passion speaking thus would be true love. Otherwise, not. Now I must leave you, Véra Pavlovna; I have said all that I had to say."

Vérotchka shook his hand. "Well, *au revoir!* You do not congratulate me? Today is my birthday."

Lopoukhoff gave her a singular look. "Perhaps, perhaps!" he said; "if you are not mistaken, so much the better for me!"

V.

"What! so quickly, and against all expectation!" thought Vérotchka, on finding herself alone in her chamber after the guests had gone. "We have talked only once, half an hour ago we did not know each other, and already we are so intimate! How strange!" No, it is not strange at all, Vérotchka. Men like Lopoukhoff have magic words which draw to them every injured and outraged being. It is their *sweetheart* who whispers such words to them. And what is strange indeed, Vérotchka, is that you should be so calm. Love is thought to be a startling feeling. Yet you will sleep as calmly and peacefully as a little child, and no painful dreams will trouble your slumbers; if you dream, it will be only of childish games or dances amid smiling faces.

To others it is strange; to me it is not. Trouble in love is not love itself; if there is trouble, that means that something is wrong; for love itself is gay and careless.

"Yes, it is very strange," still thought Vérotchka; "about the poor, about women, about love, he told me what I had already thought.

"Where did I find it? In books?

"No; for everything in them is expressed with so much doubt and reserve that one believes she is reading only dreams.

"These things seem to me simple, ordinary, inevitable in fact; it seems to me that without them life is impossible. Yet the best books present them as incapable of realization.

"Take Georges Sand, for instance; what goodness! what morality! but only dreams.

"Our novelists are sure to offer nothing of the kind. Dickens, too, has these aspirations; but he does not seem to hope for their realization; being a good man, he desires it, but as one who knows that it cannot come to pass. Why do they not see that life cannot continue without this new justice, which will tolerate neither poverty nor wretchedness, and that it is towards such justice that we must march? They deplore the present, but they believe in its eternity, or little short of it. If they had said what I thought, I should have known then that the good and wise think so too, whereas I thought myself alone, a poor dreamer and inexperienced young girl, in thus thinking and hoping for a better order!

"He told me that his sweetheart inspires all who know her with these ideas and urges them to labor for their realization. This sweetheart is quite right; but who is she? I must know her; yes, I must know her.

"Certainly, it will be very fine when there shall be no more poor people, no more servitude, and when everybody shall be gay, good, learned, and happy."

It was amid these thoughts that Vérotchka fell into a profound and dreamless sleep. No, it is not strange that you have conceived and cherished these sublime thoughts, good and inexperienced Vérotchka, although you have never even heard pronounced the names of the men who first taught justice and proved that it must be realized and inevitably will be. If books have not presented these ideas with clearness, it is because they are written by men who caught glimpses of these thoughts when they were but marvellous and ravishing utopias; now it has been demonstrated that they can be realized, and other books are written by other men, who show that these thoughts are good, with nothing of the marvellous about them. These thoughts, Vérotchka, float in the air, like the perfume in the fields when the flowers are in bloom; they penetrate everywhere, and you have even heard them from your drunken mother, telling you that one can live in this world only by falsehood and robbery; she meant to speak against your ideas, and, instead of that, she developed them; you have also heard them from the shameless and depraved Frenchwoman who drags her lover after her as if he were a servant, and does with him as she will. Yet, when she comes back to herself, she admits that she has no will of her own, that she has to indulge and restrain herself, and that such things are very painful. What more could she desire, living with her Serge, good, tender, and gentle? And yet she says: Even of me, unworthy as I am, such relations are unworthy. It is not difficult, Vérotchka, to share your ideas. But others have not taken them to heart as you have. It is well, but not at all strange. What can there be strange, indeed, in your wish to be free and happy? That desire is not an extraordinary discovery; it is not an act of heroism; it is natural. But what is strange, Vérotchka, is that there are men who have no such desire though they have all others, and who would, in fact, regard as strange the thoughts under the influence of which you fall asleep, my young friend, on the first evening of your love, and that, after questioning yourself as to him whom you love and as to your love itself, you think that all men should be happy and that we should aid them to become so as fast as possible. It is very natural, nevertheless; it is human; the simple words, "I wish joy and happiness," mean, "It would be pleasant to me if all men were joyous and happy;" yes, Vérotchka, it is human; these two thoughts are but one. You are good, you are intelligent; but excuse me for finding nothing extraordinary in you; half of the young girls whom I have known and whom I know, and perhaps even more than half—I have not counted them, and it matters little, there are so many of them—are not worse than you; some there are—pardon me for saying so—who are even better.

Lopoukhoff believes you a marvellous young girl. What is there astonishing in that? He loves you,—and that is not astonishing either. It is not astonishing that he loves you, for you are lovable, and if he loves you, he must necessarily believe you such.

VI.

Maria Alexevna had loitered about Lopoukhoff and Vérotchka during their first quadrille; during the second she could not do as much, for she was entirely absorbed in the preparation of a *repas à la fourchette*, a sort of improvised supper. When she had finished, she looked about for the tutor, but he had gone. Two days later he returned to give his lesson. The *samovar* was brought, as always during the lesson. Maria Alexevna entered the room where the tutor was busy with Fédia to call the latter, a duty which had hitherto been Matrœna's; the tutor, who, as we know, did not take tea, wished to remain to correct Fédia's copy-book; but Maria Alexevna insisted that he should come with them a moment, for she had something to say to him. He consented, and Maria Alexevna plied him with questions concerning Fédia's talents and the college at which it would be best to place him. These were very natural questions, but were they not asked a little early? While putting them, she begged the tutor to take some tea, and this time with so much cordiality and affability that Lopoukhoff consented to depart from his rule and took a cup. Vérotchka had not arrived; at last she came; she and Lopoukhoff saluted each other as if nothing had occurred between them, and Maria Alexevna continued to talk about Fédia. Then she suddenly turned the conversation to the subject of the tutor himself, and began to press him with questions. Who was he? What was he? What were his parents? Were they wealthy? How did he live? What did he think of doing? The tutor answered briefly and vaguely: He had parents; they lived in the country; they were not rich; he lived by teaching; he should remain in St. Petersburg as a doctor. Of all that nothing came. Finding him so stubborn, Maria Alexevna went straight to business.

"You say that you will remain here as a doctor (and doctors can live here, thank God!): do you not contemplate family life as yet? Or have you already a young girl in view?"

What should he say? Lopoukhoff had almost forgotten already the sweetheart of his fancy, and came near replying, "I have no one in view," when he said to himself: "Ah! but she was listening, then." He laughed at himself, and was somewhat vexed at having employed so useless an allegory. And they say that propagandism is useless! Go to, then!

See what an effect propagandism had had upon this pure soul disposed so little to evil! She was listening! Had she heard? Well, it was of little consequence.

"Yes, I have one," answered Lopoukhoff.

"And you are already engaged?"

"Yes."

"Formally? Or is it simply agreed upon between you?"

"Formally."

Poor Maria Alexevna! She had heard the words, "my sweetheart," "your sweetheart," "I love her much," "she is a beauty." She had heard them, and for the present was tranquil, believing that the tutor would not pay court to her daughter, and for this reason, the second quadrille not disturbing her, she had gone to prepare the supper. Nevertheless, she had a desire to know a little more circumstantially this tranquilizing story.

Lopoukhoff replied clearly, and, as usual, briefly.

" Is your sweetheart beautiful?"

" Of extraordinary beauty."

" Has she a dowry?"

" Not at present; but she is to receive an inheritance."

" A large inheritance?"

" Very large."

" How much?"

" Very much."

" A hundred thousand?"

" Much more."

" Well, how much, then?"

" There is no occasion to say; it is enough that it is large."

" In money?"

" In money also."

" In lands perhaps, as well?"

" And in lands as well."

" Soon?"

" Soon."

" And when will the nuptials take place?"

" Soon."

" You do well, Dmitry Sergnéitch, to marry her before she has received her inheritance; later she would be besieged by suitors."

" You are perfectly right."

" But how does it happen that God sends her such good fortune without any one having found it out?"

" So it is: scarcely any one knows that she is to receive an inheritance."

" And you are aware of it?"

" Yes."

" But how?"

" Why, certainly; I have examined the documents myself."

" Yourself?"

" Myself. It was there that I began."

" There?"

" Of course; no one in possession of his senses would venture far without authentic documents."

" Yes, you are right, Dmitry Sergnéitch. But what good fortune! you owe it probably to the prayers of your parents?"

" Probably."

The tutor had pleased Maria Alexevna first by the fact that he did not take tea; he was a man of thoroughly good quality; he said little: hence he was not a giddy fellow; what he said, he said well, especially when money was in question; but after she found out that it was absolutely impossible for him to pay court to the daughters of the families where he gave lessons, he became a godsend incapable of over-estimation. Young people like him rarely have such characteristics. Hence he was entirely satisfactory to her. What a positive man! Far from boasting of having a rich sweetheart, he allowed, on the contrary, every word to be drawn from him as if by forceps. He had had to look long for this rich sweetheart. And one can well imagine how he had to court her. Yes, one may safely say that he knows how to manage his affairs. And he began by going straight to the documents. And how he talks! " No one in possession of his senses can act otherwise." He is a perfect man.

Vérotchka at first had difficulty in suppressing a smile, but little by little it dawned upon her — how could it have been otherwise — it dawned upon her that Lopoukhoff, although replying to Maria Alexevna, was talking to her, Vérotchka, and laughing at her mother. Was this an illusion on Vérotchka's part, or was it really so? He knew, and she found out later; to us it is of little consequence; we need nothing but facts. And the fact was that Vérotchka, listening to Lopoukhoff, began by smiling, and then went seriously to thinking whether he was talking not to Maria Alexevna, but to her, and whether, instead of joking, he was not telling the truth. Maria Alexevna, who had all the time listened seriously to Lopoukhoff, turned to Vérotchka and said:

" Vérotchka, are you going to remain forever absorbed and silent? Now that you know Dmitry Serguéitch, why do you not ask him to play an accompaniment while you sing?" These words meant: We esteem you highly, Dmitry Serguéitch, and we wish you to be the intimate friend of our family; and you, Vérotchka, do not be afraid of Dmitry Serguéitch; I will tell Mikhaïl Ivanytch that he already has a sweetheart, and Mikhaïl Ivanytch will not be jealous. That was the idea addressed to Vérotchka and Dmitry Serguéitch, — for already in Maria Alexevna's inner thoughts he was not " *the tutor*," but Dmitry Serguéitch, — and to Maria Alexevna herself these words had a third meaning, the most natural and real: We must be agreeable with him; this acquaintance may be useful to us in the future, when this rogue of a tutor shall be rich.

This was the general meaning of Maria Alexevna's words to Maria Alexevna, but besides the general meaning they had also a special one: After having flattered him, I will tell him that it is a burden upon us, who are not rich, to pay a rouble a lesson. Such are the different meanings that the words of Maria Alexevna had.

Dmitry Serguéitch answered that he was going to finish the lesson and that afterward he would willingly play on the piano.

VII.

Though the words of Maria Alexevna had different meanings, none the less did they have results. As regards their special meaning,— that is, as regards the reduction in the price of the lessons,— Maria Alexevna was more successful than she could hope; when, after two lessons more, she broached the subject of their poverty, Dmitry Serguéitch haggled; he did not wish to yield, and tried to get a *trckhroublovy* (at that time there were still trekhroublovys, coins worth seventy-five copecks, if you remember); Maria Alexevna herself did not count on a larger reduction; but, against all expectation, she succeeded in reducing the price to sixty copecks a lesson. It must be allowed that this hope of reduction did not seem consistent with the opinion she had formed of Dmitry Serguéitch (not of Lopoukhoff, but of Dmitry Serguéitch) as a crafty and avaricious fellow. A covetous individual does not yield so easily on a question of money simply because the people with whom he is dealing are poor. Dmitry Serguéitch had yielded; to be logical, then, she must disenchant herself and see in him nothing but an imprudent and consequently harmful man. Certainly she would have come to this conclusion in dealing with any one else. But the nature of man is such that it is very difficult to judge his conduct by any general rule: he is so fond of making exceptions in his own favor! When the college secretary, Ivanoff, assures the college councillor, Ivan Ivanytch, that he is devoted to him body and soul, Ivan Ivanytch knows, as he thinks, that absolute devotion can be found in no one, and he knows further that Ivanoff in particular has *five times sold his own father* and thus surpassed Ivan Ivanytch himself, who so far has succeeded in selling his father but three times; yet, in spite of all, Ivan Ivanytch believes that Ivanoff is devoted to him, or, more properly speaking, without believing him, he is inclined to look upon him with good-will; he believes him, while not believing in him. What would you? There is no remedy for this deplorable incapacity of accurately judging that which touches us personally. Maria Alexevna was not exempt from this defect, which especially distinguishes base, crafty, and greedy individuals. This law admits exceptions, but only in two extreme cases,— either when the individual is a consummate scamp, a transcendental scamp, so to speak, the eighth wonder of the world of rascality, like Ali Pasha of Janina, Jezzar Pasha of Syria, Mahomet Ali of Egypt, who imposed upon European diplomats (Jezzar on the great Napoleon himself) as if they had been children, or when knavishness has covered the man with a breast-plate so solid and compact that it leaves uncovered no human weakness, neither ambition, nor passion for power, nor self-love, nor anything else. But these heroes of knavishness are very rare, and in European countries scarcely to be found at all, the fine art of knavery being already spoiled there by many human weaknesses.

Therefore, when any one shows you a crafty knave and says: "There is a man who cannot be imposed upon," bet him ten roubles to one, without hesitation, that, although you are not crafty, you can impose on him if you desire to; with equal promptness bet him a hundred roubles to one that for some special thing he can be led by the nose, for the most ordinary trait, a general trait, in the character of crafty men, is that of letting themselves be led by the nose in some special direction. Did not Louis Philippe and Metternich, for instance, who are said to have been the shrewdest politicians of their time, allow themselves nevertheless to be led to their ruin, like sheep to the pasture? Napoleon I was crafty, much craftier than they, and is said to have had genius. Was he not neatly stranded on the island of Elba? That was not enough for him; he wished to go further, and succeeded so well that that time he went to St. Helena. Read Charras's history of the campaign of 1815, and be moved by the zeal with which Napoleon deceived and destroyed himself! Alas! Maria Alexevna too was not exempt from this unfortunate tendency.

There are few people whom great perfection in the art of deceiving others prevents from being deceived themselves. There are others, on the contrary, and many of them, whom a simple honesty of heart serves to surely protect. Ask the Vidocqs and Vanka Cains of all sorts, and they will tell you that there is nothing more difficult than to deceive an honest and sincere man, provided he has intelligence and experience. Honest people who are not stupid cannot be seduced individually. But they have an equivalent defect,—that of being subject to seduction *en masse*. The knave cannot capture them individually, but collectively they are at his disposition. Knaves, on the contrary, so easy to deceive individually, cannot be duped as a body. That is the whole secret of universal history.

But this is not the place to make excursions into universal history. When one undertakes to write a romance, he must do that and nothing else.

The first result of Maria Alexevna's words was the reduction in the price of the lessons. The second result was that by this reduction Maria Alexevna was more than ever confirmed in the good opinion that she had formed of Lopoukhoff as a valuable man; she even thought that his conversations would be useful to Vérotchka in urging her to consent to marry Mikhail Ivanytch; this deduction was too difficult for Maria Alexevna ever to have arrived at it herself, but a speaking fact occurred to convince her. What was this fact? We shall see presently.

The third result of Maria Alexevna's words was that Vérotchka and Dmitry Serguéitch began, with her permission and encouragement, to spend much time together. After finishing his lesson at about eight o'clock, Lopoukhoff would stay with the Rosalskys two or three hours longer; he often played cards with the mother and father, talked with the suitor, or played Vérotchka's accompaniments on the piano; at other times Vérotchka played and he listened; sometimes he simply talked with the young girl, and Maria Alexevna did not interfere with them or look at them askance, though keeping a strict watch over them nevertheless.

Certainly she watched them, although Dmitry Serguéitch was a very good young man; for it is not for nothing that the proverb says: The occasion makes the thief. And Dmitry Serguéitch was a thief, — not in the blameworthy, but the praiseworthy sense; else there would have been no reason for esteeming him and cultivating his acquaintance. Must one associate with imbeciles? Yes, with them also, when there is profit in it. Now, Dmitry Serguéitch having nothing yet, association with him could be sought only for his qualities, — that is, for his wit, his tact, his address, and his calculating prudence.

If every man can plot harm, all the more a man so intelligent. It was necessary, then, to keep an eye on Dmitry Serguéitch, and that is what Maria Alexevna did, after keen reflection. All her observations only tended to confirm the idea that Dmitry Serguéitch was a positive man of good intentions. How, for instance, could any one see in him the propensities of love?

He did not look too closely at Vérotchka's bodice. There she is, playing; Dmitry Serguéitch listens, and Maria Alexevna watches to see if he does not cast indiscreet glances. No, he has not the least intention! He does not even look at Vérotchka at all; he casts his eyes about at random, sometimes upon her, but then so simply, openly, and coldly, as if he had no heart, that one sees in a moment that he looks at her only out of politeness, and that he is thinking of his sweetheart's dowry; his eyes do not inflame like those of Mikhaïl Ivanytch.

How else can one detect the existence of love between young people? When they speak of love. Now they are never heard to speak of love; moreover, they talk very little with each other; he talks more with Maria Alexevna. Later Lopoukhoff brought books for Vérotchka.

One day, while Mikhaïl Ivanytch was there, Vérotchka went to see one of her friends.

Maria Alexevna takes the books and shows them to Mikhaïl Ivanytch.

"Look here, Mikhaïl Ivanytch, this one, which is in French, I have almost made out myself: 'Gostinaïa.' * That means a manual of self-instruction in the usages of society. And here is one in German; I cannot read it."

"No, Maria Alexevna, it is not 'Gostinaïa;' it is destiny." He said the word in Russian.

"What, then, is this destiny? Is it a novel, a ladies' oracle, or a dream-book?"

"Let us see." Mikhaïl Ivanytch turned over a few pages.

"It deals with series; † it is a book for a *savant*."

---

* *Gostinaïa* is the Russian equivalent of the French word *salon*, meaning drawing-room primarily, and derivatively fashionable society.

† Series paper-money at interest. The book was Considérant's "Social Destiny."

"Series? I understand. It treats of transfers of money."

"That's it."

"And this one in German?"

Mikhaïl Ivanytch read slowly: "On Religion, by Ludwig," — by Louis Fourteenth.* It is the work of Louis XIV; this Louis XIV was a king of France, father of the king whom the present Napoleon succeeded."

"Then it is a pious book."

"Pious, Maria Alexevna, you have said it."

"Very well, Mikhaïl Ivanytch; although I know that Dmitry Serguéitch is a good young man, I wish to see: it is necessary to distrust everybody!"

"Surely it is not love that is in his head: but in any case I thank you for this watchfulness."

"It could not be otherwise, Mikhaïl Ivanytch; to watch is the duty of a mother who wishes to preserve her daughter's purity. That is what I think. But of what religion was the king of France?"

"He was a Catholic, naturally."

"But his book may convert to the religion of the Papists?"

"I do not think so. If a Catholic archbishop had written it, he would try to convert, it is unnecessary to say, to the religion of the Papists. But a king cares nothing about that: a king, as a prince and wise politician, wishes piety simply."

That was enough for the moment. Maria Alexevna could not help seeing that Mikhaïl Ivanytch, while having a narrow mind, had reasoned with much justice; nevertheless, she wished to place the matter in the clearest light. Two or three days later she suddenly said to Lopoukhoff, who was playing cards with her and Mikhaïl Ivanytch:

"Say, Dmitry Serguéitch, I have a question that I wish to ask you: did the father of the last king of France, whom the present Napoleon succeeded, ordain baptism in the religion of the Papists?"

"Why, no, he did not ordain it, Maria Alexevna."

"And is the religion of the Papists good, Dmitry Serguéitch?"

"No, Maria Alexevna, it is not good. And I play the seven of diamonds."

"It was out of curiosity, Dmitry Serguéitch, that I asked you that; though not an educated woman, I am interested just the same in knowing things. And how much have you abstracted from the stakes, Dmitry Serguéitch?"

"Oh, that's all right, Maria Alexevna; we are taught that at the Academy. It is impossible for a doctor not to know how to play."

To Lopoukhoff these questions remained an enigma. Why did Maria Alexevna want to know whether Philippe Egalité ordained baptism in the religion of the Papists?

---

* Ludwig Feuerbach, whom the officer in his simplicity had identified with Louis XIV.

May not Maria Alexevna be excused if she ceases now to watch the student? He did not cast indiscreet glances; he confined himself to looking at Vérotchka openly and coldly, and he lent her pious books: what more could one ask? Yet Maria Alexevna tried still another test, as if she had read the "Logic" which I too learned by heart, and which says that " the observation of phenomena which appear of themselves should be verified by experiments made in accordance with a deliberate plan in order to penetrate more deeply into the mysteries of their relations."

She arranged this test, as if she had read the story told by Saxon, the grammarian, of the way in which they put Hamlet to the test in a forest with a young girl.

VIII.
TEST À LA HAMLET.

One day Maria Alexevna said, while taking tea, that she had a severe headache; after having drank the tea and locked up the sugar-bowl, she went to lie down. Vérotchka and Lopoukhoff remained alone in the parlor, which adjoined Maria Alexevna's sleeping-chamber. A few moments later, the sick woman called Fédia.

" Tell your sister that their conversation prevents me from sleeping; let them go into another room; but say it politely, in order that Dmitry Serguéitch may not take offence; he takes such care of you! " Fédia did the errand.

" Let us go into my room, Dmitry Serguéitch," said Véra Pavlovna, " it is some distance from the chamber, and there we shall not prevent Mamma from sleeping."

That was precisely what Maria Alexevna expected. A quarter of an hour later she approached with stealthy step the door of Vérotchka's chamber. The door was partly open, and between it and the casing was a crack which left nothing to be desired. There Maria Alexevna applied her eyes and opened her ears.

And this is what she saw:

Vérotchka's room had two windows; between the windows was a writing-table. Near one window, at one end of the table, sat Vérotchka; she was knitting a worsted waistcoat for her father, thus strictly carrying out Maria Alexevna's recommendation. Near the other window, at the other end of the table, sat Lopoukhoff: supporting one elbow on the table, he held a cigar in his hand, and had thrust the other hand into his pocket; between him and Vérotchka was a distance of two *archines*,* if not more. Vérotchka looked principally at her knitting, and Lopoukhoff looked principally at his cigar. A disposition of affairs calculated to tranquilize.

* Two and one-third feet.

And this is what she heard:

 . . . "And is it thus, then, that life must be regarded?" Such were the first words that reached the ears of Maria Alexevna.

"Yes, Véra Pavlovna, precisely thus."

"Practical and cold men are therefore right in saying that man is governed exclusively by self-interest?"

"They are right. What are called elevated sentiments, ideal aspirations,—all that, in the general course of affairs, is absolutely null, and is eclipsed by individual interest; these very sentiments are nothing but self-interest clearly understood."

"But you, for example,— are you too thus governed?"

"How else should I be, Véra Pavlovna? Just consider what is the essential motive of my whole life. The essential business of my life so far has consisted in study; I was preparing to be a doctor. Why did my father send me to college? Over and over again he said to me: 'Learn, Mitia; when you have learned, you will become an office-holder; you will support us, myself and your mother, and you will be comfortable yourself.' That, then, was why I studied; if they had not had that interest in view, my father would not have sent me to school: the family needed a laborer. Now, for my part, although science interests me now, I should not have spent so much time upon it if I had not thought that this expense would be largely rewarded. My studies at college were drawing to an end; I influenced my father to allow me to enter the Academy of Medicine instead of becoming an office-holder. How did that happen? We saw, my father and I, that doctors live much better than government functionaries and heads of bureaus, above whom I could not expect to rise. That is the reason why I entered the Academy, — the hope of a bigger piece of bread. If I had not had that interest in view, I should not have entered."

"But you liked to learn at college, and the medical sciences attracted you?"

"Yes. But that is ornamental; it helps in the achievement of success; but success is ordinarily achieved without it; never without interest as a motive. Love of science is only a result; the cause is self-interest."

"Admit that you are right. All the actions that I understand can be explained by self-interest. But this theory seems to me very cold."

"Theory in itself should be cold. The mind should judge things coldly."

"But it is pitiless."

"For senseless and mischievous fancies."

"It is very prosaic."

"The poetic form is not suited to science."

"So this theory, which I do not see my way to accept, condemns men to a cold, pitiless, prosaic life?"

"No, Véra Pavlovna; this theory is cold, but it teaches man to procure warmth. Matches are cold, the side of the box against which we scratch them is cold, fagots are cold; but the fire which prepares warm nourishment for man and keeps him warm none the less springs from them; this theory is pitiless, but by following it men cease to be wretched objects of the compassion of the idle. The lancet must not yield; otherwise it would be necessary to pity the patient, who would be none the better for our compassion. This theory is prosaic, but it reveals the real motives of life; now, poetry is in the truth of life. Why is Shakspere a very great poet? Because he has sounded remoter depths of life than other poets."

"Well, I too shall be pitiless, Dmitry Serguéitch," said Vérotchka, smiling; "do not flatter yourself with the idea that you have had in me an obstinate opponent of your theory of self-interest, and that now you have gained a new disciple. For my part, I thought so long before I ever heard of you or read your book. But I believed that these thoughts were my own, and that the wise and learned thought differently; that is why my mind hesitated. All that I read was contrary to what went on within me and made my thought the object of blame and sarcasm. Nature, life, intelligence lead one way; books lead another, saying: This is bad, that is base. Do you know, the objections which I have raised seemed to me a little ridiculous."

"They are indeed ridiculous, Véra Pavlovna."

"But," said she, laughing, "we are paying each other very pretty compliments. On one side: Be not so proud, if you please, Dmitry Serguéitch. On the other: You are ridiculous with your doubts, Véra Pavlovna!"

"Ah! Yes!" said he, smiling also, "we have no interest in being polite to each other, and so we are not."

"Good, Dmitry Serguéitch; men are egoists, are they not? There, you have talked about yourself; now I wish to talk a little about myself."

"You are perfectly right; every one thinks of himself first."

"See if I do not entrap you in putting some questions to you about myself."

"So be it."

"I have a rich suitor. I do not like him. Should I accept his proposal?"

"Calculate that which is the most useful to you."

"That which is the most useful to me? You know I am poor enough. On the one hand, lack of sympathy with the man; on the other, domination over him, an enviable position in society, money, a multitude of adorers."

"Weigh all considerations, and choose the course most advantageous for you."

"And if I should choose the husband's wealth and a multitude of adorers?"

"I shall say that you have chosen that which seemed to you most in harmony with your interests."

"And what will it be necessary to say of me?"

"If you have acted in cold blood, after reasonable deliberation upon the whole subject, it will be necessary to say that you have acted in a reasonable manner, and that you probably will not complain."

"But will not my choice deserve blame?"

"People who talk nonsense may say what they will; but people who have a correct idea of life will say that you have acted as you had to act; if your action is such and such, that means that you are such an individual that you could not act otherwise under the circumstances; they will say that your action was dictated by the force of events, and that you had no other choice."

"And no blame will be cast upon my actions?"

"Who has a right to blame the consequences of a fact, if the fact exists? Your person under given circumstances is a fact; your actions are the necessary consequences of this fact, consequences arising from the nature of things. You are not responsible for them; therefore, to blame them would be stupid."

"So you do not recoil from the consequences of your theory. Then, I shall not deserve your blame, if I accept my suitor's proposal?"

"I should be stupid to blame you."

"So I have permission, perhaps even sanction, perhaps even direct advice to take the action of which I speak?"

"The advice is always the same: calculate that which is useful to you; provided you follow this advice, you will be sanctioned."

"I thank you. Now, my personal matters are settled. Let us return to the general question with which we started. We began with the proposition that man acts by the force of events, that his actions are determined by the influences under which they occur. If stronger influences overcome others that shows that we have changed our reasoning; when the action is one of real importance, the motives are called interests and their play in man a combination or calculation of interests, and consequently man always acts by reason of his interest. Do I sum up your ideas correctly?"

"Correctly enough."

"See what a good scholar I am. Now this special question concerning actions of real importance is exhausted. But in regard to the general question some difficulties yet remain. Your book says that man acts from necessity. But there are cases where it depends upon my good pleasure whether I act in one way or another. For example, in playing, I turn the leaves of my music book; sometimes I turn them with the left hand, sometimes with the right. Suppose, now, that I turn with the right hand; might I not have turned them with the left? Does not that depend on my good pleasure?"

"No, Véra Pavlovna; if you turn without thinking about it, you turn with the hand which it is more convenient for you to use. There is no good pleasure in that. But if you say: 'I am going to turn with the right hand,' you will turn with the right hand under the influence of that idea; now that idea sprang not from your good pleasure, but necessarily from another thought."

Here Maria Alexevna stopped listening.

" Now they are going into learned questions; those are not what I am after, and furthermore I care nothing about them. What a wise, positive, I might say noble, young man! What prudent rules he instils in Vérotchka's mind! That is what a learned man can do: when I say these things, she does not listen, she is offended; she is very obstinate with me, because I cannot speak in a learned way. But when he speaks in this way, she listens, sees that he is right, and admits it. Yes, it is not for nothing that they say: 'Knowledge is light, and ignorance darkness.'* (If I were a learned woman, should we be where we are? I should have lifted my husband to the rank of general; I should have obtained a position for him in the quartermaster's or some similar department; I should have made the contracts myself, for that is no business for him; he is too stupid. Would I have built such a house as this? I would have bought more than a thousand lives.

" As it is I cannot do it.

" One must first appear in the society of generals in a favorable light, — and I, how could I appear in a favorable light? I do not speak French!

" They would say: 'She has no manners; she is fit only to bandy insults on the Place Sennaïa.' And they would be right. Ignorance is darkness. Knowledge is light. The proverb is a true one."

This conversation, to which Maria Alexevna had listened, produced in her, then, the definitive conviction that the interviews between the two young people were not only not dangerous to Vérotchka (she had been of that opinion for some time), but that they would be even useful to her in inducing her to abandon, as her mother desired, the foolish ideas which she had adopted as an inexperienced girl, and in thus hastening her marriage to Mikhaïl Ivanytch.

IX.

The attitude of Maria Alexevna towards Lopoukhoff is not without a certain comic side, and Maria Alexevna is represented here under a somewhat ridiculous light. But really it is against my will that things present themselves in this aspect. If I had seen fit to act in accordance with the rules of what we call art, I should have carefully glided over these incidents which give the romance a tinge of the *vaudeville*. To hide them would have been easy. The general progress of the story might well be explained without them. What would there have been astonishing if the teacher had had opportunities (without entering into relations with Maria Alexevna) to talk, were it only rarely and a little at a time, with the

---

* A Russian proverb.

young girl, in the family where he gave lessons? Is it necessary to talk a great deal to make love spring up and grow? Maria Alexevna's aid has been wholly unnecessary to the results that have followed the meeting of the two young people. But I tell this story, not to win a reputation as a man of talent, but just as it happened. As a novelist, I am sorry to have written a few pages that touch the level of the comic.

My determination to tell things, not in the easiest way, but as they actually occurred, causes me still another embarrassment: I am not at all contented to have Maria Alexevna represented in a ridiculous light by her reflections upon the sweetheart which her fancy had pictured as Lopoukhoff's; by her fantastic way of guessing the contents of the books given by Lopoukhoff to Vérotchka; by her questions about Philippe Egalité and his pretended Papist absolutism and about the works of Louis XIV. Every one is liable to mistake; the errors may be absurd, when the individual tries to judge in matters of which he is ignorant; but it would be unjust to infer from the blunders of Maria Alexevna that these were the sole cause of her favorable attitude towards Lopoukhoff. No, her queer ideas about the rich sweetheart and the piety of Philippe Egalité would not have obscured her good sense for a moment, if she had only noticed anything suspicious in Lopoukhoff's acts and words. But he so conducted himself that really there was nothing to be said. Though naturally bold, he did not cast indiscreet glances at a very pretty young girl; he did not follow her assiduously; he sat down without ceremony to play cards with Maria Alexevna without betraying any sign that it would give him greater pleasure to be with Véra; when left with Véra, he held such conversations with her that Maria Alexevna regarded them as the expression of her own thought. Like her, he said that self-interest is the motive of human actions; that there is no sense in getting angry with a rascal and reminding him of the principles of honor, inasmuch as the rascal acts in accordance with the laws of his own nature under the pressure of circumstances; that, given his individuality, he could not help being a rascal, and that to pretend otherwise would be an absurdity. Yes, Maria Alexevna had reason to think that she had found in Lopoukhoff a kindred spirit.

But here is Lopoukhoff seriously compromised in the eyes of an enlightened public from the very fact that Maria Alexevna sympathizes with his way of looking at things. Not wishing to deceive any one, I do not hide, as I might have done, this circumstance so injurious to Lopoukhoff's reputation; I shall even go farther and explain that he really deserved the friendship of Maria Alexevna.

From Lopoukhoff's conversation with Vérotchka, it is plain that his way of looking at things might appear better to persons of Maria Alexevna's stamp than to those holding fine ideas; Lopoukhoff saw things in the aspect which they present to the mass of mankind, minus those holding lofty ideas.

If Maria Alexevna could rejoice at the thoughts that he had voiced regarding

Vérotchka's projected marriage, he, on his side, could have written beneath the drunken usurer's confession: *This is true.* The resemblance in their actions is so great that enlightened novelists holding noble ideas, journalists, and other public teachers have long since proclaimed that individuals like Lopoukhoff are in no wise distinguishable from individuals like Maria Alexevna. If writers so enlightened have thus viewed men like Lopoukhoff, is it for us to blame Maria Alexevna for coming to the same conclusions about this Loponkhoff that our best writers, thinkers, and teachers have arrived at?

Certainly, if Maria Alexevna had known only half as much as our writers know, she would have had good sense enough to understand that Lopoukhoff was no companion for her. But, besides her lack of knowledge, she had still another excuse: Lopoukhoff, in his conversations, never pursued his reflections to their conclusions, not being of those amateurs who try very hard to inspire in Maria Alexevnas the high thoughts in which they take delight themselves. He had good sense enough not to undertake to straighten a tree fifty years old. He and she understood facts in the same way and reasoned accordingly. Being educated, he was able to draw from facts certain inferences never dreamed of by people like Maria Alexevna, who know only their habitual cares and the routine aphorisms of every-day wisdom, proverbs, maxims, and other old apothegms *ejusdem farinæ*. If, for instance, in talking with Vérotchka, he had undertaken to explain what he meant by " self-interest," Maria Alexevna probably could have seen that his idea of self-interest was not exactly the same as her own; but Lopoukhoff did not explain himself on this point to the usurer, nor even to Vérotchka, the latter knowing his meaning from the books which had occasioned their conversation. On the other hand, in writing " This is true " under the confession made by Maria Alexevna when drunk, Lopoukhoff would have added: " But, whereas, by your own admission, the new order of things will be better than the old, we should not oppose those who joyfully and devotedly labor to establish it. As for the stupidity of the people, though it is indeed an obstacle, you will admit that men would soon become wise if they saw that it was for their advantage to become so, a fact which they have not yet been able to perceive; you will admit also that it has not been possible for them to learn to reason. Give them this possibility, and you will see that they will hasten to profit by it."

But the conversation with Maria Alexevna never went to that point, not from reserve, although he was reserved, but simply from good sense and the same feeling of propriety which prevented him from talking to her in Latin or entertaining her with accounts of the progress recently made in medicine, which would have interested him only. He had good sense and delicacy enough not to torment people with discourse beyond their grasp.

I say all this only to justify Maria Alexevna's oversight in not understanding in time what sort of a man Lopoukhoff was, and not at all to justify Lopoukhoff himself. To justify Lopoukhoff would not be a good thing. Why? That you shall see later, reader. Those who, without justifying him, would like, from motives of humanity, to excuse him, could not do so. For instance, they might say in his excuse that he was a doctor and an investigator of the natural sciences, circumstances which dispose one to accept the materialistic way of looking at things. But with me such an excuse is not a valid one. Many other sciences lead to materialism, as, for instance, the mathematical, historical, social, and, in short, all the sciences. Is that to say that all the geometers, astronomers, historians, economists, jurists, publicists, and other *savants* are materialists? Very far from that. Lopoukhoff could not then be justified. The compassionate people who do not justify him might say further in his excuse that he is not entirely without praiseworthy qualities: voluntarily and firmly he decided to renounce the advantages and preferences which he might have demanded of life in order to work for the benefit of others, finding in the pleasure resulting from this work his own enlightened self-interest; the good and pretty young girl with whom he has fallen in love he regards with so pure an eye that there are not many brothers who so regard their sister. But to this latter excuse it would be necessary to reply that, generally speaking, there is no man entirely without good qualities, and that the materialists, whatever they may be, are always materialists, and are shown by that very fact to be low and immoral men who must never be excused, since to excuse them would be to compromise with materialism. So, not justifying Lopoukhoff, we cannot excuse him. And there is no longer any room to justify him, since the defenders of *fine ideas* and *noble aspirations*, who have stigmatized the materialists, have made such a fine showing of wisdom and character in these latter days in the eyes of good men, materialists or not, that to defend any one from their blame is useless and to lend attention to their words at least superfluous.

X.

The question as to what is the true way of looking at things certainly was not the principal object of Vérotchka's interviews with Lopoukhoff. As a general thing they talked very little with each other, and their long conversations, which occurred but rarely, turned on general questions alone. They knew further that they were watched by two very experienced eyes. Consequently they seldom exchanged words on the subject which most interested them, and, when they did, it was usually while turning the leaves of music books.

It should be said also that the subject which so preoccupied them and about which they had so little chance to talk was not, as may be supposed, the expression of their inmost feeling. Of this feeling they had said not a word since the vague phrases of their first interview, and they had no time to discuss it during such moments as they were able to seize in which to talk freely and which were entirely devoted to Vérotchka's situation. How could she escape from it? How could she get a foothold on the stage? They knew that the theatre presents many dangers for a young girl, but that these dangers might be avoided by Vérotchka's firmness.

Nevertheless one day Lopoukhoff said to Vérotchka:

"I advise you to abandon the idea of becoming an actress."

"Why?"

"Because it would be better for you to marry your suitor." There the conversation stopped. These words were said at the moment when Vérotchka and he were taking their music books, he to play, she to sing. Vérotchka became very sad and more than once lost the time, although singing a very well known piece. While looking for another piece, Vérotchka said: "I was so happy! It is very hard for me to learn that it is impossible. I will take another course; I will be a governess."

Two days later she said to him:

"I have found no one who can secure me a place as governess. Will you do it yourself, Dmitry Serguéitch? I have only you to ask."

"It is very unfortunate that I have so few acquaintances to aid me. The families where I have given and still give lessons are all relatively poor, and the people of their acquaintance are almost as badly off. No matter, I will try."

"My friend, I take all your time, but what am I to do?"

"Véra Pavlovna, my time is not to be spoken of when I am your friend."

Vérotchka smiled and blushed; she had not noticed that her lips had substituted the name "My friend," for that of Dmitry Serguéitch.

Lopoukhoff smiled too.

"You did not intend to say that, Véra Pavlovna. Withdraw the name if you regret having given it."

"It is too late,—and then . . . . I do not regret it," replied Vérotchka, blushing more deeply yet.

"You shall see, if opportunity offers, that I am a faithful friend."

They shook hands.

Such were their first two interviews after the famous *soirée*.

Two days afterwards appeared in the "Journal of Police" an announcement that a noble young girl, speaking French and German, etc., desired a place as governess, and that inquiries concerning her could be made of such a functionary at Kolomna, Rue N. N., house N. N.

Lopoukhoff did indeed have to spend much time in Vérotchka's matters. He went every morning, generally on foot, from Wyborg to Kolomna to see the functionary of his acquaintance who had consented to do him a service in this connection. It was a long distance, but Lopoukhoff had no friends in his position nearer to Wyborg: for it was necessary that this friend should satisfy many conditions; among other things essential were a decent house, a well-regulated household, and an air of respectability. A poor house would have presented the governess in too disadvantageous a light; unless the person recommending had an air of respectability and lived, at least apparently, in comfort, no good opinion would have been formed of the young girl recommended. His own address? What would have been thought of a young girl who had no one to answer for her but a student! Therefore Lopoukhoff had much to do. After getting from the functionary the addresses of those who had come to find a governess, he started out to visit them: the functionary told them that he was a distant relative of the young person and only an intermediary, but that she had a nephew who would not fail to go in a carriage the next day to consult with them more fully. The nephew, instead of going in a carriage, went on foot, examined the people closely, and, as goes without saying, almost always found something which did not suit him. In this family they were too haughty; in another the mother was good, the father stupid; in a third it was just the reverse; in still another it would have been possible to live, but the conditions were above Vérotchka's means; or else English was required, and she did not speak it; or else they wanted not exactly a governess, but a nursery-maid; or again the people suited, but they were poor themselves, and had no other room for the governess than the children's chamber, where slept two large girls, two little boys, a nursery-maid, and a nurse.

The advertisement was kept in the "Journal of Police," and applicants continued to call on the functionary. Lopoukhoff did not lose hope. He spent a fortnight in his search. Coming home on the fifth day weary after his long tramp, Lopoukhoff threw himself on the sofa, and Kirsanoff said to him:

"Dmitry, you no longer work with me as you did. You disappear every morning and one evening out of two. You must have found many pupils. But is this the time to accept so many? For my part, I desire to give up even those that I have. I possess seventy roubles, which will last during the remaining three months of the term. And you have saved more than I, — one hundred roubles, it seems to me."

"Even more, — one hundred and fifty roubles; but it is not my pupils that keeps me, for I have given them all up save one: I have business on hand. After I have finished it, you will have no more reason to complain that I lag behind you in my work."

"What, then, is the business?"

"This: in the family where I still give lessons, an excessively bad family, there is a very remarkable young girl. She wishes to become a governess and leave her parents, and I am searching for a place for her."

"She is an excellent young girl?"

"Oh! yes!"

" 'Tis well, then. Search."

And the conversation ended there.

Well, Messrs. Kirsanoff and Lopoukhoff, learned men that you are, you have not thought to remark that which is most remarkable. Admit that the qualities which you seem to prize most are good; but are they all? What! Kirsanoff has not even thought to inquire whether the young girl is pretty! And Lopoukhoff has not thought to say a word about it! Why did not Kirsanoff think to say to his friend: "Have you, then, fallen in love that you take such an interest in her?" And it did not occur to Lopoukhoff to say: "She interests me much;" or, if he did not wish to say that, he at least failed to ward off such a conjecture by saying: "Do not think, Alexander, that I have fallen in love." They both thought that, when the deliverance of a person from a dangerous situation was in question, it was of very little importance whether the person's face was beautiful, even though it were a young girl's face, and still less whether one was in love or not. The idea that this was their opinion did not even occur to them; they were not aware of it, and that is precisely the best feature of it. For the rest, does this not prove to the class of penetrating readers — to which belong the majority of æsthetic *littérateurs*, who are endowed with exceptional penetration — does this not prove, I say, that Kirsanoff and Lopoukhoff were dry people, absolutely without the "æsthetic vein?" That was the expression in vogue but a very short time since among the æsthetic and transcendental *littérateurs*. Perhaps they still use it. No longer associating with them, I cannot say. Is it natural that young people as devoid as they of taste and heart should otherwise interest themselves in a young girl? Certainly they are without the æsthetic sentiment. According to those who have studied the nature of man in circles endowed with the *æsthetic sentiment* even to a greater degree than our *normalien æsthetic littérateurs*, young people in such a case should speak of woman from a purely plastic standpoint. So it has been, and so, gentlemen, it still is. But not among youth worthy of the name. That were a strange youth, gentlemen!

XI.

"Well, my friend, have you found nothing yet?"

"Not yet, Véra Pavlovna; but do not lose courage, keep up your hope. We shall finally find a suitable place."

"Oh, if you knew, my friend, how hard it is for me to stay here! As long as I saw no possible way of deliverance from this perpetual humiliation, I forced myself into a sort of excessive insensibility. Now I stifle in this heavy and putrid atmosphere."

"Patience, Véra Pavlovna, we shall find something."

Such conversations as this occurred at intervals for a week.

Tuesday.

"Patience, Véra Pavlovna, we shall find something."

"My friend, what an embarrassment for you! How much time lost! How shall I repay you?"

"You will repay me, my friend, if you do not take offence"......

Lopoukhoff stopped and became confused.* Vérotchka glanced at him; he had really said what he intended to say, and was awaiting a reply.

"But why should I take offence? What have you done?"

Lopoukhoff became still more confused and appeared distressed.

"What is the matter, my friend?"

"Ah! you did not notice it?" He said this in a very sad tone, and then burst out laughing. "Ah! how stupid I must be! Pardon me, my friend!"

"But what is the trouble?"

"Nothing. You have already repaid me.

"Oh, that! What a queer man you are! Well, so be it, call me so."

The following Thursday witnessed the test à la Hamlet according to Saxon, the Grammarian, after which Maria Alexevna relaxed her supervision a little.

Saturday, after tea, Maria Alexevna went to count the linen which the laundress had just brought.

"It looks, my friend, as if the affair was about to be arranged."

"Yes? Oh! so much the better! And let it be quickly. I believe that I should die if this should last longer. But when and how?"

"All will be decided to-morrow. I am almost certain of it."

"Tell me about it, then."

"Be calm, my friend, you may be noticed. There you are, leaping with joy, and your mother liable to come in at any moment!"

"But you came in yourself so radiant with joy that Mamma looked at you for a long time."

"Therefore I told her why I was gay; for I thought it would be better to tell her, and so I did say to her: 'I have found an excellent place.'"

"Insufferable that you are! you give me all sorts of advice, and not a word have you told me yet. Speak, then!"

"This morning Kirsanoff—that, you know, my friend, is my comrade's name—"

"I know, I know; speak, speak quickly."

"You prevent me yourself, my friend."

"Indeed! Still reprimands instead of reasonable speech. I do not know what

---

* Perhaps the English reader will be at a loss to understand Lopoukhoff's confusion unless informed that the words rendered here and on a previous page as "my friend" have in the original a significance more tender which no English word exactly conveys.

I shall do with you; I would put you on your knees, if it were not impossible here; I order you to kneel when you get home, and Kirsanoff shall write me whether you have done proper penance."

"So be it, and I will keep silence until I have done my penance and been pardoned."

"I pardon, but speak quickly, insufferable!"

"I thank you. You pardon me, Véra Pavlovna, when you are the guilty one yourself. You are constantly interrupting."

"Véra Pavlovna? What do you mean by that? Why do you no longer say my friend?"

"It is a punishment, my friend, that I desired to inflict upon you; I am an irritable and severe man."

"A punishment? You dare to inflict punishments on me! I will not listen to you"

"You will not?"

"No, I will not. What more is there to hear? You have told me almost all,— that the affair is nearly finished, and that tomorrow it will be decided; you know no more than that yourself today. What could I hear? *Au revoir*, my friend!"

"But listen a little, my friend; my friend, I beg of you."

"I do not listen, and am going away." She came back nevertheless. "Speak quickly, and I will interrupt you no more. Ah, if you knew what joy you have caused me! Give me your hand. See how heartily I shake it."

"And tears in your eyes . . . . . . why?"

"Thank you, thank you!"

"This morning Kirsanoff gave me the address of the lady who expects me to call tomorrow. I am not personally acquainted with her; but I have often heard her spoken of by the functionary, our mutual friend, and again he has been the intermediary. The lady's husband I know personally, having met him several times at the house of the functionary in question. Judging from appearances, I am satisfied that the family is a good one. The lady said, when giving her address, that she was satisfied that we could agree upon terms. Therefore we may consider the business almost finished."

"Oh! what happiness!" repeated Vérotchka. "But I wish to know immediately, as quickly as possible. You will come here straightway?"

"No, my friend, that would awaken suspicion. I must come here only at lesson-time. This is what we will do. I will send a letter by city post to Maria Alexevna announcing that I cannot come on Tuesday to give the usual lesson, and will come on Wednesday instead. If I say Wednesday morning, that will mean that the affair has terminated successfully; if Wednesday evening, that it has fallen through. But it is almost certain to be Wednesday morning. Maria Alexevna will tell Fédia, as well as yourself and Pavel Konstantinytch."

"When will the letter get here?"

"Tomorrow evening."

"So late! No, patience will fail me. And what am I going to learn from the letter? A simple 'yes,' and then to wait till Wednesday! It is actual torture! My friend, I am going to this lady's house. I wish to know the whole at once. But how shall we fix that? Oh, I know; I will wait for you in the street, until you come away from her house."

"But, my friend, that would be still more imprudent than for me to come back here. It is better, then, that I should come."

"No, perhaps we could not talk together here. And in any case Mamma would be suspicious. It is better to follow my suggestion. I have a veil so thick that no one will recognize me."

"Perhaps indeed, it is possible. Let me think a little."

"There is no time to lose in long reflections. Mamma may enter at any moment. Where does this lady live?"

"Rue Galernaïa, near the bridge."

"When will you be there?"

"At noon; that is the hour she fixed."

"From noon onward I will be seated on the Boulevard Konno-Gvardeisky, on the last bench on the side near the bridge. I told you that I would wear a very thick veil. But here is a signal for you: I will have a music roll in my hand. If I am not there, it will be because I have been detained. No matter, sit down on the bench and wait. I may be late, but I will not fail to come. How good I feel! How grateful I am to you! How happy I shall be! What is your sweetheart doing, Dmitry Serguéitch? You have fallen from the title of friend to that of Dmitry Serguéitch. How contented I am! How happy I am!"

Vérotchka ran to her piano, and began to play. "What a degradation of art, my friend! What has become of your taste? You abandon operas for galops."

"Abandoned, utterly abandoned!"

A few minutes later Maria Alexevna entered. Dmitry Serguéitch played a game of cards with her; he began by winning; then he allowed her to recover her losses, and finally he lost thirty-five copecks; it was the first time he had let her win, and when he went away, he left her well contented, not with the money, but with the triumph. There are joys purely ideal, even in hearts completely sunk in materialism, and this it is that proves the materialistic explanation of life unsatisfactory.

XII.

VÉROTCHKA'S FIRST DREAM.

Vérotchka dreamed that she was shut up in a dark and damp cellar. Suddenly the door opened, and she found herself at liberty in the country; she began to run about joyfully, saying to herself: " How did I keep from dying in the cellar?" And again she ran about and gamboled. But suddenly she felt a stroke of paralysis. " How is it that paralysis has fallen upon me?" thought she; " only old people are subject to that, old people and not young girls."

" Young girls also are subject to it," cried a voice. " As for you, you will be well, if I but touch you with my hand. You see, there you are, cured; arise."

" Who speaks thus to me? And how well I feel! The illness has quite gone."

Vérotchka arose; again she began to run about and play, saying to herself: " How was I able to endure the paralytic shock? Undoubtedly because I was born a paralytic, and did not know how to walk and run; if I had known how, I never could have endured to be without the power."

But she sees a young girl coming. How strange she is! her expression and manner are constantly changing; by turns she is English and French, then she becomes German, Polish, and finally Russian, then English again, German again, Russian again,—and yet why do her features always remain the same? An English girl does not resemble a French girl, nor a German a Russian. She is by turns imperious, docile, joyful, sad, gentle, angry, and her expression always indicates the feeling of the moment. But she is always good, even when she is angry. That is not all; she suddenly begins to improve; her face takes on new charms with every moment, and, approaching Vérotchka, she says to her : " Who are you?"

" Formerly he called me Véra Pavlovna; now he calls me ' my friend.' "

" Ah! it is you, the Vérotchka who has formed an affection for me."

" Yes, I love you much. But who are you?"

" I am the sweetheart of your sweetheart."

" Of which sweetheart?"

" I do not know. I am not acquainted with my sweethearts. They know me, but I cannot know them, for I have many. Choose one of them; never take one elsewhere."

" I have chosen " . . . .

" I have no need of his name; I do not know them. But I say to you again, choose only among them. I wish my sisters and my sweethearts to choose each other exclusively. Were you not shut up in a cellar? Were you not paralyzed?"

" Yes."

"Are you not free now?"

"Yes."

"It is I who delivered you, who cured you. Remember that there are many who are not yet delivered, who are not yet cured. Go, deliver them and cure them! Will you do it?"

"I will do it. But what is your name? I wish to know it."

"I have many names. I tell to each the name by which he is to know me. As for you, call me Love of Mankind. That is my real name; but there are not many people who know it; you, at least, shall call me so."

Then Vérotchka found herself in the city; she saw a cellar where young girls were shut up. She touched the lock, the lock fell; she said to the young girls: "Go out!" and they went out. She saw then a chamber where lay young girls who had been paralyzed; she said to them: "Arise!" They arose and all ran into the country, lighted-hearted and laughing: Vérotchka followed them, and in her happiness cried out:

"How pleasant it is to be with them! How sad it was to be alone! How pleasant it is to be with the free young girls who run in the fields, agile and joyous!"

XIII.

Lopoukhoff, overburdened with cares, had no longer any time to see his friends at the Academy. Kirsanoff, who had not ceased to associate with them, was obliged to answer a hundred questions about Lopoukhoff: he revealed the nature of the affair that occupied his friend, and thus it was that one of their mutual friends gave the address of the lady on whom Lopoukhoff is about to call at this stage of our story. "How fortunate it will be, if this succeeds!" thought he, as he walked along; "in two years, two and a half at most, I shall be a professor. Then we can live together. In the meantime she will live quietly with Madame B., provided Madame B. proves really to be a good person whom one cannot mistrust."

Lopoukhoff found in Madame B. an intelligent and good woman, without pretentions, although the position of her husband would have warranted her in having many. The conditions were good, Vérotchka would be well situated there; all was going on famously, then, and Lopoukhoff's hopes had not been groundless.

Madame B., on her side, being satisfied with Lopoukhoff's replies regarding Vérotchka's character, the affair was arranged, and after a half hour's talk, Madame B. said: "If my conditions suit your young aunt, I beg her to take up her quarters here, and I should be pleased to see her as soon as possible."

"She will be satisfied; she has authorized me to act for her. But now that we have come to an agreement, I must tell you (what it was needless to tell you before) that this young girl is not my relative. She is the daughter of the functionary in whose family I give lessons. She had no one but me whom she could trust in this affair. But I am almost a stranger to her."

"I knew it, Monsieur Lopoukhoff. You, Professor N. (the name of the friend who had given the address), and your comrade esteem yourselves so highly that one of you can form a friendship for a young girl without compromising her in the eyes of the two others. Now N. and I think the same, and, knowing that I was looking for a governess, he felt justified in telling me that this young girl is not related to you. Do not blame him for being indiscreet; he knows me very well. I believe myself also worthy of esteem, Monsieur Lopoukhoff, and be sure that I well know who is worthy of being esteemed. I trust N. as I trust myself, and N. trusts you as he trusts himself. Let us say no more on that point, then. But N. did not know her name, and it will be necessary for me to know it, since she is to come into our family."

"Her name is Véra Pavlovna Rosalsky."

"Now, I have an explanation to make to you. It may seem strange to you that, careful as I am of my children, I have decided upon a governess for them whom I have not seen. But I made the bargain with you because I know well, very well indeed, the men who compose your circle, and I am convinced that, if one of you feels so keen an interest in a young person, this young person must be a veritable treasure to a mother who desires to see her daughter become worthy of the esteem of all. Consequently to make inquiries about her seemed to me a superfluous indelicacy. In saying this I compliment, not you, but myself."

"I am very glad for Mademoiselle Rosalsky. Life in her family was so painful to her that she would have been contented in any family at all endurable. But I never should have hoped to find her a home like yours."

"Yes, N. told me that her family life was very bad."

"Very bad indeed!" And Lopoukhoff told Madame B. such facts as she would need to know in order to avoid, in her conversations with Vérotchka, touching on subjects which would give her pain by reminding her of her former troubles.

Madame B. listened with much interest, and finally, grasping his hand, she said to him:

"Enough, Monsieur Lopoukhoff; I shall have a nervous attack; and at my age of forty years it would be ridiculous to show that I cannot yet listen in cold blood to a story of family tyranny, from which I suffered so much when young."

"Permit me to say another word; it is of so little importance that perhaps it is not necessary to speak of it. Nevertheless it is better that you should be informed. She is fleeing from a suitor whom her mother wishes to force upon her."

Madame B. became thoughtful, and Lopoukhoff, looking at her, in his turn became thoughtful too.

"This circumstance, if I mistake not, seems of more importance to you than to me?"

Madame B. seemed utterly disconcerted.

"Pardon me," he continued, seeing that she did not know what to say,— "pardon me, but I perceive that you regard this as an obstacle."

"Yes, it is a very serious matter, Monsieur Lopoukhoff. To leave the house of her parents against their will would alone be certain to cause a grave quarrel. But, as I have already told you, that might be overlooked. If she only ran away from their coarseness and tyranny, that could be settled with them in one way or another; in the last extremity a little money would set everything right. But when such a mother forces a marriage, it is evident that the suitor is rich, very rich in fact."

"Evidently," said Lopoukhoff in a very sad tone.

"Evidently! Monsieur Lopoukhoff, he is rich, evidently; that is what has disconcerted me. Under such circumstances the mother could not be satisfied in any way whatever. Now, you know the rights of parents. They would halt at nothing; they would begin an action which they would push to the end."

Lopoukhoff rose.

"There is nothing further to say except to ask you to forget all that I have said to you."

"No, no, stay. I wish first to justify myself in your eyes. I must seem to you very bad. That which should attract my sympathy and protection is just what holds me back. Believe me, I am much to be pitied. Oh, I am much to be pitied!"

She was not shamming. She was really much to be pitied. She felt keenly; for some time her speech was incoherent, so troubled and confused was she. Gradually, nevertheless, order was restored in her thoughts, but even then she had nothing new to say, and it was Lopoukhoff's turn to be disconcerted. Consequently, after allowing Madame B. to finish, though not listening very closely to her explanations, he said:

"What you have just said in your justification was needless. I remained in order that I might not seem impolite and that you might not think that I blame you or am offended. Oh! if I did not know that you are right! How I wish you were not right! Then I could tell her that we failed to come to an agreement, that you did not suit me. That would be nothing, and we should still retain the hope of finding another place and reaching the deliverance so long awaited. But now what shall I say to her?"

Madame B. wept.

"What shall I say to her?" repeated Lopoukhoff, as he went down the stairs.

"What will she do? What will she do?" thought he, as he turned from the Rue Galernaïa into the street leading to the Boulevard Konno-Gvardeisky.

It goes without saying that Madame B. was not as entirely right as the man who refuses the moon to a child. In view of her position in society and her husband's powerful connections, it was very likely, and even certain, that if she had really wished Vérotchka to live with her, Maria Alexevna would have been unable to prevent it or even to cause any serious trouble either to herself or to her husband, who would have been officially responsible in the matter and for whom Madame B. was afraid. Madame B. would simply have been put to a little inconvenience, perhaps even to a disagreeable interview or two; it would have been necessary to demand such protections as people generally prefer to utilize in their own behalf. What prudent man would have taken any other course than Madame B.'s. And who is obliged to do more? We have no right to blame her. Nor, on the other hand, was Lopoukhoff wrong in despairing of Vérotchka's deliverance.

XIV.

For a long time, a very long time, had Vérotchka been sitting on the bench at the place agreed upon, and many times had her heart begun to beat faster as she saw in the distance a military cap.

"At last! There he is! It is he! My friend!" She rose suddenly and ran to meet him. Perhaps he would have regained his courage by the time he reached the bench, but, being taken unawares, he could show only a gloomy countenance.

"Unsuccessful?"

"Yes. my friend."

"And it was so sure? How did it happen? For what reasons? Speak, my friend."

"Let us go to your house; I will escort you, and we will talk as we walk; presently I will tell you the whole story, but first let me collect my thoughts; it is necessary to devise some new plan and not lose courage."

Having said this, he seemed calmer.

"Tell me directly. I cannot bear to wait. Do I understand that it is necessary to devise some new plan and that your first plan is not at all feasible? Is it, then, impossible for me to be a governess? Oh! unfortunate that I am!"

"You are not to be deceived? Yes, then, it is impossible. That is what I intended to tell you, but patience, patience, my friend! Be firm. Whoever is firm always succeeds at last."

"Yes, my friend, I am firm; but it is hard!"

They walked for some time without saying a word.
Lopoukhoff saw that she had a bundle under her cloak.
"I beg you," said he, "my friend, allow me to carry that."
"No, no, it does not trouble me; it is not at all heavy."
Again silence was resumed, and thus they walked for a long time.
"If you knew, my friend, that I have not slept for joy since two o'clock this morning. And when I slept, I had a marvellous dream. I dreamed that I had been delivered from a damp cellar, that I was paralyzed, that I was cured; then, that I ran gaily in the country with a multitude of young girls, who like me had come from dark cellars and been cured of paralysis, and we were so happy at being able to run freely in the fields! Alas! my dream is not realized. And I, who thought to go back to the house no more!"
"My friend, let me carry your bundle; you cannot keep its contents secret from me."
And once more they walked in silence.
"All was so arranged," said Lopoukhoff, at last; "you cannot leave your parents against their will. It is impossible, impossible . . . . . But give me your arm."
"No, do not be troubled; this veil stifles me, that is all."
She raised her veil.
"Ah! I am better now."
"How pale she is! My friend, do not look at things in the worst light; that is not what I meant to say to you; we shall find some means of accomplishing all."
"What! accomplishing all! You say that, my friend, to console me. There is nothing in it."
He did not answer.
"How pale she is! How pale she is! There is a way, my friend."
"What way?"
"I will tell you, when you are a little calmer. You will have to think it over coolly."
"Tell me directly. I shall not be calm until I know."
"No, you are getting excited again; now you are in no condition to come to a serious decision. Some time hence . . . . . . Soon . . . . . . Here are the steps. *Au revoir*, my friend. As soon as I find you in a condition to give me a cool answer, I will tell you the rest."
"When, then?"
"Day after to-morrow, at the lesson."
"That is too long."
"I will come to-morrow expressly."
"No, sooner."

"This evening."

"No, I will not let you. Come in with me. You say I am not calm enough, that I cannot form a well considered judgment. So be it; but dine with us, and you shall see that I am calm. After dinner mamma is going out, and we can talk."

"But how can I go in? If we enter together, your mother's suspicions will be aroused again."

"Suspicions! What matters it? No, my friend, that is still another reason why you should go in. My veil is raised, and perhaps I have been seen."

"You are right."

XV.

Maria Alexevna was much astonished at seeing her daughter and Lopoukhoff come in together. She fixed her piercing eyes upon them.

"I have come, Maria Alexevna, to tell you that I shall be busy day after to-morrow, and will give my lesson to-morrow. Allow me to take a seat. I am very tired and weary. I should like to rest a little."

"Indeed! What is the trouble, Dmitry Serguéitch? You are very sad. Have they come from a lovers' meeting," she continued to herself, "or did they simply meet by chance? If they had come from a lovers' meeting, they would be gay. Nevertheless, if the difference in their characters had led them into any disagreement, they would have reason to be sad; but in that case they would have quarreled, and he would not have accompanied her home. On the other hand, she went straight to her room without so much as looking at him, ... and yet they did not seem to be at variance. Yes, they must have met by chance. Nevertheless, he must be watched."

"Do not trouble yourself on my account, Maria Alexevna," said Lopoukhoff. "Don't you think that Véra Pavlovna looks a little pale?"

"Vérotchka? She sometimes does."

"Perhaps it was only my imagination. My head whirls, I must confess, under so much anxiety."

"But what is the trouble, then, Dmitry Serguéitch? Have you quarreled with your sweetheart?"

"No, Maria Alexevna, I am well satisfied with my sweetheart. It is with her parents that I wish to quarrel."

"Is it possible? Dmitry Serguéitch, how can you quarrel with her parents? I had a better opinion of you."

"One can do nothing with such a family. They demand unheard-of impossibilities."

"That is another thing, Dmitry Serguéitch. One cannot be generous with everybody; it is necessary to keep within bounds. If that is the case, and if it is a question of money, I cannot blame you."

"Pardon my importunity, Maria Alexevna, but I am turned so completely upside down that I need rest in pleasant and agreeable society. Such society I find only here. Permit me to invite myself to dinner with you, and permit me also to send your Matrœna on a few errands. I believe Dencher's cellar is in this neighborhood, and that he keeps some very fair wines."

A scowl came over Maria Alexevna's countenance at the first word about dinner, but her face relaxed when she heard Matrœna's name and assumed an inquiring expression which seemed to ask: "Are you going to pay for your share of the dinner? At Dencher's! It must be something nice, then!" Lopoukhoff, without even raising his eyes, drew from his pocket a cigar case, and, taking from it a piece of paper which it happened to contain, began to write upon it with a pencil.

"May I ask you what wine you prefer, Maria Alexevna?"

"To tell the truth, Dmitry Serguéitch, I do not know much about wine, and seldom drink it: it is not becoming in women." (One readily sees from a glance at your face that you do not generally take it.)

"You are quite right, Maria Alexevna, but a little *maraschino* does no one any harm; it is a young ladies' wine. Permit me to order some."

"What sort of wine is that Dmitry Serguéitch?"

"Oh! it is not exactly wine, it is more of a syrup." Drawing a bill from his pocket, he continued: "I think that will be enough," and after having looked at the order, he added: "But, to make sure, here are five roubles more."

It was three weeks' income and a month's support. No matter, there was nothing else to be done; Maria Alexevna must be generously dealt with.

Maria Alexevna's eyes glistened with excitement, and the gentlest of smiles unconsciously lighted up her face.

"Is there also a confectioner's near here? I do not know whether they keep walnut cake ready made,—in my opinion, that is the best kind of cake, Maria Alexevna,—but, if they do not keep it, we will take what they have. It will not do to be too particular."

He went into the kitchen, and sent Matrœna to make the purchases.

"We are going to feast to-day, Maria Alexevna. I desire to drown in wine my quarrel with her parents. Why should we not feast? My sweetheart and I are getting on swimmingly together. Sometime we shall no longer live in this way; we shall live gaily; am I not right, Maria Alexevna?"

"You are quite right, little father, Dmitry Serguéitch. That is why you scatter money,—something I never expected of you, as I thought you a selfish man. Perhaps you have received some earnest money from your sweetheart?"

"No, I have received no earnest money, Maria Alexevna, but if one has some money perchance, why should he not amuse himself? Earnest money! There is no need of any earnest money. The affair must be as clear as day; otherwise suspicions would be excited. And, moreover, such things are degrading, Maria Alexevna."

"Such things are degrading, Dmitry Serguéitch; you are right; such things are degrading. In my opinion one ought always to be above such things."

"You are quite right, Maria Alexevna."

They passed the three-quarters of an hour which they had to wait for dinner in agreeable conversation on lofty matters only. Among other things Dmitry Serguéitch, in an outburst of frankness, said that the preparations for his marriage had been progressing finely of late. And when will Véra Pavlovna's marriage take place?

On that point Maria Alexevna can say nothing, for she is far from desiring to coerce her daughter.

"That is right; but, if my observations are correct she will soon make up her mind to marry; she has said nothing to me about it, but I have eyes in my head. We are a pair of old foxes, Maria Alexevna, not easily to be entrapped. Although I am still young, I am an old fox just the same; am I not an old fox, Maria Alexevna?"

"Truly you are, my little father; you are a cunning rogue."

This agreeable and effusive interview with Maria Alexevna thoroughly revived Lopoukhoff. What had become of his sorrow? Maria Alexevna had never seen him in such a mood. Making a pretence of going to her room to get a pocket-handkerchief, she saw fine wines and liquors that had cost twelve roubles and fifty copecks. "We shall not drink more than a third of that at dinner," thought she. "And a rouble and a half for that cake? Truly, it is throwing money out of the window to buy such a cake as that! But it will keep; we can use it instead of confectionery to regale the gossips with."

XVI.

All this time Vérotchka remained in her chamber.

"Did I do right in making him come in? Mamma looked at him so steadily!

"In what a difficult position I have put him! How can he stay to dinner?

"O my God, what is to become of me?

"There is a way, he told me; alas! no, dear friend, there is none.

"Yes! there is one: the window.

"If life should become too burdensome, I will throw myself out.

"That is a singular thing for me to say: if life should become too burdensome,—and is my life now such a joy?

"To throw one's self out of the window! One falls so quickly! Yes, the fall is as rapid as flight; and to fall on the sidewalk, how hard and painful it must be!

"Perhaps there is only the shock, a second after which all is over, and before the fatal moment you are going through the air which opens softly beneath you like the finest down. Yes, it is a good way.

"But then? Everybody will rush to look at the broken head, the crushed face, bleeding and soiled. If, before leaping, you could only sprinkle the spot where you are to fall with the whitest and purest sand, all would be well.

"The face would not be crushed or soiled, nor would it wear a frightful aspect.

"Oh, I know; in Paris unfortunate young girls suffocate themselves with charcoal gas. That is good, very good. To throw yourself out of the window,— no, that is not fitting. But suffocation,— that's the thing, that's the thing.

"How they do talk! What are they saying? What a pity that I cannot tell what they say!

"I will leave a note telling all.

"How sweet the memory of my birthday when I danced with him! I did not know what true life was.

"After all, the young girls of Paris are intelligent. Why should I not be as intelligent as they are? It will be comical: they will enter the chamber, they will be unable to see anything, the room will be full of charcoal gas, the air will be heavy; they will be frightened: 'What has happened? Where is Vérotchka?' Mamma will scold Papa: 'What are you waiting for, imbecile? Break the windows!' They will break the windows, and they will see; I shall be seated near my dressing-table, my face buried in my hands. 'Vérotchka! Vérotchka!' I shall not reply.

"'Vérotchka, why do you not answer? Oh, God, she is suffocated.' And they will begin to cry, to weep. Oh, yes, that will be very comical, to see them weep, and Mamma will tell everybody how much she loved me.

"But he, he will pity me. Well, I will leave him a note.

"I will see, yes, I will see, and I shall die after the fashion of the poor girls of Paris. Yes, I will certainly do it, and I am not afraid.

"And what is there to be so afraid of? I will only wait until he tells me the way of which he speaks. Ways! There are none. He said that simply to calm me.

"What is the use of calming people when there is nothing to be done? It is a great mistake; in spite of all his wisdom, he has acted as any other would. Why? He was not obliged to.

"What is he saying? He speaks in a gay tone, and as if he was joyful.

"Can he, indeed, have found a way of salvation?

"It does not seem possible.

"But if he had nothing in view, would he be so gay?

"What can he have thought of?"

XVII.

"Vérotchka, come to dinner!" cried Maria Alexevna.

Pavel Konstantinytch had just come in, and the cake had been on the table for some time,— not the confectioner's but one of Matrœna's, a cake stuffed with meat, left over from the day before.

"Maria Alexevna, you have never tried taking a drop of brandy before dinner? It is very good, especially this brandy made from bitter orange. As a doctor, I advise you to take some. Taste of it, I beg of you."

"No, no, thank you."

"But if, as a doctor, I prescribe it for you?"

"The doctor must be obeyed, but only a small half-glass."

"A half-glass! It would not be worth while."

"And yourself, Dmitry Serguéitch?"

'I? Old as I am? I have made oath" . . . .

"But it is very good! And how warming it is!"

"What did I tell you? Yes, indeed, it is warming."

("But he is very gay. Can there really be a way? How well he acts toward her, while he has not a glance for me! But it is all strategy just the same.")

They seated themselves at the table.

"Here, Pavel Konstantinytch and I are going to drink this ale, are we not? Ale is something like beer. Taste, Maria Alexevna."

"If you say that it is beer, why not taste of it?"

("What a lot of bottles! Oh, I see now! How fertile friendship is in methods!")

("He does not drink, the cunning rogue. He only carries the glass to his lips. This ale, however, is very good; it has a taste of *krass*, only it is too strong. After I have united Michka and Verka, I will abandon brandy, and drink only this ale. He will not get drunk; he does not even taste of it. So much the better for me! There will be the more left; for, had he wanted to, he could have emptied all the bottles.")

"But yourself, why do you not drink, Dmitry Serguéitch?"

"Oh, I have drank a great deal in my time, Maria Alexevna. And what I have drank will last me a good while. When labor and money failed me, I drank; now that I have labor and money, I need wine no longer, and am gay without it."

The confectioner's cake was brought in.

"Dear Matrœna Stepanovna, what is there to go with this?"

"Directly, Dmitry Serguéitch, directly," and Matrœna returned with a bottle of champagne.

"Véra Pavlovna, you have not drank, nor have I. Now then let us drink too. To the health of your sweetheart and mine!"

"What is that? What can he mean?" thought Vérotchka.

"May they both be happy, your sweetheart and Vérotchka's!" said Maria Alexevna: "and, as we are growing old, may we witness Vérotchka's marriage as soon as possible!"

"You shall witness it soon, Maria Alexevna. Shall she not, Véra Pavlovna?"

"What does he really mean?" thought Vérotchka.

"Come, then! Is it yes, Véra Pavlovna? Say yes, then."

"Yes," said Vérotchka.

"Bravo! Véra Pavlovna, your mother was doubtful; you have said yes, and all is settled. Another toast. To the earliest possible consummation of Véra Pavlovna's marriage! Drink, Véra Pavlovna! Be not afraid. Let us touch glasses. To your speedy marriage!"

They touched glasses.

"Please God! Please God! I thank you, Vérotchka. You console me, my daughter, in my old age!" said Maria Alexevna, wiping away the tears. The English ale and the *maraschino* had quickened her emotions.

"Please God! Please God!" repeated Pavel Konstantinytch.

"How pleased we are with you, Dmitry Serguéitch!" continued Maria Alexevna, getting up from the table; "yes, we are well pleased with you! You have come to our house and you have regaled us; in fact, we might say that you have given us a feast!" So spoke Maria Alexevna, and her moist and hazy eyes did not testify in favor of her sobriety.

Things always seem more necessary than they really are. Lopoukhoff did not expect to succeed so well; his object was simply to cajole Maria Alexevna that he might not lose her good will.

Maria Alexevna could not resist the brandy and other liquors with which she was familiar, and the ale, the *maraschino*, and the champagne having deceived her inexperience, she gradually grew weaker and weaker. For so sumptuous a repast she had ordered Matrona to bring the *samovar* when dinner was over, but it was brought only for her and Lopoukhoff.

Vérotchka, pretending that she wanted no tea, had retired to her room. Pavel Konstantinytch, like an ill-bred person, had gone to lie down as soon as he had finished eating. Dmitry Serguéitch drank slowly; he was at his second glass when Maria Alexevna, completely used up, pleaded an indisposition which she had felt since morning, and withdrew to go to sleep. Lopoukhoff told her not to trouble herself about him, and he remained alone and went to sleep in his arm-chair after drinking his third glass.

"He, too, like my treasure, has entered into the Lord's vineyard," observed Matrona. Nevertheless her treasure snored loudly, and this snoring undoubtedly awakened Lopoukhoff, for he arose as soon as Matrœna, after clearing the table, had betaken herself to the kitchen.

XVIII.

"Pardon me, Véra Pavlovna," said Lopoukhoff, on entering the young girl's room, — and his voice, which at dinner had been so loud, was soft and timid, and he no longer said " My friend," but " Véra Pavlovna," — " pardon my boldness. You remember our toasts; now, as husband and wife cannot be separated, you will be free."

"My dear friend, it was for joy that I wept when you entered."

He took her hand and covered it with kisses.

"You, then, are my deliverer from the cellar of my dream? Your goodness equals your intelligence. When did this thought occur to you?"

"When we danced together."

"And it was at the same moment that I too felt your goodness. You make me free. Now I am ready to suffer; hope has come back to me. I shall no longer stifle in the heavy atmosphere that has oppressed me; for I know that I am to leave it. But what shall we do?"

"It is already the end of April. At the beginning of July I shall have finished my studies; I must finish them in order that we may live. Then you shall leave your cellar. Be patient for only three months more, and our life shall change. I will obtain employment in my art, though it will not pay me much; but there will be time left to attend to patients, and, taking all things together, we shall be able to live."

"Yes, dear friend, we shall need so little; only I do not wish to live by your labor. I have lessons, which I shall lose, for Mamma will go about telling everybody that I am a wretch. But I shall find others, and I too will live by my labor; is not that just? I should not live at your expense."

"Who told you that, dear Vérotchka?"

"Oh! he asks who told me! Have not you yourself always entertained me with such ideas, you and your books? For your books are full of such thoughts. A whole half of your books contains nothing but that."

"In my books? At any rate I never said such a thing to you. When, then, did I say so?"

"When? Have you not always told me that everything rests on money?"

"Well?"

"And do you really think me, then, so stupid that I cannot understand books and draw conclusions from premises?"

"But again I ask you what conclusion. Really, my dear Vérotchka, I do not understand you."

"Oh! the strategist! He too wants to be a despot and make me dependent upon him! No, that shall not be, Dmitry Serguéitch; do you understand me now?"

"Speak, and I will try to understand."

"Everything rests on money, you say, Dmitry Sergueitch; consequently, whoever has money has power and freedom, say your books; then, as long as woman lives at man's expense, she will be dependent on him, will she not? You thought that I could not understand that, and would be your slave? No, Dmitry Sergueitch, I will not suffer your despotism; I know that you intend to be a good and benevolent despot, but I do not intend that you shall be a despot at all. And now this is what we will do. You shall cut off arms and legs and administer drugs; I, on the other hand, will give lessons on the piano. What further plans shall we form about our life?"

"Perfect, Vérotchka! Let every woman maintain with all her strength her independence of every man, however great her love for and confidence in him. Will you succeed? I know not, but it matters little: whoever arrives at such a decision is already almost secure against servitude; for, at the worst, he can always dispense with another. But how ridiculous we are, Vérotchka! You say: 'I will not live at your expense,' and I praise you for it. How can we talk in this way?"

"Ridiculous or not, that matters little, dear friend. We are going to live in our own way and as we deem most fitting. What further plans shall we form about our life?"

"I gave you my ideas, Véra Pavlovna, about one side of our life; you have seen fit to completely overturn them and substitute your own; you have called me tyrant, despot; be good enough therefore to make your own plans. It seems hardly worth while for me to provide you with a pestle with which to thus grind to powder those that I propose. What plans, then, would be your choice, my friend? I am sure that I shall have only congratulations to offer."

"What! Now you pay me compliments! You wish to be agreeable? You flatter yourself that you are going to rule, while appearing to submit? I know that trick, and I beg you to speak more plainly hereafter. You give me too much praise. I am confused. Do nothing of the kind; I shall grow too proud."

"Very well, Véra Pavlovna. I will be rude, if you prefer. Your nature has so little of the feminine element that you are undoubtedly about to put forth utterly masculine ideas."

"Will you tell me, dear friend, what the feminine nature is? Because woman's voice is generally clearer than man's is it necessary to discuss the respective merits of the contralto and the barytone? We are always told to remain women. Is not that stupidity?"

"Worse than that, Vérotchka."

"Then I am going to throw off this femininity and put forth utterly masculine ideas as to the way in which we shall live. We will be friends. Only I wish to be your first friend. Oh! I have not yet told you how I detest your dear Kirsanoff."

"Beware of detesting him; he is an excellent man."

"I detest him, and I shall forbid you to see him."

"A fine beginning! She is so afraid of despotism that she desires to make a doll of her husband. How am I to see no more of Kirsanoff when we live together?"

"Are you always in each other's arms?"

"We are together at breakfast and dinner, but our arms are otherwise occupied."

"Then you are not together all day?"

"Very near together. He in his room, I in mine."

"Well, if that is the case, why not entirely cease to see each other?"

"But we are good friends; sometimes we feel a desire to talk, and we talk as long as we can with each other."

"They are always together! They embrace and quarrel, embrace and quarrel again. I detest him!"

"But who tells you that we quarrel? That has never happened once. We live well-nigh separately; we are friends, it is true; but how can that concern you?"

"How nicely I have trapped him! You did not intend to tell me how we shall live, and yet you have told me all! Listen, then; we will act upon your own words. First, we will have two rooms, one for you and one for me, and a little parlor where we will take breakfast, dine, and receive our visitors, — those who come to see us both, not you or me alone. Second, I shall not dare to enter your room lest I might disturb you. Kirsanoff does not dare to, and that is why you do not quarrel. No more shall you dare to enter mine. So much for the second place. In the third — ah! my dear friend, I forgot to ask you whether Kirsanoff meddles with your affairs and you with his. Have you a right to call one another to account for anything?"

"I see now why you ask this question. I will not answer."

"But really I detest him! You do not answer me; it is needless. I know how it is: you have no right to question each other about your personal affairs. Consequently I shall have no right to demand anything whatever of you. If you, dear friend, deem it useful to speak to me of your affairs, you will do so of your own accord, *vice versâ*. There are three points settled. Are there any others?"

"The second rule requires some explanation, Vérotchka. We see each other in the little parlor. We have breakfasted; I stay in my room, and do not dare to show myself in yours; then I shall not see you until dinner-time?"

"No."

"Precisely. But suppose a friend comes to see me, and tells me that another friend is coming at two o'clock. I must go out at one o'clock to attend to my affairs; shall I be allowed to ask you to give this friend who is to come at two o'clock the answer that he seeks, — can I ask you to do that, provided you intend to remain at home?"

"You can always ask that. Whether I will consent or not is another question. If I do not consent, you will not ask the reason. But to ask whether I will consent to do you a service, that you can always do."

"Very well. But when we are at breakfast, I may not know that I need a service; now, I cannot enter your room. How shall I make my want known?"

"Oh, God! how simple he is! A veritable infant! You go into the neutral room and say: 'Véra Pavlovna!' I answer from my room: 'What do you wish, Dmitry Serguéitch?' You say: 'I must go out; Monsieur A. (giving the name of your friend) is coming. I have some information for him. Can I ask you, Véra Pavlovna, to deliver it to him?' If I say 'no,' our conversation is at an end. If I say 'yes,' I go into the neutral room, and you tell me what reply I am to make to your friend. Now do you know, my little child, how we must conduct ourselves?"

"But, seriously, my dear Vérotchka, that is the best way of living together. Only where have you found such ideas? I know them, for my part, and I know where I have read them, but the books in which I have read them you have not seen. In those that I gave you there were no such particulars. From whom can you have heard them, for I believe I am the first new man* that you have met?"

"But is it, then, so hard to think in this way? I have seen the inner life of families; I do not refer to my own, that being too isolated a case; but I have friends, and I have been in their families; you cannot imagine how many quarrels there are between husbands and wives."

"Oh! I very easily imagine it."

"Do you know the conclusion that I have come to? That people should not live as they do now, — always together, always together. They should see each other only when they need or desire to. How many times I have asked myself this question: Why are we so careful with strangers? Why do we try to appear better in their presence than in our families? And really we are better in the presence of strangers. Why is this? Why are we worse with our own, although we love them better? Do you know the request I have to make of you? Treat me always as you have done heretofore. Although you have never given me a rude reply or passed any censure upon me, that has not prevented you from loving me. People say: How can one be rude to a woman or young

---

* By "new man" the author means a man of advanced thought.

girl whom he does not know, or how pass censure upon her? Well, here I am your sweetheart and about to become your wife; treat me always as it is customary to treat strangers; that seems to me the best way of preserving harmony and love between us. Am I not right?"

"Truly, I don't know what to think of you, Vérotchka; you are always astonishing me."

"Too much praise, my friend; it is not so difficult to understand things. I am not alone in entertaining such thoughts: many young girls and women, quite as simple as myself, think as I do. Only they do not dare to say so to their suitors or their husbands; they know very well what would be thought of them: immoral woman! I have formed an affection for you precisely because you do not think as others do in this matter. I fell in love with you when, speaking to me for the first time on my birthday, you expressed pity for woman's lot and pictured for her a better future."

"And I,— when did I fall in love with you? On the same day, as I have already told you, but exactly at what moment?"

"But you have almost told me yourself, so that one cannot help guessing, and, if I guess, you will begin praising me again."

"Guess, nevertheless."

"At what moment? When I asked you if it were true that we could so act as to make all men happy."

"For that I must kiss your hand again, Vérotchka."

"But, dear friend, this kissing of women's hands is not exactly what I like."

"And why?"

"Oh! you know yourself; why ask me? Do not, then, ask me these questions, dear friend."

"Yes, you are right; one should not ask such questions. It is a bad habit; hereafter I will question you only when I really do not know what you mean. Do you mean that we should kiss no person's hand?"

Vérotchka began to laugh. "There, now, I pardon you, since I too have succeeded in catching you napping. You meant to put me through an examination, and you do not even know the reason of my repugnance. It is true that we should not kiss any person's hand, but I was not speaking from so general a standpoint; I meant simply that men should not kiss women's hands, since that ought to be offensive to women, for it means that men do not consider them as human beings like themselves, but believe that they can in no way lower their dignity before a woman, so inferior to them is she, and that no marks of affected respect for her can lessen their superiority. But such not being your view, my dear friend, why should you kiss my hand? Moreover, people would say, to see us, that we were betrothed."

"It does look a little that way, indeed, Vérotchka; but what are we then?"

"I do not know exactly, or rather it is as if we had already been married a long time."

"And that is the truth. We were friends; nothing is changed."

"Nothing changed but this, my dear friend,— that now I know I am to leave my cellar for liberty."

XIX.

Such was their first talk,— a strange one, it will be admitted, for lovers making a declaration. When they had again clasped hands, Lopoukhoff started for his home, and Vérotchka had to lock the outside door herself, for Matrœna, thinking that her *treasure* was still snoring, had not yet begun to think of returning from the *cabaret*. And indeed "her treasure" did sleep a number of hours.

Reaching home at six o'clock, Lopoukhoff tried to go to work, but did not succeed. His mind was occupied, and with the same thought that had absorbed him when going from the Sémenovsky Bridge to the district of Wyborg. Were they dreams of love? Yes, in one sense. But the life of a man who has no sure means of existence has its prosaic interests; it was of his interests that Lopoukhoff was thinking. What could you expect? Can a materialist think of anything but his interests? Our hero, then, thought of interests solely; instead of cherishing lofty and poetic dreams, he was absorbed by such dreams of love as are in harmony with the gross nature of materialism.

"Sacrifice! That is the word that I shall never get out of her head, and there is the difficulty; for, when one imagines himself under serious obligations to any one, relations are strained.

'She will know all; my comrades will tell her that for her sake I renounced a brilliant career, and if they do not tell her, she will easily see it herself. 'See, then, what you have renounced for my sake,' she will say to me. Pecuniary sacrifices it is pretty sure that neither she nor my comrades can impute to me. It is fortunate that at least she will not say: 'For my sake he remained in poverty, while without me he would have been rich.' But she will know that I aspired to scientific celebrity, and that that aspiration I have given up. Thence will come her sorrow: 'Ah! what a sacrifice he has made for me!' That is something I have never dreamed of. Hitherto I have not been foolish enough to make sacrifices, and I hope that I never shall be. My interest, clearly understood, is the motive of my acts. I am not a man to make sacrifices. For that matter, no one makes them; one may really believe that he does, and that is always the most agreeable way of viewing one's conduct. But how explain that to her? In theory it is comprehensible; but when we see a fact before us, we are moved. 'You are my benefactor,' we say. The germ of this coming revolt has already made its appearance: 'You deliver me from my cellar.' 'How good you are to me!' she said to me. But are you under any obligations to me for that? If in so doing I labored for my own happiness, I delivered myself. And do you believe that I would do it if I did not prefer to? Yes, I have delivered myself; I wish to live, I wish to love, do you understand? It is in my own interest that I always act.

"What shall I do to extinguish in her this detrimental feeling of gratitude which will be a burden upon her? In whatever way I can I will do it; she is intelligent, she will understand that these are sentimental illusions.

"Things have not gone as I expected. If she had been able to get a place for two years, I could during that time have become a professor and earned some money. This postponement is no longer possible. Well, what great disadvantage shall I experience? Have I ever thought much of my pecuniary position? To a man that is of little consequence. The need of money is felt principally by woman. Boots, an overcoat not out at the elbows, *steki* on the table, my room warmed,— what else do I need? Now all that I shall have. But for a young and pretty woman that is not enough. She needs pleasure and social position. For that she will have no money. To be sure, she will not dwell upon this want; she is intelligent and honest; she will say: 'These are trifles, which I despise,' and indeed she will despise them. But because you do not feel what you lack, do you really lack nothing? The illusion does not last. Nature stifled by the will, by circumstances, by pride, is silent at first, but a silent life is torture. No, such is not the way for a young woman, a beauty, to live; it is not right that she should not be dressed as well as others and should not shine for want of means. I pity you, my poor Vérotchka; it would have been better could I have arranged my affairs first.

"For my part, I gain by this haste: would she accept me two years hence? Now she accepts me."

"Dmitry, come to tea," said Kirsanoff.

Lopoukhoff started for Kirsanoff's room, and on his way his thoughts continued thus: "But as it is just that the *ego* should always be the first consideration, it is with myself that I have finished. And with what did I begin? Sacrifice. What irony! Do I indeed renounce celebrity, a chair in the academy? What change will there be in my life? I shall work in the same way, I shall obtain the chair in the same way, and, finally, I shall serve medical science in the same way. From the objective standpoint it is curious to watch how selfishness mocks at our thoughts in practice."

I forewarn my reader of everything; consequently I will tell him that he must not suppose that Lopoukhoff's monologue contains any allusion to the nature of his future relations with Véra Pavlovna; the life of Véra Pavlovna will not be tormented by the impossibility of shining in society and dressing richly, and her relations with Lopoukhoff will not be spoiled by the "detrimental feeling" of gratitude.

I do not belong to that school of novelists which beneath every word hides some motive or other; I report what people think and do, and that is all; if any action whatever, or any conversation, or any monologue passing through the brain is indispensable in showing the character of a person or a situation, I relate it, although it may have no influence at all on the further course of my story.

"Henceforth, Alexander, you will have no reason to complain that I neglect my work; I am going to recover the lost time."

"Then you have finished your affair with this young girl?"

"Yes, I have finished."

"Is she going to be a governess at Madame B.'s?"

"No, she will not be a governess. The affair is arranged otherwise. Meantime she will lead an endurable life in her family."

"Very good. The life of a governess is really a very hard one. You know I have got through with the optic nerve; I am going to begin another subject. And where did you leave off?"

"I have still to finish my work upon ".... and anatomical and physiological terms followed each other in profusion.

XX.

"It is now the twenty-eighth of April. He said that his affairs will be arranged by the beginning of July. Say the tenth: that is surely the beginning. To be surer still, say the fifteenth: no, the tenth is better. How many days, then, are there left? Today does not count; there are but five hours left. Two days in April; thirty-one in May, added to two, make thirty-three; June has thirty, which, added to thirty-three, make sixty-three; ten days in July,—a total of seventy-three days. That is not so long a time, seventy-three days! And then I shall be free! I shall go out of this stifling cellar. Oh! how happy I am! Oh! my dear lover, how well he has solved the problem! How happy I am!"

That was Sunday evening. Monday came the lesson, changed from Tuesday.

"My friend, my darling, how happy I am to see you again even for so short a time! Do you know how much time I have yet to live in my cellar? Will your affairs be arranged by the tenth of July?"

"Certainly."

"Then there are but seventy-two days and this evening left. I have already scratched off one day, for I have prepared a table, as the young boarding-scholars and pupils do, and I scratch off the days. How it delights me to scratch them off!"

"My darling Vérotchka, you have not long to suffer. Two months and a half will pass quickly by, and then you will be free."

"Oh, what happiness! But, my darling, do not speak to me any more, and do not look at me; we must not play and sing together so frequently hereafter, nor must I leave my room every evening. But I cannot help it! I will come out every day, just for a moment, and look at you with a cold eye. And now I am going straight back to my room. Till I see you again, my dear friend. When will it be?"

"On Thursday."

"Three days! How long that is! And then there will be but sixty-eight days left."

"Less than that: you shall leave here about the seventh of July."

"The seventh. Then there are but sixty-eight days left now? How you fill me with joy! *Au revoir*, my well-beloved!"

Thursday.
"Dear friend, only sixty-six days now."
"Yes, Vérotchka, time goes quickly."
"Quickly? Oh, my dear friend, the days have grown so long! It seems to me that formerly an entire month would have gone by in these three days. *Au revoir*, my darling, we must not talk too long with each other; we must be strategic, must we not? *Au revoir!* Ah! sixty-six days more!"

("Hum, hum! I do not do so much counting; when one is at work, the time passes quickly. But then, I am not in 'the cellar.' Hum, hum!")

Saturday.
"Ah! my darling, still sixty-four days! How wearisome it is here! These two days have lasted longer than the three that preceded them. Ah! what anguish! What infamies surround me! If you knew, my friend! *Au revoir*, my darling, my angel,—till Tuesday. The following three days will be longer than the five just past. *Au revoir! Au revoir!*"

("Hum, hum! yes! hum! Red eyes. She does not like to weep. It is not well. Hum!")

Tuesday.
"Ah, my love, I have already stopped counting the days. They do not pass, they do not pass at all."

"Vérotchka, my good friend; I have a request to make of you. We must talk freely together. Your servitude is becoming too burdensome to you. We must talk together."

"Yes, we must, my well-beloved."

"Well, what hour to-morrow will suit you best? You have but to name it. On the same bench in the Boulevard Konno-Gvardeisky. Will you be there?"

"I will be there, I will be there surely. At eleven o'clock. Does that suit you?"

"Very well, thank you, my good friend."

"*Au revoir!* Oh, how glad I am that you have decided upon that! Why did I not think of it myself, foolish girl that I am! *Au revoir!* We are going to talk with each other; that will refresh me a little. *Au revoir*, dear friend. At eleven o'clock precisely."

Friday.

"Vérotchka, where are you going?"

"I, Mamma?" Vérotchka blushed. "To the Perspective Nevsky."

"Well, I am going with you; I have got to go to the Gastinoï Dvor. But how is this? You say that you are going to the Nevsky, and have put on such a dress! Put on a finer one; there are many fashionable people on the Nevsky."

"This dress suits me. Wait a moment, Mamma, I must get something from my room."

They go out. They have reached the Gastinoï Dvor. They follow the row of stores along the Sadovaïa near the corner of the Nevsky. Now they are at Rousanoff's perfumery.

"Mamma, I have a word to say to you."

"What, Vérotchka?"

"Till I see you again, I know not when; if you are not offended, till to-morrow."

"What, Vérotchka? I do not understand" . . . . . .

"*Au revoir*, Mamma, I am going now to my husband's. Day before yesterday took place my marriage to Dmitry Serguéitch. Rue Karavannaïa, coachman!" said she, jumping into a cab.

"A Tchervertatchok,* my good young lady."

"Yes, provided you go quickly."

"He will call on you this evening, Mamma. Do not be angry, Mamma."

Maria Alexevna had scarcely had time to hear these words.

"Coachman, you are not to go to the Rue Karavannaïa; I told you that in order that you might lose no time in deliberation, as I desired to get away from that woman. Turn to the left, along the Nevsky. We will go much farther than the

---

* A Tchervert is a coin worth twenty-five copecks. A Tchervertatchok is its diminutive.

Karavannaïa, to the island of Vassilievsky,* fifth line, † beyond the Perspective Moyenne. Go quickly, and I will pay you more."

"Ah, my good young lady, how you have tried to deceive me. For that I must have a Poltinnitchek." ‡

"You shall have it, if you go fast enough."

XXI.

The marriage had been effected without very many difficulties, and yet not without some. During the first days that followed the betrothal, Vérotchka rejoiced at her approaching deliverance; the third day "the cellar," as she called it, seemed to her twice as intolerable as before; the fourth day she cried a little; the fifth she cried a little more than the fourth; the sixth she was already past crying, but she could not sleep, so deep and unintermittent was her anguish.

Then it was that Lopoukhoff, seeing her red eyes, gave utterance to the monologue, "Hum, hum!" After seeing her again, he gave utterance to the other monologue, "Hum, hum! Yes! hum!" From the first monologue he had inferred something, though exactly what he did not know himself; but in the second monologue he explained to himself his inference from the first. "We ought not to leave in slavery one to whom we have shown liberty."

After that he reflected for two hours,—an hour and a half while going from the Sémenovsky Bridge to the district of Wyborg and half an hour lying on his bed. The first quarter of an hour he reflected without knitting his brows; but the remaining seven quarters he reflected with brows knit. Then, the two hours having expired, he struck his forehead, saying: "I am worse than Gogol's postmaster, § calf that I am! (Looking at his watch). Ten o'clock. There is yet time." And he went out.

The first quarter of an hour he said to himself: "All that is of little consequence; what great need is there that I should finish my studies? I shall not be ruined for having no diploma. By lessons and translations I shall earn as much as, and probably even more than, I should have earned as a doctor."

He had no reason, therefore, to knit his brows; the problem had shown itself so easy to solve, at least partially, that since the last lesson he had felt a presentiment of a solution of this sort. He understood this now. And if any one could have reminded him of the reflections beginning with the word "sacrifice" and ending with the thoughts about the poor, he would have had to admit that at that time he foresaw such an arrangement, because otherwise the thought, "I re-

---

* The Island of Vassilievsky is a part of the city of St. Petersburg.
† In this island each side of almost every street is called a *line*, so that, if one side of the street, for instance, is called the fifth line, the other is called the fourth line.
‡ A Poltinnik is a coin worth fifty copecks. A Poltinnitchek is its diminutive.
§ See Gogol's "Dead Souls."

nounce a career of learning," would have had no basis. It seemed to him then that he did not renounce, and yet instinct said to him: "This is not a simple postponement; it is a renunciation." But, if Lopoukhoff would thus have been convicted, as a practical thinker, of violating logic, he would have triumphed as a theorist and would have said: "Here is a new instance of the sway of selfishness over our thoughts; I ought to have seen clearly, but I saw dimly because I did not wish to see things as they were. I have left the young girl to suffer a week longer, when I should have foreseen and arranged everything on the spot."

But none of these thoughts came into his head, because, knitting his brows, he said to himself for seven quarters of an hour: "Who will marry us?" And the only reply that presented itself to his mind was this: "No one will marry us." But suddenly, instead of *no one*, his mind answered "Mertzaloff." Then it was that he struck his forehead and justly reproached himself for not having thought of Mertzaloff at first; it is true that his fault was palliated by the circumstance that he was not accustomed to consider Mertzaloff as one who marries.

In the Academy of Medicine there are all sorts of people,— among others, seminarists. These have acquaintances in the Spiritual Academy, and through these Lopoukhoff had some there also.

A student in the Spiritual Academy, with whom he had no intimate acquaintance but was on friendly terms, had finished his studies the previous year, and was a priest in a certain edifice with endless corridors situated on the island of Vassilievsky. To his house Lopoukhoff repaired, and, in view of the extraordinary circumstances and the advanced hour, he even took a cab.

Mertzaloff, whom he found at home alone, was reading some new work, I know not what,— perhaps that of Louis XIV, perhaps one by some other member of the same dynasty.

"That is the business that brings me here, Alexey Pétrovitch! I know very well that it involves a great risk on your part. It will amount to nothing if the parents are reconciled; but, if they bring a suit, you perhaps will be ruined, nay, you surely will be, but" . . . .

Lopoukhoff could think of nothing with which to follow this "but." How, indeed, present reasons to an individual to influence him to put his head upon the block for our sake?

Mertzaloff reflected for a long time; he too was trying to find a "but" that would authorize him to run such a risk, but he too could find none.

"What's to be done? I should very much like. . . . What you ask me to do now I did a year ago; but now I am not free to do all that I would like to do. It is a case of conscience: it would be in accordance with my inclinations to aid you. But when one has a wife, one fears to take a step without looking to see whither it will lead him."

"Good evening, Alocha.* My relatives send their regards to you. Good evening, Lopoukhoff; we have not seen each other for a long time. What were you saying about wives? You men are always grumbling about your wives," said a pretty and vivacious blonde of seventeen years, just returning from a call upon her parents.

Mertzaloff stated the situation to her. The young woman's eyes sparkled.

"But, Alocha, they will not eat you!"

"There is danger, Natacha." †

"Yes, very great danger," added Lopoukhoff.

"But what's to be done? Risk it, Alocha, I beg of you."

"If you will not blame me, Natacha, for forgetting you in braving such a danger, our conversation is over. When do you wish to marry, Dmitry Sergueitch?"

Then there was no further obstacle. Monday morning Lopoukhoff had said to Kirsanoff:

"Alexander, I am going to make you a present of my half of our labor. Take my papers and preparations, I abandon them all. I am to leave the Academy; here is the petition. I am going to marry." And Lopoukhoff told the story briefly.

"If you were not intelligent, or even if I were a booby, I should tell you, Dmitry, that none but fools act in this way. But I do nothing of the sort. You have probably thought more carefully than I upon all that could be said. And even though you had not thought upon it, what difference would it make? Whether you are acting foolishly or wisely I do not know; but I shall not be thoughtless enough to try to change your resolution, for I know that that would be vain. Can I be useful to you in any way?"

"I must find some rooms in some quarter at a low price; I need three. I must make my application to the Academy to obtain my papers as soon as possible, tomorrow in fact. To you, then, I must look to find me rooms."

Tuesday Lopoukhoff received his papers, went to Mertzaloff, and told him that the marriage would take place the next day.

"What hour will suit you best, Alexey Pétrovitch?"

"It is all one to me; tomorrow I shall be at home all day."

"I expect, moreover, to have time to send Kirsanoff to warn you."

Wednesday at eleven o'clock Lopoukhoff waited for Vérotchka on the boulevard for some time, and was beginning to grow anxious, when he saw her running in all haste.

"Dear Vérotchka, has anything happened to you?"

"No, my dear friend, I am late only because I slept too long."

---

* Alocha is the diminutive of Alexey.
† Natacha is the diminutive of Natalia.

"What time did you go to sleep then?"

"I do not like to tell you. At seven o'clock; no, at six; up to that time I was continually agitated by unpleasant dreams."

"I have a request to make of you, dear Vérotchka; we must come to an understanding as quickly as possible in order that both of us may be tranquil."

"That is true, dear friend."

"So, in four days, or in three" . .

"Ah, how good that will be!"

"In three days I probably shall have found some rooms; I shall have purchased everything needful for our household; can we then begin to live together?"

"Certainly."

"But first we must marry."

"Ah, I forgot; yes, we must first marry."

"But we can marry at once."

"Well, let us do so. But how have you managed to arrange everything so soon? How well you know how to do things!"

"I will tell you on the way; come, let us go."

On leaving the cab, they went through long corridors leading to the church; there they found the doorkeeper, whom they sent to Mertzaloff's, who lived in this same building with the interminable corridors.

"Now, Vérotchka, I have another request to make of you. You know that in church they bid the newly-married to kiss each other."

"I know it, but how embarrassing it must be!"

"That we may be less confused when the time comes, let us kiss each other now."

"Very well, let us kiss each other, but can it not be dispensed with there?"

"At the church it is impossible to avoid it; therefore we had better prepare for it."

They kissed each other.

"Dear friend, how fortunate we are in having had time to prepare; there is the doorkeeper coming back already."

It was not the doorkeeper coming back,—he had gone to look for the sexton; it was Kirsanoff who entered; he had been waiting for them at Mertzaloff's.

"Vérotchka, I introduce to you that Alexander Matvéitch Kirsanoff, whom you detest and wish to forbid me to see."

"Véra Pavlovna, why would you separate two such tender hearts?"

"Because they are tender," said Vérotchka, extending her hand to Kirsanoff. She became thoughtful, though continuing to smile. "Shall I love him as well as you do? For you love him much, do you not?" she added.

"I? I love no one but myself, Véra Pavlovna."

"And him also?"

"We have lived without quarreling, that is enough."

"And he loves you no more than that?"

"At least I have not remarked it. For that matter, let us ask him: do you love me, Dmitry?"

"I have no particular hatred for you."

"Well, if that is the case, Alexander Matvéitch, I will not forbid him to see you, and I will love you myself."

"That is much the better way, Véra Pavlovna."

Alexey Pétrovitch came.

"Here I am; let us go to the church." Alexey Pétrovitch was gay and even in a joking mood; but when he began the service, his voice became a little tremulous. "And if they should bring suit? Go to your father, Natacha, your husband can no longer support you; now, it is not a happy existence to live at your father's expense while your husband is still living." But after having said a few words, he completely regained his self-possession.

During the ceremony Natalia Andrevna, or Natacha, as Alexey Pétrovitch called her, came. When all was over, she invited the newly-married couple to go home with her; she had prepared a little breakfast; they went, they laughed, they danced a couple of quadrilles, they even waltzed. Alexey Pétrovitch, who did not know how to dance, played the violin. Two short hours passed quickly by. It was a joyous wedding.

"I believe that they are already waiting dinner for me at home," said Vérotchka; "it is time to go. Now, my darling, I will be patient three, four days in my 'cellar' without fretting too much. I could even live there longer Why should I be sorrowful? What have I to fear now? No, do not escort me; I will go alone; we might be seen."

"Oh, the devil! they will not eat me; do not be so anxious on my account," said Alexey Pétrovitch, in escorting Lopoukhoff and Kirsanoff, who had remained a moment longer to give Vérotchka time to go; "I am now very glad that Natacha encouraged me."

On the morrow, after four days' search, they found satisfactory rooms at the end of the fifth line on the island of Vassilievsky.

His savings amounting in all to one hundred and sixty roubles, Lopoukhoff and his comrade had decided that it would be impossible for them to furnish rooms themselves; so they rented three furnished rooms with board of a *petit bourgeois* * couple.

The *petit bourgeois* was an old man, passing his days peacefully beside a basket filled with buttons, ribbons, pins, etc., and placed against the wall of the

---

* A French translation of the Russian word *metschanine*, signifying a separate social class above the peasants and below the merchants.

little garden situated on the Perspective Moyenne between the first and second lines, or in conversation with his wife, who passed her days in repairing all sorts of old clothes brought to her by the armful from the second-hand stores. The service was performed by the proprietors themselves.

The Lopoukhoff's paid thirty roubles a month.

At that time — that is, ten years ago * — life in St. Petersburg was still comparatively inexpensive. Under these circumstances the Lopoukhoff's with their resources could live for three or even four months; ten roubles a month would pay for their food. Lopoukhoff counted, in the course of these four months, on obtaining pupils, literary work, or occupation in some commercial house.

On Thursday, the day when the rooms were found (and excellent rooms they were, that had not been easily found), Lopoukhoff, coming to give his lesson, said to Vérotchka:

"Come tomorrow; here is the address. I will say no more now, lest they may observe something."

"Dear friend, you have saved me!"

But how to get away from her parents? Should she tell them all? So Vérotchka thought for a moment; but her mother might shower blows upon her with her fists and lock her up. Vérotchka decided to leave a letter in her room. But when Maria Alexevna manifested an intention of following her daughter to the Perspective Nevsky, the latter went back to her room and took the letter again; for it seemed to her that it would be better and more honest to tell her to her face what had been done. Would her mother come to blows with her in the street? It would be necessary only to keep a certain distance from her, then speak to her, jump into a cab, and start off before she could seize her by the sleeve.

And thus it was that the separation was effected near Rousanoff's perfumery.

XXII.

But we have witnessed only half of this scene.

For a minute Maria Alexevna, who was suspecting nothing of the sort, stood as if thunderstruck, trying to understand and yet not at all comprehending what her daughter said. What did all that mean? But her hesitation lasted only a minute, and even less. She suddenly began to hurl insults, but her daughter had already entered the Nevsky; Maria Alexevna hurried a few steps in that direction; it was necessary to take a cab.

"Coachman!"

---

* Now thirty years ago.

"Where do you wish me to take you, Madame?"

Which way should she go? She thought she heard her daughter say Rue Karavannaïa; but she had turned to the left along the Nevsky. What course should she take?

"Overtake that wretch!"

"Overtake, Madame? But tell me where I am to go? What course shall I take? The price, in short."

Maria Alexevna, utterly beside herself, insulted the coachman.

"I see that you are drunk, Mistress," said he, and he drove off.

Maria Alexevna followed him with her insults, called other coachmen, and ran now one way, now another, brandishing her arms; at last she started under the colonnade, stamping with rage. A half-dozen young people, venders of all sorts of eatables and knick-knacks, gathered around her, near the columns of the Gastinoï Dvor. They admired her much; they exchanged remarks more or less spicy, and bestowed upon her praises, not without wit, and advice that testified to their good intentions. "Ah! what an excellent lady! So early, and drunk already! Excellent lady!"

"Mistress, do you hear? Mistress, buy a half-dozen lemons of me; they are good things to eat after drinking, and I will sell them to you cheap."

"Do not listen to him, Mistress; lemons will not help you any; you would do better to take a drink of something strong."

"Mistress, Mistress, what a powerful tongue you have! Are you willing to match it against mine on a wager?"

Maria Alexevna, now no longer knowing what she was about, slapped the face of one of her tormenters, a boy of about seventeen, who put his tongue out, not without some grace: the little merchant's cap rolled off into the dirt, and Maria Alexevna, thus enabled to get her hand into his hair, did not fail to grasp it by handfuls. The other scamps, seeing which, were seized with an indescribable enthusiasm:

"That's it! Hit him! Now then! Bravo, the mistress!"

"Lick him, lick him, Mistress!"

Others said: "Fedka,* defend yourself, hit her back!"

But the majority were on Maria Alexevna's side.

"What can Fedka do against this jolly old girl? Lick him, lick him, Mistress; the scamp is getting no more than he deserves."

In addition to the speakers many spectators had already gathered: coachmen, warehouse-men, and passers-by were approaching in crowds; Maria Alexevna seemed to come to her senses, and, after having by a last mechanical movement pushed away the head of the unfortunate Fedka, she crossed the street. Enthu-

---

* Fedka, a diminutive of Fœdor in popular usage.

siastic tributes of praise followed her. She became conscious that she was going home when she had passed the carriage-way of the Corps des Pages; she took a cab, and reached the house in safety. On arriving she administered a few blows to Fédia, who opened the door; rushed to the brandy closet; administered a few blows to Matrœna, who had been attracted by the noise; made for the closet again; ran into Vérotchka's room, and came back to the closet a third time; ran again into Vérotchka's room, and stayed there a long time; and then began to walk up and down the rooms scolding and reviling: but whom should she hit? Fédia had fled to the kitchen stairs; Matrœna, peeping through a crack into Vérotchka's room and seeing Maria Alexevna start in her direction, had precipitately fled toward the kitchen, but, not being able to reach it, had rushed into Maria Alexevna's bed-room and hidden under the bed, where she remained in safety awaiting a more peaceable summons.

How long did Maria Alexevna scold and vociferate, walking up and down the empty rooms? It is impossible to say exactly, but for a long time apparently, since Pavel Konstantinytch on his arrival was received also with blows and insults. Nevertheless, as everything must end, Maria Alexevna cried at last: "Matrœna, get the dinner ready!" And Matrœna, seeing that the storm was over, came out from under the bed and set the table.

During dinner Maria Alexevna left off scolding and contented herself with muttering, but without offensive intentions and simply for her own satisfaction; then, instead of going to lie down, she took a seat and remained alone, now saying nothing, now muttering: then she stopped muttering, and at last cried out: "Matrœna, wake your master, and tell him to come to me."

Matrœna, who, expecting orders, had not dared to go away, either to the *cabaret* or anywhere else outside of the house, hastened to obey.

Pavel Konstantinytch made his appearance.

"Go to the proprietor and tell her that your daughter, thanks to you, has married this blackguard. Say: 'I was opposed to my wife.' Say: 'I did it to please you, for I saw your consent was lacking.' Say: 'The fault was my wife's alone; I carried out your will.' Say: 'It was I who arranged this marriage.' Do you understand me?"

"I understand, Maria Alexevna; you reason very wisely."

"Well, start then! If she is at dinner, let that make no difference; have her called from the table. Make haste, while she is still in ignorance."

The plausibility of the words of Pavel Konstantinytch was so evident that the proprietor would have believed the worthy steward, even if he had not been endowed with the faculty of presenting his ideas with humility, veneration, and in a persuasive and respectful manner; but this power of persuasion was so great that the proprietor would have pardoned Pavel Konstantinytch, even if she had not had palpable proofs of his misunderstanding with his wife.

Was it not evident that he had put his daughter in relations with Lopoukhoff in order to avoid a marriage embarrassing to Mikhaïl Ivanytch?

"What were the terms of the marriage?"

Pavel Konstantinytch had spared nothing in order to give his daughter her marriage portion; he had given five thousand roubles to Lopoukhoff, had paid the expenses of the wedding, and established the couple in housekeeping. It was he who had carried the notes from one to the other. At the house of his colleague, Filatieff, chief of the bureau and a married man, added Pavel Konstantinytch,—yes, it was at his house, your excellency, for although I am an humble man, your excellency, the virgin honor of my daughter is dear to me,—it was at his house, I say, that the meetings took place, in my presence; we were not rich enough to employ a teacher for an urchin like Fédia; no, that was only a pretext, your excellency, etc.

Then Pavel Konstantinytch painted in the blackest colors the character of his wife. How could one help believing and pardoning Pavel Konstantinytch? It was, moreover, a great and unexpected joy. Joy softens the heart. The proprietor began her notice of discharge by a long condemnation of Maria Alexevna's abominable plans and guilty conduct, and at first called on Pavel Konstantinytch to turn his wife out of doors. He begged her not to be so severe.

She spoke thus only for the sake of saying something. Finally they agreed on the following terms:

Pavel Konstantinytch held his stewardship; the apartments fronting on the street were taken away from him; the steward was to live in the rooms farthest in the rear; his wife was not to show herself about the front of the establishment where the proprietor's eye might fall upon her, and she was to go into the street only through the carriage-way, which was far from the proprietor's windows.

Of the twenty roubles a month formerly added to his pay fifteen were taken back and five left as a reward for the zeal shown by Pavel Konstantinytch in carrying out the proprietor's will and to make good the expenses occasioned by his daughter's marriage.

XXIII.

Maria Alexevna had thought of several plans as to the way in which to deal with Lopoukhoff when he should come in the evening. That nearest her heart consisted in hiding two man-servants in the kitchen who, at a given signal, should throw themselves upon and beat him unmercifully. The most pathetic consisted in hurling from her own lips and those of Pavel Konstantinytch the paternal and maternal curse on their rebellious daughter and the ruffian, her husband, insisting at the same time on the import of this curse, the earth itself rejecting, as is well known, the ashes of those whom their parents have cursed.

But these were dreams, like those of the proprietor in wishing to separate Pavel Konstantinytch from his wife; such projects, like poetry in general, are destined less to be realized than to relieve the heart by serving as a basis for solitary reflections leading to no results and for explanations in future interviews: that is how I might have developed affairs, that is how I desired to develop them, but through goodness of heart I allowed myself to relent. The idea of beating Lopoukhoff and cursing her daughter was the ideal side of Maria Alexevna's thoughts and feelings. The real side of her mind and soul had a tendency much less elevated and much more practical,—an inevitable difference, given the weakness of every human being. When Maria Alexevna came to her senses, near the carriage-way of the Corps des Pages, and comprehended that her daughter had actually disappeared, married, and escaped, this fact presented itself to her mind in the form of the following mental exclamation: "She has robbed me!" All the way home she did not cease to repeat to herself, and sometimes aloud: "She has robbed me!" Consequently, after delaying a few minutes through human weakness to tell her chagrin to Fédia and Matrœna,— every individual allows himself to be dragged by the expression of his feelings into forgetting in his fever the real interests of the moment,—Maria Alexevna ran into Vérotchka's room. She rushed to the dressing-table and the wardrobe, which she reviewed with a hasty glance. "No," said she, "everything seems to be here." Then she proceeded to verify this first tranquillizing impression by a detailed examination. Everything, indeed, was really there, except a pair of very simple gold ear-rings, the old muslin dress, and the old sack that Vérotchka had on when she went out. Regarding this real side of the affair, Maria Alexevna expected that Vérotchka had given Lopoukhoff a list of the things belonging to her which he would claim; she was fully determined to give up no article of gold or anything in that line, but only the four plainest dresses and the most worn linen: to give nothing was impossible; *noblesse oblige*,—an adage of which Maria Alexevna was a rigid observer.

Another question of real life was the relations with the proprietor; we have already seen that Maria Alexevna had succeeded in settling it satisfactorily.

There remained the third question: what was to be done with the guilty, that is, with her daughter and the son-in-law that had been thrust upon her? Curse them? Nothing easier, only such a curse must serve as a dessert to something more substantial. Now, this substantial something could take but one practical shape, that of presenting a petition, bringing a suit, and arraigning before a court of assizes. At first, in her fever, Maria Alexevna viewed this solution of the question from her ideal side, and from this point of view it seemed very seductive to her. But in proportion as her mind became calmer, the affair gradually assumed another aspect. No one knew better than Maria Alexevna that all lawsuits require money, much money, especially lawsuits like this which pleased her by its ideal beauty, and that, after dragging for a long time and devouring much money, they end absolutely in nothing.

What, then, was to be done? She finally concluded that there were but two things to do, — give herself the satisfaction of abusing Lopoukhoff as much as possible, and save Vérotchka's things from his claims, to which end the presentation of a petition would serve as a means. But at any rate she must roundly abuse him, and thus derive all the satisfaction she could.

Even this last part of the plan was not to be realized.

Lopoukhoff arrived, and began in this tone: " We beg you, my wife and I, to be kind enough, Maria Alexevna and Pavel Konstantinytch, to excuse us for having without your consent " . . . .

At this point Maria Alexevna cried out:

" I will curse her, the good —. . . . ! " She could not finish the epithet *good-for-nothing*. At the first syllable Lopoukhoff raised his voice:

" I have not come to listen to your insults, but to talk business. And since you are angry and cannot talk calmly, I will explain myself in a private interview with Pavel Konstantinytch; and you, Maria Alexevna, will send Fédia or Matrœna to call us when you have become calmer."

As he spoke, he led Pavel Konstantinytch from the parlor into the small room adjoining, and his voice was so strong and positive that there was no way to overmaster it. So she had to reserve her remarks.

Having reached the parlor door with Pavel Konstantinytch, Lopoukhoff stopped, turned back, and said: " I would like nothing better than to make my explanation to you also, Maria Alexevna, if you desire, but on one condition, — that I may do so undisturbed."

Again she began her abuse, but he interrupted her: " Well, since you cannot converse calmly, we leave you."

" And you, imbecile, why do you go with him ? "

" Why, he drags me after him."

" If Pavel Konstantinytch were not disposed to give me a quiet hearing, I would go away, and that would be perhaps the better course: what matters it to me, indeed! But why, Pavel Konstantinytch, do you consent to be called such names? Maria Alexevna knows nothing of affairs; she thinks perhaps that they can do God knows what with us; but you, an officeholder, must know how things go on. Tell her, therefore, that things having reached this point, she can do nothing with Vérotchka and still less with me."

" He knows, the rascal, that nothing can be done with him," thought Maria Alexevna, and then she said to Lopoukhoff that, though at first her mother's feelings had carried her away, she was now in a condition to talk calmly.

Lopoukhoff and Pavel Konstantinytch retraced their steps. They sat down, and Lopoukhoff begged her to listen patiently until he had finished all that he had to say, after which she might have the floor. Then he began, taking care to raise his voice every time that Maria Alexevna tried to interrupt him, which enabled him to carry his story to its conclusion. He explained that it was impossible to unmarry them, that there was no chance therefore for Storechnikoff, and that it would be useless trouble, as they knew themselves, to begin a suit. That for the rest they could do as they pleased, and that, if they had an abundance of money, he would even advise them to try the courts; but that, all things considered, there was no occasion for them to plunge into the depths of despair, since Vérotchka had always rejected Storechnikoff's proposals and the match therefore had always been chimerical, as Maria Alexevna had seen for herself; that a young girl nevertheless must marry some time, which means as a general thing a series of expenses for the parents,—that is, the dowry first, the wedding next, but especially the dowry.

Whence Lopoukhoff concluded that Maria Alexevna and Pavel Konstantinytch ought to thank their daughter for having got married without occasioning them any expense.

Thus he spoke for a full half-hour.

When he had finished, Maria Alexevna saw that to such a rascal there was nothing to say, and she placed herself first on the ground of sentiment, explaining that what had wounded her was precisely the fact that Vérotchka had married without asking the consent of her parents, thus lacerating the maternal heart; the conversation, transferred thus to the subject of maternal feelings and wounds, naturally had for either party no more than a purely dialectical interest; they could not help going into it, the proprieties required it; so they satisfied the proprieties. They spoke, Maria Alexevna of how, as an affectionate mother, she had been wounded, Lopoukhoff of how, as an affectionate mother, she need not have been wounded; when, finally, they had filled the measure of the proprieties by digressions of a proper length upon sentimental grounds, they approached another subject equally demanded by the proprieties,—that, on the one side, she had always desired her daughter's happiness, while he answered, on the other, that that was clearly indisputable; when the conversation on this point had likewise attained the proper length, they entered on the subject of farewells, giving that also the amount of attention required by the demands aforesaid, and reached the following result: Lopoukhoff, comprehending the confusion into which the maternal heart had been thrown, did not beg Maria Alexevna for the present to give her daughter permission to see her, because that perhaps would add to the strain on the maternal heart, but Maria Alexevna would not be slow in finding out that Vérotchka was happy, which of course was always Maria Alexevna's first desire, and then, the maternal heart having recovered its equanimity, she would be in a position to see her daughter without having to suffer thereby. This agreed upon, they separated amicably.

"Oh, the rascal!" said Maria Alexevna, after having shown her son-in-law to the door.

That same night she had the following dream:

She was seated near a window, and she saw a carriage, a splendid carriage, passing in the street; this carriage stopped, and out of it got a beautiful lady followed by a gentleman, and they entered her room, and the lady said to her: "See, Mamma, how richly my husband dresses me!" This lady was Vérotchka. Maria Alexevna looked at her: the material of Vérotchka's dress was really of the most expensive sort. Vérotchka said: "The material alone cost five hundred roubles, and that is a mere bagatelle, Mamma, for us; of such dresses I have a dozen; and here is something that cost still more, see my fingers!" And Maria Alexevna looked at Vérotchka's fingers, and saw rings set with huge diamonds! "This ring, Mamma, cost two thousand roubles, and that one four thousand more; and just glance at my breast, Mamma; the price of this brooch was still greater; it cost ten thousand roubles!" And the gentleman added, the gentleman being Dmitry Serguéitch: "All these things are just nothing at all for us, my dear Mamma, Maria Alexevna! The really precious stuff is in my pocket; here, dear Mamma, see this pocket-book, how it is swollen! It is full of hundred-rouble notes. Well, this pocket-book is yours, Mamma, for it is a small matter to us! Here is another more swollen still, dear Mamma, which I will not give you; it does not contain small currency, but large bank-bills and bills of exchange, and each of these bank-bills, each of these bills of exchange, is worth more than the whole pocket-book which I have given you, dear Mamma."

"You knew well, my dear son, Dmitry Serguéitch, how to make my daughter and our whole family happy; but where do you get so much wealth?"

"I have bought the liquor-selling monopoly, Mamma!"

And, on waking, Maria Alexevna said to herself: "Truly, he must go into the business of liquor-selling."

XXIV.

EULOGY OF MARIA ALEXEVNA.

You now cease to be an important personage in Vérotchka's life, Maria Alexevna, and in taking leave of you the author of this story begs you not to complain if he makes you quit the scene with a *dénoûment* not wholly to your advantage. Do not think yourself diminished in our eyes. You are a dupe, but that can in no degree change for the worse our opinion of your judgment, Maria Alexevna: your error does not testify against you. You have fallen in with individuals such as previously you had not been in the habit of meeting, and it is not your fault if you have made a mistake in judging things according to your experience. Your whole past life had led you to the conclusion that men are divided into two classes, — fools and knaves; whoever is not a fool is a knave, an absolute knave, you have supposed; not to be a knave is necessarily to be a fool. This way of looking at things was very just, Maria Alexevna, was perfectly just until these latter days. You have met very well-spoken people, and you have observed that all of them, without exception, were either rascals, deceiving men with fine words, or big, stupid children, unacquainted with life and not knowing how to manage their affairs. Consequently, Maria Alexevna, you have placed no faith in fine words; you have regarded them either as nonsense or as falsehoods, and you were right, Maria Alexevna. Your way of looking at men had already been completely formed when you for the first time met a woman who was neither a fool nor a rascal; therefore it is not at all astonishing that you were disconcerted by her, not knowing what course to take, what to think of her, or how to treat her. Your way of looking at things had already been completely formed when you for the first time met a man of heart who was not an artless child, but who knew life quite as well as you, judged it quite as justly, and knew how to conduct his affairs quite as well; therefore, again, it is not at all astonishing that you were deceived and took him for a sharper of your own sort. These errors, Maria Alexevna, in no wise diminish my esteem for you as a prudent and reasonable woman. You have lifted your husband from his obscurity, you have provided for your old age,—good things not easily accomplished. Your methods were bad, but your surroundings offered you no others. Your methods belong to your surroundings, but not to your person; therefore the dishonor is not yours, but the honor is to your judgment and strength of character.

Are you content, Maria Alexevna, to see your good qualities thus recognized? Certainly, you ought to be, since you never pretended to be agreeable or good. In a moment of involuntary sincerity you even confessed your wickedness and rudeness, and you never considered wickedness and rudeness as qualities that dishonored you, understanding that you could not have been otherwise, given the conditions of your life. Therefore you should be but little disturbed because these tributes to your intelligence and strength of character are not followed by tributes to virtues which you admit that you do not possess, and which you would consider rather as follies than as good qualities. You would have asked no other tribute than that which I have accorded you. But I can say in your honor one word more: of all the persons whom I do not like and with whom I should wish to have no dealings, you are of those whom I should like the best. To be sure, you are pitiless when your interest is at stake. But if you have no interest in doing evil to any one, you will not do it, having nothing in view but the satisfaction of your petty and stupid passions. You reason that it is not worth while to lose one's time, labor, and money for nothing. It is needless to say that you would have taken pleasure in roasting your daughter and her husband over a slow fire, but you succeeded in repressing the spirit of revenge that had taken possession of you and in reflecting coldly upon the matter, and you recognized that roasting was out of the question; now it is a great quality, Maria Alexevna, to be able to recognize the impossible. After recognizing this impossibility, you did not allow yourself to begin an action which would not have ruined the individuals who have offended you; you perceived that all the little annoyances which you might have caused them by such an action would have cost you many greater embarrassments and sacrifices, and so you did not bring an action. If one cannot conquer his enemy, if for the insignificant loss that one can inflict on him one must suffer a greater loss, there is no reason for beginning the struggle. Understanding that, you had good sense and valor enough to submit to the impossible without uselessly injuring yourself and others, — another great quality. Yes, Maria Alexevna, one may still have dealings with you, for your rule is not evil for evil even to your own injury, and that is an extremely rare quality, a very great quality! Millions of men are more dangerous than you, both to themselves and to others, although they may not have your surly countenance. You are among the best of those who are not good, because you are not unreasonable, because you are not stupid. I should have liked very well to reduce you to dust, but I esteem you; you interfere with nothing. Now you are engaged in bad business in accordance with the exigencies of your surroundings; but if other surroundings were given you, you would willingly cease to be dangerous, you would even become useful, because, when your interest is not at stake, you do not do evil, and are capable of doing anything that seems advantageous to you, even of acting decently and nobly. Yes, you are capable, Maria Alexevna, and it is not your fault if this capacity of yours is in a state of inertia, and if in its stead capacities of an opposite nature are at work; you none the less possess it, which cannot be said of everybody. Base people are capable of nothing good, but you, you are only bad, not base. Consequently you are above many men in point of morality!

"Are you content, Maria Alexevna?"

"Have I any reason to be content, my good sir, when my affairs are in such a bad way?"

"It is for the best, Maria Alexevna."

CHAPTER THIRD.

The Life of Véra Pavlovna with her Husband, and the Second Love.

I.

Three months had passed since the marriage. Lopoukhoff's affairs were going on well. He had found some pupils, work at a book-publisher's, and, more than all, the task of translating a geographical treatise. Véra Pavlovna, too, had found two pupils; who, though they did not pay her very largely, were better than none. Together they were now earning eighty roubles a month. With this sum they could live only in a very moderate way, but they had at least the necessaries. Their means continuing to increase, they counted on being able in four months more to furnish their rooms (and later that is what they did).

Their life was not arranged quite as Véra Pavlovna had planned it on the day of their betrothal, half in sport, half in earnest, but nevertheless it did not lack much of it.

Their aged landlady and her husband had a great deal to say about the strange way in which the newly-married couple lived, — as if they were not husband and wife at all, as if they were one knows not what.

"Therefore, according to what I see and what you say, Pétrovna, they live — how shall I say — as if they were brother and sister."

"Nonsense! What a comparison! Between brother and sister there is no ceremony; is there none between them? He rises, puts on his coat, sits down, and waits until I bring the *samovar*. After having made the tea, he calls her; she too comes in all dressed. Is that the way brother and sister do? This would be a better comparison: it sometimes happens that among people in moderate circumstances two families live for economy's sake in one and the same suite. They resemble two such families."

"How is it, Pétrovna, that the husband cannot enter his wife's room? She is not dressed. Do you see? How does that seem to you?"

"And what is better yet, when they separate at night, she says: 'Good night, my darling; sleep well!' Then they go, he to his room, she to hers, and there they read old books, and sometimes he writes. Do you know what happened one night? She had gone to bed and was reading an old book; I suddenly heard through the partition — I was not asleep — I heard her rise. What do you think she did? I heard her place herself before her mirror to arrange her hair, do you understand? Just as if she were going to make a visit. Then I heard her start.

I went out into the corridor, got up on a chair, and looked through the transom into her husband's room. On reaching the door she said:

"'Can I come in, my darling?'

"And he answered: 'Presently, Vérotchka; wait a moment.' He was in bed also; he made haste to dress. I thought he was going to put on his cravat next, but he did not. After he had arranged everything, he said:

"'Now you can come in, Vérotchka.'

"'I do not understand this book,' she said to him; 'explain this to me.'

"He gave her the explanation.

"'Pardon me, my darling, for having disturbed you'

"'Wherefore, Vérotchka? I was not busy; you did not disturb me.'

"And out she went."

"She simply went out?"

"She simply went out."

"And he did nothing?"

"And he did nothing. But that is not the most astonishing part of it; the most astonishing thing is that she should have dressed to go to his room and that he should have dressed to receive her. What does that mean?"

"I think, Pétrovna, that this must be a sect; there are all sorts of sects, you know, in that line."

"So there are. Very likely you are right."

Another conversation.

"Danilytch, I have asked them about their ways.

"'Do not be offended,' I said, 'at what I am going to ask you, but of what faith are you?'

"'Of the Russian faith. What a question!'

"'And you belong to no sect?'

"'To none; but what put that idea into your head?'

"'This, Mistress (I do not know whether I am to call you Madame or Mademoiselle), — do you live with Monsieur your husband?'

"She smiled: 'Certainly,' said she."

"She smiled?"

"She smiled, and answered: 'Certainly.'

"'Why, then, this habit of never seeing him half dressed, as if you were not united?'

"'In order,' she answered, 'not to exhibit ourselves in unbecoming garb. As for sect, there is none.'

"'What, then, does this signify?'

"'We act in this way in order that there may be more love and fewer quarrels.'"

"But that seems to be correct, Pétrovna; they are very reserved toward each other."

"She further said to me: 'I do not wish others to see me too carelessly dressed; now, I love my husband more than I love others; therefore it is not fitting that I should appear before him without first washing myself.'"

"And that, too, has an air of truth, Pétrovna; why do we covet our neighbors' wives? Because we always see them dressed up, while we see our own in careless array. So it is said in the proverbs of Solomon. He was a very wise king."

II.

All went well, then, at the Lopoukhoffs'. Véra Pavlovna was always gay. But one day — about five months after their marriage — Dmitry Serguéitch, on returning from one of his pupils, found his wife in a somewhat inexplicable humor; her eyes shone with pride as well as joy. Then Dmitry Serguéitch remembered that for some days past she had shown signs of an agreeable restlessness, a smiling thoughtfulness, a gentle pride.

"Something pleasant seems to have come to you, my friend; why do you not let me share it?"

"Indeed, I believe I have reason to be joyful, dear friend, but wait a little while: I will tell you about it as soon as I feel sure of it. It will be a great joy for us both, and will also please Kirsanoff and the Mertzaloffs."

"But what is it, then?"

"Have you forgotten our agreement, my darling? Do not question. As soon as it is a sure thing, I will tell you."

A week passed.

"My darling, I am going to tell you my joy. I need only your advice: you are an expert in these things. For a long time I have wanted to do something useful, and I have conceived the plan of establishing a dressmaker's shop; is that a good idea?"

"It is agreed that I am not to kiss your hand, but that referred only to general situations; under such circumstances as the present no agreement holds. Your hand, Véra Pavlovna."

"Later, my darling, when I have succeeded."

"When you have succeeded, not to me alone will you give your hand to kiss; Kirsanoff, Alexey Pétrovitch, and everybody will demand the privilege. Now I am alone, and your intention of itself is worth the kiss."

"If you do me violence, I will cry out."

"Well, cry out."

"You make me ashamed of myself, and I will have nothing more to say to you."

"Is it, then, very important?"

"Indeed it is, and that is why we talk all the time and do nothing."

"And you, who commenced later than any of us, are the first to begin action."
Vérotchka had hidden her face in her husband's breast.
"Too much praise, my dear friend."
"No, you have a wise mind."
Her husband kissed her.
"Oh, stop! No one can say a word to you."
"Very well; say on, my good Vérotchka."
"Do not call me that."
"Then I will say my wicked Vérotchka."
"Listen, Mr. Impertinence! The most important thing now, in my opinion, is first to make a prudent choice of honest working-girls, industrious servants of proven steadiness of character, dreading quarrels and capable of choosing others."
"Exactly so."
"I have found three young girls satisfying these conditions; but how I have had to search for the last three months, how I have been through the stores, making acquaintances, until at last I have found what I wanted and am sure of my choice!"
"They must also understand business management; the house must be self-sustaining and the business must be successful in a commercial sense."
"Not otherwise, it is needless to say."
"What else is there upon which advice is needed?"
"The details."
"What are the details? You probably have thought of everything already, and will govern yourself by circumstances. The important thing now is the principle, character, and skill. Details settle themselves, in accordance with the conditions of each special case."
"I know it; nevertheless, I shall feel more confident having your approval."
They talked for a long time. Loupoukhoff found nothing to correct in his wife's plan, but to herself the plan developed itself more clearly as she told it.
The next day Lopoukhoff carried to the "Journal of Police" an advertisement announcing: *Véra Pavlovna Lopoukhoff does sewing and laundry-work at a moderate price.*
The same morning Véra Pavlovna called upon Julie. "She does not know my present name; say Mademoiselle Rosalsky," said she to the servant.
"You come to see me without a veil, your face exposed; you give your name to the domestic; why, this is madness! You will ruin yourself, dear child!"
"Oh, now I am married, and I can go everywhere and do as I like."
"And if your husband should find it out?"
"In an hour he will be here."
Julie plied her with questions about her marriage. She was enchanted, she

kissed her, weeping all the while. When her enthusiasm had at last quieted down, Véra Pavlovna spoke of the object of her visit.

"You know that we remember old friends only when we need them. I have a great favor to ask of you. I am about to establish a dressmaker's shop. Give me your orders and recommend me to your friends. I sew well, and my assistants are equally good seamstresses; you know one of them."

Indeed, Julie did know one of them as an excellent needle-woman.

"Here are some samples of my work. I made this dress myself. See how well it fits!"

Julie examined very carefully the cut of the dress and its seams, and the examination satisfied her.

"You ought to be very successful; you have talent and taste. But to that end you need a fine store on the Nevsky."

"In time I shall have one, be sure; meantime I take orders at my house."

These things arranged, they returned to the subject of Vérotchka's marriage.

"Storechnikoff led a very dissipated life for a fortnight, but afterward became reconciled to Adèle. I am very glad for Adèle; he is a good fellow; only it is a pity that Adèle has no character."

Started in this direction, Julie launched into gossip about Adèle's adventures and those of others.

Now that Mademoiselle Rosalsky was no longer a young girl, Julie did not deem it necessary to restrain herself. At first she talked reasonably; then, as her excitement increased, she painted orgies glowingly and in colors more and more licentious. Véra Pavlovna became confused, but Julie did not notice it; then, recovering from her first impression, Véra Pavlovna listened with that pitiful interest with which one examines a dear face disfigured by disease. Lopoukhoff came, and Julie for a moment transformed herself into a woman of society, serious and full of tact. But she could not play that *rôle* long. After congratulating Lopoukhoff on having so beautiful a wife, she again became excited.

"We must celebrate your marriage."

She ordered an impromptu breakfast, to be washed down with champagne. Vérotchka had to drink half a glass in honor of her marriage, half a glass in honor of her workshop, and half a glass to the health of Julie herself. Her head began to turn, and she and Julie became terribly noisy; Julie pinched Vérotchka, and began to run; Vérotchka started after her; they ran through the apartments, leaping over chairs; Lopoukhoff sat in his arm-chair, laughing; Julie presumed to boast of her strength, which brought all this tumult to an end:

"I will lift you with one hand."

"You will not lift me."

Beginning to struggle, both of them fell on the sofa, and, not wishing to rise, began to shout and laugh; finally they went to sleep.

It was a long time since Lopoukhoff had found himself in a situation where he did not know what to do. Should he waken them? He feared lest he might bring the joyous interview to a disagreeable ending. He rose carefully, and took a few steps about the room in search of some book. He fell upon the "Chronicles of the Œil de Bœuf," a book beside which that of Faublas is insipid. Lopoukhoff extended himself comfortably upon the sofa at the other end of the room, began to read, and in less than a quarter of an hour was asleep himself.

Two hours later Pauline came to waken Julie; it was dinner-time. They sat down to the table alone, without Serge, who had been invited to some public dinner; Julie and Vérotchka again began to shout and laugh. Then they became calm and resumed a serious attitude. Suddenly Julie asked Vérotchka (the idea had not occurred to her before) why she established a workshop. If she desired to get money, it would be much better to become an actress or even a singer; her voice was a very fine one. Upon that they seated themselves anew. Vérotchka told her plans, and Julie's enthusiasm revived; congratulations followed fast upon each other, mingled with eulogistic exclamations. She, Julie Letellier, was a lost woman, but she could appreciate virtue; finally she began to weep and embrace Vérotchka, whom once more she overwhelmed with praises and good wishes.

Four days later Julie carried Véra Pavlovna a large number of orders of her own and the addresses of some of her friends from whom she might also receive orders. She took Serge with her, saying to him: "We cannot do otherwise; Lopoukhoff came to see me, you must return his visit."

Julie acted like a positive woman, and her enthusiasm did not cease, so that she stayed at the Lopoukhoffs' a long time.

There were no walls there, but thin partitions; everything could be heard, and she was on the lookout. She was not enraptured, but she was moved. After having examined all the details of the Lopoukhoffs' somewhat meagre life, she saw that that was precisely the way to live, that there is no true life otherwise, that real happiness is possible only where there is no luxury; she even announced to Serge that they would go to Switzerland and live in a little cottage amid the fields and mountains on the shore of a lake, there to love each other, fish, and cultivate their little garden. Serge replied that he was of her mind, but that he would like to wait to see what she would think of the matter a few hours later.

The noise of Julie's elegant carriage and fine horses made a great impression upon the dwellers in the fifth line between the Moyenne and the Petite Perspective, where nothing like it had been seen since the days of Peter the Great, if not since a period still more remote. Many watched the surprising phenomenon, and saw it stop near the carriage gate (which was closed) of a one-story wooden house with seven windows; they saw get out a phenomenon more wonderful still, a young woman splendid and brilliant, an officer whose bearing was of the most dignified. They were greatly disappointed when the carriage gate opened and the vehicle entered the court; public curiosity was thus deprived of a sight of the stately officer and the still more stately lady on their departure.

When Danilytch came home after his day's work, he had the following interview with his wife:

"Danilytch, it appears that our tenants belong to high society. A general and his wife have been to see them. The general's wife was dressed so richly that her toilet is indescribable. The general wore two stars!"

How could Pétrovna have seen stars on Serge, who as yet had none, and who, if he had any, would not have worn them on his excursions with Julie? That is very astonishing. But she did really see them, she was not mistaken, she was not lying. It is not only she that says it; I, too, answer for its truth; she saw them. We know that there were none there; but Serge's aspect was such that, from Pétrovna's standpoint, it was impossible not to see two stars on him. Pétrovna saw them. I affirm it seriously.

"And what a livery their footman had, Danilytch! Of English cloth at five roubles an *archine*. And this footman, though grave, was nevertheless polite; he answered when questioned; he even allowed you to feel of the cloth of his sleeve. What good cloth! It is plain that they have plenty of money to throw out of the window. They stayed about two hours, and our tenants talked with them very simply, just as I do with you for instance, and did not salute them, and laughed with them; our tenant and the general simply sat back in their arm-chairs and smoked. Once, our tenant's cigarette having gone out, he took the general's to relight it. And with what respect the general kissed the hand of our tenant's beautiful wife! It is past description. What do you think of all this, Danilytch?"

"Everything comes from God, that is what I think; acquaintances of all sorts and relatives, all come from God."

"It is true, Danilytch. Everything comes from God, there is nothing else to say. For my part this is what I think,—that our tenant, or his wife, is the brother, or sister, of the general, or of the general's wife. And, to tell the truth, I am nearly convinced that she is the general's sister."

"Are you very sure, Pétrovna? I do not believe it. If such were the case, they would have money."

"That can be explained, Danilytch. Either the mother or the father may have had her outside of marriage. The face is quite different; there is no resemblance there."

"That may be it, Pétrovna,—outside of marriage. Such things happen."

Thanks to this adventure, Pétrovna acquired for four whole days a great importance at the grocery which she was accustomed to frequent. For three whole days this grocery drew a portion of the trade of the neighboring grocery. Pétrovna, devoting herself to the interest of public instruction, even neglected her mending a little during this time in order to satisfy those who had a thirst for knowledge.

All this had results. A week later Pavel Konstantinytch appeared at his son-in-law's. Maria Alexevna obtained information about the life of her daughter and her rascal of a son-in-law, not in a constant and careful way, but from time to time and out of pure curiosity. One of her friends, a gossip of the lowest rank, who lived in the island of Vassilievsky, was charged with inquiring about Véra Pavlovna, whenever she happened to pass that way. The gossip brought her information sometimes once a month, sometimes oftener, according to circumstances. The Lopoukhoff's live on good terms. They do nothing extraordinary, the only thing remarkable being that they are visited by a great many young people, all of them men and modestly dressed. It cannot be said that they live richly; nevertheless they have money. Very far from selling anything, they buy. She has made two silk dresses for herself. They have bought a sofa, a table, and a half-dozen second-hand arm-chairs for forty roubles, which were worth perhaps a hundred. They have given their proprietors notice to look for new tenants in a month, for then they intend to move into their furnished apartments, — " though remaining grateful to you for your civility," they added. The proprietors of course said that on their side the feeling was the same.

Maria Alexevna was happy to hear this news. She was a very brutal and very bad woman; she tortured her daughter, she would have killed her if she had found it to her advantage, she cursed her as she thought of the ruin of her plan for adding to her riches; all that was true, but did it follow that she had no love for her daughter? Not at all. The affair over and her daughter irrevocably escaped from her hands, what had she to do? Whatever falls into the trench is for the soldier. Vérotchka was none the less her daughter; and now, in case of need, Véra Pavlovna might readily be useful to Maria Alexevna. The mother therefore sincerely wished her daughter well. There was nothing peculiar about this affection; Maria Alexevna did not watch her carefully; what she did was simply for form's sake, to satisfy the what-will-people-say consideration, and to show that Véra was really her daughter. Why not become reconciled? Especially since the brigand son-in-law, according to all accounts, is a positive man, with whom one may in time do something. So Maria Alexevna gradually came to the conclusion that it would be better to renew her relations with her daughter. It would have taken six months longer and perhaps even a whole year to reach this result; for there was nothing pressing, and time enough ahead. But the news about the general and his wife suddenly advanced matters at least one-half. The *brigand* had indeed shown himself shrewd enough. He, a poor devil of a student who had left college without a degree, with two sons in his pocket, had formed a friendship with a young general; he had also made his wife a friend of the general's wife; such a man will go far. Or else Véra has formed a friendship with the general's wife, and has made her husband a friend of the general. What is the difference? That would simply show that Véra may go far. So, as soon as the visit was known, the father was sent to tell his daughter that her mother had pardoned her, and that she was invited to the house.

Véra Pavlovna and her husband went back with Pavel Konstantinytch and remained a portion of the evening. The interview was cold and formal. Fédia was the principal subject of conversation, because the least thorny subject. He was at school. Maria Alexevna having been persuaded to place him at boarding-school; Dmitry Serguéitch promised to go to see him, and holidays he was to spend at Véra Pavlovna's. Thus they managed to kill time until the tea-hour; then they hastened to separate, the Lopoukhoffs pretending that they were expecting visitors that evening.

For six months Véra Pavlovna had been breathing a vivifying air. Her lungs had already become completely unaccustomed to the atmosphere of strategy, in which every word was uttered with a pecuniary end in view; her ear was no longer used to the discussion of swindling schemes and vile conspiracies. As a result this return to the cellar made a horrible impression on her. This corruption, this triviality, this cynicism struck her like a new thing.

"How did I help succumbing in such surroundings? How was I able to breathe in that cellar? And not only did I live there, but I kept my health! Incomprehensible thing! How could I have been brought up there, and still acquire a love of the good? It is incredible!" thought Véra Pavlovna, on returning to her apartments, with that sense of comfort which one feels on breathing freely after having been stifled.

Shortly after their arrival their accustomed visitors came, — namely, Alexey Pétrovitch with Natalia Andreyna, and Kirsanoff; they passed the evening as usual. What a new pleasure Véra Pavlovna felt after this interview in living amid pure ideas and in the society of pure people! The conversation was, as usual, now gay and mingled with souvenirs, now serious and upon all imaginable subjects, including the historical events of that day, such as the civil war in the Caucasus (the prologue of the great war now going on between the South and the North in the United States, which in its turn is the prologue of events still greater and of which the scene will not be America only). Now everybody talks politics, but at that time those interested in them were few in number; of this small number were Lopoukhoff, Kirsanoff, and their friends. They even entered into the discussions then prevailing of Liebig's theory of agricultural chemistry, as well as the laws of historical progress a subject never forgotten in such circles. They concerned themselves also with the importance of distinguishing real desires which seek and find satisfaction from whimsical desires which it is impossible and unnecessary to satisfy. For example, when one has a hot fever, he is always thirsty, but the only truly desirable satisfaction is not in drink but in cure. The unhealthy condition of the system provokes artificial desires while changing normal desires. Besides this fundamental distinction then put forward by anthropological philosophy, they went into other analogous subjects, or, if different, subjects leading back to the same point. The ladies also from time to time took part in these scientific discussions conducted in a simple fashion; they sometimes asked questions; but as a general thing they did not listen, and had even been known to sprinkle Lopoukhoff and Alexey Pétrovitch with clean water when they seemed too much impressed with the great importance of mineral manure. But Alexey Pétrovitch and Lopoukhoff discussed their favorite subjects with an invincible tenacity; Kirsanoff did not aid them much; he generally took the ladies' side, and all three played and sang and laughed until a late hour, when, fatigued, they would at last succeed in separating the indefatigable zealots of serious conversation.

III.

VÉRA PAVLOVNA'S SECOND DREAM.

Véra Pavlovna, sleeping, saw a field in a dream; her husband — that is, her darling — said: "You wish to know, Alexey Pétrovitch, why one sort of soil produces the good, the pure, the delicate wheat, and why another sort does not produce it? You shall account for this difference yourself. See the root of this fine ear: around the root there is soil, but fresh soil, pure soil, you might say; smell of it; the odor is damp and disagreeable, but there is no mouldy or sour smell. You know that in the language of our philosophy that is real soil. It is dirty, to be sure; but look at it closely, and you will see that all the elements of which it is composed are healthy. This is the soil that they constitute in this combination; but let the disposition of the atoms be a little changed, and something different will result; and this something will be equally healthy, since the fundamental elements are healthy. What is the reason of that? Look closely at this portion of the field; you see that there is an outlet for the water, so that there can be no putridity."

"Yes, motion is reality," said Alexey Pétrovitch, "because motion is life. Now, the principal element of life is labor, and consequently the principal element of reality is labor, and the characteristic by which it can be most surely recognized is activity."

"Thus, Alexey Pétrovitch, if the sun should warm this soil and the heat should displace the elements and form them into more complex chemical combinations,

— that is, combinations of a higher degree, — then the ear which would grow out of this soil would be a healthy ear?"

"Yes, because this is real soil," said Alexey Pétrovitch.

"Now, let us pass to this part of the field. Here take likewise a plant, and examine in the same way its root. This too is dirty. Look well at this soil. It is not difficult to see that this is putrescent soil."

"That is, abnormal soil," said Alexey Pétrovitch.

"I mean, the elements of this soil being unhealthy, it is natural that, whatever their combination and whatever the resulting product, this product must be in a state of corruption."

"Evidently, since the elements themselves are unhealthy," said Alexey Pétrovitch.

"It is not difficult for us to discover the cause of this corruption."

"That is, this abnormal putridity," said Alexey Pétrovitch.

"That's it; examine this part of the field again. You see that the water, having no outlet, stagnates and rots."

"Yes, absence of motion is absence of labor," said Alexey Pétrovitch, "for labor appears in anthropological analysis as the fundamental form of motion, the form which is the basis of all the other forms, — distraction, rest, games, amusements; without labor preceding them these forms would not be real. Now, without motion there is no life, — that is, no reality; consequently this soil is abnormal, — that is, rotten. Not until modern times was it known how to make such parts of the earth healthy; now the way has been found in drainage: the superfluous water flows away, and there remains only just what is necessary; this moves, and thus makes the fields healthy. But, as long as this means is not employed, the soil remains abnormal, — that is, rotten; under these conditions it cannot produce good vegetation, while it is very natural that real soil should produce good plants, since it is healthy. Which was to be demonstrated; o-e-a-a-dum, as they say in Latin."

How do they say in Latin: "Which was to be demonstrated." Véra Pavlovna could not clearly understand this.

"You seem to like kitchen Latin and the syllogism, Alexey Pétrovitch," said her "darling," — that is, her husband.

Véra Pavlovna approached them and said:

"Enough of your analyses, identities, and anthropologisms. Vary your conversation a little, gentlemen, I beg of you, in order that I may join in it; or, rather, let us play."

"Let us play," said Alexey Pétrovitch: "let us confess."

"Let us confess, that will be amusing," said Véra Pavlovna: "but, as you started the idea, it is for you to set the example."

"With pleasure, my sister," said Alexey Pétrovitch: "but how old are you? Eighteen, are you not?"

"Nearly nineteen."

"But not quite; we will say eighteen, then, and confess, all of us, up to that age, for we must have equality of conditions. I will confess for myself and for my wife. My father was the sexton in the chief town of a government where he followed the trade of bookbinder, and my mother rented rooms to theological students. From morning till night they did nothing but talk and worry about our daily bread. My father was inclined to drink, but only when poverty bore too heavily and painfully upon him or when the income was more than sufficient: in the latter case he would bring my mother all the money and say to her: 'Now, my little mother, we have, thank God, all we shall need for two months; and I have kept a Poltinnitchek with which to drink a little drop in honor of this joyful occasion.' To him it was a real happiness. My mother got angry very often, and sometimes beat me, but this was at times when, as she said, she had lamed her back by lifting too many iron pots, or by doing the washing for us five and the five students, or by scrubbing the floor soiled by our twenty feet without galoches, or by taking care of the cow; in short, it was because of excessive nervous fatigue occasioned by wearing and ceaseless labor. And when, with all that, 'the two ends did not meet,' as she expressed it, — that is, when there was no money with which to buy boots for her sons and shoes for her daughters, — then it was that she beat us. She caressed us also when, though children, we offered to aid her in her labor, or when we did something intelligent, or when she got a rare moment of rest and her back became limber, as she said. To us those were real joys." . . .

"To the devil with your real sorrows and joys!" said Véra Pavlovna.

"Well, then, in that case, condescend to listen to my confession for Natacha."

"I do not wish to listen; she has similar real joys and sorrows, I am sure."

"You are perfectly right."

"But you will be pleased, perhaps, to hear my confession," said Serge, mysteriously making his appearance.

"Let us see," said Véra Pavlovna.

"My parents, although they were rich, did nothing but worry and talk about money; rich people are no more exempt from such anxieties" . . .

"You do not know how to confess, Serge," said Alexey Pétrovitch, in an amiable tone: "tell us why they worried about money, what the expenses were that tormented them, what were the needs that it embarrassed them to satisfy."

"I well understand why you ask me that," said Serge, "but let us lay that subject aside and view their thoughts from another standpoint. They, too, were anxious about their children."

"Were their children sure of their daily bread?" asked Alexey Pétrovitch.

"Certainly, but it was necessary to look out that" . . .

"Do not confess, Serge!" said Alexey Pétrovitch: "we know your history; care of the superfluous, preoccupation with the useless, — that is the soil out of which you have grown; it is an abnormal soil. Just look at yourself; you are by birth a fairly intelligent and very polite man; perhaps you are no worse or more stupid than we are; but what are you good for, for what are you useful?"

"I am good to escort Julie wherever she wishes to go, I am useful to Julie in helping her to lead a dissipated life," answered Serge.

"Thereby we see," said Alexey Pétrovitch, "that the abnormal unhealthy soil" . . .

"Ah, how you weary me with your realism and your abnormalism! They know that it is incomprehensible, and yet they never stop talking about it!" said Véra Pavlovna.

"Then you do not wish to talk a little with me?" said Maria Alexevna, also appearing mysteriously: "you, gentlemen, withdraw, for mother wishes to speak with daughter."

Everybody disappeared, and Vérotchka found herself face to face with Maria Alexevna. Maria Alexevna's countenance assumed a scornful expression.

"Véra Pavlovna, you are an educated person; you are so pure, so noble," said Maria Alexevna in a tone of irony; "you are so good; am I, a gross and wicked drunkard, the person to be talking to you? You, Véra Pavlovna, have a bad mother; but tell me, if you please, Madame, about what this mother has been troubled? About daily bread; that is what, in your learned language, is called the real, the veritable human anxiety, is it not? You have heard bad words; you have seen wicked and corrupt conduct; but tell me, if you please, what the object was. Was it a futile, a senseless object? No, Madame. No, whatever the life of your family, it was not a futile, whimsical life. See, Véra Pavlovna, I have acquired your learned style. But you are ashamed and distressed at having so bad a woman for a mother? You would like it if I were good and honest? Well, I am a sorcerer, Véra Pavlovna, I know how to use magic; therefore I can realize your desire. Condescend to look; your desire is fulfilled; your wicked mother has disappeared; there is a good mother with her daughter; look!"

A room. Near the door snores a dirty drunken man. What is this, — he is unrecognizable, his face being covered half by his hand and half by bruises. A bed. On the bed lies a woman, — yes, it is she, it is Maria Alexevna, but the good Maria Alexevna! Further, she is pale, decrepit at the age of forty-five, worn out! Near the bed is a young girl of about eighteen; yes, it is you, Vérotchka, yourself, but in what rags! What does this mean? You are so yellow and your features so gross, and the room itself is so poor! Of furniture there is almost none.

"Vérotchka, my friend, my angel," says Maria Alexevna: 'lie down a little while; rest yourself, my treasure; why do you look at me? It is wholly unnecessary. This is the third night that you have not slept."

"That is nothing, Mamma; I am not tired," says Vérotchka.

"And I feel very sick, Vérotchka; what will become of you when left without me? Your father's earnings are small, and he is a poor support for you. You are pretty; there are many wicked people in the world. There will be nobody to put you on your guard. How I fear for you!"

Vérotchka weeps.

"My dear child, do not take offence; I do not mean to reproach you, but simply to put you on your guard: why did you go out Friday, the day before I fell so seriously ill?"

Vérotchka weeps.

"He will deceive you, Vérotchka; abandon his company."

"No, Mamma."

Two months later. How two months have slipped away in a single moment! On a chair is seated an officer. On the table in front of the officer a bottle, and it is she, Vérotchka, upon the officer's knees!

Two months more slip by in a moment.

On a sofa is seated a lady. Before the lady stands Vérotchka.

"And do you know how to iron, Vérotchka?"

"Yes, I know how."

"What are you, my dear, a serf or free?"

"My father is an office-holder."

"Then you are of gentle birth, my dear? I cannot take you. What kind of a servant would you make? Go, my dear, I cannot take you."

Vérotchka is in the street.

"Mamzelle, mamzelle!" says some drunken youth, "where are you going? I will escort you."

Vérotchka runs to throw herself into the Néva.

"Well, my dear child, how do you like having such a mother?" said the old, the real Maria Alexevna: "am I not clever in the use of magic? Why are you silent? Have you no tongue? But I will make you speak just the same. Have you been in the stores much?"

"Yes," said Vérotchka, all of a tremble.

"Have you seen, have you heard?"

"Yes."

"Is their life honorable? Are they educated? Do they read old books, do they dream of your new order of things, of the way in which men may be made happy? Do they dream of it? Speak out!"

Vérotchka, trembling, said not a word.

"You have lost your power of speech, it seems to me. Is their life honorable, I ask you?"

Vérotchka maintained her silence and felt a shudder.

"You have then really lost your power of speech? Is their life honorable? Are they virtuous young girls, I ask you again? Would you like to be as they are? You are silent! Do not turn away your face! Listen, then, Verka, to what I am going to say to you. You are learned; thanks to the money that I have stolen, you are educated. You dream of the good, but, if I had not been wicked, you would never have known what the good is. Do you understand? It *all* comes from me; you are my daughter, *mine*. I am your mother."

Vérotchka weeps and shudders.

"What do you wish of me, Mamma? I cannot love you."

"Do I ask you to love me?"

"I should like at least to esteem you, but I cannot do that either."

"Do I need your esteem?"

"What do you want, then? Why have you come to talk to me in so dreadful a way? What do you wish of me?"

"Be grateful, without loving or esteeming me, ingrate that you are. I am wicked; is there any chance for love? I am dishonest; is there any chance for esteem? But you should understand, Verka, that, if I were not what I am, you too would not be what you are. You are honest because I have been dishonest; you are good for the reason that I have been wicked. Understand it, Vérotchka, and be grateful."

"Withdraw, Maria Alexevna; it is now my turn to speak to my sister."

Maria Alexevna disappeared.

The sweetheart of so many lovers, the sister of so many sisters took Vérotchka by the hand.

"I have always wanted to be good with you, Vérotchka, for you are good yourself. Now, I am whatever the person is to whom I am talking. At present you are sad; so am I. Look! Though sad, am I still good?"

"Always the best in the world."

"Kiss me, Vérotchka; we are both in distress. Your mother told you the exact truth. I do not like your mother, but I need her."

"Can you not do without her?"

"Later I shall be able to when it shall be useless for men to be wicked. But at present I cannot. The good, you see, cannot get a foothold of themselves, for the wicked are strong and cunning. But the wicked are not all of the same sort. To some of them it is necessary that the world should grow worse and worse, to others it is essential that it should improve, essential in their own interest. It was a good thing for your mother that you should be educated; and why? In order that you might give lessons and thus earn money; in order that you might catch a rich husband. Her intentions were bad, but did you profit by them any the less? With the other class of wicked people this is not the case. For instance, if you had had Anna Pétrovna for a mother, could you have had an education? Would you have known the good? Would you have loved it? No. Either you would not have been allowed to learn, or you would have been made a puppet of. The daughter of such a mother must be a puppet, for the mother herself is nothing else, and lives only to play to puppets with puppets. Now, your mother is bad, but she has been of the more value to you, for it was essential to her that you should not be a puppet. You see, then, that the wicked are not all of the same sort. Some prevent the existence of men worthy of the name, and would have them only puppets. But wicked people of the other sort come unconsciously to my aid by giving men the possibility of development and gathering the means that permit this development. That is exactly what I need. Yes, Vérotchka, I cannot do without this kind of wicked people to oppose the other wicked people. My wicked people are wicked, but good grows under their wicked hand. Therefore be grateful to your mother. Do not love her, since she is wicked, but do not forget that you owe everything to her, that without her you would not exist."

"Will this always be the case? It will not, will it?"

"Later, when the good shall be strong, it will be otherwise. The time is approaching when the wicked will see that it is against their interest to be wicked, and most of them will become good: they were wicked simply because it was disadvantageous to them to be good, but they know, however, that good is better than evil, and they will prefer the good as soon as they can love it without injury to their own interests."

"And the wicked who were puppets, what will become of them? I pity them too."

"They will play to puppets without injuring any one whomsoever. Their children will not resemble them, for of all members of the human family I shall make good, strong, intelligent human beings."

"Oh, how good that will be!"

"But those who prepare the way for this future are among the good from now on When you aid the cook in getting your dinner, do you not feel good, though the air of the kitchen was stifling? Every one feels good at the table, but whoever has aided in getting the dinner feels better than the others: the dishes seem much better to her. You like sweets, if I mistake not?"

"Yes," said Vérotchka, smiling to see herself thus convicted of a fondness for pastry and of having aided in making it in the kitchen.

"What reason have you to mourn? Pshaw! all that is passed."

"How good you are!"

"And joyous, Vérotchka, joyous always, even when sad. Am I not?"

"Yes, when I am sad, you come appearing sad also, but every time you drive away my sorrow; it is very pleasant to be with you."
"You have not forgotten my song: *Donc vivons*?"
"Oh, no."
"Let us sing it."
"Let us sing."

"Vérotchka! Why, I seem to have awakened you! But, at any rate, tea is all ready. You really frightened me: I heard you groan; I come in, and find you singing."
"No, my darling, you did not awaken me; I should have awakened without you. What a dream I have just had! I will tell you about it while we are taking tea. Leave me; I am going to dress. But how did you dare to enter my room without permission, Dmitry Sergnéitch? You forget yourself. You were frightened about me, my darling? Come here and let me kiss you. And now leave me quickly, for I must dress."
"You are so late that I had better act as your dressing-maid to-day; shall I?"
"Very good, my darling, but how abashed I am!"

IV.

Véra Pavlovna's shop was quickly established. At first the organization was so simple that nothing need be said about it. Véra Pavlovna had told her first three seamstresses that she would give them a little higher wages than the current rate paid to seamstresses. The three working girls, appreciating the character of Véra Pavlovna, had willingly consented to work for her. They were not at all disturbed at a poor woman's desiring to establish a dressmaker's shop.

These three young girls found four more, choosing them with all the circumspection that Véra Pavlovna had recommended to them: these conditions of choice had nothing in them to excite suspicion, nothing of an extraordinary character; what is there extraordinary in the fact that a young woman should desire her shop-girls to be of good and open character? She wants no quarrels, that is all; it is only prudence on her part.

Véra Pavlovna also formed a somewhat intimate acquaintance with the girls newly selected before telling them that she accepted them; this was very natural; she still acted like a prudent woman.

They worked a month for the wages agreed upon. Véra Pavlovna was always at the shop, so that the seamstresses had plenty of time to know her more closely and see that she was economical, circumspect, reasonable, and at the same time good; therefore she obtained their confidence very quickly. Than this there was but one thing further to say, — that she was a good employer, who knew how to manage her affairs.

When the month was over, Véra Pavlovna came to the shop with an account book, and asked her seamstresses to suspend their work and listen. Then she said to them in simple language things such as the seamstresses had never heard before:

"Now we know each other. For my part, I can say of you that you are good workers and good characters. And I do not believe that you will speak very ill of me. I am going to talk to you without reserve, and if what I say seems strange, you will reflect before deciding upon it; you will not regard my words as futile, for you know me for a serious woman.

"This is what I have to say:

"People of heart say that dressmakers' shops can be established in which the seamstresses shall work with greater profit than in the shops generally known. It has been my wish to make the attempt. Judging from the first month, we must conclude that these people are right. Your wages you have had. I am now going to tell you how much profit remains to me after deducting your wages and the running expenses."

Véra Pavlovna read them the account of the expenses and receipts for the month just over. Under the head of expenses were placed, besides the wages paid, all the other costs, — the rent of the room, lights, and even Véra Pavlovna's carriage-hire in conducting the business of the shop.

"I have so much left," she continued; "what's to be done with this money? I have established a workshop in order that the profits resulting from the work may go to the workers; that is why I come, for this first time, to distribute it among you equally. Then we shall see if that is the best way, or if it would be better to employ this money otherwise."

Having said this, she made the distribution. For some minutes the seamstresses could not recover from their astonishment; then they began to thank her. Véra Pavlovna let them go on, fearing that she would offend them if she refused to listen, which would have seemed in their eyes indifference and disdain.

"Now," she continued, "I have to tell you the most difficult thing that I shall ever have to say to you, and I do not know whether I shall succeed in making it clear. Nevertheless I must try. Why have I not kept this money? And of what use is it to establish a workshop if not to make a profit from it? I and my husband have, as you know, the necessaries: although we are not rich, we have everything that we need and enough of it. Now, if I needed anything, I should only have to say so to my husband; or, rather, even that would be needless, for if I wanted anything, he would perceive it himself and give it to me. His business is not of the most lucrative sort, but it is what he best likes. But as we love each other much, it is infinitely agreeable to him to do that which pleases me; on my side, I love to do that which pleases him. Therefore, if I needed money, he would engage in more lucrative business than that which now occupies him. And he would find it quickly, for he is intelligent and skilful,— but you are somewhat acquainted with him. Now, if he does not do it, that means that the money which we have is enough for me. I have no passion for money; every one has his passion, which is not always the passion for money. Some have a passion for dancing, others for dress, others for cards, and all are ready to ruin themselves to satisfy their ruling passion; many actually do it, and nobody is astonished at it. Now, I have a passion for the things in which I am engaged with you, and, far from ruining myself for my passion, I spend scarcely any money upon it, and I am happy to indulge myself in it without making any profit thereby. Well, there is nothing strange in that, it seems to me: who thinks of making a profit out of his passion? Every one even sacrifices money for it. I do not even do that; I spend nothing on it. Therefore I have an advantage over others in that my passion, though agreeable to me, costs me nothing, while others pay for their pleasure. Why have I this passion? This is why: Good and intelligent people have written many books concerning the way in which we should live in order that all may be happy; and the principal means that they recommend is the organization of workshops on a new basis.

"I, wishing to see if we can establish a workshop of this sort, act just as any one does who desires to build a beautiful house or lay out a fine garden or orange-grove in order to contemplate them; I wish to establish a good dressmaker's shop in order that I may have the pleasure of contemplating it. Certainly it would be something gained already, if I confined myself to distributing the profits among you monthly, as I do now. But good people say that we can manage in a much better and more profitable way. I will tell you little by little all that we can do besides, if we take the advice of intelligent people. Moreover, you yourselves, by watching things closely, will make your own observations, and when it shall seem to you possible for us to do something good, we will try to do it, but gradually and in proper season. I must only add that without your consent I shall establish nothing new. Nothing will be changed until you desire it. Intelligent people say that nothing succeeds unless it is done voluntarily. I am of their opinion, and shall do nothing without your consent.

"Here is my last order: You see that it is necessary to keep books, and look out that there may be no useless expenditures. During this first month I have done this alone, but I do not care to do so any more. Choose two of your number to join me in this work; without their advice I shall do nothing. The money is yours and not mine; therefore it is for you to watch its employment. We are hardly well enough acquainted with each other yet to know which of you is best fitted for such work; we must make a trial and choose only for a limited time;

in a week you will know whether to appoint other delegates or let the old ones continue."

These extraordinary words gave rise to long discussions. But Véra Pavlovna had gained the confidence of the working girls. She had talked to them in a very simple way, without going too far or unfolding attractive prospects before them which, after a temporary enthusiasm, give birth to distrust; consequently the young girls were far from taking her for a crank, and that was the principal point. The business went on very satisfactorily.

Here, for the rest, in an abridged form, is the history of the shop during the three years that this shop constituted the principal feature in the history of Véra Pavlovna herself.

The founders were directly interested in the success of the business, and naturally it went on very well. The shop never lost customers. It had to undergo the jealousies of a few other shops and stores, but this proved no serious obstacle. All that Véra Pavlovna had to do was to obtain the right to put a sign over the shop-door. They soon had more orders than the working girls originally employed could execute, and the force went on steadily growing. When the business had been in operation eighteen months, it kept twenty young girls at work; afterwards, more still. One of the first measures of the collective administration was a decision that Véra Pavlovna no more than the others should work without reward. When this was announced to her, she told the working girls that they were perfectly right. They wished to give her a third of the profits. She laid this aside for a certain time until she was able to convince the young girls that this was contrary to the fundamental idea of their institution. For a long time they did not understand; at last they were convinced that it was not from pride that Véra Pavlovna did not wish to accept a larger share of the profits than the others had, but because it was contrary to the spirit of the association. The business was already so large that Véra Pavlovna could not do all the cutting; they gave her another cutter to aid her. Both received the same wages, and Véra Pavlovna succeeded at last in inducing the society to receive into its treasury the sum of the profits that it had obliged her to accept, first deducting that to which she was entitled as a cutter. They used this money to open a bank.

For a year Véra Pavlovna spent a great portion of the day at the shop, where she worked as many hours as any of the seamstresses, perhaps more than any of them. When it became needless for her to work all day at the shop, she caused her wages to be decreased in proportion to the decrease of her hours of labor.

How should the profits be divided? Véra Pavlovna desired to arrive at an equal division. Not until the middle of the third year did she succeed in this. Prior to that, they passed through several stages, beginning by dividing in proportion to the wages. First they saw that, if a working girl was kept from work for several days by sickness or some other cause deserving of consideration, it was not right to diminish her share of the profits, which she acquired not exactly by her own day's works, but rather by the progress of the work as a whole and the general condition of the shop. Later they decided that the cutters, and such of the other workers as received separate pay for delivering the work at houses or fulfilling other functions, were sufficiently compensated by their individual wages, and that it was not just that they should receive more of the profits than the others. The simple seamstresses were so delicate about the matter that they did not ask for this change, even when they saw the injustice of the old method of distribution established by themselves. For the rest, it must be added that there was nothing heroic in this temporary delicacy, inasmuch as the affairs of all were improving constantly. The most difficult thing of all was to make the simple working girls understand that one ought to receive just as much of the profits as another, although some earned more than others, and that those who labored most skilfully were already sufficiently rewarded by their larger wages. This was the last change to be made in the division of the profits, and it was not reached, as has already been said, until towards the middle of the third year, when the associates had come to understand that the profits were not a reward for the talent of one or another, but rather a result of the general character of the workshop, a result of its organization and its object. Now, this object was the greatest possible equality in the distribution of the fruits of collective labor among all the working girls, regardless of the personal peculiarities of each. Upon this character of the workshop depended the participation of the laborers in the profits. But as the character of the workshop, its spirit, and its order were produced by the mutual understanding of all, the tacit consent of the most timid or the least capable was not useless in maintaining and developing this understanding.*

I pass by many details, because it is not the workshop that I am describing; I speak of it only so far as is necessary to exhibit the activity of Véra Pavlovna. If I mention some of its peculiarities, it is solely with a view of showing how Véra Pavlovna acted in this affair, and how she guided it gradually, with an indefatigable patience and a remarkable steadfastness of purpose. She never commanded, confining herself to advising, explaining, proposing her coöperation, and aiding in the execution of whatever the collectivity had resolved upon.

The profits were divided every month. At first each working girl took her entire share and spent it separately: each had urgent needs, and they were not accustomed to acting in concert. When, through constant participation in the

---

* It is hardly the proper thing for a translator to interrupt the progress of a romance for purposes of controversy, but I cannot refrain from suggesting to Véra and her associates that, after they had received equitable wages for their work, all profits remaining belonged in equity to the consumers of their products, and should have been restored to them by a general reduction in the scale of prices. These consumers being laborers themselves in other fields and adopting similar methods of procedure, the principle of universal participation in the advantages of associated over isolated labor would thus have been realized in the widest sense. — *Translator.*

business, they had acquired the habit of combining their efforts in the shop. Véra Pavlovna fixed their attention upon the circumstance that in their trade the amount of patronage is very uneven, depending upon the months of the year, and that it would not be a bad plan to lay aside during the most profitable months a portion of the income in order to make up for the decrease of profits in the other months.

The accounts were kept very exactly, and the young girls knew well that, if any one of them should leave the shop, she would receive without any delay the share belonging to her. Consequently they consented to this proposition. A small reserve capital was formed; it went on growing steadily; they began to seek various uses for it. Everybody understood, in the first place, that loans would be made to those of the participants who should chance to have a great need of money, and no one desired to lend at interest: poor people believe that pecuniary aid should be extended without interest. The establishment of this bank was followed by the foundation of a purchasing agency: the young girls found that it would be advantageous to buy their tea, coffee, sugar, shoes, and in short many other things, through the agency of the association, which bought merchandise in large quantities and consequently at lower rates. Some time later they went further still: they saw that it would be advantageous to organize in the same way for the purchase of bread and other provisions which they bought every day at the bake-shops and groceries; but they perceived at the same time that to do that it would be necessary for the associates to live not far apart. They began to draw together, several living in one house, or taking rooms near the shop. After which the association established an agency for its dealings with the bakers and grocers. About eighteen months later almost all the working girls were living in one large house, had a common table, and bought their provisions as they do in large establishments.

Half of these young girls were without family. Some had aged relatives, mothers or aunts; two of them supported their old father; several had little brothers and sisters. Because of these family relations three of them were unable to live in the house with the others: one had a mother difficult to get along with; another had a mother in government employ who objected to living with girls from the country; the third had a drunken father. These profited only by the purchasing agency; it was the same with the married seamstresses. But with these exceptions all those who had relatives to support lived in the common house. They lived two and three in a room; their relatives arranged themselves each in his or her own fashion; two old women had each a separate chamber, but the others roomed together. The little boys had a room of their own; for the little girls there were two.

It was agreed that the boys could not remain there after the age of eight; those who were older were sent to learn a trade as apprentices.

The accounts were kept in the most exact manner in order that no one in the association might injure any other or profit by another's injury.

It would be too long and tedious to enter into fuller details, but there is one point more that must be explained.

Véra Pavlovna, from the very first, took books to the shop. After having given her directions, she began to read aloud, continuing half an hour if not interrupted sooner by the necessity of distributing more work. Then the young girls rested from the attention which they had given to the reading; afterwards they resumed it, and then rested again. It is needless to say that the young girls from the first acquired a passion for reading; some had already acquired it before they came to the shop. Three weeks later, reading during work had become a regular thing. When three or four months had passed, some of the more skilful seamstresses offered to do the reading; it was agreed that they should replace Véra Pavlovna, that each should read half an hour, and that this half-hour should be counted as a part of their labor.

As long as Véra Pavlovna was obliged to do the reading, she sometimes replaced it by stories; when relieved of the reading, she multiplied the stories, which soon became a sort of course of lessons. Then — and this was a great step — Véra Pavlovna succeeded in establishing a regular system of instruction: the young girls became so desirous of learning and their labor went on so successfully that they decided to interrupt their labor to listen to the lessons in the middle of the day's work and before dinner.

"Alexey Pétrovitch," said Véra Pavlovna, when calling on the Mertzaloff's one day, "I have a request to make of you: Natacha is already with me in the idea. My shop is becoming a college of all sorts of learning. Be one of our professors."

"What then shall I teach them? Latin or Greek perhaps, or even logic and rhetoric?" said Alexey Pétrovitch, laughing: "my specialty is not very interesting in your opinion and in the opinion of some one whom I well know."

"No, you are needed precisely as a specialist; you will serve us as a moral buckler and a proof of the good tendency of our teaching."

"You are right. I see clearly that without me this would be immoral. What shall I teach?"

"Russian history, for instance, or an outline of universal history."

"Exactly. That is what I will teach, and it shall be supposed that I am a specialist. Delightful! Two functions, — a professor and a buckler."

Natalia Andrevna, Lopoukhoff, three students, and Véra Pavlovna herself were the other professors, as they jokingly called themselves.*

They mingled instruction with amusements. They had evening parties,

---

* The title of professor, in Russia, is given only to University professors.

suburban walks, at first seldom, and then, when money was plentier, more frequently; they also went to the theatre. The third winter they subscribed regularly to gallery seats at the Italian opera.

What joy! What happiness for Véra Pavlovna! But how much labor also, and anxiety, and even sorrow! The most painful impression of this sort, not only to Véra Pavlovna, but to all her little circle, was caused by the misfortune of one of the best of the working girls, Alexandrine Pribytkoff. She was pretty, and was engaged to an officeholder. One evening, when walking in the street a little later than usual, a man ran after her and took her by the hand. Wishing to release herself, she pulled her arm away quickly, thus causing the man's watch to fall. "Thief, thief!" he cried. The police came and the young girl was arrested. The lover, on hearing this news, began a search for the individual, found him, and challenged him to a duel; he refused; then the lover struck his adversary; the latter took a stick to strike back, but, before he could do so, received a blow in the breast and fell stone dead. Then the lover was imprisoned in his turn, and endless court proceedings began. And then? Then nothing, except that after that it was pitiful to look at Alexandrine Pribytkoff.

Connected with the shop were many other histories, less dramatic but equally sorrowful. These adventures, inevitable amid the prevailing ideas and surroundings, certainly caused Véra Pavlovna much sorrow and still more embarrassment.

But much greater — oh, much greater! — were the joys. All was joy except the sorrows, for the general progress of the association was gay and prosperous. Therefore, though distressing accidents sometimes happened, much more frequent on the other hand were the happy occurrences. Véra Pavlovna succeeded in finding good situations for the little brothers or sisters of such or such a working girl. In the course of the third year two of the working girls passed an examination for a governess's situation,— to them a great piece of good fortune! Cases of this sort abounded; but most joyous of all were the marriages. There were many of them and all were happy.

Véra Pavlovna was twice invited to stand godmother and twice refused. This *rôle* was almost always taken by Madame Mertzaloff, or by her mother, who was also a very good lady. The first time that she refused it was thought that she was displeased at something, and refused for that reason; but no: Véra Pavlovna was very happy to be invited, and it was simply out of modesty that she did not accept, not wishing to appear officially as the patron of the bride. She always avoided the appearance of influence; she tried to put others forward and succeeded in it, so that a number of ladies, on coming to the shop to give orders, did not distinguish her from the two other cutters. Her greatest pleasure was to demonstrate that the association had been established and was maintained by the working girls themselves. She wished to persuade herself of the possibility of her desire that the shop might be able to go on without her and others of the same sort spring up quite unexpectedly. "And why not? How good that would be! What better thing could happen?"—than that they should spring up without the guidance of some one not a dressmaker, guided solely by the intelligence and tact of the working girls themselves.

Such was Véra Pavlovna's fondest, dearest dream.

V.

Thus had rolled away nearly three years since the establishment of the workshop, and more than three years since Véra Pavlovna's marriage. By what smoothness and activity had these years been marked! With what tranquillity, joys, and contentment of all sorts had they not been filled!

Véra Pavlovna, waking in the morning, dozes a long time in bed; she loves to doze; while appearing to sleep, she thinks of what there is to do; after which her thought wanders, and she says to herself: "How warm this bed is! How nice it is thus to doze in the morning!" and so she dozes until from the neutral room (now we must say from one of the neutral rooms, for there are two in this fourth year of their marriage) — until from one of the neutral rooms her husband — that is, "her darling"—calls out: "Vérotchka, are you awake?"

"Yes, my darling."

This "yes" means that the husband may begin to make the tea; for he makes the tea in the morning, while Véra Pavlovna — no, in her room she is not Véra Pavlovna, but Vérotchka — is dressing. She is very long in dressing! Not at all! She dresses quickly, but she likes to let the water stream over her a long time; then she is a long time in combing her hair, or, rather, not exactly that; she combs her hair quickly, only she likes to play with her tresses, of which she is very fond; sometimes too, it must be added, she pays particular attention to one feature of her toilet,—her boots: Vérotchka dresses with much simplicity, but she has beautiful boots; to have beautiful boots is her passion.

Now she goes out to drink her tea; she kisses her husband.

"Did you sleep well, my darling?"

While drinking the tea, she talks about various subjects, trivial or serious. Furthermore Véra Pavlovna — no, Vérotchka (during the morning meal she is still Vérotchka) — does not take as much tea as cream; the tea is only a pretext for taking the cream, and she puts in much more cream than tea; cream also is her passion. It is very difficult to get good cream in St. Petersburg, but she knows where to find real cream, excellent cream. She dreams of owning a cow; if affairs go on for another year as they have already gone on, perhaps she may have one. But it is nine o'clock. Her darling goes off to give his lessons or attend to his other business: he is also employed in a manufacturer's counting-room. Véra Pavlovna now becomes Véra Pavlovna until the next morning. She attends to her household duties; she has but one servant, a very young girl, who has to be shown everything; and as soon as she has become familiar with affairs, a new one has to be shown, for servants do not stay long with Véra Pavlovna. They are always marrying. After six months or a little more Véra Pavlovna makes a pelerine or some ruffles as a preparation for standing godmother. On this occasion she cannot refuse. "But then, Véra Pavlovna, you have arranged everything; no one but you can be godmother," they would say, with reason.

Yes, she has many household cares. Then she has to go to give her lessons, numerous enough to occupy her ten hours a week: to have more would be fatiguing to her, and furthermore she has no time. Before the lessons she has to go to the shop and spend some time there; on returning from the lessons she has to call in again and take a glance at affairs. Then it is time to dine with her "darling." Often there are one or two persons to dine with them. Not more than two; they cannot have more; and even two cause considerable trouble. If Véra Pavlovna comes home tired, then the dinner is simpler; she goes to her room to rest, and the dinner begun under her direction is finished without her. But if on coming home she is not tired, she runs to the kitchen and goes actively to work: in that case the dinner is ornamented with some bit of pastry, generally something to be eaten with cream, — that is, something that may serve as a pretext for eating cream. During the meal she talks and asks questions, but generally talks; and why should she not talk? How many new things she has to communicate concerning the shop alone! After the meal she remains a quarter of an hour longer with her "darling;" then they say "*au revoir*," and retire to their respective rooms. Now Véra Pavlovna again lies down upon her bed, where she reads and dozes; very often she sleeps; perhaps that is the case half of the time. It is her weakness, a vulgar weakness perhaps; but Véra Pavlovna sleeps after dinner. And she even loves to sleep; she is neither ashamed nor repentant of this vulgar weakness. She rises after having slept or simply dozed for an hour and a half or two hours; she dresses and goes once more to the shop, where she stays until tea-time. Then, if they have no guests to take tea with them, she talks again with her "darling," and they spend about half an hour in the neutral room. After which, "Till tomorrow, my darling;" they kiss each other and separate until the following morning.

Then for some time, occasionally until two o'clock in the morning, she works, reads, finds recreation at the piano (which is in her room). This grand piano has just been bought; previously she had hired one. It was a great pleasure to her when this piano was bought; in the first place it was a saving. The piano, which was a small second-hand one, cost one hundred roubles; it only had to be repaired at a cost of seventy roubles, and then she had a piano of excellent tone. Sometimes her darling comes in to hear her sing, but only rarely: he has so much to do! So the evening passes: working, reading, playing, singing; but especially reading and singing. This when nobody is there. But very often they receive visitors, generally young people not as old as Véra Pavlovna herself, among the number the workshop professors. All hold Lopoukhoff in high esteem, consider him one of the best minds of St. Petersburg, and perhaps they are not wrong. This is the motive of their intimacy with the Lopoukhoffs: they find Dmitry Serguéitch's conversations useful to them. For Véra Pavlovna they have a boundless veneration; she even permits them to kiss her hand without feeling herself humiliated, and conducts herself toward them as if she were fifteen years their elder; that is, she so conducts herself when not indulging in gayeties; but, to tell the truth, the most of the time she does indulge in gayeties: she runs, she plays with them and they are enchanted, and all dance, and waltz, and run, and chatter and laugh, and make music, and, above all, sing. So much gayety does not at all prevent these young people from profoundly venerating Véra Pavlovna, and from esteeming her as one rarely esteems an elder sister and as one does not always esteem a good mother. Moreover, the song is not always a gay one; in fact, Véra Pavlovna oftenest sings serious things; sometimes she stops singing and plays serious airs on her piano; her hearers listen in silence. They receive also older visitors, their equals, — for the most part Lopoukhoff's old comrades, acquaintances of his old comrades, and two or three young professors, almost all bachelors: the only married people are the Mertzaloff's.

The Lopoukhoffs visit more rarely, scarcely ever going to see any one but the Mertzaloffs and Madame Mertzaloff's parents: these good and simple old people have a large number of sons filling positions of considerable importance in all the different ministries; at the houses of these, who live in a certain degree of luxury, Véra Pavlovna meets a society of all colors and shades. This free, active life, not without a touch of sybaritism, — dozing in her soft, warm bed, taking cream, eating pastry with cream, — this life is very pleasant to Véra Pavlovna.

Does the world afford a better life? To her as yet it seems not.

Yes, and for the beginning of youth perhaps she is right.

But the years roll on, and with the lapse of time life grows better, provided it comes to be what it already is for some and what it one day will be for all.

VI.

One day — the end of the summer was already near at hand — the young girls were getting ready to take their customary Sunday walk in the suburbs. On almost every holiday during the summer they went in boats to the islands.* Ordinarily Véra Pavlovna alone went with them, but on this occasion Dmitry Serguéitch was going too, which was very extraordinary; it was the second time that year that he had done so. This news caused much joy in the shop: Véra Pavlovna, thought the girls, will be gayer than usual, and the walk will be a very lively one. Consequently some of the girls, who had intended to pass this Sunday otherwise, changed their plans and joined the promenaders. They had to engage five yawls instead of four, and found that even five would not be enough; they had to take a sixth. There were more than fifty persons, over twenty of whom were seamstresses. Only six were absent. There were three women advanced in years; a dozen children; mothers, sisters, and brothers of the seamstresses; three young men who had sweethearts among them, one being a clockmaker's foreman, another a small merchant, and both scarcely yielding in point of manners to the third, who was a schoolteacher in the district; and finally five other young men of various pursuits, of whom two were officers, and eight students from the University and Medical Academy.

They took four great *samovars* filled with bits of all sorts of provisions, bread, cold veal, etc. For the young people were very active, and in the open air could be relied on to have good appetites: they did not forget half a dozen bottles of wine: for fifty people, fifteen of whom were children, this was certainly none too much.

The trip was a very joyous one; nothing was wanting. They danced quadrilles with sixteen and even twenty couples. In the races twenty-two couples took part; they hung three swings between the trees; in the intervals they drank tea or ate. For half an hour a part of the joyous company listened to a discussion between Dmitry Serguéitch and two students, the most intimate of his younger friends; they mutually charged each other with erroneous reasoning, moderantism, and *bourgeoisisme*. These were general charges, but in each individual some special fault was pointed out. In one of the students it was romanticism, in Dmitry Serguéitch schematism, and in the other student rigorism; it is needless to say that it was very difficult for a simple listener to give attention to such a discussion for more than five minutes.

One of the disputants was not able to keep it up over an hour and a half, after which he fled to join the dancers, but his flight was not altogether inglorious. He had become indignant against some moderate or other. Undoubtedly this moderate was myself, though I was not present, and knowing that the object of his wrath was already well along in years, he cried out: "What are you talking about? Let me quote you some words that I heard uttered lately by

---

* That is, the Islands situated in the suburbs of St. Petersburg and formed by the various arms of the Neva.

a very estimable and very intelligent lady: 'Man is incapable of useful thought after the age of twenty-five years.'"

"But I know the lady to whom you refer," said the officer, approaching, unfortunately for the romanticist; "she is Madame N., and she said that in my presence; she is indeed an excellent lady, only she was convicted on the spot of having boasted half an hour before of being twenty-six years old, and you remember, do you not, how she joined all the others in laughing at herself."

And now all four laughed, and the romanticist, while laughing, took advantage of the opportunity to run away. But the officer took his place in the discussion, which grew still more animated and lasted until tea was ready. The officer answered the rigorist and the schematist more rudely than the romanticist had done, but showed himself a thorough-going follower of Auguste Comte.

After tea the officer declared that, inasmuch as he was still at that age when one can think correctly, he was ready to join the other individuals of the same age; Dmitry Serguéitch and even the rigorist followed his example in spite of themselves; it is true that they did not dance, but they joined in the races. When the contests in running and leaping the brook began, the three thinkers showed themselves among the most enthusiastic. The officer proved himself the superior when it came to leaping the brook. Dmitry Serguéitch, who was endowed with great strength, became greatly excited on being thrown by the officer; he counted on being the first in this sort of exercise after the rigorist, who very easily lifted into the air and threw to the ground Dmitry and the officer together. That did not clash with the ambition of the officer or of Dmitry Serguéitch, for the rigorist was a recognized athlete; but Dmitry Serguéitch did not like to pocket the disgrace of being conquered by the officer, and so he returned to the struggle five times, and five times the officer, though not without difficulty, threw him. The sixth time he acknowledged himself conquered. Both could do no more. The three thinkers, stretching themselves upon the grass, resumed their discussion; this time Dmitry Serguéitch took the Comtean view and the officer was the schematist, but the rigorist remained a rigorist. At eleven o'clock they started homeward. The old women and children slept in the boats; fortunately they had taken many warm wraps along; the others on the contrary talked incessantly, and the games and laughter in the six yawls did not stop until their arrival.

VII.

Two days afterward, at the breakfast table, Véra Pavlovna told her husband that he had a bad color. He answered that that night he had not slept very well, and had been feeling badly since the previous evening; but that it was nothing; he had taken a little cold on the excursion, especially while lying on the ground after the racing and wrestling; he acknowledged that he had been a little imprudent, but convinced Véra Pavlovna that it was nothing at all.

Then he went about his usual business, and at tea-time said that his indisposition had left him. But the next morning he was obliged to confess that he must remain a while in the house. Véra Pavlovna, very anxious, became seriously frightened, and urged Dmitry Sergueitch to send for a doctor

"But I am a doctor myself, and can care for myself if need be; at present it is not necessary."

But Véra Pavlovna insisted, and he wrote a note to Kirsanoff, in which he told him that his sickness was insignificant and that he called him only to please his wife.

Consequently Kirsanoff made no haste about coming. He remained at the hospital until dinner-time, and, when he reached the Lopoukhoffs, it was already after five o'clock.

"I did well, Alexander, in calling you," said Lopoukhoff: "although there is no danger, and probably will be none, I have an inflammation of the lungs. I should certainly have cured myself without you, but care for me just the same. It is necessary to ease my conscience: I am not a bachelor like you."

They sounded each other's chests for a long time, and both came to the conclusion that Lopoukhoff's lungs were really inflamed. There was no danger, and probably would be none, but this disease is always grave. The patient must keep his bed a dozen days.

Kirsanoff had to talk a long time to Véra Pavlovna to ease her mind. She finally was persuaded that they were not deceiving her; that the disease, in all probability, was not only not dangerous, but even quite light; only it was "in all probability," and how many things happen against all probability! Kirsanoff came twice a day to see his patient: they both saw that the disease was not dangerous. On the morning of the fourth day Kirsanoff said to Véra Pavlovna:

"Dmitry is getting on well: for the next three or four days he will be a little worse, after which his recovery will begin. But I wish to speak seriously to you of yourself; why do you not sleep nights? You are doing wrong. He has no need of a nurse, or of me. In acting in this way you are injuring yourself, and quite uselessly. At this very moment your nerves are agitated."

To all these arguments Véra Pavlovna answered:

"Never!" "Impossible!" Or else, "I should like to, but I cannot," — that is, sleep nights and leave Lopoukhoff without a nurse.

At last she said: "But all that you are saying to me now he has already told me many times over, as you well know. Certainly I would have yielded to him rather than to you; therefore I cannot."

Against such an argument there was nothing to be said. Kirsanoff shook his head and went away.

Coming back to his patient after nine in the evening, he remained by his side in company with Véra Pavlovna about half an hour; then he said:

"Now, Véra Pavlovna, go and rest. We both beg you to. I will spend the night here."

Véra Pavlovna was much confused; she was half convinced that her presence all night by the bedside was not absolutely necessary. But then why does Kirsanoff, a busy man, remain? Who knows? No, her "darling" cannot be left alone; no one knows what might happen. He will want to drink, perhaps he will want some tea; but he is so considerate that he will refrain from asking for it; therefore it is necessary to remain by his side. But that Kirsanoff should spend the night there is out of the question; she will not allow it. Therefore she refused to go away, pretending that she was not very tired and that she had rested a great deal during the day.

"I beg you to go; I ask your pardon, but I absolutely pray you to."

And Kirsanoff took her by the hand, and led her almost by force to her room.

"You really confuse me, Alexander," said the sick man; "what a ridiculous rôle you play in remaining all night with a patient who does not need you! and yet I am much obliged to you, for I have never been able to induce her to get a nurse, since she fears to leave me alone; she cannot trust me to any one else."

"If I did not see that she could not rest easy in trusting you to any other, you may be sure that I would not disturb my comfort. But now I hope that she is going to sleep, for I am a doctor and your friend besides."

In fact, Véra Pavlovna had no sooner reached her bed than she threw herself upon it and went to sleep. Three sleepless nights alone would be nothing, and the hurry and worry alone would be nothing. But the hurry and worry and the three sleepless nights together, without any rest in the daytime, were really dangerous; forty-eight hours more of it, and she would have been more seriously sick than her husband.

Kirsanoff spent three nights with his patient; it tired him scarcely any, for he slept very tranquilly, only taking the precaution to lock the door that Véra Pavlovna might not observe his negligence. She strongly suspected that he slept, but was made not at all uneasy thereby. He is a doctor; what, then, is there to fear? He knows when to sleep and when to go without it. She was ashamed at not having been able to calm herself sooner in order to no further disturb Kirsanoff. But in vain did she assure him that she would sleep even if he were not there; he did not believe her, and answered:

"It is your fault, Véra Pavlovna, and you must take the consequences. I have no confidence in you."

Four days afterward she saw clearly that the sick man was almost cured; the most decisive proofs conquered her doubts. That evening they played cards, three-handed. Lopoukhoff was no longer completely on his back, but in a half-sitting posture, and had regained the voice of a man in health. It was safe for Kirsanoff to suspend his attentions, and he told them so.

"Alexander Matvéitch, why have you so completely forgotten me? With Dmitry you are on a good footing; he sees you often enough; but, as for you, you have not been to see us, it seems to me, for more than six months; and it has been so for years. Do you remember that at the beginning we were intimate friends?"

"Men change, Véra Pavlovna. And I do an enormous amount of work; I can boast of it. I visit nobody, for lack of time and will. I tire myself so from nine till five in the hospital that, when I go home, I can put on nothing but my dressing-gown. Friendship is good, but — do not be offended at what I am going to say — to lie in one's dressing-gown, with a cigar between one's lips, is better still."

In fact, Kirsanoff, for more than two years, had not been a visitor at the Lopoukhoffs'. The reader has not noticed his name among their ordinary visitors, or even among their rare visitors; for a long time he had been the rarest of all.

VIII.

The reader with the penetrating eye (I make this explanation only to the masculine reader: the feminine reader is intelligent enough to annoy an author with her penetration; therefore, let me say once for all, I do not explain myself to her; among masculine readers also there are some intelligent people; no more do I explain myself to these; but most masculine readers, among them nearly all men of letters and men who wield a pen, have the penetrating eye; with them it is always well to have an understanding), — well, the reader with the penetrating eye says: "I see where this is going to end; in Véra Pavlovna's life a new romance is beginning, in which Kirsanoff is to play the principal *rôle*. I see even farther. Kirsanoff has long been in love with Véra Pavlovna, and that is why he has ceased to visit the Lopoukhoffs." How facile your conception, O reader with the penetrating eye! As soon as something is told you, you note it on the instant and glory in your penetration. Accept my admiration, reader with the penetrating eye!

Thus in the history of Véra Pavlovna appears a new personage, and I should have to introduce him, had this not already been done. Whenever I spoke of Lopoukhoff, I set my wits to work to distinguish him from his intimate friend, and yet I could say almost nothing of him that I should not have to repeat in speaking of Kirsanoff. Yes, all that the reader with the penetrating eye will be able to divine of Kirsanoff's character will be a repetition of what has been said about Lopoukhoff. Lopoukhoff was the son of a *petit bourgeois*, tolerably well-to-do for his station, — that is, generally having meat in his *stchi*; Kirsanoff was the son of a law copyist, — that is, of a man who often had no meat in his *stchi*. Lopoukhoff, from his earliest years, had earned his own living; Kirsanoff, at the age of twelve, began to aid his father in copying. As soon as he reached the fourth form at school he began to give lessons. Both paved their own way, without aids or acquaintances.

What kind of a man was Lopoukhoff? At school French had not been taught him. As for German, he had been taught just enough to enable him to decline *der die, das* almost faultlessly. After entering the Academy he soon saw that with Russian alone one cannot make much progress in science; he took a French-Russian dictionary and a few French books ready to his hand, — *Télémaque*, Madame de Genlis's novels, a few numbers of our wise *Revue Étrangère*, not very attractive works, — he took these, and, though a great lover of reading, said to himself: "I will not open a single Russian book until I am able to read French easily;" and he succeeded. With German he managed another way; he hired a bed in a room occupied by many German workingmen. The lodging was frightful, the Germans tiresome, the Academy a long way off, but nevertheless he slept there long enough to learn German.

With Kirsanoff it had been otherwise. He had learned German with books and a dictionary, as Lopoukhoff had learned French, and his French he acquired in still another way, — by means of a single book and no dictionary. The Gospel is a well-known book; he procured a copy of a Geneva translation of the New Testament; he read it eight times; the ninth time he understood it all, — he knew French.

What kind of a man was Lopoukhoff? This will show. One day in his much-worn uniform he was going along the Perspective Kamenno-Ostrovsky to give a lesson for fifty copecks two miles away from the Lyceum. He saw approaching him some one with an imposing air, evidently out for exercise, who marched straight upon him without turning aside; now, at that time Lopoukhoff had made this rule: "I turn aside first for nobody except women." Their shoulders touched. The individual, half turning back, said: 'Hog! Beast that you are!" and was about to continue in this tone, when Lopoukhoff, quickly turning around, seized the individual around the waist and threw him into the gutter with great dexterity; then standing over his adversary, he said to him: "Do not stir; else I will drag you into a muddier place yet." Two peasants passing saw and applauded; an officer older passing saw, did not applaud, and confined himself to a half smile. Carriages passed, but their occupants could not see who was in the gutter. After remaining some time in this attitude, Lopoukhoff again took his man, not around the waist, but by the hand, aided him to rise, led him into the road, and said to him: "Ah, sir, what a misstep you made! I hope you have not hurt yourself? Allow me to wipe you off." A peasant passing helped to wipe him, as did two *petits bourgeois* also passing: after the man was clean, each went his way.

To Kirsanoff a similar but somewhat different thing once happened. A certain lady had formed an idea of cataloguing the library which her husband, an admirer of Voltaire, had left her at his death twenty years before. Exactly why a catalogue became necessary after twenty years is not known. It was Kirsanoff who chanced to put himself at the disposition of the lady for her purpose, and they agreed on eighty roubles as the price; Kirsanoff worked for six weeks. Suddenly the lady changed her fancy and decided that the catalogue was useless; so she went into the library, and said:

"You have done enough; I have changed my mind: here is the pay for your work," and she handed him ten roubles.

"I have already done, your —— (he gave the lady her title), more than half of the work: of the seventeen cases I have copied ten."

"Do you consider yourself badly paid? Nicolas, come here and talk to this gentleman." Nicolas hurried to the scene.

"How dare you be rude to my mother?"

"But, my beardless boy (an expression without foundation on Kirsanoff's part, Nicolas being about five years his elder), you would do well to understand the matter before expressing yourself."

"Ho! there! my servants!" shouted Nicolas.

"Ah! your servants! I will teach you." The lady gave a shrill scream and fainted, and Nicolas saw clearly that it was impossible for him to make any movement with his arms fastened against his sides by Kirsanoff's right hand as if by a band of iron. Kirsanoff, after pulling his hair with his left hand, placed it at his throat and said:

"Do you see how easy it is for me to strangle you?"

He gave his throat a grip, and Nicolas saw that it was indeed very easy to strangle him. The grasp was loosened. Nicolas found that he could breathe, but was still at the mercy of his conqueror. To the Goliaths who made their appearance Kirsanoff said:

"Stop there, or I will strangle him. Keep your distance, or I will strangle him."

Nicolas, at once comprehending the situation, made signals which meant:

"His reasoning is good."

"Now, will you escort me, my dear, to the stairs?" said Kirsanoff, again addressing Nicolas though continuing to hold his arm around him. He went out into the hall and descended the stairs, the Goliaths looking at him in astonishment; on the last step, letting go his hold of Nicolas's throat, he hurled him from him, and started for a hat store to buy a cap in place of that which he had left upon the battle-ground.

Well, then, are not these two men alike in character? All the prominent traits by which they are marked are traits, not of individuals, but of a type, so different from those you are accustomed to see, reader with the penetrating eye, that these general peculiarities hide from you their personal differences. These people are like a few Europeans scattered among the Chinese, whom the Chinese cannot distinguish from each other, seeing but one and the same nature, "barbarians with red hair and without manners." In their eyes the French have "red hair" as well as the English. Now, the Chinese are right: compared to them all Europeans are as a single individual; not individuals, but representatives of a type and nothing more. None of them eat cockroaches or wood-lice; none of them cut men up into little pieces; all alike drink brandy and wine made of grapes instead of rice; and even the common drink, tea, is prepared by the Europeans with sugar, and not without as the Chinese prepare it. It is the same with people of the type to which Lopoukhoff and Kirsanoff belonged: they seem identical to men who do not belong to this type. Each is bold and resolute, knowing what to do under all circumstances, and doing it with a strong arm when necessary. That is one side of their character. On the other side each is of irreproachable honesty, of honesty such that one cannot even ask concerning either: 'Can this man be relied on fully and absolutely?" It is as clear as the air that they breathe; as long as those breasts heave, they will be warm and unshakeable; lay your head upon them boldly, it will rest there safely. These general traits are so prominent that they eclipse all individual peculiarities.

It is not long since this type was established in Russia. Formerly from time to time a few individuals shadowed it forth; but they were exceptions, and as such felt their isolation and weakness; hence their inertia, their *ennui*, their exaltation, their romanticism, their whimsicality; they could not possess the principal traits of this type, — tact, coolness, activity, all well balanced, the realization of common sense in action. They were really people of the same nature, but this nature had not yet developed itself into the condition of a type. This type, I repeat, has been established but a little while; I can remember when it did not exist, although I am not yet of mature age. I have not succeeded in becoming one of them, for I was not brought up in their time; consequently I can without scruple express my esteem for these new men, for unfortunately I do not glorify myself in saying of them: "These are excellent men." Recently this type has been multiplying rapidly. It is born of an epoch; it is a sign of the times, and — must I say it? it will disappear with the fast-flying epoch which produced it. Its life, new as it is, is fated to last but a short time.

We did not see these men six years ago; three years ago we despised them; and now — but it matters little what we think of them now; in a few years, in a very few years, we shall appeal to them; we shall say to them: 'Save us!" and whatever they say then will be done by all. A few years more, perhaps even a few months, and we shall curse them; they will be driven from the scene amid hisses and insults. What matters it? You may drive them away, you may curse them, but they will be useful to you, and that will satisfy them. They will quit the scene, proud and modest, austere and good, as they ever were. Not one will remain upon the scene? Not one! How shall we live without them? None too well. But after them things will go on better than before. Many years will pass, and then men will say: "Since their day things have been better, but still they are bad." And when they shall speak thus, that will mean that it is time for this type to be born again; it will reappear in a greater number of individuals under better forms, because goodness will then be plentier, and all that is now good will then be better. And so history will begin again in a new phase. And that will last until men say: "Now we are good," and then there will be no longer any special type, for all men will be of this type, and it will be difficult for any one to understand that there ever was a time when it was regarded as special and not as the common nature of all mankind.

IX.

But just as Europeans seem to the Chinese to have the same faces and the same customs when contrasted with those of the Chinese, while in reality there is a much greater difference between Europeans than between Chinese, so it is with these modern men who seem to constitute but a single type. Individual diversity develops itself in more numerous differences, and they are more sharply distinguished from each other than are individuals of any other type. They include all sorts of people, — sybarites and stoics, the stern and the tender, in short, all varieties. But as the most savage European is very gentle, the most cowardly very courageous, the most epicurean very moral compared with the Chinese, so it is with the new men; the most austere believe that man needs more comfort than others dream of for him; the most sensual are more rigid in their morality than the moralists found in the common run of men. But they have conceptions of their own in all these things: they view in a way wholly peculiar to themselves both morality and comfort, sensuality and virtue.

But they all view these things in the same way and as if they were one and the same thing, so that to them comfort, sensuality, virtue, morality seem identical. But all this is true only from the Chinese standpoint; they themselves, on the contrary, find very great differences in their views corresponding to the diversity of their natures. How grasp all these differences?

When Europeans talk over their affairs with each other, but only with each other and not with the Chinese, the diversity of their natures is visible. So is it with our new men; we see in them a great diversity when the relations between themselves and not with others are before us. We have seen two individuals of this type, Véra Pavlovna and Lopoukhoff, and we have seen what their relations were. A third individual now appears upon the scene. Let us see what differences will grow out of the possibility now open to one of the three of making a comparison between the two others. Véra Pavlovna now has before her Lopoukhoff and Kirsanoff. Formerly she had no choice to make; now she may make one.

X.

Nevertheless two or three words must be said of Kirsanoff's outer man.

He too, like Lopoukhoff, had regular and beautiful features. Some thought the latter more beautiful, others the former. Lopoukhoff, who was darker, had hair of a deep chestnut color, sparkling brown eyes that seemed almost black, an aquiline nose, thick lips, and a somewhat oval face.

Kirsanoff had moderately thick light hair, blue eyes, a Grecian nose, a small mouth, and an oblong face of rare whiteness.

Kirsanoff's position was a fairly good one. He already had a chair. The electors were against him by an enormous majority, and he not only would not have obtained a chair, but would not even have been made a doctor at the final examination at the Academy, had it not been impossible to avoid it. Two or three young people and one of his old professors, a man already advanced in age, all his friends, had long since reported to the others that there existed in the world a man named Virchow and that this Virchow lived in Berlin, and a man named Claude Bernard and that this Claude Bernard lived in Paris, and I know not how many more names of men of this sort, which my memory does not retain and who also lived in different cities; they had also said that these Virchows, Claude Bernards, and others were scientific luminaries.

All that was improbable in the last degree, for we well know the luminaries of science, — Boerhoave, Hufeland; Harvey was also a great *savant*, being the discoverer of the circulation of the blood; likewise Jenner, who taught us vaccination; these we know, but, as for these Virchows, and these Claude Bernards we do not know them. What sort of luminaries are they, then? The devil knows. This same Claude Bernard showed appreciation of Kirsanoff's work before he had finished his last year as a student; of course, then, it was impossible to avoid electing him. So they gave Kirsanoff a physician's diploma and about eighteen months afterward a chair. The students said that he was a valuable addition to the number of good professors. Of practice he had none, and said that he had abandoned the practice of medicine. But he spent many hours at the hospital; he often dined there and sometimes slept there. What did he do there? He said that he worked there for science and not for the sick: "I do not treat patients, I only observe and experiment." The students sustained this opinion and added that none but imbeciles treat the sick now, for no one yet knows how to treat them. The hospital attendants thought otherwise: "See, Kirsanoff takes this patient into his ward; the case must be a serious one," said they to each other; and then they said to the patient: "Be tranquil; no disease can stand against this doctor; he is a master, and a father besides."

XI.

For the first few months after Véra Pavlovna's marriage Kirsanoff visited the Lopoukhoff's very often, almost every other day, I might say almost every day and be nearer the truth. He became soon, if not from the very first, as intimate a friend of Véra Pavlovna as of Lopoukhoff himself. That lasted about six months. One day, when they were talking freely, as was their custom, Kirsanoff, who had had the most to say, suddenly became silent.

"What is the matter with you, Alexander?"

"Why do you stop, Alexander Matvéitch?"

"Oh, it is nothing; I am seized with a fit of melancholy."

"That is something that rarely happens to you, Alexander Matvéitch," said Véra Pavlovna.

"It never happens to me without cause," said Kirsanoff, in a tone which seemed strained.

A little later, rather sooner than usual, he rose and went away, taking his leave, as he always did, unceremoniously.

Two days afterward Lopoukhoff told Véra Pavlovna that he had been to see Kirsanoff, and he had been received by him in a rather singular fashion, as if Kirsanoff were trying to be agreeable to him, which was quite unnecessary, considering their relations. Lopoukhoff, after watching him a while, had said to him frankly: "It seems to me that you are out of sorts towards us, Alexander; with whom are you offended? Perhaps with me?"

"No."

"With Vérotchka?"

"No."

"But what is the matter, then?"

"Nothing; you take notions, I don't know why."

"You do not feel right toward me today; something is the matter with you."

Kirsanoff was profuse with his assurances: nothing was the matter; in what way had he shown himself put out? Then, as if ashamed, he again threw off ceremony and became very cordial. Lopoukhoff, seizing the opportunity, said to him:

"Now, Alexander, tell me, why are you out of sorts?"

"I never dreamed of such a thing,"—and again he became mawkish and affected.

What an enigma! Lopoukhoff recalled nothing that could have offended him; indeed, such a thing was not possible, considering their reciprocal esteem and profound friendship. Véra Pavlovna, too, asked herself if she had not offended him, but was as unable to find anything, knowing perfectly well that she, no more than her husband, could have offended him.

Two days more passed. Not to come to the Lopoukhoffs' for four days together was an extraordinary thing for Kirsanoff. Véra Pavlovna even wondered if he were not unwell. Lopoukhoff went to see if he were not really sick. Sick? No, not at all: but still he was out of sorts. To Lopoukhoff's urgent inquiries and after several times saying " No " and several times " It is your imagination," he began to talk all sorts of nonsense about his feelings toward Lopoukhoff and Véra Pavlovna: he loved them and esteemed them highly. From all that it was to be inferred that they had wronged him, and the worst of it was that in his remarks there was no allusion to anything of the kind. It was evident that they had offended him. It seemed so strange to Lopoukhoff to see this in a man like Kirsanoff that he said: " Listen, we are friends; all this ought really to make you blush." Kirsanoff answered with an affected sorrow that perhaps he was too sensitive, but that on several occasions he had felt hurt.

" But at what ? "

He began to enumerate a great number of things that had happened lately, all of them things of this sort:

" You said that the lighter the color of a man's hair, the weaker he is. Véra Pavlovna said that tea had risen in price. One was an ill-natured jest on the color of my hair. The other was an allusion to the fact that I was your guest."

Lopoukhoff stood stupefied: " Pride governs all his thoughts, or, rather, he has become simply a fool, a fool in four letters."

Lopoukhoff went home a little saddened; it was painful to him to see such failings in a man whom he so much loved. To Véra Pavlovna's questions on the subject he replied sadly that it was better not to talk about it, that Kirsanoff said disagreeable things, and that probably he was sick.

Three or four days later Kirsanoff came back to himself, recognized the imbecility of his words, and called on the Lopoukhoffs, behaving himself as he had been wont to do. Then he began to tell how stupid he had been. From Véra Pavlovna's words he saw that his conversation had not been reported; he sincerely thanked Lopoukhoff for his discretion, and to punish himself told all to Véra Pavlovna; he feelingly excused himself, saying that he was sick and had been in the wrong. Véra Pavlovna bade him abandon the subject, declaring that these were stupidities; he caught at the word " stupidities," and began to talk all sorts of twaddle no less senseless than the things he had said to Lopoukhoff; he said with much reserve and *finesse* that certainly these things were " stupidities," for he fully realized his inferiority to the Lopoukhoffs, but that he deserved nothing else, etc., the whole being said with veiled allusions and accompanied by the most amiable assurances of esteem and devotion.

Véra Pavlovna, at hearing him go on in this way, stood as stupefied as her husband had before her. After Kirsanoff's departure they remembered that some days before their friend had shown signs of very singular stupidity. At the time they had neither remarked upon nor understood it; now his remarks became clear to them; they were of the same sort, only less pronounced.

Kirsanoff again began to visit the Lopoukhoff's frequently; but the continuation of the former simple relations was no longer possible. From under the mask of a good and intelligent man had protruded for several days asses' ears of such length that the Lopoukhoffs would have lost a large share of their esteem for their former friend even if the ears had not reappeared; but they continued to show themselves from time to time, and, although they did not seem so long as before and were each time withdrawn precipitately, there was always something pitiable, vile, and stupid about them.

Soon the Lopoukhoffs grew cold toward him. Finding in this an excuse, he stopped his visits. But he saw Lopoukhoff at the house of one of their friends. Some time after, his conduct improving, Lopoukhoff's aversion to him began to weaken, and he began to visit him again. Within a year Kirsanoff resumed his visits at the Lopoukhoffs'; he again became the excellent Kirsanoff of former days, unaffected and loyal. But he came rarely: it was plain that he was not at his ease, remembering the foolish part that he had played. Lopoukhoff and Véra Pavlovna had almost forgotten it. But relations once broken off are never quite reestablished. Judging from appearances, he and Lopoukhoff had become friends again, and Lopoukhoff really esteemed him now almost as much as before and visited him often; Véra Pavlovna, too, had restored to him a portion of her good graces, but she saw him only rarely.

XII.

Lopoukhoff's sickness, or, better, Véra Pavlovna's extreme attachment to her husband, having forced Kirsanoff to maintain intimate daily relations with the Lopoukhoffs for more than a week, he clearly saw that he was entering upon a perilous path in deciding to pass his nights near Lopoukhoff in order to prevent Véra Pavlovna from being her husband's sick-nurse. He was very happy and proud at having succeeded so well in doing all that he had deemed necessary to arrest the development of his passion when he had perceived its symptoms three years before. Two or three weeks afterward he had been unable to avoid returning to the Lopoukhoffs'. But even at those times he had felt more pleasure over his firmness in the struggle than suffering at his privation, and a month later he did not suffer at all; the only feeling left being that of satisfaction with his upright conduct. So tranquil and pure was his soul.

But now the danger was greater than then: in these three years Véra Pavlovna had certainly greatly developed morally; then she was half a child, now it was quite a different thing: the feeling that she inspired could no longer be the light attachment that one feels for a little girl whom one loves and at the same time admires in her innocence. And not only had she developed morally; with us here in the North, when a woman is really beautiful, she grows more and more so every year. Yes, at that age three years of life do a great deal to dvelope the good and the beautiful in the soul, in the eyes, in the features, and in the entire person, if the person be moral and good.

The danger was great, but for him only; as for Véra Pavlovna, what risk had she to run? She loved her husband, and Kirsanoff was not thoughtless and foolish enough to believe himself a dangerous rival of Lopoukhoff. It was from no false modesty that he thought so: all who knew them looked on them as equals. Now, Lopoukhoff had on his side this enormous advantage, that he had already deserved love, that he had already completely won Véra Pavlovna's heart. The choice was made; she was very contented and happy; could she dream of anything better? Was she not happy? It was even ridiculous to think of such a thing. To her and to Lopoukhoff such an apprehension would have been but an absurd vanity on Kirsanoff's part.

Well, for such a little thing, to save himself a month or two of weariness, ought Kirsanoff to let this woman fatigue herself and run the risk of contracting a serious disease by watching nights at a sick man's bedside? To avoid disturbing the tranquillity of his own life for a little while, ought he to allow another individual no less worthy to incur a serious danger? That would not have been honest. Now, a dishonest action would have been much more disagreeable to him than the slightly painful struggle with himself through which he had to pass, and of the result of which he felt as sure as of his firmness.

These were Kirsanoff's thoughts, on deciding to take Véra Pavlovna's place at her husband's bedside.

The necessity for watching passed. To save appearances and not make the change in their relations so abrupt as to call attention to it, it was necessary for Kirsanoff to visit his friends at first two or three times a week, then from month to month, and then every six months. He could readily explain his absence by his occupations.

XIII.

What Kirsanoff foresaw was realized; his attachment was renewed, and became more intense than before; but to struggle against it gave him no difficulty, no serious torment. Visiting the Lopoukhoffs for the second time during the week following the cessation of his treatment of Dmitry Serguéitch, he stays till nine o'clock in the evening. This was enough, appearances were saved; he need not come again for a fortnight, and it would be over. But this time he must stay an hour longer. The week was not yet over, and his passion was already half stilled; in a month it would entirely disappear. Therefore he was well contented. He took an active part in the conversation and with so much ease that he rejoiced at his success, and this contentment added still further to his self-possession.

But Lopoukhoff was arranging to go out for the first time since his sickness. At this Véra Pavlovna was much pleased, her joy perhaps being greater than that of the convalescent himself.

The conversation turning upon the sickness, they made fun of Véra, and ironically extolled her conjugal self-denial. Barely had she escaped falling sick herself in her exaggerated alarm at that which did not call for it.

"Laugh, laugh," said she, "but I am sure that in my place you would not have done differently."

"What an influence the cares of others have upon a man!" said Lopoukhoff; "he is so affected by them that he finally comes to believe that all the precautions of which he is the object are useful. For instance, I might as well have been out for the last three days, and yet I stay in the house. This very morning I desired to go out, but still I said: 'To be on the safe side I will wait till tomorrow.'"

"Yes, you might have gone out long ago," added Kirsanoff.

"That is what I call heroism, for really it is a great bore to me, and I should much like to run away at once."

"My dear friend, it is to pacify me that you are playing the hero. Get ready on the instant if you are so desirous of ending your quarantine forthwith. I must now go to the shop for half an hour. Let us all three go there; it will be a very nice thing on your part to make our shop the object of your first visit. The working-girls will notice it and be much pleased at the attention."

"Good! Let us go together," said Lopoukhoff, visibly delighted at the prospect of breathing the fresh air that very afternoon.

"Here is a friend full of tact," said Véra Pavlovna: "it did not even occur to her that you might not have any desire to come with us, Alexander Matvéitch."

"On the contrary, I am much interested; I have long wanted to see the shop. Your idea is a very happy one."

In truth, Véra Pavlovna's idea was a happy one. The young girls were much pleased at receiving Lopoukhoff's first visit. Kirsanoff was much interested in the shop; given his way of thinking, he could not have helped it. If a special reason had not withheld him, he would have been from the first one of the most zealous professors. In short, an hour passed before they knew it. Véra Pavlovna went with Kirsanoff through the different rooms, showing him everything. They were going from the dining-room to the work-rooms, when Véra Pavlovna was approached by a young girl who originally was not there. The working girl and Kirsanoff gave one glance at each other:

"Nastennka!"

"Sacha!" *

And they kissed each other.

"Sachennka,† my friend, how happy I am at having met you!"

The young girl, laughing and crying, covered him with kisses. When she had recovered from her joy, she said:

"Véra Pavlovna, I cannot talk business today. I cannot leave him. Come, Sachennka, to my room."

Kirsanoff was no less happy than she. But Véra Pavlovna noticed also much sorrow in his first look after that of recognition. And it was not at all astonishing: the young girl was in the last stage of consumption.

Nastennka Krukoff had entered the shop a year before, being even then very sick. If she had remained in the store where up to that time she had worked, over-work would have killed her long before. But in the shop a way was found of prolonging her life a little. The working girls excused her from sewing altogether, finding her a task less tiresome and less injurious to the health; she performed different functions in the shop, took part in the general administration, and received the orders for work, so that no one could say that she was less useful in the shop than the others.

The Lopoukhoff's went away without awaiting the end of Nastennka's interview with Kirsanoff.

XIV.

NASTENNKA KRUKOFF'S STORY.

The next morning Nastennka Krukoff came to see Véra Pavlovna.

"I wish to talk with you about what you saw yesterday, Véra Pavlovna," said she,—and for some minutes she did not know how to continue,—"I should not like you to think unfavorably of him, Véra Pavlovna."

"Think unfavorably of him! as you yourself think unfavorably of me, Nastassia Borissovna."

"Another would not have thought as I do; but you know I am not like others."

"Nastassia Borissovna, you have no right to treat yourself thus. We have known you for a year, and several members of our little society have known you from a still earlier date."

"Ah! I see that you know nothing of me."

"On the contrary, I know much about you. Latterly you were the waiting-maid of the actress N.; when she married, you left her to avoid her husband's

---

* Nastennka and Sacha are the diminutives of Nastassia and Alexander.

† A more affectionate diminutive than Sacha.

father: you were employed in the store of ———, whence you came to us; I know all that and many details besides."

"Of course I was sure that Maximoff and Cheine, who knew what I used to be, would not run to you with the story. But I thought that you or the others might have heard of it in some other way. Ah! how happy I am that they do not know. But to you I will tell all in order that you may know how good he is. I was a very wicked girl, Véra Pavlovna."

"You, Nastassia Borissovna?"

"Yes, Véra Pavlovna, I. And I was very insolent; I had no shame, and was always drunk; that was the origin of my sickness: I drank too much for my weak chest."

Véra Pavlovna had seen three or four similar cases. Young girls whose conduct had been irreproachable ever since she knew them had told her that formerly they led a bad life. The first time she was astonished at such a confession; but after reflecting upon it a little, she said to herself: "And my own life? The mud in which I grew up was also very bad; nevertheless it did not soil me, and thousands of women, brought up in families like mine, remain pure just the same. Why is it, then, at all extraordinary that from this humiliation should come out unstained those whom a favorable opportunity has aided to escape?" The second time she was not astonished to learn that the young penitent had preserved truly human qualities, — disinterestedness, fidelity in friendship, deep feelings, and even some degree of innocence.

"Nastassia Borissovna, I have before had interviews similar to that which you desire to begin. Such interviews are painful both to the speaker and the listener; my esteem for you will not diminish, but will rather increase, since I know now that you have suffered much; but I understand it all without hearing it. Let us talk no more about it: to me explanations are superfluous. I, too, have passed many years amid great sorrows; I try not to think of them, and I do not like to speak of them, for it is very painful to me."

"No, Véra Pavlovna, I have another motive: I wish to tell you how good he is: I should like some one to know how much I owe to him, and whom shall I tell if not you? It will be a relief to me. As to the life that I led, of course there is no occasion to speak of it; it is always the same with poor women of that sort. I only wish to tell you how I made his acquaintance. It is so agreeable to me to talk about him. I am going to live with him; so you ought to know why I leave the shop."

"If it will please you to tell this story, Nastassia Borissovna, I am very happy to listen to you. Only let me get my work."

"My work! Alas, I cannot say that. How good were these young girls to find me an occupation suited to my health! I wish to thank them one and all. Tell them, Véra Pavlovna, that I begged you to thank them for me. I was walking along the Perspective Nevsky: I had just gone out, and it was still early; I saw a student coming, and directed my steps toward him. He did not say a word, but simply crossed to the other side of the street. I followed him, and grasped him by the arm. 'No,' I said to him, 'I will not leave you, you are so fine looking.'

"'But I beg you to leave me,' said he.

"'Oh, no; come with me.'

"'I have no reason to.'

"'Well, I will go with you. Where are you going? For nothing in the world will I leave you.' I was impudent, as impudent as any and more so."

"Perhaps that was because you were really timid and were making an effort to be bold."

"Yes, that may be. At least I have noticed it in others, — not at that time, mind you; it was afterwards that I understood the reason. So, when I told him that I absolutely must go with him, he smiled and said:

"'Come, if you must; only it will be in vain.'

"He wanted to rebuke me, as he afterwards told me; he was impatient at my persistence. So I went, talking all sorts of nonsense to him; but he said not a word. We arrived. For a student he lived very comfortably; his lessons brought him about twenty roubles a month, and he lived alone. I stretched myself upon the divan and said:

"'Some wine!'

"'No,' said he, 'I shall not give you any wine; only tea, provided you want it.'

"'With punch,' said I.

"'No, without punch.'

"I began to act riotously; he remained calm, and looked at me without paying the slightest attention to my conduct: that offended me much. In these days we meet such young people, Véra Pavlovna, — young people have grown much better since then, — but then it was very exceptional. Therefore I felt offended and began to insult him.

"'If you (*tu*) are made of wood,' — and I added an insult, — 'then I am going away.'

"'But why go now?' said he; 'have some tea first; the landlord will bring the *samovar* presently. Only no insults.'

"And he invariably addressed me as 'you' (*vous*).*

---

* There is no way of expressing in English the distinction made by the Continental peoples between the second person singular and second person plural of the personal pronoun. The singular is used by them in conversation between people who are on very familiar terms. Hence in the above interview Nastassia, wishing to assume a tone of familiarity, tried to use the singular, while Kirsanoff maintained his reserve by insisting on the plural. — *Translator.*

"'Tell me rather who you are and how you have reached this condition.'

"I began to tell him a story of my own invention: we invent all sorts of stories, and that is why nobody believes us; sometimes, nevertheless, these stories are not invented: there are noble and educated persons among us. He listened a little while and then said:

"'No, it is not a clever story; I should much like to believe it, but I cannot.'

"We were already taking tea. Then he said:

"'Do you know, I see by your complexion that it injures you to drink; your chest is in bad condition in consequence of an excessive use of wine. Permit me to examine you.'

"Well, Véra Pavlovna, you will not believe me, but I suddenly felt a sense of shame; and yet in what did my life consist? and but a moment before I had been behaving very boldly! He noticed it.

"'Why, no,' said he, 'I only want to sound your chest.'

"He began to listen at my chest.

"'Yes,' he said, 'you must not drink at all; your chest is not in good condition.'

"'That is impossible,' said I.

"And indeed it was impossible, Véra Pavlovna.

"'Then abandon this life.'

"'And why? it is so joyous!'

"'Not so very,' said he; 'now leave me; I am going to attend to my affairs.'

"And I went away, provoked at having lost my evening, to say nothing of the fact that his indifference had offended me. We girls have our pride in these matters. A month later I happened to be passing that way.

"'Shall I call,' thought I, 'upon my wooden gentleman, and amuse myself a little with him?'

"It was not yet dinner-time; the night before I had slept well, and I had not been drinking. He was reading a book.

"'How do you do, my wooden sir?'

"'How do you do? Is there anything new with you?'

"Again I began my improprieties.

"'I will show you the door,' said he, 'if you do not stop; I have already told you that this does not please me. Now you are not drunk and can understand me. Think rather of this: your face is still more sickly than before; you must abandon wine. Arrange your clothing, and let us talk seriously'

"In fact, I had already begun to feel pains in my chest. Again he sounded it, told me that the disease was growing worse, and said a great deal; my chest pained me so badly that, seized with a sudden access of feeling, I began to weep; I did not want to die, and he filled me with fears of consumption.

"'But,' I said to him, 'how shall I abandon this life? My mistress will not let me go away, for I owe her seventeen roubles.'

"They always keep us in debt so that we may be patient.

"'Seventeen roubles? I cannot give them to you now, for I haven't them; but come day after to-morrow.'

"That seemed to me very strange, for it was not with this in view that I had spoken as I did; besides, how could I have expected such an offer? I could not believe my ears, and I began to cry still harder, believing that he was making sport of me.

"'It is not good in you to make sport of a poor girl, when you see that I am crying.'

"For some minutes longer I refused to believe it. Finally he assured me that he was not joking. Would you believe it? He got the money and gave it to me two days afterwards. I could scarcely believe it then.

"'But how is this?' said I; 'but why do you do this, since you have wanted nothing in return.'

"I freed myself from my mistress and hired a little room. But there was nothing that I could do: in freeing us they give us a special kind of certificate; where could I turn with such a document? And I had no money. Consequently I lived as before, though not exactly as before. I received only my best acquaintances, those not offensive to me; wine I left alone. What was the difference, then, you ask? My life was already much less distressing than it had been. But it was still distressing; and let me tell you something: you will think that it was distressing because I had many friends, five perhaps; no, for I felt an affection for all of them; hence it was not that. Pardon me if I speak thus to you, but it is because I am sincere with you: today I am still of the same mind. You know me; am I not modest? Who has heard anything but good of me? How much time I spend in playing with the children in the shop, and they all love me, and the old ladies will not say that I teach them anything but the best. It is only with you, Véra Pavlovna, that I am sincere; today I am still of the same mind: if you feel affection, there is no harm, provided there is no deceit; if there is deceit, that is another thing. And in that way I lived. Three months went by, and in that time, so tranquil was my life, I obtained considerable rest, and although I had to thus get the money that I needed, I no longer considered that I was leading a wicked life.

"Sachenuka often visited me in those days. I too went sometimes to see him. And now I have got back to my subject, from which I should not have wandered. But his purpose in visiting me was not the same as that of the others; he watched over me to see that my old weakness did not regain possession of me and that I drank no wine. During the first few days, in fact, he sustained me; so great was my desire to take it that nothing but my great deference for him withheld me: if he should come in and see me, thought I. Otherwise I should not have kept my word, for my friends - generous young fellows — said: 'I will send out for some wine.' But wishing to heed Sachenuka's advice, I answered them: 'No, that cannot be.'

"In three weeks' time my will was already much stronger: the desire for drink had gone, and I had already thrown off the manners peculiar to victims of intoxication. During that time I saved in order to repay him, and in two months I did repay him the whole. He was so glad to see me repay him! The next day he brought me muslin for a dress and other articles bought with the same money. After that he still kept up his visits, always as a doctor caring for a patient. One day when at my room, about a month after I had paid my debt, he said to me: 'Nastenuka, you please me.'

"Drunkenness spoils the face; in consequence of my sobriety my complexion had grown softer and my eyes clearer; further, having thrown off my old manners, I had acquired modesty of speech; I was no longer shameless since I had stopped drinking; it is true that in my words I sometimes forgot myself, but a seemly behavior had become habitual with me.

"On hearing these words I was so happy that I wanted to throw myself on his neck, but I did not dare to and so stopped. He said to me:

"'You see, Nastenuka, that I am not without feeling.'

"He told me also that I had grown pretty and modest, and he covered me with caresses. He took my hand, placed it in his own, and caressed it with his other hand while looking at it. My hands in those days were white and plump. These caresses made me blush. After such a life, too! I felt a sort of maiden bashfulness; it is strange, but it is true. In spite of my shame, — yes, my shame, although the word seems ridiculous when uttered by me, — I said to him:

"'What gave you the idea to caress me, Alexander Matvéitch?'

"He answered:

"'Because, Nastenuka, you are now a virtuous girl.'

"These words made me so happy that I burst into tears.

"'What is the matter with you, Nastenuka?' said he, embracing me. This kiss turned my head, and I lost consciousness. Would you believe, Véra Pavlovna, that such a thing could have happened to me after such a life?

"The next morning I wept, saying to myself: What shall I do now, poor girl? How shall I live? There is nothing left for me but to throw myself into the Néva. I felt that I could no longer remain in the pursuit by which I lived; I would rather be dead; I had loved him a long time, but as he had shown no sentiment toward me and as I had no hope of pleasing him, this love had become torpid in me, and I did not even realize it. Now all was clear. When one feels such a love, how can one even look at another man? Therefore it was that I was weeping and saying to myself: What shall I do now, without any means of existence? I had already conceived this idea: I will go to him, see him once more, and then drown myself. I wept thus all the morning. Suddenly he entered, kissed me, and said:

"'Nastennka, will you live with me?'

"I told him what I thought. And we began to live together.

"Those were happy days, Véra Pavlovna, and I believe that few persons have ever enjoyed such happiness. But I can say no more to you today, Véra Pavlovna. I only wanted to tell you how good Sachennka is."

XV.

Subsequently Nastennka Krukoff finished telling her story to Véra Pavlovna. She lived with Kirsanoff more than two years. The symptoms of incipient disease seemed to have disappeared. But toward the end of the second year, with the opening of spring, consumption showed itself in a considerably advanced stage. To live with Kirsanoff would have been to condemn herself to speedy death; by renouncing this tie she could count on again staving off her disease for a long time. They resolved to separate. To give herself to constant labor would have been equally fatal; therefore she had to find employment as a housekeeper, maid-servant, nurse, or something of the sort, and that too in a house where the work was not too heavy and where — a no less important consideration — there would be nothing disagreeable, conditions rare enough. Nevertheless such a place was found. Kirsanoff had acquaintances among the rising artists; thanks to them, Nastennka Krukoff became the maid of a Russian actress, an excellent woman. They were a long time in effecting the separation. "Tomorrow I will go," said Nastennka, and tomorrow came with other tomorrows to find her still there. They wept and could not tear themselves from each other's arms. Finally the actress, who knew all, came herself to find Nastennka, and, cutting everything short, took her away in order that the hour of separation might not be further protracted to the injury of her future servant.

As long as the actress remained upon the stage Nastennka was very well situated; the actress was full of delicacy, and the young Krukoff set a high value upon her place; to find another like it would have been difficult; so she devoted herself to her mistress, who, seeing this, showed her the more kindness. The servant therefore lived very tranquilly, and there was little or no development of her disease. But the actress married, abandoned the stage, and went to live in her husband's family. There, as Véra Pavlovna already knew, the actress's father-in-law made advances to her servant. The latter was in no danger of seduction, but a family quarrel broke out. The whilom actress began to blame the old man, and he began to get angry. Nastennka, not wishing to be the cause of a family quarrel and living besides a less peaceful life than before, threw up her situation.

That occurred about two years after her separation from Kirsanoff. During all that time they had not seen each other. At first he visited her again; but the joy of the interview had such an injurious effect upon her that he obtained her permission, in consideration of her own interest, to stay away thereafter.

She tried to live as a servant in two or three other families, but everywhere she found so many incompatibilities that it was preferable to become a seamstress; it was as well to condemn herself to the rapid development of the disease which was bound to develop in any case as a result of her too stirring life; it was better to submit herself to the same destiny as a result of labor alone, unaccompanied by any disagreeable features. A year of sewing finished the young Krukoff. When she entered Véra Pavlovna's shop, Lopoukhoff, who was the doctor, did his best to slacken the progress of the consumption. He did much, — that is, much considering the difficulty of the case, his success being really insignificant, — but the end approached.

Up to the last moment the young girl remained under the influence of the delusion common to all consumptives, believing that her disease had not yet made very much progress; therefore she forced herself to avoid Kirsanoff that she might not aggravate her situation. Nevertheless for two months she had been pressing Lopoukhoff with questions; how much time had she yet to live?

Why she desired to know this she did not say, and Lopoukhoff did not believe he had a right to tell her that the crisis was approaching, seeing in her questions nothing more than the ordinary attachment to life. He often tried to calm her, but in vain. She merely restrained her desire to realize that which could make her end a happy one; she saw herself that she had not long to live, and her feelings were in harmony with this thought; but, the doctor assuring her that she ought still to take care of herself, and she knowing that she ought to place more confidence in him than in herself, she obeyed him and did not seek to see Kirsanoff again.

This doubt could not have lasted long: in proportion as the end grew nearer, the more questions the young consumptive would have asked, and either she would have confessed the motive that led her to seek the truth, or else either Lopoukhoff or Véra Pavlovna would have divined it, and the termination precipitated by Kirsanoff's visit to the shop would have been reached two or three weeks later.

"How happy I am! how happy I am! I was getting ready to go to see you, Sachennka!" said the young Krukoff enthusiastically, when she had ushered him into her room.

"I am no less happy, Nastennka; this time we shall not separate; come home with me," said Kirsanoff, influenced by a feeling of compassionate love.

After these words he said to himself: "How could I have said that? It is probable that she does not yet suspect the proximity of the crisis."

Life of Véra with her Husband, and the Second Love.

As for the young girl, either she did not at first understand the real meaning of Kirsanoff's words, or she understood them, but, her thoughts being elsewhere, paid no attention to their significance, her joy at finding her lover again drowning her sorrow at her approaching end. However that may be, she rejoiced and said: "How good you are! You still love me as in the old days."

But when he went away she wept a little; then only did she comprehend or realize that she comprehended: "It would be useless to take care of yourself now; you are incurable; at least, then, let your end be happy."

And indeed she was happy; he did not leave her a moment except in the hours that he was obliged to spend at the hospital and the Academy. Thus she lived about a month longer, and all this time they were together; and how many accounts there were to give, accounts of all that each had felt after the separation, and still more memories of their former life together, and how many amusements they enjoyed in common! He hired a barouche, and every evening they went into the suburbs of St. Petersburg and contemplated them. Nature is so dear to man that even this pitiful, contemptible, artificial nature in the suburbs of St. Petersburg, which cost tens of millions of roubles, is admired. They read, played cards and loto, and she even began to learn to play chess, as if there were no lack of time.

Véra Pavlovna went many times to spend the evening with them, even late at night after their return from their drive, and still oftener she went in the morning to amuse Nastennka when she was left alone. During their long *tête-à-têtes* the latter could only say over and over again: "How good Sachennka is, how tender he is, and how he loves me!"

XVI.

Four months have passed. The care that he had had to bestow upon Nastennka and the memory of the poor girl had absorbed Kirsanoff. It seemed to him now that his love for Véra Pavlovna was thoroughly conquered; he did not avoid her when during her visits to the young Krukoff she met him and talked with him, nor afterwards when she tried to distract him. Indeed, as long as he felt any fear of his feelings toward Véra Pavlovna, he checked them, but now he felt no more than a friendly gratitude toward her proportional to the service she had done him.

But — the reader knows already in advance the meaning of this "but," as he always will know in advance what is going to happen in the course of the story — but it is needless to say that the feeling of Kirsanoff toward the young Krukoff, at the time of their second coming together, was not analogous to that of her toward him. He no longer loved her; he was only well disposed toward her, as one is toward a woman whom he has loved. His old love for her had been no more than a youth's desire to love some one, no matter whom. It is needless to say that

Nastenka was never fitted for him, for they were not equals in intellectual development. When he grew to be more than a youth, he could do no more than pity her; he could be kind to her for memory's and compassion's sake, and that was all. His sorrow at having lost her disappeared very quickly, after all. But after this sorrow had really disappeared, he believed that he still felt it. When he finally realized that he felt it no longer, and that it was only a memory, he saw that his relations with Véra Pavlovna had assumed a fatal character.

Véra Pavlovna tried to divert him from his thoughts, and he allowed her to do so, believing himself incapable of succumbing, or, rather, not even believing that he felt a lover's passion for her. During the two or three months that followed he passed almost every evening at the Lopoukhoffs', or else accompanied Véra Pavlovna in her walks; often Lopoukhoff was with them, but oftener they went alone. That was all, but that was too much, not only for him, but for her also.

How now did Véra Pavlovna pass her days? Until evening just as before. But at six o'clock? Formerly at that hour she went alone to the shop, or else remained alone in her room and worked; now, if she needed to be at the shop in the evening, Kirsanoff was told the night before, and he appeared to escort her. During the walk, not a long one by the way, they usually talked about the shop, for Kirsanoff was her most active co-worker. While she was busy in distributing the work, he also had much to do. Is it not something to answer the questions and fulfil the commissions of thirty young girls? No one better than he knew how to get through it. Besides, he remained to talk with the children, some of the young girls also participating in the conversations, which were very instructive and very diversified. They talked, for example, of the beauty of the Arabian tales, "The Thousand and One Nights," — he related several of them, — and of white elephants, which are esteemed so much in India, just as there are many men among us who love white cats; half of his hearers regarded this preference as stupid: white elephants, white cats, and white horses are only albinos, a sickly species which it was easy to see that they regarded as weaker than those of darker color. The other half of his hearers defended white cats. "Do you know nothing of the life of Mrs. Beecher Stowe, of whose novel you have told us?" asked one of the larger questioners. Kirsanoff knows nothing now, but he will find out about her, for that interests him also; at present he can tell them something about Howard, a person of the same stamp as Mrs. Beecher Stowe. The time was taken up now by Kirsanoff's stories, now by discussions, and however the make-up of his audience might vary so far as the young girls were concerned, so far as the children were concerned it was always the same. But Véra Pavlovna has finished her business, and she returns to the house with him to take tea.

In these days Véra Pavlovna and Dmitry Serguéitch are together much more than formerly. All three while away an hour or two every evening with music;

Dmitry Serguéitch plays, Véra Pavlovna sings, Kirsanoff listens; sometimes Kirsanoff plays, and then Dmitry Serguéitch and his wife sing. Sometimes Véra Pavlovna hurries back from the shop in order to have time to dress for the opera, which they now attend, half the time all three together and the rest of the time only Kirsanoff and Véra Pavlovna. Moreover, the Lopoukhoff's now have more visitors than they did. Formerly, leaving out the very young people (are these visitors? they are only *neuveux*), the Mertzaloffs were almost the only ones that came, while now the Lopoukhoffs have ties of friendship with two or three good families of their own stamp. The Mertzaloffs and two other families decided to take turns in giving, weekly, little evening parties to the members of their circle, at which they danced. They numbered as many as eight couples. Lopoukhoff without Kirsanoff scarcely ever went to the opera or to visit the families of their acquaintance, but Kirsanoff often took Véra Pavlovna alone. Lopoukhoff said that he preferred to wrap himself in his great coat and stretch out upon his divan. So the three spent only half of the evenings together, and even when the Lopoukhoff's had no caller except Kirsanoff, the divan often attracted Lopoukhoff from the parlor, where the piano was now kept. But this retreat did not save Dmitry Serguéitch; a quarter of an hour later, or at most a half an hour, Kirsanoff and Véra Pavlovna left the piano and came to the divan; and before long Véra Pavlovna would even half lie down upon the divan without crowding Lopoukhoff too much, the divan being large, and then for greater comfort the young woman would even throw her arm about her husband.

Three months passed away.

Idyls are not in fashion now, and I even do not like them, — that is, personally, as I do not like wall ing or asparagus; there are many things that I do not like; a man cannot like all dishes or all sorts of amusements; but yet I know that these things are very fine things judging not by my personal taste, but by the taste of another; that they are to the taste or would be to the taste of a much greater number of men than those who, like myself, prefer chess to promenades and sour cabbage with hempseed oil* to asparagus; I even know that the majority, who do not share my taste for chess and sour cabbage with hempseed oil, have no worse tastes than mine; so I say: Let there be as much promenading as possible in the world, and let sour cabbage with hempseed oil disappear almost entirely, remaining only as an antique rarity for the few originals like myself!

I know likewise that to the immense majority of men, who are no worse than I, happiness must have an idyllic character, and consequently I say: Let the idyl predominate over all other modes of life. For the few originals, who are not amateurs, there shall be other methods of enjoyment. But the majority of men have no desire for idyllic life, which does not mean that they shun it; they

---

* An ordinary dish among Russian peasants.

shun it as the fox in the fable shuns the grapes. It seems to them that the idyl is inaccessible, so they have invented the excuse that it should not be in fashion. But it is utterly absurd that the idyl should be inaccessible: the idyl is not only a good thing for almost all men, but also a possible, very possible thing, as I could easily show. Not possible, however, for one or for ten individuals exclusively, but for everybody through the practice of solidarity.

Italian opera also was an impossible thing for five or six persons, but for the whole of St. Petersburg nothing is easier, as everybody sees and clearly understands. The "Complete Works of N. V. Gogol," published in Moscow in 1861,* were no less impossible for eight or ten persons, but for the entire public nothing is easier and cheaper, as every one knows. But until Italian opera existed for the whole city, the most passionate lovers of music had to put up with the most ordinary concerts; and until the second part of the "Dead Souls" was printed for the entire public, the few Gogol enthusiasts were obliged to expend much effort in taking a manuscript copy. Manuscript is incomparably inferior to a printed book, an ordinary concert is a very poor thing in comparison with Italian opera, but the manuscript and the ordinary concert have nevertheless their value.

XVII.

If any one had come to ask Kirsanoff's advice about such a situation as that in which he found himself when he came to himself, and he had been an utter stranger to all the persons involved, he would have answered:

"It is too late to remedy the evil by flight; I do not know how events will shape themselves, but to you the same danger presents itself whether you go or stay. As for those about whose tranquillity you are disturbed, perhaps the greater danger to them would result from your departure."

It is needless to say that Kirsanoff would have thus advised a man like himself or like Lopoukhoff, a man of firm character and invincible integrity. With any other men it is useless to discuss such matters, because other men in such cases always act basely and dishonestly: they would have dishonored the woman and themselves, and then would have gone to all their acquaintances to whine or to boast, seeking always their own enjoyment, either by posing as virtuous or by indulging in the pleasures of love. Of such people neither Lopoukhoff nor Kirsanoff cared to ask how really noble natures ought to act. But in saying to a man of the same stamp as himself that to fly was perhaps even worse than to remain Kirsanoff would have been right. There would have been implied in this advice: "I know how you would conduct yourself if you remained. The thing to be done is not to betray your feeling, since it is only on that condition

---

* The first complete edition of Gogol's works.

that you can remain without becoming a dishonest man. The point is to disturb as little as possible the tranquillity of the woman whose life is calm. That she should not be troubled at all has already become impossible. The feeling in opposition to her present relations probably — but why probably? it would be more accurate to say undoubtedly — has already arisen in her, only she has not yet perceived it. Whether or not it will manifest itself soon without any provocation on your part no one can tell, whereas your departure would be a provocation. Consequently your departure would only accelerate the thing you wish to avoid."

Only Kirsanoff viewed the question not as if it concerned a stranger, but as personal to himself. He imagined that to go was more difficult than to stay; sentiment urged him to the latter course; therefore in staying would he not be yielding to sentiment, surrendering himself to the seduction of his inspirations? What security could he have that neither by word nor look would he manifest his feelings and arouse in her a consciousness of her situation? Therefore the safer way would be to go. In one's own affairs it is extremely difficult to realize how far the mind is seduced by the sophistries of passion, honesty telling you to act contrary to your inclination and thereby stand a greater chance of acting in a manly fashion. That is the translation of the language of theory into every-day language; now, the theory to which Kirsanoff held considers the great words "honesty," "nobility," etc., as equivocal and obscure, and Kirsanoff, using his own terminology, would have expressed himself thus: "Every man is an egoist, and I am no exception to the rule; the question now is to find out which would be better for me, to go or to stay. By going I stifle in myself a special sentiment; by staying I run the risk of revolting the sentiment of my own dignity by a stupid word or look inspired by this special sentiment. A special sentiment can be stifled, and in the course of time my tranquillity will be reëstablished, and I shall once more be contented with my life. But if I once act against my human nature, I shall lose forever the possibility of tranquillity, the possibility of being contented with myself, and poison my whole life. This, in a word, is the situation in which I find myself: I like wine, and I see before me a cup of very good wine, but I have a suspicion that this wine is poisoned. Whether or not there is any ground for my suspicion it is impossible for me to know. Shall I drink this cup, or overturn it that it may not tempt me? I should not characterize my decision as noble or honest even; those are too high-sounding words; it is at most a matter of reason, of enlightened self-interest; I overturn the cup. Thereby I deprive myself of a certain pleasure, I cause myself a certain pain; but on the other hand I assure myself health,— that is, the possibility of drinking for many years and in sufficient quantities wine which, I feel sure, is not poisoned. I do not act stupidly; that is my only merit."

XVIII.

But how to retire? To play the old comedy over again, to feign offence, to show a base side to his character in order to explain his course,—that would not do; one cannot mislead twice in the same way; a second affair of the same sort would only have explained the real meaning of the first, and set Kirsanoff up as a hero not only of the new occasion, but of the old as well. In general any abrupt suspension of relations should be avoided; not that such a separation would not have been easier, but it would have excited attention,—that is, would have been a low and base thing (according to the egoistic theory of Kirsanoff). Therefore there was but one way left, the most difficult and painful,—to beat a retreat in a slow, imperceptible way, so that his departure should not be noticed. It was a delicate and sufficiently trying task; to go away without attracting the attention of one whose eyes are ever upon you is difficult. But, whether he would or no, this was what he had to do. However, according to Kirsanoff's theory, this course was not only not painful, but really agreeable; the more difficult an affair is, the more one rejoices (through pride) in his power and skill, if he executes it well.

And indeed he did execute it well: neither by a word, nor by ill-timed silence, nor by a look did he betray himself; he still maintained his ease of manner, and jested as before with Véra Pavlovna; it was evident that as before he found pleasure in her society; but obstacles were always arising to prevent him from coming to see the Lopoukhoffs as often as he used to, and from staying all the evening, so that Lopoukhoff had occasion oftener than before to seize him by the hand or else by the lappel of his coat and say to him:

"No, dear friend, I will not let you leave this discussion in that way." And so it was that while at the Lopoukhoffs' he always sat nearer his comrade's divan. All this was arranged so methodically that the change was not even perceptible.

Kirsanoff had obstacles, but he did not put them forward; on the contrary, he expressed regrets (rarely, for to express them too often would not have been proper) that these obstacles should present themselves. And these obstacles were so natural, so inevitable, that very often the Lopoukhoff's themselves drove him away by reminding him that he had forgotten his promise to be at home that evening, that such or such a one was waiting for him there, or that he forgot that if he did not go that day to see such a person that person would be offended, or that he forgot that he had at least four hours' work to do before the next morning; had he no desire to sleep at night? It was already ten o'clock; a truce to babbling! it was time to go to work. Thus they refreshed Kirsanoff's memory, but he did not always listen. He did not go to see this or that acquaintance; he might take offence if he liked. The work could wait; there was time enough, and he desired to stay the evening through. But the obstacles continually multiplied, and scientific pursuits pressed ever faster upon him and took away his evenings one after another. "May the devil take the scientific pursuits!" sometimes he would cry. He met a steadily increasing number of individuals who threw their acquaintance at his head. The ease with which these individuals made his acquaintance was really astonishing, he would sometimes remark incidentally. It seemed so to him, but the Lopoukhoffs saw clearly that he was making a reputation and that for that reason an ever growing number of men needed him. He must not neglect them, and it was wrong to let himself go on like that. What was to be done? He had grown very lazy during the last few months, and could not set himself to work. "But you must, my dear Alexander;" "It is time, Alexander Matvéitch," they often said to him. It was a difficult manœuvre. Through long weeks he had to drag this deception and execute it with the slowness and precision of a clock-hand, which you cannot see move however attentively you look at it, but which nevertheless does its work, stealthily, and moves farther and farther from its primitive position. What pleasure, therefore, Kirsanoff the theorist found in the contemplation of his practical skill! The egoists and materialists do nothing except for their own pleasure. Kirsanoff too could say, with his hand upon his conscience, that he was acting for his own pleasure, and rejoiced at his skill and decision.

A month passed in this way, and if any one had examined things, he would have found that in the course of this month Kirsanoff's intimacy with the Lopoukhoff's had grown no less, but that the time he spent with them had become four times less, and the part of the time spent with Véra Pavlovna had diminished one-half. A month more and, while the friendship will remain the same, the interviews will be few and far between and the movement will be finished.

Does the clear-sighted Lopoukhoff notice nothing?

No, nothing at all.

And Véra Pavlovna? Does she notice nothing either? Not when herself. But here she has a dream.

XIX.

VÉRA PAVLOVNA'S THIRD DREAM.

This was Véra Pavlovna's dream.

After having taken tea and talked with her "darling," she went to her room and lay down all dressed for a moment, not to sleep, – it was too early, being only half-past eight, — but only to read. There she is, on her bed, reading. But the book falls from her hands. She reflects and says to herself: Why does *ennui* sometimes come over me of late, or rather, not *ennui*, but something like it? It simply occurred to me that I wanted to go to the opera this evening. But this Kirsanoff is so inattentive! He went too late to get the tickets. He ought to know, however, that, when Bosio sings, tickets are not to be had at eleven o'clock for two roubles each. Can Kirsanoff be blamed? If he had had to work until five o'clock, I am sure he would not have admitted it. But it is his fault just the same. No, in future I will rather ask my "darling" to get the tickets, and I will go with him to the opera: my "darling" will not leave me without tickets, and, as for accompanying me, he will be always very happy to; he is so agreeable, my "darling." Now, thanks to this Kirsanoff, I have missed "La Traviata;" it's horrid! I would have gone to the opera every evening, if there had been an opera every evening, however bad the piece, provided Bosio filled the principal rôle. If I had a voice like Bosio's, I would sing all day. If I could make her acquaintance? How can I do it? That artillery officer knows Tamberlik well, cannot he be secured as a mediator? It is not possible. But what a queer idea! Of what use to make Bosio's acquaintance? Would she sing for me? Must she not look out for her voice?

But when did Bosio get time to learn Russian? And to pronounce it so well? Where did she unearth those verses that are so licentious? She probably studied Russian with the same grammar that I used: those verses are quoted in it as an example of punctuation, which is very stupid. If only those verses were not so licentious; but there is no time to think of the words, for one has to listen to her voice.

> Consacre à l'amour
> Ton heureuse jeunesse,
> Et cherche nuit et jour
> L'heure de l'ivresse.*

How queer these words are! But what a voice and what sentiment! Yes, her voice is much improved; it is admirable now. How did Bosio succeed in reaching such a point? I did not know how to make her acquaintance, and here she is, come to make me a visit. How did she learn of my desire?

"You have been summoning me a long time," said Bosio, in Russian.

"I? How could I have done so, when I am unknown to you? No matter, I am glad, very glad, to see you."

Véra Pavlovna opens her curtains to extend her hand to Bosio, but the singer begins to laugh; it is not Bosio, but rather De-Merick playing the Bohemian in "Rigoletto." But if the gay laugh is De-Merick's, the voice is really Bosio's; she draws back abruptly and hides behind the curtain. What a pity!

"Do you know why I have come?" said the apparition, laughing as though she were De-Merick instead of Bosio.

"But who are you? You are not De-Merick?"

"No."

---

* Rendered in English prose: Consecrate to love your happy youth, and seek night and day the hour of intoxication.

"Then you are Bosio?"

Fresh laughter. "You recognize quickly, but we must now attend to the business on which I have come. I wish to read your diary with you."

"I have no diary; I never kept any."

"But look! what is that on the little table?"

Véra Pavlovna looks: on the little table near the bed lies a writing-book inscribed: *Diary of V. L.* Where did this writing-book come from? Véra Pavlovna takes it, opens it, — it is written in her hand: but when?

"Read the last page," says Bosio.

Véra Pavlovna reads: "Again it happens that I remain alone entire evenings. But that is nothing: I am used to it."

"Is that all?" says Bosio.

"All."

"No, you do not read all. You cannot deceive me. And what is this here?"

Véra Pavlovna sees a hand stretch forth. How beautiful this hand is! No, this marvellous hand is not Bosio's. And how did it pierce the curtains without opening them? The hand touches the page; at its contact new lines stand out which were not there before.

"Read."

Véra Pavlovna feels a pressure on her heart; she has not yet looked at these lines; she does not know what they contain, and nevertheless her heart is oppressed. She does not wish to read.

"Read," repeats the apparition.

Véra Pavlovna reads: "No, now I grow weary in my solitude. Formerly I did not grow weary. Why did I not grow weary before, and why do I grow weary now?"

"Turn one page back."

Véra Pavlovna turns the leaf: "Summer of this year" (who is it that writes her diary in this way? says Véra Pavlovna; it should have said 1855, June or July, with the date). "Summer of this year. We are going, as usual, out of the city to the islands. This time my darling accompanies us; how contented I am!" (Ah! it is August. What day of the month, — the fifteenth or the twelfth? Yes, yes, about the fifteenth; it was after this excursion that my poor darling fell sick, thinks Véra Pavlovna.)

"Is that all?"

"All"

"No, you do not read all. And what is this here?" (And the marvellous hand again stretches forth, and more new lines appear.)

Véra Pavlovna reads without wishing to: "Why does not my darling accompany us oftener?"

"Turn another leaf."

"My darling is so busy, and it is always for me, always for me that he works, my darling." (That is really the answer, thinks Véra Pavlovna with joy.)

"Turn one page more."

"How honest and noble these students are, and how they esteem my darling! And I am gay in their company; with them I feel as if I were with brothers, quite at my ease."

"Is that all?"

"All."

"No, read farther" (and for the third time the hand stretches forth causing new lines to appear).

Véra Pavlovna reads unconsciously: "August 16" (that is, the day after the excursion to the islands; it did occur then on the fifteenth, thinks she). "On the excursion my darling talked the whole time with that Rakhmetoff, the rigorist, as they jokingly call him, and with his other comrades. He stayed with me scarcely a quarter of an hour." (That is not true; it was over half an hour; over half an hour, I am sure, thinks she, without counting the time when we sat side by side in the boat.) "August 17. Yesterday we had the students here all the evening;" (yes, it was the night before my darling fell sick). "My darling talked with them all the evening. Why does he devote so much time to them and so little to me? He does not work all the time. For that matter he says himself that without rest labor is impossible, that he rests a great deal, and that he reflects upon some special idea in order to rest himself; but why does he meditate alone, without me?"

"Turn another leaf."

"In July of this year we have had the students twice, as usual; I have played with them a great deal, I was so gay. Tomorrow or day after tomorrow they will come again, and again I shall be gay."

"Is that all?"

"All."

"No, read farther" (the hand reappears, and new lines respond to its contact). Again Véra Pavlovna reads unconsciously:

"From the beginning of the year to the end of spring. Yes, formerly I was gay with these students, but I was gay and that was all. Now I often say to myself: These are children's games; they will probably seem amusing to me for a long time to come, and even when I shall be old. When I shall be no longer of an age to take part in them, I shall contemplate the games of youth and thus recall my childhood. But even now I look upon these students as younger brothers, and I should not like to transform myself forever into playful Vérotchka, since I desire to rest myself with serious thoughts and labor. I am already Véra Pavlovna; to amuse myself as Vérotchka is pleasant from time to time, but not always. Véra Pavlovna would like distractions which would permit her to remain Véra Pavlovna. Distractions with her equals in development."

"Turn a few pages farther back."

"I went to Julie's to get her orders. She did not let us go away without breakfast; she ordered champagne, and made me take two glasses. We began to sing, run, shout, and wrestle. I was so gay! My darling looked at us and laughed."

"Is that quite all?" says the apparition, again stretching forth the hand, which always produces the same result, — the appearance of new lines.

Véra Pavlovna reads:

"My darling only looked and laughed. Why did he not play with us? It would have been even merrier. Would he have acted clumsily? Not at all. But it is his character. He confines himself to the avoidance of interference, he approves, rejoices, and that is all."

"Turn a page forward."

"This evening we went, my darling and I, for the first time since our marriage, to see my parents. It was so painful to me to see again this interior which oppressed and stifled me before my marriage. Oh, my darling! From what a hideous life he has delivered me! At night I had a horrible dream: I saw Mamma, who reproached me with being ungrateful; it seemed to me that that was the truth, and this conviction made me groan. My darling, hearing my groans, ran to my side; when he entered my room, I was singing (though still asleep); the presence of the fair one, whom I love so much, had soothed me. My darling wished to dress me — I was much abashed. But he is so reserved; he only kissed my shoulder."

"Is that really all that is written there? You cannot deceive me. Read."

Again under the fatal hand other characters arise, and Véra Pavlovna reads them, still unconsciously:

"And as if that were offensive!"

"Turn a few pages back."

"Today I waited for my friend D. on the boulevard near the Pont Neuf; there lives the lady by whom I wished to be employed as a governess. But she would not give her consent. D. and I returned to the house very much worried. Going to my room before dinner, I had ample time to consider that it would be better to die than to live as I had lived. Suddenly at dinner D. said to me: 'Véra Pavlovna, let us drink to the health of my sweetheart and yours.' I could scarcely keep from weeping tears of joy before everybody for this unexpected deliverance. After dinner I talked a long time with D. as to the way we should live. How I love him: he enables me to leave my cellar."

"Read, read the whole."

"There is no more there."

"Look." (The hand stretches forth.)

"I do not wish to read," says Véra Pavlovna, seized with fright; she has not yet seen clearly what these new lines say, but she is already afraid.

"I command you: read!"

Véra Pavlovna reads:

"Do I really love him because he delivered me from my cellar? No, I love not him, but my deliverance."

"Turn farther back; read the first page."

"Today, the anniversary of my birth, I for the first time talked with D., and formed an affection for him. I have never heard any one speak such noble and strengthening words. How he sympathizes with everything that is worthy, how he longs to aid all that calls for aid! How sure he is that the happiness of mankind is possible and must come some day; that wickedness and pain are not perpetual, and that a new and peaceful life is approaching with ever hastening steps! How my heart beat with joy when I heard these things from a learned and serious man! They confirmed my own thoughts. How good he was when he spoke of us, poor women! Any woman would love such a man. How wise, noble, and good he is!"

"Exactly; turn again to the last page.

"But I have already read that page."

"No, that was not quite the last. Turn one leaf more."

"Read, read! Do you not see? So much is written there." And the contact of the hand calls forth lines which were not there at first.

Véra Pavlovna trembles:

"I do not wish to read; I cannot."

"I command you. You must."

"I am neither willing nor able."

"Well, I will read what you have written there. So listen: 'He has a noble soul, he is my liberator. But a noble character inspires esteem, confidence, a disposition to act in concert, friendship; the liberator is rewarded by gratitude, devotion, and that is all. His nature, perhaps, is more ardent than mine. His caresses are passionate. But he has another need; he needs a soft and slow caress; he needs to slumber peacefully in tender sentiment. Does he know all that? Are our natures, our needs, analogous? He is ready to die for me, and I for him. But is that enough? Does he live in the thought of me? Do I live in the thought of him? Do I love him as much as I need to love? In the first place, I do not feel this need of a soft and tender sentiment; no, my feeling towards him is not'" . . .

"I will hear no more," and Véra Pavlovna indignantly threw away the diary. "Wicked woman, why are you here? I did not call you: go away!"

The apparition laughs, but with a gentle and good laugh.

"No, you do not love him; these words are written with your own hand."

"Be accursed!" Véra Pavlovna awoke with this exclamation, and had no sooner regained possession of herself than she rose and ran.

"My darling, embrace me, protect me! I have had a frightful dream!" She presses herself against her husband. "My darling, caress me, be affectionate with me, protect me!"

"What is the matter, Vérotchka? You are trembling all over," said Lopoukhoff as he embraced her. "Your cheeks are moist with tears, and your brow is covered with a cold sweat. You have walked in bare feet over the floor; let me kiss your feet to warm them."

"Yes, caress me, save me! I have had a horrible dream; I dreamed that I did not love you."

"But, dear friend, whom do you love, then, if not me? That is a very strange dream!"

"Yes, I love you; but caress me, embrace me! I love you, and you I wish to love."

She embraced him with intensity, she pressed her whole form against him, and, soothed by his caresses, she gently fell asleep in his embrace.

XX.

That morning Dmitry Serguéitch did not have to call his wife to take tea; she was there, pressing herself against him; she still slept; he looked at her and thought: "What is the matter with her? What has frightened her? What does this dream mean?"

"Stay here, Vérotchka, I am going to bring the tea; do not rise; my darling, I am going to bring the water for your toilet that you may not have to disturb yourself in order to wash."

"Yes, I will not rise, I will remain in bed a while longer, I am so comfortable here; how good you are, my darling, and how I love you! There! I have washed; now bring the tea; no, embrace me first."

And Véra Pavlovna held her husband a long time in her arms. "Ah, my darling, how strange I am! How I ran to your side! What will Macha think now? We will hide this from her. Bring me my clothes. Caress me, my darling, caress me; I wish to love you, I need to love! I wish to love you as I have not yet loved you!"

Véra Pavlovna's room remains empty. Véra Pavlovna conceals nothing more from Macha, and is completely established in her husband's room. "How tender he is! How affectionate he is, my darling! And I imagined that I did not love you! How strange I am!"

"Now that you are calm, tell me your dream of day before yesterday."

"Oh, that nonsense! I only saw, as I have already told you, that you were not very demonstrative. Now I am well contented. Why have we not lived in this way always? I should not have had the dream, which I do not like to recall."

"But had it not been for this dream, we should not be living as we are now living."

"True; I am very grateful to her, this bad woman: she is not bad, she is good."

"Who is 'she'? Besides the beauty of former days, have you still a new friend."

"Yes, still a new one. I saw a woman come to me with an enchanting voice, more so than Bosio's, and what hands! Oh, what admirable beauty! I only saw her hand; she hid herself behind the curtains; I dreamed that my bed (I have abandoned it because I had this dream there) had curtains and that the woman hid herself behind them; but what an admirable hand, my darling! and she sang of love and told me what love is; now I understand it. How stupid I was; I did not understand; I was only a little girl, a stupid little girl!"

"Everything in its time, my angel. As we lived before, it was love; as we live now, it is love: some need one, others the other; at first the former was sufficient for you; now you need the latter. You have become a woman, my dear friend, and that which you did not need at first has now become necessary to you."

Two weeks pass. Véra Pavlovna takes her ease. Now she stays in her room only when her husband is not at home or when he is at work; but no, even when he is at work, she stays in his study, except when Dmitry Serguéitch's task demands all his attention. But such tasks are rare, and very often scientific tasks are purely mechanical; so three-quarters of the time Lopoukhoff saw his wife by his side. They lacked but one thing; it was necessary to buy another divan, a little smaller than her husband's. This was done, and Véra Pavlovna took her ease after dinner on her little divan, contemplating her husband sitting before her.

"My dear friend, why do you kiss my hands? I do not like that."

"Truly? I had quite forgotten that I offend you; and besides, what does it matter, for I shall do it just the same."

"You deliver me for the second time, my darling; you have saved me from wicked people, you have saved me from myself! Caress me, my dear friend caress me!"

A month passes. Véra Pavlovna still willingly takes her ease. He sits down beside her on the divan; she throws herself into his arms, but becomes pensive; he embraces her; she is still pensive, and her tears are ready to flow.

"Vérotchka, dear Vérotchka, why are you so pensive?"

Véra Pavlovna weeps and does not say a word. No, she weeps no more, she wipes away her tears.

"No, do not embrace me, my dear friend! That is enough. I thank you." And she gives him a glance so soft and so sincere.

"I thank you; you are so good to me."

"'Good,' Vérotchka? What do you mean?"

"Good, yes, my dear friend, you are good!"

— —

Two days passed. After dinner Véra Pavlovna, pensive, lay stretched upon her bed. Her husband was near her, held her in his arms, and seemed equally pensive.

"No, that is not it; that is lacking."

"How good he is, and how ungrateful I am!" thought Véra Pavlovna.

Such were their thoughts.

She said in a simple tone and without sadness:

"Go to your room, my dear friend; to work or to rest."

"Why do you drive me away, Vérotchka? Am I not all right here?"

He was able to say these words, as he wished, in a simple and gay tone.

"No, go away, my dear friend. You do so much for me. Go and rest."

He embraced her, and she forgot her thoughts and breathed again quite freely and as if nothing saddened her.

"I thank you, my dear friend," she said.

———

And Kirsanoff is thoroughly happy. The struggle had been a little difficult to sustain; the greater therefore the internal contentment brought him by the triumph, a contentment which will last and warm his breast for a long time, throughout his life. He is honest. He has brought them nearer to each other. Yes, in fact, he has brought them together. Kirsanoff on his divan smoked and thought: "Be honest,— that is, calculating; make no mistake in the calculation; remember that the whole is greater than any of its parts,—that is, that your human nature is stronger and of more importance to you than any of your aspirations taken separately; place its interests, therefore, before the interests of any of your special aspirations, if they happen to be in contradiction; to put the whole in a simple definition: Be honest and all will go well. A single rule of great simplicity, but containing all the prescriptions of science, the whole code of happy life. Yes, happy those who have the power to understand this simple rule. For my part, I am happy enough in this respect. I undoubtedly owe much more to intellectual development than to nature. But in time this will become a general rule, inspired by education and surroundings. Yes, everybody will then live comfortably, as I do now, for instance. Yes, I am content. Nevertheless, I must go to see them; I have not been there for three weeks. It is time to go even though it were not agreeable. But would it not be better to postpone it a month? That is it. The retreat is executed; they will not notice now whether it has been three weeks or three months since I went to see them. It is very agreeable to think at a distance of men towards whom one has acted honestly. I rest on my laurels."

Three days later Lopoukhoff went into his wife's room after dinner, took his Vérotchka in his arms, and, carrying her to his room, placed her upon the little divan.

"Rest here, my friend," and he began to contemplate her. She went off into a doze, smiling; he sat down and began to read. She half opened her eyes and thought:

"How modestly his room is furnished! He has only the necessaries. No, he too has his whims. There is an enormous box of cigars, which I gave him last year; it is not yet exhausted. The cigar is his only whim, his only article of luxury. No, there is another article of luxury,— the photograph of that old man. What a noble face that old man has, what a mixture of goodness and perspicacity in those eyes, in the whole expression of the face! How much trouble Dmitry had in getting that photograph! Portraits of Owen are exceedingly rare. He wrote three letters; two of those who took these letters did not find the old man; the third found him and had to torment the old man a great deal in order to get a good photograph. And how happy Dmitry was when he received it with a letter from 'the sainted old man,' as he calls him, in which Owen praises me on the strength of what Dmitry has written him. And there is another article of luxury,— my portrait. For six months he economized in order to be able to employ a good painter. How they tormented me with that young painter! Two portraits, and that is all. To buy engravings and photographs like mine would not be so dear. He has no flowers either, and I have so many in my room. Why does he not want flowers, since I want them? Is it because I am a woman? What nonsense! Or is it because he is a serious and learned man? But there is Kirsanoff; he has engravings and flowers, although he too is a serious and learned man.

"And why does it weary him to devote much time to me?

"I know well that it costs him great effort. Is it because he is a serious and learned man?

"But there is Kirsanoff . . . No, no, he is good, very good, he has done everything, he is ready to do everything for me. Who can love me as much as he does? And I too love him, and am ready to do everything for him" . . .

"You are no longer asleep, then, dear Vérotchka?"

"My darling, why do you not have flowers in your room?"

"Very well, my friend, I will have some tomorrow; they are indeed very pleasant."

"What else do you want? Ah! buy yourself some photographs, or rather I will buy both flowers and photographs."

"Then they will be doubly agreeable to me. But, Vérotchka, you were pensive, you were thinking of your dream. Permit me to beg you to relate to me in greater detail this dream which so frightened you."

"I think no more about it: it is too painful to me to recall it."

"But perhaps, Vérotchka, it would be useful for me to know it."

"Very well, my dear friend."

And Vérotchka told her dream.

"Pardon me, my friend, if I ask you one more question: is that all you saw?"

"If it were not all, should I not have told you so, and besides did I not tell you so that very night?"

This was said so sincerely and simply that Lopoukhoff felt an ineffably sweet emotion, one of those intoxicating moments of happiness never to be forgotten.

What a pity that so few husbands can know this feeling! All the joys of happy love are as nothing compared with it; it fills the heart of man forever with the purest contentment and the holiest pride.

In Véra Pavlovna's words, spoken with a certain sadness, were conveyed a reproach, but the meaning of the reproach was: My friend, do you not know that you have deserved all my confidence? In the present state of their mutual relations a wife must conceal from her husband the secret movements of her heart, but from you, my dear friend, I have nothing to conceal; my heart is as open before you as before myself.

That is a very great reward for a husband, a reward purchased only by a high moral dignity; and whoever earns it has the right to consider himself an irreproachable man, to be sure that his confidence is pure and always will be, that valor and tranquillity will never desert him whatever the situation in which he may find himself, and that destiny has almost no hold on the peace of his soul. We are well enough acquainted with Lopoukhoff to know that he is not sentimental, but he was so touched by these words of his wife that his face grew purple with emotion.

"Vérotchka, my friend, you have reproached me,"—his voice trembled for the second and last time in his life; the first time it trembled with doubt, now it trembled with joy.—"you have reproached me, but this reproach is dearer to me than any words of love. I have offended you by a question, but I am happy to have drawn such a reproach upon myself. See! there are tears in my eyes, the first tears that I have shed since my childhood!"

Throughout the evening his eyes were fixed upon her. She did not once say to herself during that evening that he was trying to be affectionate, and that evening was one of the happiest that she ever passed. In a few years she will have days, weeks, years like it; this will be the case when her children have grown up and she sees them happy men worthy of happiness. This joy is above all other personal joys; that which in every other personal joy is a rare and fleeting intensity is here the ordinary level of every day without distinction. But this is still in the future for Véra Pavlovna.

XXI.

When she had gone to sleep upon his knees and he had placed her on her little divan, Lopoukhoff concentrated his thoughts upon this dream. It was not for him to consider whether she loved him or not; that was her affair, and in this she was no more mistress than he was master. This was a point that must clear itself up, to be thought of only leisurely; now time was pressing, and his business was to analyze the causes of this presentiment.

At first it was a long time before he could discover anything. He had seen clearly for some days that he could not keep her love. Painful loss, but what was to be done? If he could change his character, acquire this inclination for gentle affection which the nature of his wife demanded, that would be another matter, certainly. But he saw that this would be a vain attempt. If this inclination is not given by nature or developed by life independently of the intentions of the man himself, it cannot be created by the effort of his will; now, without the inclination nothing is as it should be. Hence for him the question was solved. So this was the problem of his first reflections. Now, after having meditated on his own situation (as an egoist thinking first of himself and of others only secondarily), he could approach the affair of another,—that is, of his wife. What can be done for her? She does not yet understand what is going on within her, she is not yet as well versed as he in affairs of the heart, and very naturally, being four years younger, which at that early age is a great deal. Could he not, as the more experienced, trace this dream back to its cause?

Immediately came into Lopoukhoff's mind this supposition: the cause of her thoughts must be sought in the circumstance which gave rise to her dream. Some connection must be found between the cause of her dream and its substance. She said that she was vexed because she did not go to the opera. Let us see.

Lopoukhoff began to examine his way of living and that of his wife, and the light dawned on his mind. Most of the time when they had nothing to do she had remained in solitude, as he did. Then had come a change: she had had distractions. Now the more sober life had returned. She had not been able to accept it with indifference, for it was no more in her nature to do so than in that of the enormous majority of mankind. So far there is nothing extraordinary. Now, it is no farther to suppose the solution of the enigma to lie in her association with Kirsanoff, an association followed by the latter's separation. But why did Kirsanoff go away? The cause seems only too natural,—lack of time, pressure of duties. But one cannot deceive, though he use all possible stratagems, an honest, intelligent man, experienced in life, and above all utilizing the theory to which Lopoukhoff held. He may deceive himself through lack of attention; he may neglect to notice what is going on: thus it was that Lopoukhoff came to mistake the motives of Kirsanoff's original separation, because then, to tell the truth, he had no interest and consequently no desire to look closely into the causes of this separation; the only thing important for him to know was this: Who was to blame for the rupture of friendship? Was it not himself? Evidently not. Then there was no occasion to think about it further. He was neither Kirsanoff's favorite nor a pedagogue charged with guiding men in the straight road. Kirsanoff understood things as well as he did. How did his conduct concern him? In his relations with Kirsanoff was there anything so important? As long as you are on good terms with me and wish me to love you, I am well content; if not, more's the pity, but for that matter go where you please, it's all one to me. It makes no great difference whether there is one imbecile more or less in the world. I took an imbecile for an honest man; I am very sorry for it, and that is all. If our interests are not bound up with the acts of an individual, his acts trouble us little provided we are serious men.

Two cases alone excepted, which, however, seem exceptions only to men accustomed to consider the word "interest" in the not too strict sense of ordinary calculation. The first case is when actions interest us on their theoretical side, as psychical phenomena explaining the nature of man,—that is, when we feel an intellectual interest; the other case is when the destiny of the person is so dependent upon ourselves that we should be guilty in our own eyes if we should be careless of his conduct,—that is, when we feel a conscientious interest. But in the silly departure which Kirsanoff had formerly taken there was nothing not known to Lopoukhoff as a very ordinary characteristic of actual morals, for it is not rare to see a man of honest ideas governed by current trivialities. But that Lopoukhoff could play an important part in Kirsanoff's destiny was something that Lopoukhoff could never have imagined: of what use, therefore, to trouble himself about Kirsanoff? So go, my dear friend, where it seems good to you; why should I trouble myself about you? But now the situation was no longer the same: Kirsanoff's acts appeared in connection with the interests of the woman whom Lopoukhoff loved. He could not help giving them close thought. Now, to give a thing close thought and to understand its causes are almost one and the same thing to a man of Lopoukhoff's habits of thought. Lopoukhoff believed that his theory furnished the surest means of analyzing human emotions, and I confess that I am of his opinion. During a long series of years this theory that I profess has not once led me into error, and has always put me in a position to easily discover the truth, whatever the depths in which it be hidden.

It is none the less true that this theory is not accessible to all; it requires experience and habits of thought to be able to understand it.

After a half-hour's meditation all was clear to Lopoukhoff in Kirsanoff's relations with Véra Pavlovna. It was clear, indeed, but nevertheless Lopoukhoff did not cease to ponder over it, and this reverie ended in a decisive and complete discovery, which so impressed him that he could not sleep. But why wear out one's nerves through insomnia? It is three o'clock. If one cannot sleep, he must take morphine. He took two pills; "I will take just one look at Vérotchka." But instead of going and looking, he drew his armchair up to the divan upon which his wife lay asleep, and sat down there; then he took her hand and kissed it.

"You still work, my darling, and always for me; how good you are, and how I love you!" she murmured in her sleep. Against morphine in sufficient quantities no laceration of the heart can endure; on this occasion two pills were enough. Therefore sleep took possession of him. This laceration of the heart was approximately equal in intensity (according to Lopoukhoff's materialism) to four cups of strong coffee, to counteract which one pill would not have been enough while three pills would have been too many. He went to sleep, laughing at the comparison.

XXII.

A THEORETICAL CONVERSATION.

Scarcely had Kirsanoff stretched himself out the next day like a veritable sybarite, a cigar between his lips, to read and to rest after his dinner which had been delayed by his duties at the hospital, when Lopoukhoff entered.

"I am as much in the way here as a dog in a ninepin alley," said Lopoukhoff in a jocose though not at all trifling tone; "I disturb you, Alexander. It is absolutely necessary that I should talk seriously with you. It is pressing; this morning I overslept and should not have found you."

Lopoukhoff did not seem to be trifling.

"What does this mean? Can he have noticed anything?" thought Kirsanoff.

"Therefore let us talk a little," continued Lopoukhoff, sitting down; "look me in the face."

"Yes, he speaks of *that;* there is no doubt about it," said Kirsanoff to himself.

Then aloud and in a still more serious tone: "Listen, Dmitry; we are friends. But there are things that even friends must not permit themselves. I beg you to drop this conversation. I am not disposed to talk today. And on this subject I am never disposed to talk."

Kirsanoff's eyes had a steady look of animosity, as if there were a man before him whom he suspected of an intention to commit some piece of rascality.

"To be silent,—that cannot be, Alexander," continued Lopoukhoff, in a calm though somewhat hollow voice; "I have seen through your manœuvres."

"Be silent! I forbid you to speak unless you wish me for an eternal enemy, unless you wish to forfeit my esteem."

"Formerly you did not fear to lose my esteem,—do you recollect? Now, therefore, all is clear. Then I did not pay sufficient attention."

"Dmitry, I beg you to go away, or I shall have to go myself."

"You cannot. Is it with your interests that I am concerned?"

Kirsanoff did not say a word.

"My position is advantageous. Yours in conversation with me is not. I seem to be performing an act of heroism. But such notions are silly. I cannot act otherwise; common sense forces me to it. I beg you, Alexander, to put an end to your manœuvres. They accomplish nothing."

"What? Was it too late already? Pardon me," said Kirsanoff quickly, unable to tell whether it was joy or chagrin that moved him when he heard the words: "They accomplish nothing."

"No, you do not rightly understand me. It was not too late. Nothing has happened so far. What will happen we shall see. For the rest, Alexander, I do not understand of what you speak; nor do you understand of what I speak; we do not understand each other. Am I right? And we do not need to understand each other. Enigmas that you do not understand are disagreeable to you. But there is no enigma here. I have said nothing. I have nothing to say to you. Give me a cigar; I have carelessly forgotten mine. I will light it, and we will discuss scientific questions; it was not for that that I came, but to spend the time in chatting about science. What do you think of these strange experiments in the artificial production of albumen?"

Lopoukhoff drew another chair up to his own to put his feet on it, seated himself comfortably, lighted his cigar, and continued his remarks:

"In my opinion it is a great discovery, if it be not contradicted. Have you reproduced the experiments?"

"No, but I must do so."

"How fortunate you are in having a good laboratory at your disposition! Reproduce them, reproduce them, I beg of you, but with great care. It is a complete revolution in the entire alimentary economy, in the whole life of humanity,—the manufacture of the principal nutritive substance directly from inorganic matter.

That is an extremely important discovery, equal to Newton's. Do you not think so?"

"Certainly. Only I very much doubt the accuracy of the experiments. Sooner or later we shall reach that point, indisputably; science clearly tends in that direction. But now it is scarcely probable that we have already got there."

"That is your opinion? Well, it is mine, too. So our conversation is over. *Au revoir*, Alexander; but, in taking leave of you, I beg you to come to see us often, as in the past. *Au revoir*."

Kirsanoff's eyes, fixed on Lopoukhoff, shone with indignation.

"So, you wish, Dmitry, to leave with me the opinion that you have of low thoughts?"

"Not at all. But you ought to see us. What is there extraordinary in that? Are we not friends? My invitation is a very natural one."

"I cannot. You began upon a senseless and therefore dangerous matter."

"I do not understand of what affair you speak, and I must say that this conversation pleases me no more than it pleased you two minutes ago."

"I demand an explanation of you, Dmitry."

"There is nothing to explain or to understand. You are getting angry for nothing, and that is all."

"No, I cannot let you go away like that." Kirsanoff seized Lopoukhoff by the hand as he was on the point of starting. "Be seated. You began to speak without any necessity of doing so. You demand of me — I know not what. You must listen to me."

Lopoukhoff sat down.

"What right have you," began Kirsanoff in a voice still more indignant than before,— "what right have you to demand of me that which is painful to me? Am I under obligation to you in anything? And what's the use? It is an absurdity. Throw aside this nonsense of romanticism. What we both recognize as normal life will prevail when society's ideas and customs shall be changed. Society must acquire new ideas, it is true. And it is acquiring them with the development of life. That he who has acquired them should aid others is also true. But until this radical change has taken place, you have no right to engage the destiny of another. It is a terrible thing. Do you understand? Or have you gone mad?"

"No, I understand nothing. I do not know what you are talking about. It pleases you to attribute an unheard-of significance to the invitation of your friend who asks you not to forget him, it being agreeable to him to see you at his house. I do not understand what reason you have to get angry."

"No, Dmitry, you cannot throw me off this conversation by trifling. You are mad; a base idea has taken possession of you. We utterly reject prejudices, for instance. We do not admit that there is anything dishonoring in a blow *per se* (that idea is a silly, harmful prejudice, and nothing more). But have you a right at the present moment to strike any one a blow? That would be rascality on your part;

you would take away from such a man the tranquillity of his life. How stupid you are not to understand that, if I love this man and you demand that I shall strike him, I hold you for a base man and will kill either you or myself, but will not strike the blow? Besides men, there are women in the world, who are also human beings; besides blows, there are other insults,—stupidities according to our theories, and in reality, but which take away from men the tranquillity of life. Do you understand that to submit any human being whomsoever—let alone a woman—to one of these stupidities now regarded as insults is a despicable thing? Yes, you have offensive thoughts."

"You tell the truth, my friend, touching things proper and things offensive; only I do not know why you speak of them, or why you take me to task in the matter. I have not said a single word to you; I have no designs upon the tranquillity of any one whomsoever. You construct chimeras, that is all. I beg you not to forget me, it being agreeable to me to spend my time with you,—nothing more. Will you comply with your friend's request?"

"It is offensive, and I do not commit offences."

"Not to commit them is laudable. But some whim or other has irritated you, and you launch out into full theory. So be it; I too would like to theorize, and quite aimlessly; I am going to ask you a question, simply to throw light on an abstract truth, without reference to any one whomsoever. If any one, without doing anything disagreeable to himself, can give pleasure to another, in my opinion he should do so, because in so doing he himself will find pleasure. Is not that true?"

"That's all humbug, Dmitry; you have no right to say that."

"But I say nothing, Alexander; I am only dealing with theoretical questions. And here is another. If any desire whatever is awakened in any one, do our efforts to stifle this desire lead to any good? Are you not of a contrary opinion, and do you not think that suppression simply overexcites this desire, a hurtful thing, or gives it a false direction, a hurtful and dangerous thing, or stifles life in stifling this special desire, which is a calamity?"

"That is not the point, Dmitry. I will state this theoretical question in another form: has any one a right to submit a human being to a risk, if this human being is in a tolerably comfortable condition without any need of running a risk? There will come a time, we both know, when all desires will receive complete satisfaction, but we also know that that time has not yet arrived. Now, the reasonable man is content if his life is comfortable, even though such a life should not permit the development of all his faculties, the satisfaction of *all* his desires. I will suppose, as an abstract hypothesis, that this reasonable human being exists and is a woman; that the situation in which she finds it convenient to live is the marriage state; that she is content in this situation; and I ask, given these conditions, who has the right to submit this person to the danger of losing the life which satisfies her simply to see if she might not attain a better, more complete life with which she can easily dispense. The golden age will come, Dmitry, as we well know, but it is yet to come. The iron age is almost gone, but the golden age is not yet here. I pursue my abstract hypothesis: if an intense desire on the part of the person in question — suppose it, for instance, to be the desire of love — were receiving little or no satisfaction, I should have nothing to say against any danger incurred by herself, but I still protest against the risk that another might lead her to run. Now, if the person finds in her life a partial satisfaction of her new desire, she ought not to risk losing everything; and if she does not wish to run this risk, I say that he would be acting in a censurable and senseless manner who should try to make her run it. What objection have you to offer to this hypothetical deduction? None. Admit, then, that you are not right."

"In your place, Alexander, I should have spoken as you do; I do not say that you are interested in the matter; I know that it scarcely touches us; we speak only as *savants*, on an interesting subject, in accordance with general scientific ideas which seem to us to be just. According to these ideas, each one judges everything from his own standpoint, determined by his personal relations to the thing in question; it is only in this sense that I say that in your place I should speak absolutely as you do. You in my place would speak absolutely as I do. From the general scientific standpoint, this is an indisputable truth. A in B's place is B; if, in B's place, A were not B, that would mean that he was not exactly in B's place. Am I right? If so, you have nothing to say against that, just as I have nothing to say in answer to your words. But, following your example, I will construct an abstract hypothesis, likewise having no reference to any one whomsoever. Suppose that, given three persons, one of them has a secret which he desires to hide from the second and especially from the third, and that the second discovers the secret of the first and says to him: Do what I ask of you, or I will reveal your secret to the third. What do you think of such a case?"

Kirsanoff turned a little pale, and, twisting his moustache obstinately, said:

"Dmitry, you are not acting rightly toward me."

"Do I need to act rightly toward you? Is it you that I am interested in? And, moreover, I do not know what you are talking about. We have spoken of science; we have mutually proposed to each other various learned and abstract problems; I have succeeded in proposing one to you which embarrasses you, and my ambition as a *savant* is satisfied. So I break off this theoretical conversation. I have much to do, — no less than you; so, *au revoir*. But, by the way, — I forgot, — you will yield to my desire, then, and no longer disdain your good friends who would be so happy to see you as often as before."

Lopoukhoff rose.

Kirsanoff looked steadily at his fingers, as if each of them were an abstract hypothesis.

"You are not acting rightly toward me, Dmitry. I cannot satisfy your request.

But, in my turn, I impose one condition upon you. I will visit you, but unless I go away from your house alone, you must accompany me everywhere without waiting for me to say a word. Do you understand? Without you I will not take a step either to the opera or anywhere else."

"This condition is offensive to me. Must I look upon you as a robber?"

"That is not what I meant; I could not so far outrage you as to believe that you could regard me as a robber. I would put my head in your hands without hesitation. I hope that I may expect equal confidence from you. But it is for me to know what is in my thought. As for you, do as I tell you.— that is all."

"I know all that you have done in this direction, and you wish to do still more; in that case you are right to lay this necessity upon me. But, however grateful I may be to you, my friend, I know that such a course will result in nothing. I too tried to force myself. I have a will as well as you; my manœuvres were no worse than yours. But that which is done from calculation, from a sentiment of duty, by an effort of the will instead of by natural inclination, is destitute of life. One can only kill by such means. Life cannot result from suffocation."

Lopoukhoff was so moved by Kirsanoff's words, "It is for me to know what is in my thought," that he said to him: "I thank you, my friend. We have never embraced each other; shall we do so now?"

If Lopoukhoff had been able to examine his course in this conversation as a theorist, he would have remarked with pleasure: "How true the theory is, to be sure! Egoism always governs a man. That is precisely the main point, which I have hidden. 'Suppose that this person is contented with her situation,'— it was there that I should have said: 'Alexander, your supposition is not correct;' and yet I said nothing, for it would not have been to my advantage to say it. It is agreeable to a man to observe as a theorist what tricks his egoism plays him in practice. One renounces that which is lost, and egoism so shapes things that one sets himself up as a man performing an heroic act."

If Kirsanoff had examined his course in this conversation as a theorist, he would have remarked with pleasure: "How true the theory is! I desire to preserve my tranquillity, to rest on my laurels, and I preach that one has no right to compromise a woman's tranquillity; now that, you will understand, means: I will act heroically, I will restrain myself, for the tranquillity of a certain person and my own. How, then, before my greatness of soul. It is agreeable to a man to observe as a theorist what tricks his egoism plays him in practice. I abandoned this affair that I might not be a coward, and I gave myself up to the joy of triumph as if I had performed an heroic and generous act. I refuse to yield to the first word of invitation that I may not be again embarrassed in my conduct and that I may not be deprived of the sweet joy which my noble way of acting causes me, and egoism so arranges things that I have the air of a man who persists in a course of noble heroism."

But neither Lopoukhoff nor Kirsanoff had time to take a theoretical standpoint for the purpose of making these agreeable observations: for both of them practice was very difficult.

XXIII.

The temporary absence of Kirsanoff explained itself very naturally. For five months he had sadly neglected his duties and consequently had had to apply himself to his work assiduously for nearly six weeks; now he had caught up and could therefore dispose more freely of his time. This was so clear that any explanation was almost useless. It was, in fact, so plausible that no doubt on the subject suggested itself to Véra Pavlovna.

Kirsanoff sustained his *rôle* in the same artistic, irreproachable manner as before. He feared that his tact might fail him on his first visit to the Lopoukhoffs after the scientific conversation with his friend; he feared lest he should blush with emotion on taking his first look at Véra Pavlovna, or should make it too plain that he avoided looking at her, or should make some similar mistake; but no, he was contented with himself and had a right to be; the first meeting passed off very well. The agreeable and friendly smile of a man happy to see his old friends again, from whom he had had to tear himself away for a time; the calm look, the vivacious and careless language of a man who has at the bottom of his soul no other thoughts than those which he expresses so lightly, — the shrewdest gossip might have looked at him with the greatest desire to discover something suspicious and seen only a man happy at being able to pass an evening in the society of his friends.

The first test met so successfully, was it difficult to maintain his self-possession during the rest of the evening? And everything going so well on the first evening, was it difficult to produce the same result on the subsequent evenings? Not a word which was not free and easy, not a look which was not simple and good, sincere and friendly, — that was all.

But though Kirsanoff conducted himself as well as before, the eyes that looked at him were ready, on the contrary, to notice many things that other eyes, no matter whose, would have been unable to see. Lopoukhoff himself, in whom Maria Alexevna had discerned a man born for the management of the liquor business, was astonished at the ease of Kirsanoff, who did not betray himself for a second, and as a theorist he took great pleasure in his observations, in which he was unconsciously interested on account of their psychological and scientific bearings.

But not for nothing had the apparition sung and compelled the reading of the diary. Certain eyes were very clear-sighted when the apparition of the dream spoke in the ear of a certain person. These eyes themselves could see nothing, but the apparition said: "Watch closely, although you cannot see what I see;" and the aforesaid eyes examined, and, although they saw nothing, it was enough for them to examine in order to notice. For instance, Véra Pavlovna goes with her husband

and Kirsanoff to an evening party at the Mertzaloffs'. Why does not Kirsanoff waltz at this little party of intimate friends, where Loponkhoff himself waltzes, it being the general rule: a septuagenarian happening to find himself there would have committed the same follies as the rest; no one looks at you, each has one and the same thought of the steadily increasing noise and movement,—that is, the more joy for each, the more for all; why, then, does Kirsanoff not waltz? Finally he throws himself into it, but why does he hesitate a few minutes before beginning? Is it worth while to expend so much reflection on the question whether or no he shall begin an affair so serious? Not to waltz was to half betray his secret. To waltz, but not with Véra Pavlovna, was to betray it quite. But he was a very skilful artist in his *rôle;* he would have preferred not to waltz with Véra Pavlovna, but he saw at once that that would be noticed. Hence his hesitation. All this, in spite of the whisperings of the apparition, would not have been noticed if this same apparition had not begun to ask a multitude of other questions quite as insignificant. Why, for instance, when, on returning from the Mertzaloffs', they had agreed to go to the opera the following evening to see "Il Puritani," and when Véra Pavlovna had said to her husband: "You do not like this opera; it will tire you; I will go with Alexander Matvéitch; every opera pleases him; were you or I to write an opera, he would listen to it just the same," why did not Kirsanoff sustain the opinion of Véra Pavlovna? Why did he not say: "That's so, Dmitry; I will get no ticket for you"? Why was this? That her darling should go in spite of all was not strange, for he accompanied his wife everywhere. Since the time when she had said to him: "Devote more time to me," he had never forgotten it, and that could mean but one thing,—that he was good and should be loved. But Kirsanoff knew nothing of this; why, then, did he not sustain the opinion of Véra Pavlovna? To be sure, these were insignificant things scarcely noticed by Véra Pavlovna and which she seldom remembered beyond the moment, but these imperceptible grains of sand fell and fell continually.

Here, for instance, is a conversation which is not a grain of sand, but a little pebble.

The following evening, while going to the opera in a single cab (for economy's sake), they talked of the Mertzaloffs, praised their harmonious life, and remarked upon its rarity: so said they all, Kirsanoff for his part adding: "Yes, and a very good thing too about Mertzaloff is that his wife can freely open her heart to him." That was all that Kirsanoff said. Each of the three might have said the same thing, but Kirsanoff happened to be the one to say it. But why did he say it? What did it mean? Looked at from a certain point of view, it might be a eulogy of Loponkhoff, a glorification of Véra Pavlovna's happiness with him; it might also have been said with no thought of any one but the Mertzaloffs; but supposing him to have been thinking of the Mertzaloffs and the Loponkhoffs, it was evident that it was said expressly for Véra Pavlovna. With what object?

So it always is: whoever sets himself to look in a certain direction always finds what he is looking for. Where another would see nothing, he very clearly distinguishes a trace. Where another does not see a shadow, he sees the shadow and even the object which throws it, whose features become more distinct with each new look, with each new thought.

Now, in this case there was, besides, a very palpable fact, in which lay hidden the entire solution of the enigma: it was evident that Kirsanoff esteemed the Lopoukhoffs; why, then, had he avoided them for more than two years?

It was evident that he was an honest and intelligent man; how could he have shown himself so stupid and commonplace? As long as Véra Pavlovna had no need to think this over, she had not done so, any more than Lopoukhoff had at that time, but now her thoughts took this direction unconsciously.

XXIV.

Slowly and imperceptibly to herself this discovery ripened within her. Produced by Kirsanoff's words or acts, even insignificant impressions which no one else would have felt accumulated within her, without any ability on her part, on such trifles did they rest, to analyze them. She supposed, suspected, and gradually became interested in the question why he had avoided her for nearly three years.

She became more and more firmly established in this idea: such a man would not have taken himself away out of paltry ambition, for he has no ambition. All these things chased each other in confusion through her head, and to add to the confusion there came into her consciousness from the silent depths of life this thought: "What am I to him? What is he to me?"

One day after dinner Véra Pavlovna was sitting in her chamber sewing and thinking, very tranquilly, not at first of this, but of all sorts of things, in the house, at the shop, about her lessons, when very quietly, very quietly these thoughts directed themselves towards the subject which for some unknown reason occupied them more and more. Memories, questions arose slowly; not very numerous at first, they then increased, multiplied, and swarmed by thousands through her head; they grew thicker and thicker, and gradually merged themselves in a single question taking more and more definite shape. "What is the matter with me? Of what am I thinking? What is it that I feel?" And Véra Pavlovna's fingers forgot to stitch, and her sewing fell from her hands, and she grew a little pale, then blushed, turned pale again, and then her cheeks inflamed and passed in a twinkling of an eye from a fiery redness to a snowy whiteness. With almost haggard eyes she ran into her husband's room, threw herself upon his knees, embraced him convulsively, and laid her head upon his shoulder that he might sustain it and hide her face.

"My dear friend, I love you," said she in a stifled voice, bursting into tears.

"Well, my dear friend? Is there any reason in that for so much grief?"

"I do not want to offend you; it is you I wish to love."

"You will try, you will see. If you can. In the meantime, be calm; time will tell what you can and what you cannot do. You have a great affection for me; then how could you offend me?"

He caressed her hair, kissed her head, pressed her hand. She sobbed a long time, but gradually grew calm. As for him, he had been prepared for a long time to hear this confession, and consequently he received it imperturbably; moreover, she did not see his face.

"I will see him no more; I will tell him that he must stop visiting us," said Véra Pavlovna.

"Think it over yourself, my dear friend; you shall do what seems best to you. And when you are calm, we will talk it over together."

"Whatever happens, we cannot fail to be friends. Give me your hand; clasp mine; see how warmly you press it."

Each of these words was said after a long interval,—intervals which he spent in lavishing upon her the caresses of a brother for a grieved sister.

"Remember, my friend, what you said to me on the day of our betrothal: 'You give me liberty.'"

Silence and new caresses.

"How did we define love the first time that we spoke of it? To rejoice in whatever is good for the loved one; to take pleasure in doing everything necessary to make the loved one happier,—was that not what we said?"

Silence and new caresses.

"Whatever is best for you rejoices me. Seek this best. Why be sorrowful? If no misfortune has come to you, what misfortune can have come to me?"

These words, often repeated after interruptions and each time with slight variations, took up considerable time, which was alike painful to Lopoukhoff and to Véra Pavlovna. But on becoming calmer Véra Pavlovna began at last to breathe more easily. She embraced her husband with warmth, and with warmth kept on repeating to him: "It is you I wish to love, you alone; I wish to love only you."

He did not tell her that she was no longer mistress of herself in that matter: it was necessary to let the time slip by in order that her strength might be reestablished by the quieting influence of some thought or other, no matter what. But Lopoukhoff seized a favorable moment to write and place in Macha's hands a note for Kirsanoff, which read as follows. "Alexander, do not come in now, and do not visit us for some time; there is nothing the matter and there will be nothing in particular the matter; only rest is necessary." Rest necessary, and nothing in particular the matter,—a fine conjunction of words! Kirsanoff came, read the note, and told Macha that he had come on purpose to get the note, but had not time to come in now, as he had some distance yet to go, and would stop to reply on his way back.

The evening passed quietly, at least quietly to all appearance. Half the time Véra Pavlovna remained alone in her chamber after having sent her husband away, and half the time he was seated near her, quieting her continually by a few kind words, and not so much by words either, but by his gentle and soothing voice; not gay, of course, but not sad on the other hand,— simply a little melancholy like his face. Véra Pavlovna, hearing this voice and looking at this face, began gradually to think that the matter was of no significance, and that she had mistaken for a strong passion a dream which would not be slow in vanishing.

Her feeling told her that this was not the case.

Yes, it is the case, thought she with greater firmness, and the thought prevailed. How could it have been otherwise within the hearing of this gentle voice which said that the matter was of no significance?

Véra Pavlovna went to sleep to the soft whisperings of this voice, did not see the apparition, slept quietly, and woke late and thoroughly rested.

XXV.

"The best relief from sad thoughts is to be found in labor," thought Véra Pavlovna (and she was quite right); "I will stay in the shop from morning till night until I am cured. That will cure me."

And so she did. The first day she really found considerable to divert her thoughts; the second resulted in fatigue without much diversion; on the third she found no diversion at all. Thus passed a week.

The struggle was a painful one. Véra Pavlovna grew pale. But outwardly she was quite calm; she even tried to seem gay, and in this she almost always succeeded; but, though no one noticed anything and though the paleness was attributed to a slight indisposition, Lopoukhoff was not at all deceived; he did not even need to look at her; he knew the whole without.

"Vérotchka," said he a week afterwards, "in our life we are realizing the old and popular belief that the shoemaker always goes barefooted and that the tailor's clothes never fit him. We are teaching others to live according to our economic principles, and we scarcely dream of governing our own life in accordance with these same principles. One large household is much more advantageous than several small ones. I should like very much to apply this rule to our home. If we associate some one with us, we can save a great deal; I could abandon these cursed lessons, which are repugnant to me; my salary at the commercial house would be enough, and, having less work to do, I could resume my studies and make a career for myself. It is only necessary to select persons with whom we can agree. What do you think about it?"

All this time Véra Pavlovna had been looking at her husband with as much distrust and indignation as Kirsanoff had shown on the day of the theoretical conversation. When he had finished, she was red with anger.

"I beg you," said she, "to suspend this conversation. It is out of place."

"Why is it out of place, Vérotchka? I speak only of pecuniary interests; poor people like ourselves cannot neglect them. My work is hard and some of it disagreeable."

"I am not to be talked to thus." Véra Pavlovna rose. "I will permit no one to approach me with equivocations. Explain what you mean, if you dare."

"I mean, Vérotchka, that, having taken our interests into consideration, we could profit" . . .

"Again! Be silent! Who gave you the right to set yourself up as my guardian? I shall begin to hate you!" She ran hurriedly to her room and shut herself up.

It was their first and last quarrel.

Véra Pavlovna remained shut up in her room until late in the evening. Then she went to her husband's room:

"My dear friend, I spoke too severely to you. But do not be offended. You see, I am struggling. Instead of sustaining me you put within my reach that which I am pushing away with the hope,—yes, with the hope of triumph."

"Forgive me, my friend, for having approached the question so rudely. Are we, then, reconciled? Let us talk a little."

"Oh, yes, we are reconciled, my friend. Only do not work against me. I have already enough to do to struggle against myself."

"And it is in vain, Vérotchka. You have taken time to examine your feeling, and you see that it is more serious than you were willing to believe at first. What is the use of tormenting yourself?"

"No, my friend, it is you whom I wish to love, and I do not wish, I do not wish in any way to offend you."

"My friend, you wish me well. Do you think, then, that I find it agreeable or useful that you should continue to torment yourself?"

"My dear friend, but you love me so much!"

"Much, Vérotchka, but what is love? Does it not consist in this,—to rejoice in the joy and suffer in the suffering of the person loved? In tormenting yourself you will torment me also."

"That is true, my dear friend, but you will suffer also if I yield to this sentiment, which . . . . . . Ah! I do not understand why this feeling was born in me! A curse upon it."

"How and why it was born, it makes no difference; nothing can be changed now. There is nothing left but to choose one of these two things,—either that you suffer and myself with you, or that you cease to suffer and myself likewise."

"But, my dear friend, I shall not suffer; this will pass away. You will see that it will pass away."

"I thank you for your efforts. I appreciate them because they show that you have the will to do what you deem necessary. But know this, Vérotchka: they seem necessary only to you, not to me. As a looker-on I see your situation more clearly than you do. I know that this will be useless. You may struggle while you have strength; but do not think of me, do not fear to offend me. You know my way of looking at these things; you know that my opinion is fixed and really judicious; you know all that. Do you expect to deceive me? Will you cease to esteem me? I might ask further: will your good feelings towards me, in changing their character, grow weaker? Will they not, on the contrary, be strengthened by this fact,—that you have not found an enemy in me? Do not pity me: my fate will be in no way deserving of pity because, thanks to me, you have not been deprived of happiness. But enough. It is painful to talk too long about these things, and still more so for you to listen to them. Adieu, Vérotchka. Go to your room, reflect, or, rather, sleep. Do not think of me, but think of yourself. Only by thinking of yourself can you prevent me from feeling useless sorrows."

XXVI.

Two weeks later, while Lopoukhoff was busy with his factory accounts, Véra Pavlovna spent the morning in a state of extreme agitation. She threw herself upon her bed, hid her face in her hands, and a quarter of an hour afterwards rose abruptly, walked up and down her room, fell into an armchair, began again to walk with an unsteady and jerky movement, threw herself again upon her bed, and then resumed her walk. Several times she approached her writing table, remained there a few moments, and went away rapidly. At last she sat down, wrote a few words, and sealed them; but half an hour afterwards she took the letter, tore it up, and burned the pieces. And her agitation began again. She wrote another letter, which she tore up and burned in turn. Finally, after renewed agitation, she wrote for the third time, and precipitately, as soon as she had sealed it and without taking time to address it, ran into her husband's room, threw the letter on the table, fled into her room, and fell into an armchair, where she remained without stirring and hiding her face in her hands for half an hour, or perhaps an hour. A ring! It is he! She runs into his room to get the letter, tear it up, and burn it,—but where is it? It is not there. She looks for it hastily. But where is it, then? Already Macha is opening the door. Lopoukhoff, on entering, sees Véra Pavlovna gliding, with pale face and disordered hair, from her husband's room to her own. He does not follow her, but enters his room directly. Coolly and slowly he examines his table and the things around it. To tell the truth, he has been expecting for some days an explanation by conversation or by letter. At last here is a letter, unaddressed, but bearing Véra Pavlovna's seal. It is evident that she was looking for it to destroy it; she could not have come in that condition to bring it; she was looking for it to destroy it; his papers are all in disorder; but could the poor woman have found it in her present state of agitation and mental disturbance? She has thrown it as one would throw a piece of coal which burned his fingers, and the letter has fallen on the casement behind the table. It is almost useless to read it: the contents are known. Let us read it nevertheless.

"My dear friend, I was never so strongly attached to you as at this moment. If I could only die for you! Oh! how happy I should be to die if it would make you happy! But I cannot live without him. I offend you, I kill you, my dear friend, and I do not wish to. I act in spite of myself. Forgive me! Forgive me!"

For more than a quarter of an hour Lopoukhoff remained before his table, his eyes lowered and fixed. Although the blow was expected, it was none the less terrible; although everything necessary to be done after such a confession had been reflected upon and decided in advance, he was at first very much agitated internally. At last he collected himself, and went to the kitchen to speak to Macha:

"Macha, wait a little, please, before setting the table. I feel a little indisposed, and I am going to take some medicine before dinner. As for you, do not wait for us; eat, and take your time. When I am ready to sit down to dinner, I will tell you."

From the kitchen he went to his wife's room. She was lying down with her face hid in the pillows; on his entrance she trembled.

"You have found it, you have read it! How mad I am! What I have written is not true; this letter is the result of a moment of fever and delirium."

"Certainly, my friend. There is no need of paying any attention to this letter, since you have written it in so agitated a mood. Things of this importance cannot be decided in such a fashion. We have still much time to think the matter over, and to talk about it calmly several times, considering its importance to us. Meanwhile I wish to talk to you of my business. I have succeeded in making several changes which are very satisfactory to me. Are you listening to me?"

It is needless to say that she did not know herself whether she was listening or not. She could only have said that, listening or not, she heard something, but that, her thoughts being elsewhere, she did not really understand what she heard. Lopoukhoff, however, became more and more explicit, and she began to perceive that something else was in question, something having no relation to the letter. Gradually she began to listen, feeling herself compelled to do so. It was her desire, moreover, to think of something other than the letter, and, although she had not at first comprehended, she nevertheless had been gradually soothed by her husband's dispassionate and almost jovial tone. At last she really comprehended what he was saying.

"But listen, then; these are very important matters to me," continued the husband; "yes, much-desired changes, which he described in all their details. It is true that she knew three-fourths of these things; she even knew them all; but what difference did it make? it was so good to listen. Lopoukhoff complained again of the lessons which for a long time had been disagreeable to him: he told why, and named the families to which he felt the greatest aversion. He added that his work of keeping the factory books was not unpleasant. It was important and permitted him to exert an influence over the workmen in the factory, with whom he might succeed in doing something: he had given elementary instruction to a few ardent friends, and shown them the necessity of teaching reading and writing; he had succeeded in obtaining for these teachers payment from the owners of the factory, having been able to show the latter that educated workmen injured the machinery less, worked better, and got drunk less frequently: he told how he had snatched workmen from lives of drunkenness, with which object he often frequented their taverns,—and I know not what besides. But the most important thing was that his employers esteemed him as an active and skilful man, who had gradually taken the affairs of the house into his own hands, so that the conclusion of the story, and the part that Lopoukhoff had most at heart, was this: he had been given the position of assistant superintendent of the factory; the superintendent, a member of the firm, was to have only the title and the usual salary, and he was to be the real superintendent; it was only on this condition that the member of the firm had accepted the position of superintendent.

"I cannot accept it," the latter had said; "it would not become me."

"But you need only accept the title so that it may be attributed to a man of standing; you need not take a hand in anything; I will do all."

"In that case I can accept."

But it was not the power conferred that concerned Lopoukhoff; the essential thing with him was that he would receive a salary of thirty-five hundred roubles, almost a thousand roubles more than before, thus enabling him to abandon all his other employments, much to his delight. This story lasted more than half an hour, and towards the end Véra Pavlovna was already able to say that she really felt very well and, after arranging her hair, would go to dinner.

After dinner Macha was given eighty kopecks to get a cab with which to carry in all directions a note from Lopoukhoff, saying: "I am at leisure, gentlemen, and shall be very glad to see you." Shortly after appeared the horrible Rakhmétoff, followed soon by a number of young people, and a learned discussion began between these confident and obstinate debaters. They accused each other of all imaginable violations of logic; a few traitors to this elevated discussion aided Véra Pavlovna to pass a tolerable evening. Already she had divined the object of Macha's errands; "how good he is!" thought she. This time Véra Pavlovna was glad to see her young friends, and, though entering into no frolics with them, she looked at them with joy, and was ready to cover Rakhmétoff himself with kisses.

They did not separate till three o'clock in the morning. Véra Pavlovna, tired, was no sooner in bed than her husband entered.

"In speaking to you of the factory, I forgot, my dear Vérotchka, to say one thing, which, however, is not of great importance. Passing over the details,—for we are both in need of sleep,—I will tell you in two words. In accepting the place of assistant superintendent, I have reserved the privilege of taking a month, or even two if I like, before entering upon my duties. I wish to make good use of this time. It is five years since I went to see my parents at Riazan; hence I will go to embrace them. Till tomorrow, Vérotchka. Do not disturb yourself. Tomorrow you will have time. Sleep well."

XXVII.

When the morrow came and Véra Pavlovna left her room, her husband and Macha were filling two valises with his things. Macha was very busy. Lopoukhoff had given her so many things to pack that she could not manage them.

"Help us, Vérotchka."

All three drank their tea together while the packing was going on. Scarcely had Véra Pavlovna begun to come to herself when her husband said:

"Half past ten! It is time to go to the station."

"I am going with you, my dear friend."

"Dear Vérotchka, I shall have two valises; there will be no room for you. Sit with Macha in another cab."

"That is not what I said. To Riazan."

"Well, in that case Macha shall take the valises, and we will go together."

In the street the conversation could not be very intimate, the noise of the pavements was so deafening!

Many things Lopoukhoff did not hear; to many others he replied in such a way as not to be heard himself, or else did not reply at all.

"I am going with you to Riazan," repeated Véra Pavlovna.

"And your things? How can you go without your things? Get ready, if you wish to: you shall do as you think best. I will ask only this of you: wait for my letter. It shall reach you tomorrow; I will send it by some one coming this way."

How she kissed him at the station! What names she called him when he was boarding the train! But he did not stop talking of the factory affairs, of what a good state they were in, and how glad his parents would be to see him. Nothing in the world is so precious as health; she must take care of herself. At the very moment of parting he said to her through the railing:

"You wrote me yesterday that you were never so attached to me as now; it is true, dear Vérotchka. I am no less attached to you. Good feelings toward those whom we love implies a great desire for their happiness, as both of us know. Now, there is no happiness without liberty. You would not wish to stand in my way; no more do I wish to stand in yours. If you should stand in your own way for my sake, you would offend me. Therefore do nothing of the kind. And act for your greatest good. Then we will see. You will inform me by letter when I am to return. *Au revoir,* my friend! The bell is ringing the second time; it is time to go. *Au revoir!*"

XXVIII.

This happened towards the end of April. In the middle of June Lopoukhoff returned to live at St. Petersburg for three weeks; then he went to Moscow,—on factory business, as he said. He started on the ninth of July, and on the morning of the eleventh occurred the adventure at the hotel situated near the Moscow railway station, and two hours later the scene which was enacted in a country-house on the island of Kamennoy. Now the reader with the penetrating eye can no longer miss his stroke and will guess who it was that blew his brains out. " I saw long ago that it was Lopoukhoff," says the reader with the penetrating eye, enchanted by his talent for divination. What has become of Lopoukhoff, and how does it happen that his cap is pierced by a ball? " I do not know, but it was surely he who played this rascally bad trick," repeats the reader with the penetrating eye. So be it, obstinate reader; judge in your own way; it is impossible to make you understand anything.

XXIX.

AN UNCOMMON MAN.

About three hours after Kirsanoff's departure Véra Pavlovna came back to herself, and one of her first thoughts was this: the shop cannot be abandoned. Much as Véra Pavlovna might like to demonstrate that the shop would go on of itself, she really knew very well that this was only a seductive idea, and that, to tell the truth, the shop required some such management as her own to keep it from falling to pieces. For the rest, the business was now well under way, and the management caused her but little trouble. Madame Mertzaloff had two children; but she could give half an hour to it two or three times a day. She certainly would not refuse, especially as she had already accepted opportunities to do many things in the shop. Véra Pavlovna began to unpack her things for a sale, and at the same time sent Macha first to Madame Mertzaloff to ask her to come, and then to a huckster named Rachel, one of the shrewdest of Jewesses, but an old and good acquaintance of Véra Pavlovna, toward whom Rachel practised the same absolute honesty that characterizes almost all the small Jewish merchants in their dealings with honest people. Rachel and Macha were to enter the apartments in the city, get all the clothes that had been left at the fur-dealer's, where Véra Pavlovna's cloaks had been deposited for the summer, and then, with all this baggage, come to the country-house, in order that Rachel, after estimating the value of the goods, might buy them all at once.

As Macha stepped through the carriage entrance, she met Rakhmétoff, who had been rambling about in the vicinity for half an hour.

"You are going away, Macha? For a long time?"

"I do not expect to get back before night. I have so much to do."

"Is Véra Pavlovna alone?"

"Yes."

"Then I will go in and see her. Perhaps I will stay in your place, in case I can be useful."

"Oh, yes, do so; I am afraid on her account. I have forgotten to notify any of the neighbors; there are, however, a cook and a child's nurse, two of my friends, to serve her at dinner, for she has not yet dined."

"That is nothing; no more have I; I have not dined; we can serve ourselves alone. But you,—have you dined?"

"Yes, Véra Pavlovna would not let me go away without."

"Well again! I should have supposed that it would have been forgotten."

Except Macha and those who equalled or surpassed her in simplicity of soul and garb, everybody was a little afraid of Rakhmétoff. Lopoukhoff, Kirsanoff, and all those who were afraid of nothing sometimes felt in his presence a sort of fear. Véra Pavlovna did not regard him as a friend: she found him too much of a bore, and he never frequented her society. But he was Macha's favorite, although less amiable and talkative with her than were Lopoukhoff's other visitors.

"I have come without an invitation, Véra Pavlovna," he began: "but I have seen Alexander Matvéitch, and I know all. Hence I thought that I might be useful to you in some way; so I will stay with you all the evening."

Offers of service were not to be disdained at such a moment.

Any one else in Rakhmétoff's place would have been invited, and would have proposed himself, to unpack the things; but he did not do it and was not asked to; Véra Pavlovna pressed his hand and said to him with sincere feeling that she was very grateful to him for his attentions to her.

"I will stay in the study," he answered: "if you need anything, you will call me; and, if any one comes, I will open the door; do not disturb yourself."

Having said this, he went very quietly into the study, took from his pocket a large piece of ham and a slice of black bread, weighing in all about four pounds, sat down in an armchair, ate the whole, and in trying to masticate it well drank half a decanter of water; then he went up to the bookshelves and began to look for something to read.

"Familiar . . . . . Imitation . . . . . Imitation . . . . . Imitation . . . . . " This word *Imitation* referred to the works of Macaulay, Guizot, Thiers, Ranke, and Gervinus.

"Ah! here is something which falls opportunely to my hand," said he, reading on the backs of several large volumes "Newton's Complete Works"; he turned over the leaves, found what he was looking for, and with a gentle smile exclaimed:

"Here it is! Here it is! 'Observations on the Prophecies of Daniel and the Apocalypse of St. John.'

"Yes, I know little of such things as these. Newton wrote these commentaries in his extreme old age when he was half mad. They constitute a classic source for one studying the question of the mingling of intellect with insanity. This is a universally historical question; this mixture is found in all events without exception; in almost all books, in almost all heads. But here must necessarily be a typical form of it. In the first place, it concerns the greatest genius known. Then, the insanity mingled with this intellect is a recognized, indisputable insanity. Therefore this is a capital book of its kind. The most delicate indications of the general phenomenon must appear here in a more striking manner than in the case of any other individual, no matter who he may be, and no one can doubt that these are really the indications observable in phenomena concerning the mingling of insanity with intellect. In short, a book worth studying!"

So he began to read the book and with pleasure,—this book which no one had read for a century, except, perhaps, those who corrected the proofs. To any other than Rakhmétoff to read this book would have been like eating sand or sawdust. But he had a keen taste for it.

Of people like Rakhmétoff there are but few: I have met but eight (of whom two were women); they resembled each other in nothing, save one point. There were among them the amiable and the stern, the melancholy and the joyous, the fiery and the phlegmatic, the impressionable (one with a stern countenance, satirical even to insolence, and another with an apathetic face, have sobbed several times in my presence like hysterical women, and that not because of their own affairs, but in connection with a conversation on general topics; I am sure that they wept often when alone) and the imperturbably calm. They resemble each other in only one point, I have said; but that is enough to make a special type of them and distinguish them from all other men. I laughed at those whom I knew, when I was with them; they got angry or not, but they could not help doing as much themselves. And indeed there were many ridiculous things about them, and it was in that respect that they resembled each other. I like to laugh at such people.

The one whom I met in the circle of Lopoukhoff and Kirsanoff, and whom I am about to describe, serves to prove that the opinions of Lopoukhoff and Alexey Pétrovitch on the qualities of the soil, in Véra Pavlovna's second dream, allow one exception,—namely, that, whatever the quality of the soil, one may always find little patches of ground capable of producing healthy ears.

The genealogy of the principal personages of my story—Véra Pavlovna, Kirsanoff, and Lopoukhoff—has not been traced beyond their grandfathers and grandmothers. What would be the use of saying anything about the great-grandfather when the great-grandfather is already wrapped in the shades of oblivion? It is only known that he was the husband of the great-grandmother and that his name was Kiril, the grandfather's name having been Guéracime Kirilytch.

Rakhmétoff belonged to a family known since the thirteenth century, — that is, to one of the oldest families not only in Russia, but in all Europe. Among the chiefs of the Tartar regiments massacred at Tver with their army, for having tried to convert the people to Mohammedanism, according to the reports (an intention which they certainly did not have), but in reality simply for having exercised tyranny, — among these chiefs was one named Rakhmét, who had had a child by a Russian whom he had abducted, a niece of the principal court official at Tver, — that is, the high court marshal and field marshal. The child was spared on account of the mother and rebaptized as Latyfe-Mikhaïl. It is from Latyfe-Mikhaïl Rakhmétovitch that the Rakhmétoffs descend. At Tver they were boyars, at Moscow they were only grand officers of the crown, and at St. Petersburg in the last century they were generals-in-chief, — not all of them, of course; the family having become very numerous, certainly all its members could not be generals-in-chief. The father of the great-grandfather of our Rakhmétoff was a friend of Ivan Ivanytch Chouvaloff, who got him out of the disgrace into which he had fallen in consequence of his friendship for Munich. His great-grandfather was the colleague of Roumiantsoff, had attained the rank of general-in-chief, and was killed at the battle of Novi. His grandfather accompanied Alexander to Tilsitt, and would have gone farther than any of the others, but his friendship with Spéransky put an early end to his career. At last his father served the government without success or disgrace. At the age of forty he resigned, and went to live as a retired lieutenant-general on one of his estates scattered along the banks of the Medvéditza and near its source. The estates, however, were not very large, containing in all about twenty-five hundred souls. But he had many children, — eight, we believe. Of these eight children Rakhmétoff was the next to the last, there being one sister younger than himself; consequently his inheritance was rather small: he received about four hundred souls and seven thousand acres of land. What he did with these souls and fifty-five hundred acres of the land no one knew; so also no one knew that he kept fifteen hundred acres, that he was a *seigneur*, and that he derived an income of three thousand roubles from the leases of that part of the land which he kept; no one knew that while he lived among us. We did not learn it till later, but we supposed of course that he belonged to the family of Rakhmétoffs containing so many rich *seigneurs*, whose aggregate wealth was estimated at seventy-five thousand souls. These *seigneurs* live near the sources of the Medvéditza, the Khoper de la Soura, and the Tzna; they have always been marshals of the nobility of their district. The marshal of the nobility for the government in one or another of the three governments through which flow the tributary sources of the aforesaid rivers is always a member of this family. We knew also that our friend Rakhmétoff spent four hundred a year; for a student that was much in those days, but for a Seigneur Rakhmétoff it was very little. But it was difficult to get information, and we simply said to ourselves that our Rakhmétoff belonged to some branch of the family that had fallen into poverty,—that perhaps he was a son of the counsellor of some financial board who had left his children a small capital. But of course all these things interested us but little.

Now he was twenty-two years old; he had been a student since the age of sixteen, but he had spent almost three years away from the University. At the end of his second year he went to his estate, arranged his affairs, and, after having overcome the resistance of his tutor, won the curses of his brothers, and behaved himself in such a way that the husbands of his sisters had forbidden them to pronounce his name, he began to travel through Russia by land and water in ordinary and extraordinary ways,—on foot, for instance, and in decked boats, and in boats of not much speed. He met with many adventures; he took two individuals to the University of Kazan and five to that of Moscow,—they were his bursars,—but to St. Petersburg, where he intended to come himself, he brought none; this accounts for the fact that no one knew that his income was not four hundred roubles but three thousand. That was not ascertained till later. Then we only saw that he had disappeared for a long time, that two years before he had entered the philological faculty, that still earlier he had been in that of the natural sciences, and that was all.

But though none of his St. Petersburg acquaintances knew anything of his relatives or his fortune, all, on the other hand, knew him by two surnames; one of these, "the rigorist," the reader knows already; this name he accepted with his light smile of half-content. But when they called him Nikitouchka,* or Lomoff, or by his full surname, Nikitouchka Lomoff, a broad smile lit up his face, which was justifiable, since it was not by birth but by the firmness of his will that he had acquired the right to bear this illustrious name among millions of men. But this name is glorious only in a strip of land one hundred versts† wide crossing eight governments; to readers living in other parts of Russia this name requires explanation. Nikitouchka Lomoff, a boat-hauler who went up the Volga fifteen or twenty years ago, was a giant of Herculean strength; two archines and fifteen verchoks‡ in height, his chest and shoulders were so large that he weighed fifteen poudes,§ although he was not fleshy, but simply solid. As for his strength it is enough to say that he received on account of it four times the usual wages. When the vessel reached a town and our man went to the market, or, as they say on the Volga, to the bazaar, the young villagers in the neighboring alleys were heard to shout: "There's Nikitouchka Lomoff! There's Nikitouchka Lomoff!" and everybody ran into the street leading from the wharf to the bazaar, and the people followed in crowds their hero-athlete.

---

* A diminutive of Nikita.
† A verst is equivalent to a little more than half a mile.
‡ Nearly seven feet.
§ More than five hundred and forty pounds.

When Rakhmétoff, at the age of sixteen, came to St. Petersburg, he was an ordinary youth of somewhat above the average height and strength, but very far from being remarkable for his muscular force: of ten of his equals in age taken at random two surely could have thrown him. But in the middle of his seventeenth year he formed the idea of acquiring physical strength and acted accordingly. At first he practised gymnastics; it was a good plan, but gymnastics only perfects the original material; it was necessary, therefore, to equip himself with the material, and during twice as long a period as he had spent in gymnastics he became for several hours every day a laborer in search of work requiring strength; he carried water, delivered fire-wood, chopped it up, cut stone, dug in the earth, sawed wood, and forged iron; he tried many different kinds of work, changing very often, for with each new task, with each change, new muscles were developed. He adopted the diet of pugilists: he ate food known exclusively as strengthening, especially almost raw beef-steak, and from that time on he always lived so. A year later he took his journey, and found in it still more favorable opportunities for developing his physical strength: he had been an agricultural laborer, a carpenter, a boatman, and a worker at all sorts of healthy trades; once he even went along the Volga from Dombovka to Rybinsk as a boat-hauler. To say that he wanted to be a boat-hauler would have seemed in the last degree absurd both to the master of the boat and to the boat-haulers, and they would not have accepted him; but he took the bank simply as a traveller. After having put himself on friendly terms with the boat-haulers, he began to aid them in pulling the rope, and a week later became a veritable boat-hauler; they soon saw how he pulled, and they measured strength with him; he vanquished four of the strongest boat-haulers; he was then twenty years old, and his fellow-workmen christened him Nikitouchka Lomoff, in memory of the hero who was then already dead. The following summer he travelled by steamboat; one of the men with whom he had worked at boat-hauling happened to be in the crowd on deck, and it was in this way that some students, his fellow-travellers, learned that he had been called Nikitouchka Lomoff. In fact, by devoting his time to it, he had acquired and learned how to use extraordinary strength. "I must do it," he had said; "it will make me loved and esteemed by the common people. And it is useful; some day it may prove good for something." And thus it was that he acquired this extraordinary strength. At the age of sixteen he came to St. Petersburg as an ordinary school-graduate, who had worthily completed his early studies. He passed his first months of study after the manner of beginners. Soon he saw that among his comrades there were some especially intelligent who did not think as the others did, and having learned the names of five or six of them (they were few in number), he interested himself in them and cultivated the acquaintance of one of them, who was no other than Kirsanoff, and his transformation into the rigorist, into Nikitouchka Lomoff, into an uncommon man, began. He listened to Kirsanoff with passionate eagerness.

The first evening that they spent together he wept; he interrupted Kirsanoff with exclamations of hatred against that which must die and enthusiastic panegyrics of that which must endure.

"With what books should I begin?" said he.

Kirsanoff informed him on this point. The next morning at eight o'clock he walked up and down the Nevsky between the Place de l'Amirauté and the Pont de Police, awaiting the opening of a French and German book-store where he could buy what he wanted. He read three days and nights continuously, from Thursday at eleven in the morning till Sunday at nine in the evening,—eighty-two hours in all. To keep him awake the first two nights his will alone sufficed; to keep awake the third night he drank eight cups of very strong coffee; the fourth night his strength failed him, the coffee had no effect, he fell on the floor, and slept there about fifteen hours. A week later he came to Kirsanoff to ask him for the titles of some new books and explanations concerning the books he had just read; he became united with him in bonds of friendship, and through him with Lopoukhoff.

Six months later, although but seventeen years old, while they were already twenty-one, he was treated by them as an equal, and became thenceforth an uncommon man.

What circumstances had helped him to become an uncommon man?

His father was very intelligent, very well-informed, and ultra-conservative,—in this like Maria Alexevna, only more respectable. So far as his father went, then, the son's life was certainly a painful one. If this were all, however, it would be nothing. But his mother, a rather delicate woman, suffered from the trying character of her husband; besides, he was a witness of the life of the peasantry. And even this would be nothing. But, when about fifteen years old, he became amorous of one of his father's mistresses. Connected with this there was a story, relating principally, be it understood, to the mistress. He greatly pitied the woman, who, thanks to him, had suffered so much. Ideas soon began to travel vaguely through his head, and to him Kirsanoff was what Lopoukhoff had been to Véra Pavlovna. His past life may have counted for something, it is true, in the formation of his character; but he could not have become what he was going to be if he had not been specially endowed by nature. Some time before he left the University to go first to his estate and then on his journey through Russia he had already adopted special rules for the government of his physical, moral, and intellectual life; and on his return these rules had been transformed into a complete system, to which he always held unchangeably. He had said to himself: "I will not drink a single drop of wine. I will not touch a woman." Why this resolution? So extreme a course was not at all necessary. "It must be," said he; "we demand that men may have a complete enjoyment of their lives, and we must show by our example that we demand it, not to satisfy our personal passions, but for mankind in general; that what we say we say from principle and not from passion, from conviction and not from personal desire."

For the same reason he forced himself to lead a very austere life. To become and to remain Nikitouchka Lomoff he had been obliged to eat meat, much meat, and he ate it in large quantities. But he looked long at a kopeck spent for any other food than meat; consequently he ordered his landlady to get the best of meat, the best pieces for him, while all the other food that he ate at home was of the cheapest. He gave up white bread, and ate only black bread at his table. For whole weeks he did not taste sugar, for months together he did not touch fruit or veal or poultry, nor did he buy anything of the kind: "I have no right to spend money on a whim which I need not gratify." Yet he had been brought up on a luxurious diet and had a keen taste, as could be seen from his remarks about food when dining out: he ate with relish many dishes which he denied himself at his own table, while there were others which he ate nowhere, and this for a well-founded reason: "Whatever the people eat, though only at intervals, I may eat also, when occasion offers. I must not eat that which is entirely out of the reach of the common people. This is necessary in order that I may feel, though but in a very slight degree, how much harder is the life of the common people than my own." So, when fruits were served, he always ate apples, but never apricots: at St. Petersburg he ate oranges, but refused them in the provinces. Because at St. Petersburg the common people eat them, which is not the case in the provinces. He ate sweets because a good cake is no worse than pie, and pie made of puff-paste is known to the common people; but he did not eat sardines. He was always poorly clad, though fond of elegance, and in all other things lived a Spartan's life; for instance, he allowed himself no mattress and slept on felt without so much as doubling it up.

But he had one thing to trouble his conscience; he did not leave off smoking. "Without my cigar I cannot think; if that is a fact, it is not my fault; but perhaps it is due to the weakness of my will." He could not smoke bad cigars, having been brought up amid aristocratic surroundings, and he spent money for cigars at the rate of three hundred and seventy-five roubles a thousand. "Abominable weakness," as he expressed it. But it was only this weakness that made it possible for him to repel his assailants. An adversary, cornered, would say to him: "Perfection is impossible; even you smoke." Then Rakhmétoff redoubled his attacks, but aimed most of his reproaches at himself, his opponent receiving less yet without being quite forgotten. He succeeded in doing a great deal, since in the employment of his time he imposed equally strict rules upon himself. He did not lose a quarter of an hour, and had no need of rest.

"My occupations are varied; change of occupation is a rest."

The circle of friends which had its centre in Kirsanoff and Lopoukhoff he visited only just often enough to enable him to keep on an intimate footing with its members.

So much was necessary; daily experience proves the usefulness of intimate relations with some circle or other of men; one must always have under his hand open sources for all sorts of information. Aside from the meetings of this circle, he never visited any one except on business, and nowhere did he stay five minutes longer than his business required; likewise, at home, he neither received any one nor allowed any one to stay except on these conditions. He said plainly to his visitor: "Our conversation is finished. Now let me occupy myself with something else, for my time is precious."

During the first months of his new birth he spent almost all his time in reading; but that lasted only a little more than half a year; when he saw that he had acquired a systematic method of thinking in the line of the principles which he had found to be true, he instantly said to himself: "Henceforth reading is a secondary thing; so far as that is concerned I am ready for life," and he began the habit of devoting to books only such time as he had left after attending to his other business,—that is, very little time. In spite of that the range of his knowledge extended with an astonishing rapidity; at the age of twenty-two he was already a learned man. In this matter, too, he imposed rules upon himself.

"No luxury, no caprices; nothing but the necessary. Now, what is necessary? Upon each subject there are only a very few first-class works; in all the others there are nothing but repetitions, rarefactions, modifications of that which is more fully and more clearly expressed in these few. There is no need of reading any but these; all other reading is but a useless expenditure of time. Take, for example, Russian *belles lettres*. I say to myself: 'First I will read all of Gogol's works.' In the thousands of other novels I have only to read five lines on five different pages to see that I shall find nothing in them but Gogol spoiled. Then what is the use of reading them?"

It was the same in economic science; there the line of demarkation was even more sharply drawn.

"If I have read Adam Smith, Malthus, Ricardo, and Mill, I know the alpha and omega of this school: I do not need to read a single one of the hundreds of economists, however great their celebrity: from five lines taken from five pages I see that I shall not find in them a single new thought that belongs to them. All that they say is borrowed and distorted. I read only that which is original, and I read it only so far as is necessary in order to know this originality."

Consequently there was no way of inducing him to read Macaulay; after spending a quarter of an hour in reading several pages, he said to himself: "I know the quality of these rags." He read, and with pleasure, Thackeray's "Vanity Fair," and began to read "Pendennis," but closed the book at the twentieth page.

"It is all in 'Vanity Fair;' he has nothing more to say; hence to read him further is useless. Each of the books that I have read is of such a character as to relieve me of the necessity of reading hundreds of others," said he.

Gymnastics, labor for the development of his strength, and reading were Rakhmétoff's personal occupations, but after his return to St. Petersburg they took but a quarter of his time; the rest of the time he occupied in the affairs of some one else or in matters not relating especially to his own person, always holding to the rule by which he governed his reading,—not to spend time on secondary matters and with second-rate men, but to attend only to important matters and important men. For instance, outside of his circle, he made the acquaintance of no men save those that had an influence over others. A man who was not an authority for several others could by no means enter into conversation with him. He said, "Excuse me, I have no time," and went his way. Likewise, if he wished to make the acquaintance of any one, there was no way of getting rid of him. He came directly to you and said what he had to say with this introduction: "I wish to make your acquaintance; it is necessary. If you have no time now, fix some other time." To your minor affairs he lent no attention even though you were his most intimate friend and had begged him to take an interest in your concerns: "I have no time," he would say, turning away. But he concerned himself about important matters when in his opinion it was necessary, even though no one asked him to do so: "It is my duty," he would say. In all that he said and did he gave no heed to ceremony.

This, for instance, is the way in which I made his acquaintance. I was already past my youth and living very comfortably; so from time to time five or six young people of my locality were wont to meet at my house. This made me a precious man for him: these young people were well-disposed toward me, and they found in me a similar disposition toward them.

It was on such an occasion that he heard my name spoken. When I saw him for the first time at Kirsanoff's, I had never heard of him: it was shortly after his return from his travels. He came in after I did; I was the only member of the company whom he did not know. Scarcely had he entered when he took Kirsanoff aside and, pointing to me with his eyes, said a few words to him. Kirsanoff, too, said a few words in reply, and left him. A moment later Rakhmétoff sat down directly opposite me at a distance no greater than the width of a little table near the divan, perhaps an archine and a half; he began to look me in the face with all his might. I was irritated: he looked at me without the slightest ceremony, as if I were a portrait, and I frowned. That did not disturb him the least in the world. After having looked at me two or three minutes, he said to me: "M. N., I wish to make your acquaintance. I know you, but you do not know me. Go to Kirsanoff and those present in whom you have the most confidence, and ask them about me." This said, he rose and went into another room.

"Who is this original?"

"It is Rakhmétoff. He wishes you to inform yourself concerning him,—whether he deserves confidence unconditionally and whether he deserves consideration. He is worth more than all of us put together," said Kirsanoff, and the others bore him out.

Five minutes later he came back into the room where we all were. He did not try to talk with me, and talked but very little with the others; the conversation was not a learned one nor one of much importance. "Ah, ten o'clock already!" said he a little while later; "at ten o'clock I have business elsewhere. M. N. [he addressed himself to me], I must say a few words to you. When I took Kirsanoff aside to ask him who you were, I pointed you out with my eyes; even if I had not done so, you would have noticed that I was inquiring about you. Why should we not make the gestures that are natural in asking a question of this sort? When will you be at home to receive me?"

At that time I did not like to make new acquaintances, and, besides, this importunity did not please me at all.

"I only sleep in the house; I am not at home through the day."

"But you do sleep at home? What time do you enter to go to bed?"

"Very late."

"For instance?"

"Toward two or three o'clock."

"Very well, fix the hour."

"If you absolutely wish it, day after tomorrow, at half past three in the morning."

"Surely I ought to look upon your words as rude and insulting; however, it is possible that you have good reasons. In any case, I will be at your house day after tomorrow at half past three in the morning."

"If you are so bent upon it, come a little later instead; I shall be at home all the morning until noon."

"Good! I will call at ten o'clock. Will you be alone?"

"Yes."

"Good!"

He came, and with the same directness went straight to the matter concerning which he had felt the necessity of making my acquaintance. We talked about half an hour. The subject of our conversation is of little consequence; it is enough to remember that he said, "It is necessary," and I answered, "No;" that he added, "You ought to," and I replied, "Not at all." At the end of the half-hour he said: "It is clear that it would be useless to continue. Are you convinced that I am a man worthy of absolute confidence?"

"Yes; all have told me so, and now I see it for myself."

"And in spite of all you persist in your opinion?"

"I persist."

"Do you know what follows from that? That you are either a liar or a man of little value!"

What do you say to that? What should one do to another who uses such language toward him? Provoke him to a duel? But he spoke so calmly, without any trace of personality, like a historian who judges things coldly, not with an intent to offend any one, but to serve the truth, that it would have been ridiculous to take offence, and I could only laugh.

"But these amount to the same thing," said I.

"In the present case they do not amount to the same thing."

"Then perhaps I am both at once."

"In the present case to be both at once is impossible. But one or the other,— certainly. Either you do not think and act as you speak, and in that case you are a liar; or you do think and act as you speak, and in that case you are a man of little value. One of the two,—certainly. The first, I suppose."

"Think as you please," said I, continuing to laugh.

"Good day. In any case remember that I keep my confidence in you, and am ready to resume our conversation whenever you see fit."

However queer this was, Rakhmétoff was perfectly right, both in having begun as he did, since he had inquired about me before approaching the matter, and in having ended the conversation in this way. In fact, I did not say what I thought, and he had the right to call me a liar; and "in the present case," as he expressed it, I could not take offence at or even exception to his words, the case being such that he could really keep his confidence in and even his esteem for me. Yes, however odd his manner, every man he dealt with was convinced that Rakhmétoff acted in precisely the most reasonable and most simple way, and his terrible insults, his terrible reproaches were so given that no sensible man could be offended at them; and, with all his phenomenal rudeness, he was at bottom very gentle. Consequently his prefaces were in this tone. He began every difficult explanation in this way:

"You know that I am going to speak without any personal feeling. If you find the words I am about to say to you disagreeable, I will ask you to forgive them. I simply think that one should not take offence at what is said conscientiously and with no intention of offending. For the rest, whenever it may seem to you useless to listen to my words, I will stop; it is my rule to propose my opinion wherever I ought to, and never to impose it."

And, in fact, he did not impose it: he could not be prevented from giving his opinion when he deemed it useful; but he did it in two or three words, and added: "Now you know what the end of our conversation would be; do you think it would be useful to discuss further?" If you said "No," he bowed and went his way.

That is how he talked and acted. He always had a great deal of business not relating to himself personally; personal matters he had none; that everybody knew; but what the matters were to which he gave his attention the members of his circle did not know. They simply saw that he had a multitude of concerns. He was rarely at home, and was always on the go, either on foot or in a cab, but generally on foot. At the same time he received many people, and for this purpose had made it a rule to be always at home from two o'clock till three. During this time he talked business and dined. But very often, for several days together, he did not go home, and then one of his friends, devoted to him body and soul and silent as a tomb, received his visitors for him. About two years after his entrance into Kirsanoff's study, where we now see him reading Newton's commentaries on the Apocalypse, he left St. Petersburg, after telling Kirsanoff and two or three of his most intimate friends that he had nothing more to do in the city, that he had done all that he could, that nothing more could be done for two or three years, and that consequently he was free for that length of time and wished to use it for the benefit of his future activity. We have learned since that he went to his old estate, sold the land remaining to him, received about thirty-five thousand roubles, went to Riazan and Moscow, and distributed about five thousand roubles among his seven bursars that they might finish their studies. And here ended his authentic history. What became of him after his departure from Moscow is not known. Several months went by, and no news came from him. Those who knew most about him no longer kept silence regarding several matters which, at his request, they had concealed during his stay among us. Then it was that the members of our circle learned that he had bursars, and the various other details about him which I have just given. We heard also a multitude of stories which, instead of making him better known to us, only rendered his character more problematical,—stories astonishing from their singularity, stories some of which flatly contradicted the opinion we had formed of him, as a man wholly without feeling, having, if I may so express myself, no heart beating with personal emotions. To relate all these stories would be out of place. I will give but two here,—one of each class,—one queer and the other upsetting the theory of his pretended hardness of heart. I choose them from those told me by Kirsanoff.

A year before he disappeared for the second and probably the last time from St. Petersburg Rakhmétoff said to Kirsanoff: "Give me a large quantity of salve good for healing wounds inflicted by sharp tools." Kirsanoff filled an enormous jar for him, thinking that Rakhmétoff intended to take it to a carpenters' shop or that of some other workmen liable to cuts. The next morning Rakhmétoff's landlady ran to Kirsanoff in great fright:

"Father* doctor, I do not know what has got into my tenant: he is late, he has not left his room, the door is locked; I looked through the crack of the door and saw him covered with blood; when I began to cry out, he said to me through the door: 'It is nothing, Agraféna Antonovna.' How can it be nothing! Save him, father doctor! Oh, how I fear lest he may die! He is so utterly without pity for himself."

---

* A formula of respect in Russia among the people.

Kirsanoff ran in all haste; Rakhmétoff opened his door, a broad and dismal smile on his lips. Kirsanoff saw a sight at which Agraféna Antonovna might well have been startled; others would have been. The back and sides of Rakhmétoff's shirt (he was in his shirt) were covered with blood; there was blood under the bed; the felt on which he slept was covered with blood; in the felt were hundreds of little nails, sticking up about an inch; Rakhmétoff had lain all night on this bed of his invention.

"Pray, what does this mean, Rakhmétoff?" cried Kirsanoff, thoroughly frightened.

"A trial. It was necessary to make it. Improbable, certainly, but at all events it was necessary to make it. I know now what I can do."

Besides what Kirsanoff saw, the landlady evidently could have told many curious things about Rakhmétoff, but in her innocence and simplicity the old woman doted on him, and it is needless to say that nothing could be learned from her. On this occasion she ran to Kirsanoff only because Rakhmétoff himself allowed her to do so for her own peace of mind, so bitterly did she weep, thinking that he intended to commit suicide.

Two months after this affair, at the end of the month of May, Rakhmétoff disappeared for a week or more, but no one remarked upon it, as it very often happened that he disappeared for several days. Later Kirsanoff told us the following story of the way in which Rakhmétoff spent his time while absent. It was the erotic episode of his life. His love grew out of an event worthy of Nikitouchka Lomoff. Rakhmétoff was going from Premier Pargolovo* to the city, in a thoughtful mood and with eyes lowered, as usual; when passing by the Institut Forestier, he was startled from his dreams by the harrowing cry of a woman. Raising his eyes, he saw that a horse, attached to a jaunting-car in which a lady sat, had taken the bits in his teeth and was running as fast as he could; the lady had dropped the reins, which were dragging along the ground; the horse was not more than two steps from Rakhmétoff; he threw himself into the middle of the road, but the horse passed rapidly by him before he could seize the bridle; he could only grasp the rear axle of the jaunting-car, which he stopped, though he fell himself. The passers-by ran to the spot, helped the lady out of the jaunting-car, and picked up Rakhmétoff. His chest was slightly bruised, but his most serious injury was the loss of a good-sized piece of flesh which the wheel had torn from his leg. When the lady had recovered herself, she ordered him to be taken to her country-house, about half a verst distant. He consented, for he felt very weak, but he insisted that Kirsanoff be sent for, as he would have no other doctor. Kirsanoff decided that the bruises on his chest were not of serious consequence, but he found Rakhmétoff himself very weak from the loss of blood which he had suffered. He remained in bed ten days. Naturally, the lady whom he had saved cared for him herself. In view of his weakness he

---

* A village in the suburbs of St. Petersburg.

could only talk with her, — the time would have been lost at any rate, — so he spoke and for once without reserve. The lady was a young widow nineteen years old, moderately rich, independent, intelligent, and fine-looking. Rakhmétoff's ardent words (not of love, be it understood) charmed her.

"I see him in my dreams surrounded with a halo," said she to Kirsanoff. He also conceived a passion for her. From his exterior she thought him poor; consequently she was the first to propose marriage when on the eleventh day he rose and said that he could go home.

"With you I have been more outspoken than with others; you can see that men like me have not the right to bind their destiny to that of any one whomsoever."

"Yes, you are right," said she, "you cannot marry. But until you have to leave me, love me."

"No, I cannot accept that offer either; I am no longer free, and must not love."

What has become of this lady since? This adventure must have changed her life, and undoubtedly she became herself a person like Rakhmétoff. I should like to know it. But Kirsanoff did not wish to tell me her name, and he knew no more than I what she had become. Rakhmétoff had asked him not to inquire about her. "If I supposed that you knew anything about her," said he, "I could not help asking you for the facts, and that must not be." When the story was known, everybody remembered that at that time and for some two months afterwards Rakhmétoff was more sober than usual. With no matter what fury any one might throw in his face his abominable weakness, cigars, he did not pour out wrath upon himself, and no broad and gentle smile illuminated his countenance when any one flattered him with the name of Nikitouchka Lomoff. I have other memories. Three or four times that summer he happened to make answer to my ridicule (for I laughed at him when we were together, and that is why he took me into his affection):

"Yes, pity me; you are right, pity me. I, too, like the others, am not an abstract idea, but a man who wishes to live. However, it will pass away."

And in fact it did pass away. Once only, several months later, I so excited him by my raillery that he happened to say the same words over again.

The reader with the penetrating eye sees, perhaps, that I know more about Rakhmétoff than I say. It may be so. I dare not contradict him, for his eye is penetrating. If I only knew! I know many things that you, reader with the penetrating eye, can never learn. But what I really do not know is this, — where Rakhmétoff is now, what has become of him, and whether I shall ever see him again. About these matters I know no more than his other friends. Three or four months after his disappearance from Moscow we supposed, though we had heard nothing from him, that he was travelling in Europe. This conjecture seems to have been correct. At least it is confirmed by this evidence. A year after Rakhmétoff's disappearance one of Kirsanoff's acquaintances met in a railway carriage between Vienna and Munich a young Russian, who said that he had travelled through all the Slavonic countries, meeting all classes of society and staying in each country only as long *as it was necessary* in order to form a true conception of its ideas, its customs, its manner of life, its local institutions, its material condition, and the various branches of its population; that with this view he lived in cities and villages, going on foot from one village to another; that he had studied in the same way the Roumanians and the Hungarians; that he had travelled, now on foot and now by rail, through Northern Germany; that then he had visited in detail Southern Germany and the German provinces of Austria; that now he was going to Bavaria, and thence to Switzerland by way of Würtemberg and Baden; that afterwards he would go through France and England in the same way, which he counted on doing in a year; if there were enough of the year left, he would see also Spain and Italy; if not, he would not go there. Why? Because in a year it was absolutely necessary that he should be in the United States, a country which he must study more than any other. There he would remain a long time, perhaps more than a year, and perhaps for ever should he find occupation there; but it was more likely that in three years he would return to Russia, as it seemed to him that at that time it would be necessary to be there. All this is much like Rakhmétoff, including the "it is necessarys" impressed upon the memory of the narrator. The age, the voice, the features of the traveller were also confirmatory indices; but the narrator had not paid much attention to his fellow-traveller, who, moreover, had left him two hours later, descending from the train at a little village. Consequently the narrator gave only a vague description of his external appearance, so that the authenticity is not complete. It is also said that a young Russian, an *ex-seigneur*, once presented himself to one of the greatest European thinkers of our century, the father of the new German philosophy, and said to him: "I have thirty thousand thalers; I need but five thousand; the remainder I beg you to accept." The philosopher was living in great poverty.

"What for?"

"For the publication of your works."

The philosopher did not accept; but the Russian nevertheless deposited the money in his name at a banker's, and wrote him a note which read as follows: "Do with this money as you will; throw it in the water if you like; but you cannot send it back to me, for you will not find me." The money is said to be still at the banker's. If this report be true, it was Rakhmétoff and none other that called on the philosopher. Such, then, is the gentleman whom we now see seated in Kirsanoff's study. He is truly an uncommon man, an individual of a very rare sort. And I have not spoken to you of him at this length, reader with the penetrating eye, to teach you the proper method of behavior (unknown to you) toward people of his sort. You cannot see a single man of his type; your eyes are not made to see such phenomena; to you these men are invisible; none but honest and fearless eyes can see them. But it was good that you should know, were it only by hearsay, that such men exist; as for feminine readers and simple-minded masculine readers, they know the value of this description.

Yes, people like Rakhmétoff are very droll, very amusing. I tell them that they are very droll; I tell them so because I pity them; I say to the noble hearts who are charmed by them: "Do not imitate them. The way in which they lead you is poor in personal joys." But, instead of listening to me, they say: "The way is not poor at all; on the contrary, it is very rich; though it should be poor in some particular spot, it can never long continue so, and we shall have strength enough to scale the difficult points in order to enter into the immense prairies fertile in all sorts of joys." You see, then, reader with the penetrating eye, that it is not for you, but for another portion of the public, that I have said that men like Rakhmétoff are droll. I will tell you, however, that they are not wicked; otherwise, perhaps you would not understand; no, they are not wicked. They are few in number, but through them the life of all mankind expands; without them it would have been stifled. They are few in number, but they put others in a position to breathe, who without them would have been suffocated. Great is the mass of good and honest men, but Rakhmétoffs are rare; they are like the theine in the tea, the bouquet in fine wine,—strength and aroma. They are the best among the best, they are the movers of the movers, they are the salt of the salt of the earth.

XXX.

"Ah, then!" thinks the reader with the penetrating eye, "so Rakhmétoff is to be the principal personage and master of all, Véra Pavlovna is to fall in love with him, and we are to see the story of Lopoukhoff begun over again with Kirsanoff as the hero."

Nothing of the sort, reader with the penetrating eye. Rakhmétoff will pass the evening in conversation with Véra Pavlovna, and I will not keep from you a single word of what they say. You shall soon see that, if I had not chosen to communicate this conversation to you, I could very easily have kept from doing so, and the course of events in my story would not have been changed in the least. I also tell you in advance that, when Rakhmétoff, after talking with Véra Pavlovna, shall go away, he will go away for ever from my story, that he will be neither a principal nor a secondary character, and that he will not figure further in my romance. Why have I introduced him into the romance and described him in such detail? There is an enigma for you, reader with the penetrating eye. Can you guess it? It will be solved for you in the following pages. But guess now what will be said farther on. It should not be difficult, if you had the slightest idea of art, about which you are so fond of chattering; but it is Greek to you. Stop, I will whisper in your ear half of the solution of the enigma. I have shown Rakhmétoff in order to satisfy the most essential condition of art, and simply for that.

Well, now, find out if you can what this artistic condition is. Look, guess! The feminine reader and the simple-minded masculine reader, who do not chatter about art, know, but to you it is an enigma. Take your time. I draw a long, broad stroke between the lines: (see how careful I am with you). Pause over this stroke, and reflect upon it; still, perhaps you will not guess.

Madame Mertzaloff came. After having regretted and consoled, she said that she would take charge of the shop with pleasure, but that she feared she might not succeed, and again she began to regret and console while helping to sort out the effects. After having asked the neighbors' servants to go to the bake-shop, Rakhmétoff prepared the *samovar*, brought it in, and they began to take tea; Rakhmétoff spent half an hour with the ladies, drank five cups of tea, half emptied at the same time an enormous pot of cream, and ate a frightful quantity of rolls, and two plain loaves which served as a foundation.

"I am entitled to this extra indulgence, for I am sacrificing an entire half of my day."

While enjoying his meal and listening to the ladies as they exhausted themselves in grief, he expressed three times his opinion: "It is senseless,"—not that the ladies should exhaust themselves in grief, but that any one should kill himself for any reason whatever except to get rid of an intolerably painful and incurable disease or to avoid a painful and inevitable death,—such, for instance, as torture on the wheel; each time he expressed this opinion concisely, as was his habit. He poured out the sixth cup of tea, at the same time emptying the pot of cream completely, and took all the rolls that were left, and, the ladies having long ago finished their meal, he made a bow and went off with these things to finish his physical delectation in the study, where he passed some time as a sybarite, extended on the divan, which was used by everybody, but which to him was Capuan luxury.

"I am entitled to this feast, for I am sacrificing twelve or fourteen hours of my time," said he. After having finished his physical delectation, he began once more his mental delectation,—the reading of the commentaries on the Apocalypse. About ten o'clock the police official came to communicate the particulars of the affair to the wife of the suicide; Rakhmétoff told him that the wife knew all about it already, and that there was nothing to be said to her; the official was very glad to be relieved from participation in a harrowing scene. Then came Macha and Rachel and began to sort out the clothing and goods; Rachel advised the sale of everything except the nice cloak, for, if that were sold, it would be necessary in three months to have a new one made. To this Véra Pavlovna consented, and the price was fixed at four hundred and fifty roubles,—all that the things were worth, according to Madame Mertzaloff. So at ten o'clock the commercial transaction was concluded. Rachel paid two hundred roubles; she had no more about her, but would send the balance in two or three days by Madame Mertzaloff; she took the things and went away. Madame Mertzaloff remained an hour longer, but it was time to nurse her child, and she went away, saying that she would come the next day to accompany Véra Pavlovna to the station.

When Madame Mertzaloff had gone, Rakhmétoff closed Newton's commentaries on the Apocalypse, put them carefully back in their place, and sent Macha to ask Véra Pavlovna if he could go into her room. He obtained permission. He entered, as usual, slowly and coolly.

"Véra Pavlovna, I am now able to console you to a certain extent. It is permissible to do so now; it was not necessary to do so sooner. First warning you that the general result of my visit will be of a consoling nature,—you know, I never say vain words, and you must calm yourself in advance,—I am going to explain the affair to you at length. I told you that I had seen Alexander Matvéitch and that I knew all. That was strictly true. But I did not tell you that I knew all from him, and I could not have told you so, since in reality I knew all, not from him, but from Dmitry Serguéitch, who came to see me about two o'clock; I was notified in advance of his coming, and consequently was at home; so he came to see me about two o'clock, after writing the note which has caused you so much grief. And he it was who asked me" . . . .

"You knew what he intended to do and did not stop him?"

"I asked you to be calm, as the result of my visit was to be consoling. No, I did not stop him, for his mind was thoroughly made up, as you shall see for yourself. As I began to say, he it was who asked me to spend this evening with you, and, knowing that you would be in sorrow, he entrusted me with a commission for you. He chose me as his agent because he knew me to be a man who carries out with perfect exactness the instructions that are given him, and cannot be turned aside by any sentiment or any prayer. He foresaw that you would beg me to violate his will, and he hoped that I would carry it out without being moved by your prayers. So I shall, and I beg you to ask no concession of me. This commission is as follows. In going away to 'quit the scene' " . . . . .

"My God, what has he done! Why did you not restrain him?"

"Examine this expression, 'quit the scene,' and do not blame me prematurely. He used this expression in the note that you received, did he not? Well, we will adopt the same expression, for it is very happily chosen and expresses the idea exactly."

Véra Pavlovna became more and more perplexed; she said to herself: "What does it mean? What must I think?"

Rakhmétoff, with all the apparent absurdity of his circumstantial method of explanation, managed the affair in a masterly way. He was a great psychologist, and knew how to proceed gradually.

"So, in going away, with a view to quitting the scene, to use his accurate expression, he left with me a note for you" . . . . .

Véra Pavlovna rose abruptly.

"Where is it? Give it to me! And you could stay here all day without delivering it to me?"

"I could because it was necessary. You will soon understand my reasons. They are well-founded. But first I must explain to you the expression that I employed just now: 'the result will be consoling.' By the consoling nature of the result I did not mean the receipt of this note, and that for two reasons, the first of which is this: in the fact of the receipt of this note there would not have been sufficient relief, you see, to deserve the name of consolation; to give consolation something more is necessary. So the consolation must be found in the contents of the note."

Véra Pavlovna rose again.

"Calm yourself; I do not say that you are mistaken. Having prepossessed you concerning the contents of the note, let me tell you the second reason why I could not mean by the 'consoling nature of the result' the fact of the receipt of the note, but its contents rather. These contents, on the character of which we have settled, are so important that I cannot give them to you, but can only show them to you."

"What! You will not give them to me?"

"No. That is precisely why he chose me, for anybody else in my place would have given them to you. The note cannot remain in your hands because, considering the extreme importance of its contents, on the character of which we have settled, it must not remain in the hands of any one. Now, if I should give it to you, you would wish to keep it. So, not to be obliged to take it away from you again by force, I shall not give it to you, but shall only show it to you. But I shall not show it to you until you have sat down, placed your hands upon your knees, and given me your word not to raise them."

If any stranger had been there, however susceptible his heart, he could not have helped laughing at the solemnity of this procedure and especially at the quasi-religious ceremonies of this climax. It is comical, I confess, but it would be very good for our nerves if, in communicating news calculated to produce a strong impression, we knew how to observe toward each other even a tenth part of Rakhmétoff's processes.

But Véra Pavlovna, not being a stranger, could feel only the oppressive side of this delay; she even assumed an expression no less laughable when, being seated and having precipitately and submissively placed her hands upon her knees, she cried, in the pleasantest voice,—that is, a voice of painful impatience: "I swear it!"

Rakhmétoff placed on the table a sheet of letter-paper, on which were written ten or twelve lines.

Scarcely had Véra Pavlovna cast a glance at it when, forgetting her oath, she rose impetuously to seize the note, which was already far off in Rakhmétoff's lifted hand.

"I foresaw that, and for that reason, as you would have noticed had you been in a condition to notice anything, my hand did not leave the note. Therefore I will continue to hold this sheet by the corner as long as it remains on the table. This will make all your attempts useless."

Véra Pavlovna sat down again and replaced her hands. Rakhmétoff again placed the note under her eyes. She read it over twenty times with emotion. Rakhmétoff stood with much patience beside her chair, holding the corner of the sheet with his hand. A quarter of an hour passed thus. Finally Véra Pavlovna raised her hand slowly, evidently without bad intentions, and hid her eyes.

"How good he is! how good he is!" said she.

"I am not quite of your opinion, and you shall know why. This will be no part of his commission, but only the expression of my opinion, which I gave to him too at our last interview. My commission consisted only in this,—to show you this note and then burn it. Have you looked at it enough?"

"Again, again!"

She folded her hands anew, he replaced the note, and with the same patience stood in the position already described a good quarter of an hour longer. Again she hid her face in her hands and repeated: "Oh! how good he is, how good he is!"

"You have studied this note as closely as you could. If you were in a calmer frame of mind, not only would you know it by heart, but the very form of each letter would be stamped for ever in your memory, so long and attentively have you looked at it. But in your present state of agitation the laws of memory do not exist, and memory may prove false to you. In view of this possibility I have made a copy of the note; this copy you can always see at my house whenever you like. Sometime I may even find it possible to give it to you. Now I think it is time to burn the original, and then my commission will be completed."

"Show it to me once more."

He again placed the note on the table. This time Véra Pavlovna repeatedly raised her eyes from the paper: it was plain that she had learned the note by heart and was verifying her remembrance of it. A few minutes afterwards she gave a deep sigh, and stopped lifting her eyes from the note.

"Now, that is enough, it seems to me. It is time. It is midnight already, and I have yet to give you my thoughts about this matter, for I deem it useful that you should know my opinion. Do you consent?"

"Yes."

On the instant the note was ablaze in the flame of the candle.

"Ah!" cried Véra Pavlovna, "that is not what I said. Why" . . . . .

"Yes, you only said that you consented to listen to me. But sooner or later I should have had to burn it."

Saying these words, Rakhmétoff sat down.

"Besides, the copy of the note remains. Now, Véra Pavlovna, I am going to give you my opinion of the affair. I will begin with you. You are going away. Why?"

"It would be very painful for me to stay here. The sight of places which would recall the past would make me very unhappy."

"Yes, that is a very disagreeable feeling. But do you believe that life would be much less painful to you anywhere else? Very little less, in any case. And yet what do you do? To secure yourself a slight relief, you hazard the destiny of fifty individuals dependent upon you. Is it well to do that?"

What has become of the tiresome solemnity of Rakhmétoff's tone? He speaks in a spirited, natural, simple, brief, and animated way.

"That is true, but I have asked Madame Mertzaloff".....

"You do not know whether she will be in a position to replace you in the shop; her capacity is not yet proven. Now, this is a matter which calls for a person of more than ordinary capacity. The chances are ten against one that no one would be found to replace you and that your departure would ruin the shop. Is that well? You expose fifty persons to almost certain, almost inevitable ruin. And for what reason? To secure a little comfort for yourself. Is that well? What an eager tenderness for one's own trivial relief, and what an insensibility to the fate of others! How does this view of your course please you?"

"Why did you not restrain me?"

"You would not have listened to me. And, besides, I knew that you would come back soon; consequently the matter was not important. You see that you are in the wrong."

"Completely," said Véra Pavlovna, partly in jest and partly in earnest,— almost wholly in earnest, in fact.

"No, that is but one side of your crime. 'Completely' involves much more. But for your repentance you shall receive a reward: I am going to aid you to repair another crime, which it is not yet too late to correct. Are you calm now, Véra Pavlovna?"

"Yes, almost calm."

"Good! Do you need Macha for anything?"

"Certainly not."

"And yet you are already calm; you ought, then, to have remembered that it was time to tell her to go to bed,— it is already past midnight,— especially as she has to rise early. Who should have thought of this, you or I? I will tell her that she may sleep. And at the same time for this fresh repentance — for you do repent — here is a new reward; I will see what there is for supper. You have not eaten today, and you must have an appetite."

"It is true, and a keen one; I felt it as soon as you reminded me of it," said Véra Pavlovna, laughing this time.

Rakhmétoff brought the remains of the dinner. Macha had shown him the cheese and a pot of mushrooms, which made them a good supper enough; he brought two knives and forks, and, in short, did everything himself.

"See, Rakhmétoff, how eagerly I eat; that means that I was hungry; and yet I did not feel it; it was not Macha alone that I forgot; I am not, you see, so malicious a criminal."

"Nor am I so very attentive to others; I reminded you of your appetite because I too wanted to eat, for I did not dine very well, though I ate more than another would have needed for a dinner and a half; but, as you well know, I eat as much as any two peasants."

"Ah, Rakhmétoff, you are my good angel, and not for my appetite alone. But why did you stay here all day without showing me the note? Why did you keep me so long in torture?"

"The reason is a very serious one. It was necessary that others should witness your sorrow, so that the news of your extreme grief might spread and thus confirm the authenticity of the event which caused it. You would not have wanted to feign sorrow, and, in fact, it is impossible to completely replace nature by anything whatever; nature in all cases acts in a much more convincing way. Now there are three sources from which the event may be authenticated,—Macha, Madame Mertzaloff, and Rachel. Madame Mertzaloff is an especially important source, as she knows all your acquaintances. I was very glad that you conceived the idea of sending for her."

"But how shrewd you are, Rakhmétoff!"

"Yes, it was not a bad idea to wait until night, but the credit of it belongs to Dmitry Serguéitch himself."

"How good he is!" and Véra Pavlovna heaved a profound sigh, not of sorrow, but of gratitude.

"Well, Véra Pavlovna, we will analyze him further. Indeed, of late, his thoughts have been very wise and his conduct perfect. Yet we shall convict him of some pretty serious sins."

"Rakhmétoff, do not speak of him in that way, or I shall get angry."

"You rebel! That calls for another punishment. The list of your crimes is only just begun."

"Execute, execute, Rakhmétoff."

"For this submission a reward. Submission is always rewarded. If you have any wine, it would not be a bad idea for you to drink some. Where is it? In the sideboard or in the closet?"

"In the sideboard."

In the sideboard he found a bottle of sherry.

Rakhmétoff obliged Véra Pavlovna to drink two small glasses of it, and lit a cigar himself.

"It is a pity that I cannot drink three or four small glasses with you. I desire it so much."

"Is it possible, Rakhmétoff?"

"It is tempting, Véra Pavlovna, it is very tempting," said he, laughing; "man is weak."

"You, too, weak! Why, Rakhmétoff, you astonish me! You are not at all what I have been in the habit of thinking you. Why are you always so sober? Tonight you are a gay and charming man."

"Véra Pavlovna, I am now fulfilling a gay duty; why should I not be gay? But this is an exceptional case, a rarity. Generally the things that I see are not gay at all; how could I help being sober? But, Véra Pavlovna, since you have chanced on this occasion to see me as I should very much like to be always, and since we have come to talk so freely to each other, know this,—but let it be a secret,—that it is not to my liking to be sober. It is easier for me to do my duty when it is not noticed that I too should like to enjoy life. In that case no one tries to entertain me, and I am not forced to waste my time in refusing invitations. But that it may be easier for you to think of me only as a sober man, I continue my inquest concerning your crimes."

"But what more do you want, then? You have already convicted me of two,—insensibility toward Macha and insensibility regarding the shop. I am repentant."

"The insensibility toward Macha is only an offence, not a crime: Macha would not die from rubbing her heavy eyes an hour longer; on the contrary, she would have done it with a pleasant feeling, knowing that she was doing her duty. But as regards the shop I want to devour you."

"Have you not devoured me enough already?"

"Not entirely yet, and I want to devour you entirely. How could you abandon this shop to its ruin?"

"But I have repented, and, besides, I did not abandon it: Madame Mertzaloff had consented to take my place."

"We have already spoken of that: your intention of furnishing her as a substitute is not a sufficient excuse. But by this excuse you have succeeded only in convicting yourself of a new crime."

Rakhmétoff gradually resumed his serious, though not solemn, tone.

"You say that she is going to take your place. Is that decided upon?"

"Yes," said Véra Pavlovna, seriously, foreseeing that something bad was to follow.

"Look at it. The affair is decided, but by whom? By you and by her, without taking any further counsel. Whether these fifty persons would consent to such a change, whether they wished it, and whether they might not have found some better way,—what is that to you? That is despotism, Véra Pavlovna. So you are already guilty of two great crimes,—lack of pity and despotism. But the third is a heinous crime. The institution which more or less closely corresponded to healthy ideas of social organization, which to a greater or less extent demonstrated their practicability (a precious thing, proofs of this kind being very rare),

—this institution, I say, you submitted to the risk of destruction and of transformation from a proof of the practicability into evidence of the impracticability and absurdity of your convictions, into a means of refuting your ideas, so beneficial to humanity: you furnished an argument against your holy principles to the champions of darkness and of evil. Now, I say no more of the fact that you destroyed the prosperity of fifty individuals,— that is a matter of fifty individuals,— but you harmed humanity, you betrayed progress. That, Véra Pavlovna, is what is called, in ecclesiastical language, the sin against the Holy Ghost, the only unpardonable sin. Isn't that true, madam criminal? Fortunately everything has happened as it has, and you have sinned only in intention. Ah! you blush in earnest, Véra Pavlovna. It is well; now I will console you. If you had not suffered so much, you would not have committed such crimes even in your imagination. Therefore the real criminal is he who has occasioned you so much torment. And you repeat continually: 'How good he is! how good he is!'"

"What! Do you think that, if I have suffered, it is through his fault?"

"Whose fault is it, then? He has managed this affair well, I admit, but why all this hubbub? Nothing of the kind should have happened."

"Yes, I should not have had this feeling. But I did not invite it; on the contrary, I tried to suppress it."

"'I should not have had'—that is good! You do not see wherein you are guilty, and you reproach yourself when there is no occasion to. This feeling necessarily had to arise in one way or another, given your character and that of Dmitry Serguéitch, and it would have developed itself under any circumstances. The essential point in the matter is not that you are in love with another, which is only a result; it is the dissatisfaction with your former relations. What form was this dissatisfaction obliged to take? If both, or even one of you, had been deficient in intellectual development and refinement, or if you had been bad people, your dissatisfaction would have taken the ordinary form,— hostility between husband and wife; you would have devoured each other, if you had both been bad; or one of you would have tormented the other, and the other would have been pitilessly tormented. It would have been in any case one of those domestic hells that we find in most families. That evidently would not have prevented the appearance of love for another, but in addition there would have been hell, mutual torment, I know not what. With you dissatisfaction could not take this form, because both of you are honest; so it took only its lightest, mildest, most inoffensive form,— love of another. Of this love there is no occasion to speak: it is not, I repeat, the essential point. The essential point is the dissatisfaction with your former situation, and the cause of your dissatisfaction is the difference in your characters. Both of you are good, but when your character, Véra Pavlovna, matured, when it lost its childish ambiguity and acquired definite traits, it became evident that you and Dmitry Serguéitch were not well suited to each other. What is there in that that is against either of you? I, for instance, am not a bad man. Could you live a long time with me? You would die of *ennui*. In how many days, do you think?"

"In a very few days," said Véra Pavlovna, laughing.

"He is not as sober as I am, but nevertheless there is altogether too much difference between you. Who should have noticed it first? Who is the older? Whose character was formed the earlier? Who has had the greater experience in life? He should have foreseen all and prepared you, in order that you might not be frightened and eaten up with sorrow. He did not realize this until the feeling that he should have anticipated was not only developed, but had produced its results. Why did he foresee nothing, notice nothing? Was it stupidity? He does not lack wit. No, it was inattention, negligence, rather; he neglected his relations with you, Véra Pavlovna. That was the real trouble. And still you repeat: 'He is good; he loved me.'"

Rakhmétoff was gradually becoming animated, and already spoke with warmth. But Véra Pavlovna stopped him.

"I must not listen to you, Rakhmétoff," said she in a bitter and discontented tone; "you heap reproaches upon the man to whom I am under infinite obligations."

"Véra Pavlovna, if you ought not to listen to this, I would not say it to you. Do you imagine that I now notice this for the first time? You know that no one can avoid a conversation with me if it seems to me indispensable. Therefore I could have said this to you before, and yet I said nothing. Therefore the fact that I have now begun to speak means that it is necessary. I never speak sooner than is necessary. You saw me keep the note in my pocket nine whole hours, although it filled me with pity to see you. But it was necessary to keep silent, and I kept silent. So, if I now say what I long ago thought about the ways of Dmitry Sergueïtch towards you, that means that it is necessary to speak about it."

"But I will not listen to you," said Véra Pavlovna with extreme vehemence: "I beg you to be silent, Rakhmétoff. I beg you to go away. I am much obliged to you for having sacrificed an evening on my account. But I beg you to go away."

"Absolutely?"

"Absolutely."

"Good," said he, laughing. "No, Véra Pavlovna, you cannot get rid of me so easily. I foresaw this contingency, and took my precautions. The note which I burned was written of his own accord. And here is one which he wrote because I asked him to. This I can leave with you, because it is not an important document. Here it is."

Rakhmétoff handed the note to Véra Pavlovna.

My dear Vérotchka:

Listen to all that Rakhmétoff has to say to you. I do not know what he intends to say to you, I have not charged him to say anything to you, and he has

not made the slightest allusion to what he intends to say. But I know that he never says anything unnecessary. Yours,   D. L.
July 11, 2 o'clock in the morning.

God knows how many times Véra Pavlovna kissed this note.

"Why did you not give it to me sooner? Perhaps you have something else from him."

"No, I have nothing more, because nothing more was necessary. Why did I not give it to you? There was no reason for giving it to you until it became necessary."

"But to give me the pleasure of receiving a few lines from him after our separation."

"If that is all, that is not so important," and he smiled.

"Ah, Rakhmétoff, you will put me in a rage!"

"So this note is the cause of a new quarrel between us?" said he, smiling again: "if that is the case, I will take it away from you and burn it; you know well what they say of such people as we are,—that to them nothing is sacred. Hence we are capable of all sorts of violence and rascality. May I continue?"

They both became calm,—she, thanks to the note, he, because he remained silent while she kissed the note.

"Yes, I must listen to you."

"He did not notice what he should have noticed," began Rakhmétoff calmly: "that has produced bad results. Though we cannot call it a crime in him, neither can we excuse it. Suppose that he did not know that the rupture was inevitable; still, given your character and his own, he should nevertheless have prepared you at all events against anything like it, just as one would against any accident which is not to be desired and which there is no reason to expect, but which is to be provided for; for one cannot answer for the future and the changes that it may bring. With this axiom— that we are exposed to all sorts of accidents—he was familiar, we may be sure. Why did he leave you in ignorance to such an extent that, when the present circumstances arose, you were not at all prepared for them? His lack of foresight came from negligence, injurious to you, but in itself an indifferent thing, neither good nor bad; but, in failing to prepare you against any contingency, he acted from an absolutely bad motive. To be sure, he had no data to act upon, but it is precisely in those matters where one acts without data that nature best manifests itself. It would have been contrary to his interests to prepare you, for thereby your resistance to the feeling not in harmony with his interests would have been weakened. Your feeling proved so strong that your resistance could not overcome it; but it was not at all unlikely that this feeling would manifest itself with less force. If it had been inspired by a man less exceptionally worthy, it would have been weaker. Feelings against which it is useless to struggle are an exception. There are many more chances that this feeling will manifest itself in such a way that it may be stifled, if the power of resistance is not wholly destroyed. It was precisely in view of these, the most probable chances, that he did not wish to lessen your power of resistance. Those were his motives for leaving you unprepared and subjecting you to so much suffering. What do you say to this?"

"It is not true, Rakhmétoff. He did not hide his ways of thinking from me. His convictions were as well known to me as to you."

"To hide them would have been difficult. To oppose in your presence convictions corresponding to his own and to pretend for such a purpose to think otherwise than he did would have been simply dishonesty. You would never have loved such a man. Have I pronounced him bad? He is very good; I could say nothing else; I will praise him as highly as you like. I only say this: at the time of your rupture his conduct was very good, but before that his conduct towards you was bad. Why did you distress yourself? He said (was it worth while to say so, it being clear without it?) that it was because you did not wish to grieve him. Why was this thought that you could thereby greatly grieve him able to find a place in your mind? It should not have found a place there. What grief? It is stupid. Jealousy?"

"You do not admit jealousy, Rakhmétoff?"

"A man with a developed mind should not have it. It is a distorted feeling, a false feeling, an abominable feeling; it is a phenomenon of our existing order of things, based upon the same idea that prevents me from permitting any one to wear my linen or smoke my pipe: it is a result of the fashion of considering one's companion as an object that one has appropriated."

"But, Rakhmétoff, not to admit jealousy leads to horrible consequences."

"To those who are jealous they are horrible, but to those who are not there is not only nothing horrible about them, but nothing even of importance."

"You preach utter immorality, Rakhmétoff!"

"Does it seem so to you after living with him for four years? That is precisely where he has done wrong. How many times a day do you dine? Only once. Would any one find fault with you if you dined twice? Probably not. Why do you not do so? Do you fear that you may grieve some one? Probably because you do not feel the necessity of it. Yet dinner is a very agreeable thing. But the mind and (more important still) the stomach say that one dinner is agreeable and that a second would be disagreeable. But if the fancy seized you or you had an unhealthy desire to dine twice, would you be prevented by the fear of grieving some one? No, if any one felt grieved or prohibited you, you would hide and eat your food in bad condition, you would soil your hands in taking it hastily, you would soil your clothes by hiding bits in your pockets, and that would be all. The question here is not one of morality or immorality, but only this: is smuggling a good thing? Who is restrained by the idea that jealousy is a feeling worthy of esteem and respect? Who says to himself: "Ah! if I do this, I shall cause him grief"? Who is tormented by these useless struggles? Few people, the best, just those whose nature would not lead them into immorality. The mass are not restrained by these stupidities; they only resort to further strategy. They fill their lives with deceit and become really bad. That is all. Are you not well aware of this?"

"Why, certainly."

"Where, then, do you find the moral utility of jealousy?"

"Why, we have always talked in this vein ourselves."

"Not exactly in this vein, probably, or perhaps you talked so without believing your own words, not believing them because on this as on other questions you heard continually the opposite views. If that was not the case, why did you torment yourself? Why all this confusion about such trivial matters? What an embarrassment to all three of you, and especially to you, Véra Pavlovna! Whereas you might all three live as in the past, as you lived a year ago, or take apartments together, or arrange your life in any other way, according to your choice, but without any upturning, and all three take tea or go to the opera together as in the past. Why these anxieties? Why these catastrophes? Always because, owing to his wrong policy of keeping you in ignorance on this matter, he has thus caused you much useless sorrow."

"No, Rakhmétoff, you say horrible things."

"'Horrible things' again! Groundless anxieties and needless catastrophes are the things that seem horrible to me."

"Then, in your eyes, our whole story is only a stupid melodrama?"

"Yes, an utterly useless melodrama coupled with a dramatist no less useless. And instead of a simple and peaceful conversation there has been a harrowing melodrama; the guilty party is Dmitry Serguéitch. His honest conduct at the last hardly suffices to cancel his original fault. Yes, he is very guilty. But, then, he has paid dearly enough for it. Take another glass of sherry and go to bed. I have accomplished the object of my visit; it is already three o'clock, and, if not waked, you will sleep a long time. Now, I told Macha not to call you till half past ten, so that tomorrow you will hardly have time to take breakfast, but will have to hurry to the depot; even though you should not have time to pack all your things, you will come back soon, or else they will be sent to you. Do you wish Alexander Matvéitch to go directly after you, or do you prefer to come back yourself? But it would be painful for you to be in Macha's presence, for she must not notice that you are entirely calm. She will not notice this during half an hour of hurried preparations. With Madame Mertzaloff it is another thing. I will go to her tomorrow morning, and tell her not to come because you went to bed late and must not be waked; that she must go directly to the depot instead."

"How attentive you are to me!" said Véra Pavlovna.

"This attention, at least, you need not attribute to him; it comes from me. Except that I rebuke him for the past (to his face I said much more) on account of his responsibility for this useless anxiety, I find that, as soon as you actually began to suffer, he acted very commendably."

XXXI.

AN INTERVIEW WITH THE READER WITH THE PENETRATING EYE, AND HIS EXPULSION.

Tell me, then, reader with the penetrating eye, why I have shown you Rakhmétoff, who has just gone away to appear no more in my story. I have already told you that he would take no part in the action.

"It is not true," interrupts the reader with the penetrating eye. "Rakhmétoff is a personage, for he brought the note, which" . . . .

Why, how weak you are, my good sir, in the æsthetic discussions of which you are so fond! In that case Macha too is, in your eyes, a personage? She also, at the beginning of the story, brought a letter, which horrified Véra Pavlovna. And perhaps Rachel is a personage? For it was she who bought Véra Pavlovna's things, without which the latter could not have gone away. And Professor N. is a personage, because he recommended Véra Pavlovna to Madame B. as a governess, without which the scene of the return from the Boulevard Konno-Gvardeisky would not have occurred. Perhaps the Boulevard Konno-Gvardeisky is also a personage? For without this boulevard the scene of the rendezvous and the return would not have occurred either. And the Rue Gorokhovaïa must be the most essential personage, because without it the houses there situated would not have existed, including the Storechnikoff house, and as a consequence there would have been no steward of this house and no steward's daughter, and then there would would have been no story at all.

Admitting with you that the Boulevard Konno-Gvardeisky and Macha, Rachel and the Rue Gorokhovaïa are personages, why is it that only five words or even less are said of each of them? It is because their action is worth no more. On the other hand, how many pages are devoted to Rakhmétoff?

"Ah! now I know," says the reader with the penetrating eye. "Rakhmétoff appeared to pronounce judgment on Véra Pavlovna and Lopoukhoff; he was needed for the conversation with Véra Pavlovna."

Your weakness is really deplorable, my worthy friend. You construe the matter in just the wrong way. Was it necessary to bring a man in simply that he might pronounce his opinion of the other personages? Your great artists do it, perhaps. As for me, though a feeble writer, I understand the conditions of art a little better than that. No, my good sir, Rakhmétoff was not at all necessary for that. How many times has Véra Pavlovna herself, how many times have Lopoukhoff and Kirsanoff themselves, expressed their own opinion concerning their own actions and relations! They are intelligent enough to judge what is good and what is bad; they need no prompter for that. Do you believe that Véra Pavlovna herself, recalling at her leisure a few days later the tumult just passed through, would not have blamed herself for having forgotten the shop in the same way that Rakhmétoff blamed her? Do you believe that Lopoukhoff himself did not think of his relations with Véra Pavlovna quite as Rakhmétoff spoke of them to Véra Pavlovna? Honest people think of themselves all the evil that can be said of them, and that is the reason, my good sir, why they are honest people; do you know it? How weak you are when it comes to analyzing the thoughts of honest people! I will say more: did you not think that Rakhmétoff in his conversation with Véra Pavlovna acted independently of Lopoukhoff? Well, he was only Lopoukhoff's agent; he understood it so himself, and Véra Pavlovna saw it a day or two later; and she would have seen it as soon as Rakhmétoff opened his mouth, if she had not been so much agitated. So that is how things happened as they did; is it possible that you did not understand even this much? Certainly Lopoukhoff told the truth in his second note; he had said nothing to Rakhmétoff and the latter had said nothing to him about the conversation which was to take place; but Lopoukhoff was acquainted with Rakhmétoff and knew what the latter thought of such or such things and what he would say under such or such circumstances. Honest people understand each other without explaining themselves. Lopoukhoff could have written in advance, almost word for word, all that Rakhmétoff would say to Véra Pavlovna, and that is exactly why he asked Rakhmétoff to be his agent. Must I instruct you further in psychology? Lopoukhoff knew perfectly well that all he thought about himself, Rakhmétoff, Mertzaloff and his wife, and the officer who had wrestled with him on the islands thought also, and that Véra Pavlovna was sure to think so within a short time even though no one should say it to her. She would see it as soon as the first flush of gratitude passed: therefore, calculated Lopoukhoff, I really lose nothing by sending Rakhmétoff to her, although he will rebuke me, for she would reach the same opinion herself; on the contrary, I gain in her esteem: she will see that I foresaw the substance of the conversation, and that I arranged it, and she will think: "How noble he is! He knew that during these first days of agitation my exalted gratitude would dominate everything, and he took care to plant in my mind as early as possible thoughts which would lessen this burden. Although I am angry with Rakhmétoff for accusing him, I see that really Rakhmétoff was right. In a week I should have seen it myself, but then it would not have been of any importance to me, and I should have had to recover from my agitation without it, whereas by hearing these thoughts the same day I have escaped a painful emotion which otherwise would have lasted a whole week. At that time these thoughts were very useful to me; yes, he has a very noble heart."

That was the plan which Lopoukhoff devised, and Rakhmétoff was only his agent. You see, my good reader with the penetrating eye, what sly dogs honest people are and how their egoism works; their egoism is different from yours, because they do not find their pleasure in the same direction that you do. They find their greatest pleasure, you see, in having people whom they esteem think well of them, and that is why they trouble themselves to devise all sorts of plans with no less zeal than you show in other matters. But your objects are different, and the plans that you devise are different. You concoct evil plans, injurious to others, while they concoct honest plans, useful to others.

"Why! how dare you say such insulting things to me?" cries the reader with the penetrating eye; "I will bring a complaint against you; I will proclaim everywhere that you are a man of evil disposition."

Pardon, my good sir, how could I dare to say insulting things to you when I esteem your character as highly as your mind? I simply take the liberty to enlighten you concerning art, which you love so well. In this respect you were in error in thinking that Rakhmétoff appeared to pronounce sentence on Véra Pavlovna and Lopoukhoff. No such thing was necessary. He has said nothing that I might not have given you as thoughts which, without Rakhmétoff's intervention, would have come to Véra Pavlovna in time.

Now, my good sir, a question: why, then, do I give you Rakhmétoff's conversation with Véra Pavlovna? Do you understand now that when I give you, not the thoughts of Lopoukhoff and Véra Pavlovna, but Rakhmétoff's conversation with the latter, I thereby signify the necessity of giving you, not alone the thoughts which constitute the essence of the conversation, but the actual conversation itself?

Why is it necessary to give you the precise conversation? Because it is Rakhmétoff's conversation with Véra Pavlovna. Do you understand now? No, not yet? What a thick head! How weak-minded you are! I am going to make you understand.

When two men talk, one sees more or less the character of these men; do you see whither this tends? Was Véra Pavlovna's character sufficiently well known to you before this conversation? It was; you have learned nothing about her: you already knew that she flares up, that she jests, that she likes good things to eat and a glass of sherry to drink; therefore the conversation was necessary to show the character, not of Véra Pavlovna, but of whom then? There were but two in the conversation, she and Rakhmétoff. To show the character, not of Véra Pavlovna, but — well, guess!

"Rakhmétoff," shouts the reader with the penetrating eye.

Bravo! You have hit it; I like you for that. Well, you see, it is just the contrary of what you first thought. Rakhmétoff is not shown for the sake of the conversation, but the conversation is given to make you better acquainted with

Rakhmétoff and solely for that purpose. Through this conversation you have learned that Rakhmétoff had a desire for sherry, although he never drank wine; that Rakhmétoff was not absolutely solemn and morose; that on the contrary, when engaged in agreeable business, he forgot his sorrowful thoughts, his bitter sadness, and gaily jested and made merry: only, as he explained it, "that is rarely the case with me, and I am sorry that it is so rarely the case; I do not like to be solemn, but circumstances are such that a man with my ardent love of good cannot help being solemn; if it were not for that, I should jest, I should laugh; perhaps I should sing and dance all day long." Do you understand now, reader with the penetrating eye, why, though many pages were used in directly describing Rakhmétoff, I have devoted additional pages to the accomplishment of the same purpose indirectly? Tell me, now, why I have shown and described this figure in such detail. Remember what I have already told you;—"solely to satisfy the most essential condition of art." What is this condition, and how is it satisfied by the fact that I have put Rakhmétoff's figure before you? Do you understand? No, you cannot see. Well, listen. Or rather do not listen; you will never understand; go away; I have laughed at you enough. I speak to you no longer, but to the public, and I speak seriously. The first demand of art consists in this,—to so represent objects that the reader may conceive them as they really are. For instance, if I wish to represent a house, I must see to it that the reader will conceive it as a house, and not as a hovel or a palace. If I wish to represent an ordinary man, I must see to it that the reader will not conceive him as a dwarf or as a giant.

It has been my purpose to represent ordinarily upright people of the new generation, people whom I meet by hundreds. I have taken three of them: Véra Pavlovna, Lopoukhoff, and Kirsanoff. I consider them ordinary people, they consider themselves such, and are considered such by all their acquaintances (who resemble them). Have I spoken in any other vein? Have I told extraordinary things? I have represented them with affection and esteem, it is true, but that is because every upright man is worthy of such affection and esteem.

But when have I bowed before them? Where have you seen in me the slightest tendency to adoration, or hint that nothing superior to them can be imagined and that they are ideal characters? As I conceive them, so they act,—like simple, upright people of the new generation. What do they do that is remarkably elevated? They do not do cowardly things, they are not poltroons, they have honest but ordinary convictions, they try to act accordingly, and that is all. Where is their heroism? Yes, it has been my purpose to show human beings acting just as all ordinary men of this type act, and I hope I have succeeded. Those of my readers who are intimately acquainted with living men of this type have seen from the beginning and up to the present moment that my principal characters are not at all ideal and not above the general level of people of their type, and that these men do not act in real life in any other way than that in which I picture them as acting. Suppose that other upright people had been confronted with a slightly different situation: it is not a matter of absolute necessity or fatality that all husbands and all wives should separate; all upright wives do not strongly feel a passionate love for their husband's friend, all upright men do not have to struggle against their passion for a married woman during three whole years; nor is one always forced to blow his brains out on a bridge or (to use the words of the reader with the penetrating eye) to disappear from a hotel to go no one knows where. But no upright man in the place of the people pictured by me would have considered it heroic to do as they have done; he would do likewise under similar circumstances. Many times he has acted thus in many situations no less difficult, if not still more so, and yet he does not consider himself a man to be admired, but simply an ordinary, moderately upright man, nothing more. And the friends of such a man, resembling him (for these people form friendships only with those who act and think as they do), consider him an estimable man, but never dream for a moment of dropping on their knees before him; they say to themselves: We, too, are like him.

I hope, I say, that I have succeeded in making every upright man of the new generation recognize the type of his friends in my three characters. But those who from the beginning of the story have been able to think of Véra Pavlovna, Kirsanoff, and Lopoukhoff as "our friends, people like ourselves simply,"—these are yet but a minority of the public. The majority are still much below this type. A man who has never seen anything but dirty huts might take an engraving of a very ordinary house for the picture of a palace. How shall the house be made to seem to such a man a house and not a palace? Only by showing in the same picture even a little wing of a palace; he will then see from this wing that the palace must be quite a different thing from the building represented in the picture, and that the latter is really but a simple house no better than every one ought to have, perhaps not as good. If I had not shown the figure of Rakhmétoff, the majority of readers would have had a false idea of the principal characters of my story. I will wager that up to the concluding paragraphs of this chapter Véra Pavlovna, Kirsanoff, and Lopoukhoff have seemed to the majority of the public to be heroes, individuals of a superior nature, if not ideal persons, if not even persons impossible in real life by reason of their very noble conduct. No, my poor friends, you have been wrong in this thought: they are not too high, you are too low. You see now that they simply stand on the surface of the earth; and, if they have seemed to you to be soaring in the clouds, it is because you are in the infernal depths. The height where they stand all men should and can reach.

Elevated natures, such as neither you nor I, my poor friends, can equal,—elevated natures are not like these. I have shown you a faint outline of the profile of one of them; the features are different, as you clearly see. Now, it is possible for you to become entirely the equals of the men whom I represent provided you will work for your intellectual and moral development. Whoever is beneath them is very low.

Come up from your caves, my friends, ascend! It is not so difficult. Come to the surface of this earth where one is so well situated and the road is easy and attractive! Try it: development! development! Observe, think, read those who tell you of the pure enjoyment of life, of the possible goodness and happiness of man.

Read them, their books delight the heart; observe life,—it is interesting; think,—it is a pleasant occupation. And that is all. Sacrifices are unnecessary, privations are unnecessary, unnecessary. Desire to be happy: this desire, this desire alone, is indispensable. With this end in view you will work with pleasure for your development, for there lies happiness.

Oh! how great the pleasure enjoyed by a man of developed mind! That which would make another suffer he feels to be a satisfaction, a pleasure, so many are the joys to which his heart is open.

Try it, and you will see how good it is.

CHAPTER FOURTH.

The Life of Véra Pavlovna with her Second Husband.

I.

Berlin, July 20, 1856.

Madame and highly esteemed Véra Pavlovna:

My intimacy with Dmitry Serguéitch Lopoukhoff, who has just perished, and my profound esteem for you lead me to hope that you will kindly admit me among the number of your acquaintances, although I am entirely unknown to you. However that may be, I make bold to believe that you will not accuse me of importunity. I but execute effectively the will of this poor Dmitry Serguéitch; and you may consider the information which I have to communicate to you on his account as perfectly authentic, for the good reason that I am going to give you his own thoughts in his own words, as if he were speaking himself.

These are his words upon the matter which it is the object of my letter to clear up:

"The ideas which have resulted in pushing me to the act that has so much alarmed my intimate friends [I give you the very words of Dmitry Serguéitch, as I have already told you] ripened in me gradually, and changed several times before taking their definitive form. It was quite unexpectedly that I was struck by the event which threw me into these thoughts, and only when she [Dmitry Serguéitch refers to you] told me with fright a dream that had horrified her. This dream made a great impression on me, and as a man who analyzed the feelings which caused it I understood from that moment that new horizons were about to dawn upon her life, and that for a longer or shorter time the nature of our relations would completely change. One always tries to maintain to the last extremity the position which one has made for himself. At the bottom of our nature lies that conservative element which we abandon only when forced to do so. There, in my opinion, is to be found the explanation of my first supposition. I wished to believe, and I did really believe, that this change would not be of long duration, that our old relations would be reestablished. She even tried to escape this change by holding herself to me as closely as possible. That had its influence upon me, and for some days I believed it possible to realize her hope. But I soon saw, nevertheless, that this hope was vain.

"The reason lies in my character, which, in so speaking of it, I in no wise blame. I simply so understand things.

"He who employs his time well divides it into three parts, — work, pleasure, rest or distraction. Pleasure demands rest as much as work does. In work and in pleasure the human element predominates over individual peculiarities. We are driven to labor by the preponderant motive of external rational needs. To pleasure by the preponderant motive of other needs of human nature,—needs quite as general. By rest and distraction the individual seeks to reëstablish his forces after the excitement which has exhausted them. In this the individual decides freely for himself in accordance with his personal tastes and proclivities. In work and in pleasure men are drawn to each other by a powerful general force above their personal peculiarities,—in work by a clearly understood self-interest, and in pleasure by the identical needs of the organism. In rest it is not the same. Here there is no general force acting to dominate individual peculiarities: leisure is of all things the most personal, the thing in which nature demands most liberty; here man most individualizes himself, each seeking the satisfaction most agreeable to him.

"In this respect men are divided into two principal categories. For those of one category leisure or distraction is most agreeable in the society of others. Solitude is indispensable to every one. But to them it is indispensable that it should be an exception, their rule being life with others. This class is much more numerous than the other, which needs the opposite. Those of the latter class are more at ease in solitude than in society. This divergence has been remarked by general opinion, which has signified it by the expressions 'sociable men' and 'unsociable men.' I belong to the category of the unsociables, she to that of the sociables. That is the whole secret of our history. It is clear that neither of us is to blame for this, any more than either of us is to blame for not having strength enough to remove this cause: man can do nothing against his own nature.

"It is very difficult for us to understand the peculiarities of other natures; every man pictures all other men to himself from the standpoint of his own character. That which I do not need others need no more than I: so our individuality manifests itself. I need more than evidence to recall me to the opposite feeling. The situation which suits me ought, in my opinion, to suit others. This tendency of thought being natural, in it I find my excuse for having remarked too late the difference between her nature and my own. This is important. When we began to live together, she placed me on too high a pedestal: so at that time we did not stand on an equality. She had too much esteem for me; my way of living seemed to her exemplary; she considered my individual peculiarity as a characteristic befitting all men, and for a time she was under its influence. There was, besides, a reason that controlled her in a different way.

"The inviolability of the inner life is very lightly esteemed among people of but little intellectual development. Every member of the family—especially the oldest members—unceremoniously thrusts his nose into your private life. Not that our secrets are thereby violated: secrets are things more or less precious, which one does not forget to conceal and guard. Moreover, every man does not have them, so numerous are those who have nothing to hide from their relatives. But every one wishes to keep a little corner of his inner life into which no one may penetrate, just as every one wishes to have a room of his own. People of but little intellectual development pay small respect either to the one or the other: even if you have a room of your own, everybody walks into it, not exactly to watch you or intrude upon you, but because they do not dream that they may disturb you; they imagine that you can object to unexpected visits from none but those whom you dislike; they do not understand that, even with the best intentions, one may be intrusive. The threshold, which no one has a right to cross against the will of the interested party, is respected only in one case, that of the head of the family, who may put out by the shoulders whoever intrudes upon him. All the rest must submit to any and every intrusion and on the most idle pretexts, or even without any pretext at all. A young girl has two every-day dresses, one white and the other red; she puts on the red dress; that is enough to start the babble.

" ' You have put on your red dress, Anuta; why did you do so?'

" Anuta herself does not know why; she had to put on one, and, after all, if she had put on her white dress, it would have been just the same.

" ' I do not know, mamma,' (or, ' my sister').

" ' You would do better to put on your white dress.'

" Why would she do better? Anuta's questioner does not know, herself; only she must say something.

" ' You are not gay today, Anuta.'

" Anuta is neither gay nor sad.

" ' I did not know it; it seems to me that I am just as usual.'

" ' No, you are not gay.'

" Two minutes later:

" ' If you would play a little on the piano, Anuta.'

" Why, no one knows; and so it goes all day. As if your soul were a street and every one stationed himself at the window to look into it, not expecting to see anything,— knowing, in fact, that he will see nothing useful or interesting,— but looking because he has nothing else to do. Why should not one look into the street? And, indeed, to the street it is a matter of indifference; but man does not like to be intruded upon.

" It is natural that these intrusions, without purpose or intention, should provoke a reaction; and as soon as the individual finds himself in a position to live alone, he takes pleasure for some time in solitude, though naturally inclined to society.

" To come back to the person in question. Before marrying she was in a very peculiar situation; she was intruded upon, her thoughts were scrutinized, not simply to kill time, or even through indelicacy, but systematically, shamelessly, grossly, and with bad intentions. Consequently the reaction was very strong in her.

"That is why my fault must not be judged too severely. For some months, perhaps a year, I was not mistaken: she did, indeed, need solitude, and took pleasure in it. And during that time I formed my idea of her character. Her intense temporary need of solitude was identical with my constant need; why is it astonishing, then, that I should have taken a temporary phenomenon for a constant trait of her character? Every one is led to judge others by himself!

"This is a fault and a pretty serious one. I do not accuse myself, but I am moved, nevertheless, to justify myself; that is, I foresee that others will not be as indulgent for me as I am for myself. That is why, in order to soften the blame and help to an understanding, I must enter into some details about my character relatively to the subject which we are considering.

"I have no idea of rest except in solitude. To be in society means to me to busy one's self with something, or to work, or to delight one's self.

"I feel completely at my ease only when I am alone. What shall we call this feeling? What is its origin? In some it comes from dissimulation; in others, from timidity; in a third class, from a tendency to melancholy; in a fourth, from a lack of sympathy for others. It seems to me that I have none of these things. I am straightforward and sincere; I am always ready to be gay, and am never sad. Company pleases me: only it is all combined for me either with work or with pleasure. But these occupations must be relieved by rest,—that is, by solitude. As far as I can understand myself, I am moved by a desire of independence, of liberty.

"So the force of the reaction against her old family life led her to accept for a time a way of life not in conformity with her steady inclinations; her esteem for me maintained these temporary dispositions in her longer than they would otherwise have lasted. Then I said to myself that I had formed a false idea of her character: I had taken her inclinations of the moment for steady inclinations; and I rested on this thought. That is the whole story. On my side there is a fault deserving of not much blame; on hers there is no fault at all. How much suffering all this has cost her, and by what a catastrophe am I forced to put an end to it!

"When the fright occasioned by her horrible dream had opened my eyes to the state of her feelings, it was already too late to repair my fault. But if we had seen sooner what she lacked, it is possible that, by making steady efforts over ourselves, she and I would have succeeded in achieving a sort of contentment with each other. But I do not believe that, had we succeeded, anything good would have resulted from it. Suppose we had reconstructed our characters sufficiently to render them harmonious; conversions, nevertheless, are good only when brought into action against some evil proclivities; now, the proclivities that we should have had to change are in no way blameworthy. In what respect is sociability worse or better than the desire for solitude, and *vice versa?* Now, conversion, after all, is violence, dispersion; in dispersion many things are lost, and the effect of violence is to stupefy.

"The result that we perhaps (perhaps!) should have attained would not have been a compensation. We should have become insignificant and should have withered more or less the freshness of our life. And why? To keep certain places in certain rooms? If we had had children, that would have been another matter; then we should have had to consider carefully the possibly bad influence that our separation would have had upon their fortunes. In that case it would have been necessary to make every possible effort to avoid this *dénoûment*, and the result—the joy of having done all that was necessary to make those dear to us happier—would have rewarded adequately all our efforts. But in the actual state of things what rational object could our efforts have had?

"Consequently, the present situation being given, all is arranged for the best. We have not had to violate our natures. We have had much sorrow, but, had we acted any otherwise, we should have had much more, and the result would not have been as satisfactory."

Such are the words of Dmitry Serguéitch. You can easily see with what persistence he has dwelt in this matter upon what he calls his wrongs. He added: "I feel sure that those who analyze my conduct without sympathy for me will find that I have not been entirely right. But I am sure of their sympathy for her. She will judge me even better than I judge myself. Now, for my part, I believe that I have done perfectly right. Such is my opinion of my conduct up to the time of the dream."

Now I am going to communicate to you his feelings concerning the subsequent events:

"I have said [Dmitry Serguéitch's words] that from the first words that she uttered about her dream I understood that a change in our relations was inevitable. I expected that this change would be a pretty radical one, for it was impossible that it should be otherwise, considering the energy of her nature and the intensity of her discontent at that time; and her discontent was all the greater from having been long suppressed. Nevertheless, I looked only for an external change and one quite to my advantage. I said to myself: 'For a time she will be under the influence of a passionate love for some one; then, a year or two having gone by, she will come back. I am an estimable man; the chances of finding another man like me are very rare (I say what I think, and have not hypocrisy enough to underrate my merits); her feeling will lose a portion of its intensity by satisfaction; and she will see that, although one side of her nature is less satisfied in living with me, on the whole she is happier and freer with me than with any one else. Then things will again shape themselves as in the past. Having learned by experience, I shall bestow more attentions upon her, she will have a greater and keener attachment for me, and we shall live more harmoniously than in the past.'

"But (this is a thing which it is a very delicate matter for me to explain, and yet it must be done),—but what effect did the prospect of this reëstablishment of our relations have upon me? Did it rejoice me? Evidently. But was that all? No, I looked forward to it as a burden, a very agreeable burden, to be sure, but still a burden. I loved her much, and would have violated my nature to put myself in greater harmony with her; that would have given me pleasure, but my life would have been under restraint. That was the way in which I looked at things after the first impression had passed away, and I have seen that I was not mistaken. She put me to the proof of that, when she wished me to force myself to keep her love. The month of complaisance which I devoted to her was the most painful month of my life. There was no suffering in it,—that expression would be out of place and even absurd, for I felt only joy in trying to please her,—but it wearied me. That is the secret of the failure of her attempt to preserve her love for me.

"At first blush that may seem strange. Why did I not get weary of devoting so many evenings to students, for whom I certainly would not have seriously disturbed myself, and why did I feel so much fatigue from devoting only a few evenings to a woman whom I loved more than myself and for whom I was ready to die, and not only to die, but to suffer all sorts of torments? It is strange, I admit, but only to one who has not fathomed the nature of my relations with the young, to whom I devoted so much time. In the first place, I had no personal relations with these young people; when I was with them, I did not seem to have men before me, but abstract types exchanging ideas; my conversations with them were hardly to be distinguished from my solitary dreams; but one side of the man was occupied, that which demands the least rest,—thought. All the rest slept. And furthermore the conversation had a practical, a useful object,—coöperation for the development of the intellectual life and the perfecting of my young friends. This was so easy a task that it rather reëstablished my strength, exhausted by other work,—a task which did not tire me, but, on the contrary, refreshed me; nevertheless, it was a task, and it was not rest that I was after, but a useful object. In short, I let my whole being go to sleep, thought excepted, and that acted without being troubled by any personal prepossession regarding the men with whom I was talking; consequently, I felt as much at my ease as if I had been alone. These conversations did not take me out of my solitude, so to speak. There was nothing in them similar to the relations in which the entire man participates.

"I know what a delicate matter it is to utter the word 'ennui'; but sincerity will not permit me to withhold it. Yes, with all my love for her, I felt a sense of relief when later I became convinced that our relations were forever broken. I became convinced of it about the time when she perceived that to comply with her desires was a burden to me. Then my future seemed to assume a more agreeable shape; seeing that it was impossible to maintain our old relations, I began to consider by what method we could soonest — I must again use a delicate expression — consummate the separation. That is why those who judge only by appearances have been able to believe in my generosity. Nevertheless I do not wish to be hypocritical and deny the good that is in me; therefore I must add that one of my motives was the desire to see her happy. But this was only a secondary motive, a strong one enough, to be sure, but far inferior in intensity to the first and principal motive, — the desire to escape *ennui:* that was the principal motive. It was under this influence that I began to analyze attentively her manner of life, and I easily discovered that the person in question was dominated in her feelings and acts by the presence and absence of Alexander Matvéitch. That obliged me to consider him also. Then I understood the cause of her strange actions, to which I had at first paid no attention. That made me see things in a still more agreeable light. When I saw in her not only the desire for a passionate love, but also the love itself, an unconscious love for a man entirely worthy of her and able to completely replace me at her side; when I saw that this man too had a great passion for her, — I was thoroughly rejoiced. It is true, however, that the first impression was a painful one: no grave change takes place without some sorrow. I saw now that I could no longer conscientiously consider myself indispensable to her, as I had been accustomed to do and with delight; this new change, therefore, had a painful side. But not long. Now I was sure of her happiness and felt no anxiety about her. That was a source of great joy. But it would be an error to believe that that was my chief pleasure; no, personal feeling was dominant even here: I saw that I was to be free. I do not mean that single life seemed to me freer than family life; no, if husband and wife make each other mutually happy without effort and without thought, the more intimate their relations the happier they are. But our relations were not of that character. Consequently to me separation meant freedom.

"It will be seen that I acted in my own interest, when I decided not to stand in the way of their happiness; there was a noble side to my conduct, but the motive power was the desire of my own nature for a more comfortable situation. And that is why I had the strength to act well, to do without hesitation and without pain what I believed to be my duty: one does his duty easily when impelled by his own nature.

"I started for Riazan. Some time afterwards she called me back, saying that my presence would not trouble her. I took the contrary view, — for two reasons, as I believe. It was painful to her to see the man to whom (in her opinion) she owed so much. She was mistaken; she was under no obligation to me, because I had always acted much more in my own interest than in hers. But she saw it differently, and moreover she felt a very profound attachment for me, which was a source of pain. This attachment had also its agreeable side, but this could not have become dominant unless it had been less intense, for, when intense, it is very painful. The second motive (another delicate explanation, but I must say what I think) arose from the fact that her rather abnormal situation in the matter of social conditions was disagreeable to her. Thus I came to see that the proximity of my existence to hers was painful to her. I will not deny that to this new discovery there was a side incomparably more painful to me than all the feelings that I had experienced in the preceding stages of the affair. I retained very good dispositions toward her: I wished to remain her friend. I hoped that such would be the case. And when I saw that it could not be, I was much grieved. And my chagrin was compensated by no personal interest. I may say, then, that my final resolution was taken only through attachment to her, through a desire to see her happy. Consequently, my conduct toward her even in our happiest days never gave me so much inner satisfaction as this resolution. Then at last I acted under the influence of what I may call nobility, or, to speak more accurately, noble design, in which the general law of human nature acts wholly by itself without the aid of individual peculiarities; and I learned to know the high enjoyment of seeing one's self act nobly,—that is, in the way in which all men without exception ought to act. This high enjoyment of feeling one's self simply a man, and not Ivan or Peter, is too intense; ordinary natures like mine cannot stand it too often. But happy the man who has sometimes felt it!

"I do not need to explain this side of my conduct, which would have been senseless to the last degree in dealing with other men; it is, however, only too well justified by the character of the person to whom I yielded. When I was at Riazan, not a word passed between her and Alexander Matvéitch. Later, at the time when I took my final resolution, not a word passed between him and me or between her and me. But to know their thoughts I did not need to hear them."

I have transmitted literally the words of Dmitry Serguéitch, as I have already said.

I am an entire stranger to you, but the correspondence upon which I enter with you, in carrying out the will of poor Dmitry Serguéitch, is of so intimate a nature that you will be curious perhaps to know who this unknown correspondent is, who is so familiar with Dmitry's inner life. I am a medical student who has renounced his profession; I can tell you nothing more about myself. Of late years I have lived in St. Petersburg. A few days ago I conceived the idea of travelling and seeking a new career in foreign lands. I left St. Petersburg the day after you learned of Dmitry's loss. By the merest chance I did not have my passport, but I succeeded in getting that of another, which one of our common acquaintances had the kindness to furnish me. He gave them to me on condition that I would do

The Life of Véra Pavlovna with her Second Husband. 249

some errands for him on the way. If you happen to see M. Rakhmétoff, be kind enough to tell him that all his commissions have been attended to. Now I am going to wander about for a while,—probably in Germany observing the customs of the people. I have a few hundred roubles, and I wish to live at my ease and without doing anything. When I grow weary of idleness, I shall look for work. Of what sort? It is of no consequence. Where? It matters not. I am as free as a bird, and I can be as careless as a bird. Such a situation enchants me.

Probably you will wish to reply, but I do not know where I shall be a week hence,—perhaps in Italy, perhaps in England, perhaps at Prague. Now I can live according to my caprice, and where it will take me I know not. Consequently, upon your letters place only this address: "*Berlin, Friedrichstrasse 20, Agentur von H. Schmeidler*"; within this envelope place another containing your letter, and upon the inner envelope, instead of any address, write the figures 12345; to the Schmeidler agency that will mean that the letter is to be sent to me. Accept, Madame, the assurance of the high esteem of a man unknown to you, but profoundly devoted to you, who signs himself

A QUONDAM MEDICAL STUDENT.

My much esteemed Monsieur Alexander Matvéitch:

In conformity with the wishes of poor Dmitry Serguéitch, I must tell you that he considered the obligation to yield his place to you the best conclusion possible. The circumstances which have induced this change have gradually come about within the last three years, in which you had almost abandoned his society, and without, consequently, any share in them on your part. This change results solely from the acts of two individuals whom you have tried in vain to bring together, and the conclusion was inevitable. It is needless to say that Dmitry Sergúeitch could in no way attribute it to you. Of course this explanation is superfluous, and it is only for form's sake that he has charged me with making it. He was not fitted for the situation which he occupied, and in his opinion it is better for all that he has yielded his place to you.

I shake your hand.

A QUONDAM MEDICAL STUDENT.

"And, for my part, I know" . . . .

What's that? The voice is familiar to me. I look behind me; it is he, it is really he, the reader with the penetrating eye; lately expelled for knowing neither A nor B on a question of art, here he is again, and with his usual penetration again he knows something.

"Ah! I know who wrote that" . . . . .

I seize precipitately the first object that comes to my hand,—it is a napkin, inasmuch as, after copying the letter of the quondam student, I sat down to breakfast,—I seize the napkin and I close his mouth. "Well! know then! but why cry out like a madman?"

II.

St. Petersburg, August 25, 1856.

Monsieur:

You cannot imagine how happy I was to receive your letter. I thank you with all my heart. Your intimacy with Dmitry Sergueïtch, who has just perished, entitles me to consider you a friend, and permit me to call you so.

In each of the words which you have communicated to me I have recognized the character of Dmitry Sergueïtch. He was always searching for the most hidden causes of his acts, and it pleased him to apply thereto the theory of egoism. For that matter it is a habit common to all our circle. My Alexander also is fond of analyzing himself in this fashion. If you could hear how he explains his conduct towards me and Dmitry Sergueïtch for the last three years! To hear him, he did everything from selfish design, for his own pleasure. I, too, long since acquired this habit. Only it occupies us — Alexander and me — a little less than Dmitry Sergueïtch; we have the same inclination, only his was stronger. Yes, to hear us, we are all three the greatest egoists that the world has yet seen. And perhaps it is the truth. It is possible, after all.

But, besides this trait, common to all three of us, the words of Dmitry Sergueïtch contain something peculiar to himself: the object of his explanations is evident, — to quiet me. Not that his words are not wholly sincere, — he never said what he did not think, — but he makes too prominent that side of the truth calculated to quiet me. I am very grateful to you, my friend, but I too am an egoist, and I will say that his anxiety on my account was useless. We justify ourselves much more easily than others justify us. I too do not consider myself at all guilty towards him; I will say more: I do not even feel under any obligation to have an attachment for him. I appreciate highly his noble conduct, but I know that he acted nobly, not for me, but for himself; and I, in not deceiving him, acted, not for him, but for myself, — not because, in deceiving him, I should have been unjust to him, but because to do so was repugnant to me. I say, like him, that I do not accuse myself. But like him also I am moved to justify myself; to use his expression (a very correct one), that means that I foresee that others will not be as indulgent as myself regarding some phases of my conduct. I have no desire to justify myself regarding that part of the matter upon which he touches; but, on the other hand, I have a desire to justify myself regarding the part upon which he does not need to justify himself. No one will call me guilty on account of what took place before my dream. But, then, is it not my fault that the affair took so melodramatic an aspect and led to a theatrical conclusion? Ought I not to have taken a much simpler view of a change of relations already inevitable, when my dream for the first time opened the eyes of Dmitry Serguéitch and myself to my situation? In the evening of the day when Dmitry Serguéitch died, I had a long conversation with that ferocious Rakhmétoff; what a good and tender man, that Rakhmétoff! He said I know not how many horrible things about Dmitry Serguéitch. But, if one should repeat them in a friendly tone, they would be almost just.

I believed that Dmitry Serguéitch knew perfectly well what Rakhmétoff was going to say to me, and that he had calculated upon it. In my state of mind I needed to hear him, and his remarks did much to quiet me. Whoever planned that conversation, I thank you much, my friend. But the ferocious Rakhmétoff himself had to confess that in the last half of the affair the conduct of Dmitry Serguéitch was perfect. Rakhmétoff blamed him only for the first half, concerning which it pleased Dmitry Serguéitch to justify himself.

But I am going to justify myself concerning the second half, although no one has told me that I was guilty. But every one of us — I speak of ourselves and our friends, of our whole circle — has a severer censor than Rakhmétoff himself, — his or her own mind. Yes, I understand, my friend, that it would have been much easier for all if I had taken a simpler view of the affair and had not given it so tragic a bearing. And, if we leave it to the opinion of Dmitry Serguéitch, I shall have to say further that he would then have had no need to resort to a sensational climax very painful to him: he had to act as he did only because pushed by my impetuous way of looking at things.

I suppose that he must have thought so too, although he did not charge you to tell me so. I set the higher value on his good feelings towards me from the fact that, in spite of all that happened, they did not weaken. But listen, my friend; this opinion is not just; it was not from any fault of mine, it was not from my unnecessary exaggeration of feeling, that the necessity presented itself to Dmitry Serguéitch of an experience which he himself calls very painful. It is true that, if I had not attached a great importance to the change of relations, the journey to Riazan might have been dispensed with, but he says that that was not painful to him; in this respect, then, my excitement caused no great unhappiness. It was only the necessity of dying that was painful to him. He explains by two reasons why he was forced to adopt that resolution.

In the first place, I suffered from my extreme attachment for him; in the second, I suffered because I could not give my relations with Alexander the character demanded by public opinion. In fact, I was not altogether tranquil; my situation was burdensome, but he did not divine the real cause. He believed that his presence was painful to me on account of the depth of my gratitude; this was not quite the case. We are very much disposed to look for consoling thoughts, and when Dmitry Serguéitch saw the necessity of dying, that necessity had long ceased to exist; my gratitude had decreased to that moderate degree which constitutes an agreeable feeling. Now, deep gratitude was the sole cause of my painful exaggeration of feeling. The other cause mentioned by Dmitry Serguéitch — the desire to give my relations with Alexander the character demanded by society — did not depend at all upon my way of viewing the affair. It was the result of society's ideas. That cause I could not have controlled; but Dmitry Serguéitch was absolutely mistaken if he supposed that his presence was painful to me for that reason. If a husband lives with his wife, that is enough to prevent scandal, whatever the relations of his wife with another. That is a great step already. We see many examples where, thanks to the noble character of the husband, affairs are thus arranged, and in that case society lets the woman alone. Now, I consider that the best and easiest way of arranging affairs of this sort. Dmitry Serguéitch at first proposed this plan to me. I then refused on account of my exaggeration of feeling. I do not know what would have happened if I had accepted; but, if I had been able to content myself with being left alone and the avoidance of scandal regarding my relations with Alexander, it is evident that the plan proposed by Dmitry Serguéitch would have been sufficient, and that, if I had adopted it, there would have been no need of his decision to die. In that case evidently I should have had no reason to desire to formally determine my relations with Alexander. But it seems to me that such an arrangement, satisfactory in most cases similar to ours, in ours would not have been so. Our situation had one peculiar feature, — the three individuals whom it concerned were of equal force. If Dmitry Serguéitch had felt an intellectual and moral superiority in Alexander; if, in yielding his place to him, he had yielded to moral superiority; if his withdrawal, instead of being voluntary, had been only the withdrawal of the weak before the strong, — why, then certainly nothing would have weighed upon me. Likewise, if I had been superior in mind and character to Dmitry Serguéitch; if he himself, before the birth of my passion, had been one of the two heroes of a certain anecdote which once made us laugh so heartily, — all would have been arranged, he would have submitted. The anecdote was of two gentlemen who, after having conversed some time and being pleased with each other, desired to make each other's acquaintance:

"I am Lieutenant So-and-So," said one, with an air of dignity.

"And I am the husband of Madame Tedesco," said the other.

If Dmitry Serguéitch had been the husband of Madame Tedesco, why, then he would have had no need to resort to extremities, he would have submitted to his fate, he would have seen nothing offensive to him in his submission, and everything would have been delightful. But his relations with me and with Alexander were not at all of such a character. In no respect was he either our inferior or our superior; this was evident to all. My liberty could depend only on his good will and not at all on his weakness. You cannot deny it, my friend.

What, then, was my situation? I saw myself dependent on his good will. That was why my situation was painful to me, that was why he deemed it useful to adopt his noble resolution. Yes, my friend, the cause of my feeling, which forced him to this step, was much more deeply hidden than he explains in your letter. The overwhelming degree of gratitude no longer existed. To satisfy the requirements of society would have been easy in the way proposed by Dmitry Serguéitch himself, and, after all, these requirements did not affect me, living in my little circle, entirely beyond the reach of gossip. But I remained dependent upon Dmitry Serguéitch. That was the painful part of it. What had my view of the change of our relations to do with this? Dmitry Serguéitch remained the master. Now, you know and approve my feeling: I do not wish to be dependent upon the good will of any one, though he were the most devoted of men, the man whom I most esteemed, in whom I believed as in another self, and in whom I had full confidence. I do not wish it, and I know that you approve this. But why so many words? Why this analysis of our inmost feelings, which no one would have gone into? Like Dmitry Serguéitch, I have a mania for undressing my feelings in order that I may say: It is not my fault, but the result of a circumstance beyond my control? I make this remark because Dmitry Serguéitch liked remarks of this character. I wish to insinuate myself into your mind, my friend. But enough of this! You have had so much sympathy for me that you have thought nothing of the few hours required to write your long and precious letter. From it I see (whether from Dmitry Serguéitch's style or yours),—yes, I see that you will be curious to know what became of me after Dmitry Serguéitch left me to go to Moscow and then to come back and die. On his return from Riazan he saw that I was embarrassed. This was manifest in me only in his presence; as long as he was at Riazan, I did not think so much about him. But, when he started for Moscow, I saw that he was meditating something grave. He settled up his affairs at St. Petersburg. He had been waiting for a week only to get everything arranged for his departure, and why should I not have foreseen this? During the last days I sometimes saw sadness on his face, on that face which knew so well how to hide secrets. I foresaw that something decisive was to be expected. And when he boarded the train, I was so sad! The next day and the day after my sorrow increased. Suddenly Macha brought me a letter. What a painful moment! What a painful day! You know it. How much better I know now the strength of my attachment for Dmitry Serguéitch! I had no idea myself that it was so deep. You know the strength of our mutual attachment. You certainly know that I had then decided to see Alexander no more; all day I felt that my life was broken forever, and you know of my childish enthusiasm when I saw the note of my good, my very good, friend, the note that changed completely all my thoughts (notice the prudence of my expressions; you must be contented with them, my friend). You know all this, because Rakhmétoff, after escorting me to the train, went to accompany you to the station; Dmitry Serguéitch and he were right in saying that I ought nevertheless to leave St. Petersburg in order to produce the effect so much desired by Dmitry Serguéitch that he inflicted upon me to achieve it such horrible torments for an entire day. How grateful I am to him for having had so little pity on me! He and Rakhmétoff were also right in advising Alexander not to appear before me or escort me to the station. But, as I no longer needed to go as far as Moscow, it being necessary only to leave St. Petersburg, I stopped at Novgorod. A few days later Alexander came there with the documents establishing the loss of Dmitry Serguéitch. We were married a week after this loss, and have lived almost a month at Tchoudovo,* near the railroad, in order that it may be easy for Alexander to go three or four times a week to his hospital. Yesterday we returned to St. Petersburg, and that is why I am so late in answering your letter. It has remained in Macha's box, who had almost forgotten it. And you have probably framed all sorts of ideas in consequence of receiving no reply.

I clasp you in my arms, my friend.

Yours,

Véra Kirsanoff.

I grasp your hand, my dear; only I beg you not to send compliments, at least to me; else I will let my heart flow out before you in a torrent of adoration, which would certainly be disagreeable to you in the highest degree. But do you know that for us to write so briefly to each other shows considerable stupidity in me as well as in you? It seems that we are somewhat embarrassed in each other's presence. Supposing that this were pardonable in me, why should you feel any embarrassment? Next time I hope to talk freely with you, and I shall forthwith write you a heap of St. Petersburg news.

Yours,

Alexander Kirsanoff.

III.

These letters, while perfectly sincere, were indeed a little exclusive, as Véra Parlovna herself remarked. The two correspondents evidently tried to make the painful shocks which they had felt seem less intense to each other. They are very shrewd people. I have very often heard them — them and those like them — say things which made me laugh heartily in the midst of their pathetic assertions that such and such a thing was nothing and could easily be endured.

I laughed at such assertions when made privately to me, a stranger. And when I heard them said before a man who could not help listening, I corroborated them,

---

* A railway station and large village situated about sixty-five miles from St. Petersburg.

and said that such and such a thing was indeed nothing. An honest man is very queer; I have always laughed at them when I have met them. They are sometimes even absurd. Take, for example, these letters. I am a little accustomed to such things, being on terms of friendship with them, but on an entire stranger what an impression they must make,—on the reader with the penetrating eye, for instance!

The reader with the penetrating eye, who has already had time to get clear of his napkin, pronounces sentence, shaking his head:

"Immoral!"

"Bravo! Do me the favor of saying one word more."

"The author also is an immoral man to approve such things," says the reader with the penetrating eye, adding to the sentence.

"No, my dear, you are mistaken. There are many things in this that I do not approve, and, to tell the truth, I do not even approve any of it. It is all much too ingenious, much too far-fetched; life is much simpler."

"Then you are still more immoral?" asks the reader with the penetrating eye, opening his eyes wide, astonished at the inconceivable immorality into which humanity has fallen in my person.

"Much more immoral," I say, and no one knows whether I am telling the truth or laughing at the reader with the penetrating eye.

The correspondence lasted three or four months longer,—actively on the part of the Kirsanoffs, negligently and inadequately on the part of their correspondent. The latter soon ceased to answer their letters; they saw that his sole intention was to communicate to Véra Pavlovna and her husband the thoughts of Lopoukhoff, and that, after having fulfilled this duty, he deemed further correspondence useless. Having obtained no reply to two or three letters, the Kirsanoffs understood him and stopped writing.

IV.

Véra Pavlovna is resting on her soft couch, waiting for her husband to come back from the hospital to dinner. Today she does not care to make pastry for dinner; she prefers to rest, for she has worked hard all the morning. It has been so for a long time, and it will be so for a very long time to come: she is starting another workshop for seamstresses at the other extremity of the city. Véra Pavlovna Lopoukhoff lived on the island of Vassilievsky, Véra Pavlovna Kirsanoff lives on the Rue Serguievskaia, her husband requiring rooms in the neighborhood of the Wyborg district.

Madame Mertzaloff proved equal to the management of the shop on the island of Vassilievsky, which was quite natural, she and the shop being old acquaintances. On her return to St. Petersburg Véra Pavlovna saw that she did not need to visit the shop often to see that things went well, and, though she continued to visit it almost daily, it was solely because she was drawn by her sympathy. It must be added, however, that her visits were not quite useless, for Madame Mertzaloff often needed her advice; but that took very little time, besides being needed less and less frequently. Madame Mertzaloff will soon have as much experience as herself, and will be able to conduct things herself. After her return to St. Petersburg Véra Pavlovna visited the island of Vassilievsky more as a dear friend than as an indispensable person; what, then, was to be done? Establish a new workshop for seamstresses, in her own neighborhood, at the other end of the city.

So, in fact, a new shop was established in one of the smaller streets between the Rue Basseinaïa and the Rue Serguievskaïa. Here there is much less work than in the first shop: the first five of the working-girls are from the old shop, where their places have been filled by others; the rest of the force is made up of acquaintances of the seamstresses in the old shop. So, everything is half done, to start with. All the comrades are perfectly familiar with the purpose and organization of the shop; the young girls came filled with a desire to establish promptly in the new shop the organization which had been effected so slowly in the old. Oh! now the organization went ahead ten times faster than then, and with three times less embarrassment. But none the less there was a great deal of work to be done, and Véra Pavlovna was tired, as she had been yesterday, and day before yesterday, and as she had been for about two months. Two months only, although six months had elapsed since her second marriage; after all, it was very necessary that she should allow herself a honeymoon; now she had resumed work.

Yes, she had worked a great deal; now she was resting and thinking of many things, especially of the present; it is so beautiful and so full! So full of life that but little time is left for memories; memories will come later. Oh! much later! Not in ten years, nor even in twenty, but later still. Nevertheless, they do come even now, though rarely. At this moment, for example, she is recalling what has most impressed her. Here is what her memory brings back to her.

V.

"My darling, I am going with you."

"But you have not your things."

"I will go tomorrow, since you will not take me with you today."

"Reflect, meditate. And await my letter. It will reach you tomorrow."

There she is on her way back from the station to the house; what does she feel and what does she think as she comes back with Macha? She hardly knows, herself, so shaken has she been by the rapid shaping of events. It is but twenty-two hours since he found in his room the letter which she had written, and already he is gone! How quickly, how suddenly! At two o'clock in the morning she foresaw nothing of this. He waited till, conquered and exhausted by fatigue, she was overcome by sleep; then he entered her room and said a few not over-sensible words as a scarcely comprehensible preface to this bit of information:

"I have not seen my old parents in a long time; I am going to see them; they will be very glad."

Only that, and then he went out. She ran after him, although he had made her promise not to do so.

"Where is he, then? Macha, where is he, where is he?"

Macha, who was still engaged in clearing the tea-table just left by visitors, answered:

"Dmitry Serguéitch went out; he said, as he passed by, 'I am going to walk.'"

She had to go back to bed. How could she sleep? She did not know that his departure was to take place in a few hours. He had said that they still had time to talk over all these things together. And when she awoke, it was time to go to the station.

All this passes before her eyes like a flash, as if it had not happened to her, but had been the experience of some one else, which had been told to her hastily. Only on reaching the house does she regain possession of herself, and begin to think: What is she now? what is to become of her?

Yes, she will go to Riazan. She will go. To do otherwise is impossible. But the letter? What will it say? Why wait for it before deciding? She knows the contents in advance. No, it is necessary to wait until the letter comes. But what is the use of waiting? She will go. Yes, she will go. She repeats it to herself for one, two, three, four hours. But Macha, getting hungry, is already calling her to dinner for the third time, and this time she orders rather than calls; well, it is at least a distraction.

"Poor Macha, she must be very hungry on my account. Why did you wait for me, Macha? You would have done better to dine without waiting for me."

"That cannot be, Véra Pavlovna."

And again the young woman reflects for two hours:

"I will go. Tomorrow. Only I will wait for the letter, for he begged me to. But, whatever its contents,—I know what it will contain,—I will go."

That is what she thinks; but is that really all? No, her thought still runs upon five little words: *He does not wish it*, and these five little words dominate her thought more and more. The setting sun finds her still absorbed. And just at the moment when the importunate Macha comes to demand that she shall take tea, six words add themselves to the five: *Nor do I wish it either*. Macha has entered; she has driven away these six new bad little words. But not for long. At first they do not dare to make their appearance, and give place to their own refutation: *But I must go*; but they yield only to come back escorted by this refutation. In a twinkling they return to Véra Pavlovna's thought: *He does not wish it — Nor do I wish it either.* For half an hour they dance a saraband in her brain; then against these words so often uttered, *I will go,* rush these three, *Shall I go?* But here comes Macha again.

"I gave a rouble to the bearer, Véra Pavlovna, for it was written on the envelope that, if he brought the letter before nine o'clock, he should be given a rouble; if after that, only half as much. Now, he brought it before nine o'clock. To go faster he took a cab; 'I did as I promised,' he said to me."

A letter from him! She knows what it contains: "Do not come." But she will go just the same; she does not wish to listen to this letter. The letter contains something else, — something which cannot be disregarded:

"I am going to Riazan, but not directly. I have many business matters to attend to on the way. Besides Moscow, where press of business will oblige me to spend a week, I must stop at two cities this side of Moscow and three places the other side, before reaching Riazan. How much time I shall have to sacrifice in this way I cannot tell. For instance, I have to collect some money from our commercial representatives, and you know, my dear friend [these words, *dear friend,* were repeated in the letter that I might see that he was still well-disposed towards me; how I kissed these words!], — you know, my dear friend, that, when one has to collect money, he often has to wait several days where he expected to stay but a few hours. So I absolutely cannot fix the day of my arrival at Riazan, but it surely will not be immediately."

Véra Pavlovna still remembers word for word the contents of this letter. What, then, is to be done? He deprives her of all dependence upon him by which she may remain attached to him. And the words, *I must go to him,* change into these: *Nevertheless I must not see him,* and in the latter sentence the word *him* refers to another person. She repeats these words for an hour or two: *I must not see him.* Of this thought is born another: *Is it possible that I wish to see him? No.* When she goes to sleep, this last thought gives way to another: *Will it be possible for me to see him?* No answer, but a new transformation: *Is it possible that I may not see him?* And she sleeps till morning in this last thought: *Is it possible that I may not see him?*

And when she awakes very late in the morning, all the thoughts of the evening before and of the night give way to these two, which clash against each other: *I will see him! I will not see him!* That lasts all the morning. *I will see him!* No! no! no! But what is she doing? She has taken her hat, she looks in the glass instinctively to see if her hair is in order, and in the glass she sees her hat; everything vanishes then before these three words: "No going back! No going back! No going back!"

"Macha, do not wait for me to come to dinner. I shall not dine at home."

"Alexander Matvéitch has not yet returned from the hospital," says Stépane to

The Life of Véra Pavlovna with her Second Husband. 259

her, calmly. Indeed, there is no reason for Stépane to be astonished at the presence of Véra Pavlovna, who had come very often lately.

"I suspected as much, but it makes no difference; I will wait. Do not tell him that I am here."

She takes up a literary review,—yes, she can read, she sees that she can read; yes, now that there is no going back, now that her resolution is taken, she feels very calm. Evidently she reads but little, or perhaps not at all; she looks the room over and begins to arrange things, as if she were at home; evidently she does not do much arranging, but she is calm: and she can read and occupy herself with matters in general; she notices that the ash-pan is not empty, that the table-cloth needs straightening, and that this chair is not in its place. She sits down and thinks: *No going back, no choice, a new life is about to begin.* That lasts an hour or two.

A new life is about to begin. How astonished and happy he will be! A new life is about to begin. How happy we are! A ring; she blushes slightly and smiles; the door opens.

"Véra Pavlovna!"

He staggers; yes, he staggers; he has to support himself against the door, but she runs to him, and, kissing him, says:

"My dear, dear friend! How noble he is! How I love you! I could not live without you!"

What took place then, how they crossed the room, she does not remember; she only remembers running to him and kissing him; for that matter, he remembers no more than she. They only remember that they passed by arm-chairs and by the table, but how did they leave the door? . . . . . Yes, for a few seconds their heads were turned, their sight disturbed by this kiss . . . . .

"Vérotchka, my angel!"

"My friend, I could not live without you. How long you have loved me without telling me so! How noble you are, and how noble he is, too!"

"Tell me, then, Vérotchka, how this has happened."

"I told him that I could not live without you; the next day—that is, yesterday—he went away; I desired to follow him; all day yesterday I thought that I should go to him; yet here I have been waiting a long time."

"But how thin you have grown in the last two weeks, Vérotchka! How delicate your hands are!"

He kisses her hands.

"Yes, my friend, it was a painful struggle! Now I can appreciate how you have suffered to avoid disturbing my peace. How did you succeed in maintaining such self-possession that I noticed nothing? How you must have suffered!"

"Yes, Vérotchka, it was not easy."

And he still covers her hands with kisses. Suddenly she begins to laugh:

"Ah! how inattentive I am to you! You are tired, Sacha, you are hungry!"
She escapes and runs away.
"Where are you going, Vérotchka?"
But she does not answer; already she is in the kitchen, talking to Stépane in gay and urgent tones.
"Get dinner for two! Quick, quick! Where are the plates, and knives and forks? I will set the table. Bring in something to eat; Alexander is so tired from his hospital duties that his dinner must be served in a hurry."
She returns with the plates, on which rattle knives, forks, and spoons.
"You know, my darling, that the first thought of lovers at the first interview is to dine as quickly as possible," says she, laughing.
He laughs also, and helps her set the table; he helps her much, but delays her still more, for he is constantly kissing her hands.
"Ah! how delicate your hands are!" And he kisses them again.
"Come to the table, Sacha, and be quiet!"
Stépane brings the soup. During dinner she tells him how this all happened.
"Ah! my darling, how we eat for lovers! It is true, though, that yesterday I ate nothing."
Stépane enters with the last dish.
"Stépane, I have eaten your dinner."
"Yes, Véra Pavlovna, I shall have to buy something at the shop."
"Do so, and now you must know that in future you will always have to prepare for two, not counting yourself. Sacha, where is your cigar-case? Give it to me."
She cuts a cigar herself, lights it, and says to him:
"Smoke, my darling; meantime I will prepare the coffee; or perhaps you prefer tea? Do you know, my darling, our dinner ought to be better; you are too easy with Stépane."
Five minutes later she returns; Stépane follows her with the tea-service, and, as she comes in, she sees that Alexander's cigar has gone out.
"Ha! ha! my darling, how dreamy you have become in my absence!"
He laughs too.
"Smoke, then," and again she lights his cigar.
In recalling all this now, Véra Pavlovna laughs over again: "How prosaic our romance is! The first interview and the soup; our heads turned at the first kiss, then a good appetite,— what a strange love-scene! It is very queer. And how his eyes shone! But indeed they shine still in the same way. How many of his tears have fallen on my hands, which were then so delicate, but which certainly are not so now. But really my hands are beautiful; he tells the truth." She looks at her hands and says: "Yes, he is right. But what has that to do with our first interview and its accompaniments? I sit down at the table to pour the tea.

"'Stépane, have you any cream? Could you get some that is good? But no, we have not time, and surely you would not find any. So be it, but tomorrow we will arrange all that. Smoke away, my darling; you are all the time forgetting to smoke.'"

The tea is not yet finished when a terrible ring is heard; two students enter the room in all haste, and in their hurry do not even see her.

"Alexander Matvéitch, an interesting subject!" they say, all out of breath; "an extremely rare and very curious subject [here they give the Latin name of the disease] has just been brought in, Alexander Matvéitch, and aid is needed immediately; every half-hour is precious. We even took a cab."

"Quick, quick, my friend, make haste!" says she. Not till then do the students notice her and bow, and in a twinkling they drag away their professor, who was not long in getting ready, having kept on his military overcoat. Again she hurries him.

"From there you will come to me?" says she, as she takes leave of him.

"Yes."

In the evening he makes her wait a long time. It is ten o'clock, and he does not come; eleven, — it is useless to expect him. What does it mean? Certainly she is not at all anxious; nothing can have happened to him; but why is he obliged to stay with the interesting subject? Is he still alive, this poor interesting subject? Has Sacha succeeded in saving him? Yes, Sacha was, indeed, detained a long time. He does not come till the next morning at nine o'clock; till four he had remained at the hospital.

"The case was very difficult and interesting, Vérotchka."

"Saved?"

"Yes."

"But why did you rise so early?"

"I have not been in bed."

"You have not been in bed! To avoid delaying your arrival you did not sleep last night! Impious man! Go to your room and sleep till dinner-time; be sure that I find you still asleep."

In two minutes he was driven away.

Such were their first two interviews. But the second dinner went off better; they told each other of their affairs in a reasonable manner. The night before, on the contrary, they did not know what they were saying. They laughed, and then were gloomy. It seemed to each of them that the other had suffered the more. Ten days later they hired a little country-house on the island of Kamennoy.

VI.

It is not very often that Véra Pavlovna recalls the past of her new love: the present is so full of life that but little time is left for memories. Nevertheless these memories come back oftener and oftener, and gradually she feels the growth within her of a certain discontent, faint, slight, vague, at first,—a discontent with whom, with what? Ah! there it is; at last she sees that it is with herself that she is discontented, but why? She was too proud for that. Is it only with the past that she is discontented? That was the case at first, but she notices that this discontent refers also to the present. And of how strange a character this feeling is! As if it were not her, Véra Pavlovna Kirsanoff, who felt this discontent, but as if it were the discontent of thousands and millions of human beings reflected in her. For what reason are these thousands and millions of human beings discontented with themselves? If she had lived and thought as she used to when she was alone, it is probable that this feeling would not have shown itself so soon; but now she was constantly with her husband, they always thought together, she thinks of him in the midst of these other thoughts. That aids her much in determining the character of her feeling. He has been unable to find the solution of the enigma: this feeling, obscure to her, is still more so to him; it is even difficult for him to understand how one can feel discontent without this discontent referring to something personal. This is a singularity a hundred times more obscure to him than to her. Nevertheless she feels much aided by the fact that she thinks always of her husband, that she is always with him, observes him, and thinks with him. She has noticed that, when the feeling of discontent comes, it is always followed by a comparison (it is even contained in this comparison) between herself and her husband, and her thought is illuminated by the right word: "A difference, an offensive difference." Now all is clear to her.

VII.

"How agreeable N. N. is, Sacha! [The name spoken by Véra Pavlovna was that of the officer through whom she had desired to make the acquaintance of Tamberlik in her horrible dream.] He has brought me a new poem, which is not to be printed for a long time yet," said Véra Pavlovna, at dinner. "When we have dined, we will read this poem, if you like. I have waited for you, though I had a great desire to read it."

"What, then, is this poem?"

"You shall judge. We shall see if he has succeeded. N. N. says that he himself — I mean the author — is almost satisfied with it."

They sat down in Véra Pavlovna's room, and she began to read:

> Oh! comme la corbeille est pleine!
> J'ai de la perse et du brocart.
> Ayez pitié, ô mon amour,
> De l'épaule du garçon.

The Life of Véra Pavlovna with her Second Husband. 263

"Now I see," said Kirsanoff, after hearing several dozen lines: "it is a new style peculiar to the author. But it is easy to see who wrote it. Nékrassoff, is it not? I thank you very much for having waited for me."

"I believe it is!" said Véra Pavlovna. And they read twice the little poem, which, thanks to their intimacy with a friend of the author, they thus had the privilege of seeing three years before its publication.

"But do you know the lines which most impress me?" said Véra Pavlovna, after they had several times read and re-read several passages of the poem; "these lines do not belong in the principal passages, but they impress me exceedingly. When Katia* was awaiting the return of her lover, she grieved much:

> Inconsolable, elle se serait consumée de douleur
> Si elle avait eu le temps de se chagriner;
> Mais le temps des travaux pénibles pressait,
> Il aurait fallu achever une dizaine d'affaires.
> Bien qu'il lui arrivât souvent
> De tomber de fatigue, la pauvre enfant,
> Sous sa faux vaillante tombait l'herbe,
> Le blé criait sous sa faucille;
> C'est de toutes ses forces
> Qu'elle battait le blé tous les matins,
> Et jusqu'à la nuit noire elle étendait le lin
> Sur les prairies pleines de rosée.†

These lines are only the preface of the episode where this worthy Katia dreams of Vania;‡ but, I repeat, they are the ones which most impress me."

"Yes, this picture is one of the finest in the poem, but these lines do not occupy a prominent place. You find them so beautiful because they accord so closely with the thoughts that fill your own mind. What, then, are these thoughts?"

"There, Sacha. We have often said that it is probable that woman's organization is superior to man's, and that it is probable, therefore, that intellectually man will be thrown back by woman to a second place when the reign of brute force is over. We have reached this supposition by watching real life and especially by noting the fact that the number of women born intelligent is greater than that of men. Moreover, you rest this opinion on various anatomical and physiological details."

---

* Katia is the diminutive of Katérina.
† Prose translation: Inconsolable, she would have been consumed by sorrow if she had had time to grieve; but the time for arduous tasks was pressing, and there were a dozen things to be finished. Although the poor child often fell from fatigue, under her gallant scythe fell the grass, the corn rustled under her sickle; with all her strength she threshed the corn every morning, and until dark night she spread the flax over the dewy fields.
‡ Vania is the diminutive of Ivan.

"How well you treat men, Vérotchka! Fortunately, the time that you foresee is still far off. Otherwise I should quickly change my opinion to avoid being relegated to a second place. For that matter, it is only probability; science has not yet observed facts enough to solve this grave question properly."

"But, dear friend, have we not also asked ourselves why the facts of history have been hitherto so contradictory of the deduction which may be drawn, with almost entire certainty, from observations of private life and the constitution of the organism? Hitherto woman has played but a minor part in intellectual life, because the reign of violence deprived her of the means of development and stifled her aspirations. That is a sufficient explanation in itself; but here is another. So far as physical force is concerned, woman's organism is the weaker, but it has at the same time the greater power of resistance, has it not?"

"This is surer than the difference in native intellectual powers. Yes, woman's organism is more effective in its resistance to the destructive forces,—climate, inclement weather, insufficient food. Medicine and physiology have paid but little attention to this question as yet, but statistics has already given an eloquent reply: the average life of women is longer than that of men. We may infer from this that the feminine organism is the more vigorous."

"The fact that woman's manner of life is generally even less healthy than man's makes this all the truer."

"There is another convincing consideration given us by physiology. Woman's growth may be said to end at the age of twenty, and man's at the age of twenty-five; these figures are approximately correct in our climate and of our race. Admitting that out of a given number there are as many women who live to the age of seventy as men who attain the age of sixty-five, if we take into consideration the difference in the periods of development, the preponderance of vigor in the feminine organism becomes even more evident than the statisticians suppose, as they have never taken into account the difference in the ages of maturity. Seventy years is twenty times three and five-tenths; sixty-five years is twenty-five times two and six-tenths. Therefore woman's life is three and one-half times as long as the period of her development, while man's is but little more than two and one-half times as long as the period of his development, which is a little slower. Now, the respective strength of the two organisms should be measured by this standard."

"The difference is greater than my readings had led me to believe."

"You have read only the statistical summaries bearing on the average length of life. But if to these statistical facts we add physiological facts, the difference will appear very much greater yet."

"That is so, Sacha; I thought — and the thought now strikes me still more forcibly — that, if the feminine organism is better fitted to resist destructive forces, it is probable that woman could endure moral shocks with the greater ease and firmness. But in reality the opposite seems to be the truth."

"Yes, it is probable. But it is only a supposition. It is true, nevertheless, that your conclusion is derived from indisputable facts. The vigor of the organism is very intimately connected with the vigor of the nerves. Woman's nerves are probably more elastic and of more solid texture, and, if that is the case, they ought to endure painful shocks and sensations with the greater ease and firmness. In actual life we have far too many examples of the contrary. Woman is very often tormented by things that man endures easily. Not much effort has been made as yet to analyze the causes which, given our historical situation, show us phenomena the opposite of what we are justified in expecting from the very constitution of the organism. But one of these causes is plain; it governs all historical phenomena and all the phases of our present condition. It is the force of bias, a bad habit, a false expectation, a false fear. If a person says to himself, 'I can do nothing,' he finds himself unable to do anything. Now, women have always been told that they are weak, and so they feel weak and to all intents and purposes are weak. You know instances where men really in good health have been seen to waste away and die from the single thought that they were going to weaken and die. But there are also instances of this in the conduct of great masses of people, entire humanity. One of the most remarkable is furnished by military history. In the Middle Ages infantry imagined that it could not hold its own against cavalry, and actually it could not. Entire armies of foot soldiers were scattered like flocks of sheep by a few hundred horsemen; and that lasted until the English foot-soldiers, small proprietors, proud and independent, appeared on the Continent. These did not share this fear, and were not accustomed to surrender without a struggle. They conquered every time they met the innumerable and formidable French cavalry. Do you remember those famous defeats of French horsemen by small armies of English foot-soldiers at Crécy, Poitiers, and Agincourt? The same fact was repeated when the Swiss foot-soldiers once got the idea that they had no reason to think themselves weaker than the feudal cavalry. The Austrian horsemen, and afterwards those of Burgundy, still more numerous, were beaten by them in every fight. The other horsemen wanted to meet them also, and were always routed. Everybody saw then that infantry was a more solid body than cavalry; but entire centuries had gone by in which infantry was very weak in comparison with cavalry, simply because it thought itself so."

"True, Sacha. We are weak because we consider ourselves so. But it seems to me that there is still another cause. I have us two in mind. Does it not seem to you that I changed a great deal during the two weeks when you did not see me?"

"Yes, you grew very thin and pale."

"It is precisely that which is revolting to my pride when I remember that no one noticed you grow thin or pale, though you suffered and struggled as much as I. How did you do it?"

"This is the reason, then, why these lines about Katia, who escapes sorrow through labor, have made such an impression on you! I endured struggle and suffering with reasonable ease, because I had not much time to think about them. During the time that I devoted to them I suffered horribly, but my urgent daily duties forced me to forget them the greater part of the time. I had to prepare my lessons and attend to my patients. In spite of myself I rested during that time from my bitter thoughts. On the rare days when I had leisure, I felt my strength leaving me. It seems to me that, if I had abandoned myself for a week to my thoughts, I should have gone mad."

"That's it, exactly. Of late I have seen that the origin of the difference between us was there. One must have work that cannot be neglected or postponed, and then one is incomparably securer against sorrow."

"But you had a great deal of work too."

"My household duties, to be sure, but I was not obliged to attend to them, and often, when my sadness was too strong, I neglected them to abandon myself to my thoughts; one always abandons that which is least important. As soon as one's feelings get firm possession of them, these drive all petty cares out of the mind. I have lessons; these are more important; but I can neglect them when I like, and the work is not absorbing. I give it only such attention as I choose; if my mind wanders during the lesson, no great harm is done. And again: do I live by my lessons? Is my position dependent on them? No, my main support then came from Dmitry's work as it now comes from yours. The lessons allow me to flatter myself that I am independent, and are by no means useless. But then I could get along without them.

"Then I tried, in order to drive away the thoughts which were tormenting me, to busy myself in the shop more than usual. But I did it only by an effort of the will. I understood well enough that my presence in the shop was necessary only for an hour or an hour and a half, and that, if I stayed longer, I was tying myself down to a fatigue which, though certainly useful, was not at all indispensable. And then, can such altruistic occupation sustain persons as ordinary as I am? The Rakhmétoffs are another sort of people: they are so much concerned about the common welfare that to work for public ends is a necessity to them, so much so that to them altruistic life takes the place of private life. But we do not scale these high summits, we are not Rakhmétoffs, and our private life is the only thing, properly speaking, that is indispensable to us. The shop was not my matter, after all; I was concerned in it only for others and for my ideas; but I am one of those who take little interest in the affairs of others, though they are suffering themselves. What we need in such cases is a personal, urgent occupation, upon which our life depends; such an occupation, considering my feelings and condition, would weigh more with me than all the impulses of passion; it alone could serve to support me in a struggle against an omnipotent passion; it alone gives strength and rest. I want such an occupation."

"You are right, my friend," said Kirsanoff, warmly, kissing his wife, whose eyes sparkled with animation. "To think that it has not occurred to me before, when it would have been so simple; I did not even notice it! Yes, Vérotchka, no one can think for another. If you wish to be comfortable, think for yourself of yourself; no one can take your place. To love as I love, and not to have understood all this before you explained it to me! But," he continued, laughing, and still kissing his wife, "why do you think this occupation necessary now? Are you becoming amorously inclined towards any one?"

Véra Pavlovna began to laugh heartily, and for some minutes mad laughter prevented them from speaking.

"Yes, we can laugh at that now," she said, at last: "both of us can now be sure that nothing of the kind will ever happen to either of us. But seriously, do you know what I am thinking about now? Though my love for Dmitry was not the love of a completely developed woman, neither did he love me in the way in which we understand love. His feeling for me was a mixture of strong friendship with the fire of amorous passion. He had a great friendship for me, but his amorous transports needed but a woman for their satisfaction, not me personally. No, that was not love. Did he care much about my thoughts? No, no more than I did about his. There was no real love between us."

"You are unjust to him, Vérotchka."

"No, Sacha, it is really so. Between us it is useless to praise him. We both know very well in what high esteem we hold him; it is vain for him to say that it would have been easy to separate me from him; it is not so; you said in the same way that it was easy for you to struggle against your passion. Yet, however sincere his words and yours, they must not be understood or construed literally."

"Oh! my friend, I understand how much you suffered. And this is how I understand it." . . . . .

"Vérotchka, you stifle me. Confess that, besides the force of sentiment, you also wanted to show me your muscular force. How strong you are, indeed! But how could you be otherwise with such a chest?"

"My dear Sacha!"

VIII.

"But you did not let me talk business, Sacha," began Véra Pavlovna, when, two hours later, they sat down to tea.

"I did not let you talk? Was it my fault?"

"Certainly."

"Who began the indulgence?"

"Are you not ashamed to say that?"

"What?"

"That I began the indulgence. Fie! the idea of thus compromising a modest woman on the plea of coldness!"

"Indeed! Do you not preach equality? Why not equality of initiative as well?"

"Ha, ha, ha! a fine argument! But would you dare to accuse me of being illogical? Do I not try to maintain equality in initiative also? I take now the initiative of continuing our serious conversation, which we have too thoroughly forgotten."

"Take it, if you will, but I refuse to follow you, and I take the initiative of continuing to forget it. Give me your hand."

"But we must finish our talk, Sacha."

"We shall have time enough tomorrow. Now, you see, I am absorbed in an analysis of this hand."

IX.

"Sacha, let us finish our conversation of yesterday. We must do so, because I am getting ready to go with you, and you must know why," said Véra Pavlovna the next morning.

"You are coming with me?"

"Certainly. You asked me, Sacha, why I wanted an occupation upon which my life should depend, which I should look upon as seriously as you on yours, which should be as engaging as yours, and which should require as much attention as yours requires. I want this occupation, my dear friend, because I am very proud. When I think that during my days of trial my feelings became so visible in my person that others could analyze them, I am thoroughly ashamed. I do not speak of my sufferings. You had to struggle and suffer no less than I, and you triumphed where I was conquered. I wish to be as strong as you, your equal in everything. And I have found the way; I have thought a great deal since we left each other yesterday, and I have found it all alone; you were unwilling to aid me with your advice; so much the worse for you. It is too late now. Yes, Sacha, you may be very anxious about me, my dear friend, but how happy we shall be if I prove capable of success in what I wish to undertake!"

Véra Pavlovna had just thought of an occupation which, under Kirsanoff's guidance and her hand in his, she could engage in successfully.

Lopoukhoff, to be sure, had not hindered her at all; on the contrary, she was sure of finding support from him in all serious matters. But it was only under serious circumstances that he was as devoted and firm as Kirsanoff would have been. This he had shown when, in order to marry her and deliver her from her oppressive situation, he had sacrificed all his scientific dreams and exposed himself to the sufferings of hunger. Yes, when the matter was serious, his hand was held out to her, but usually it was wanting. Véra Pavlovna, for instance, organized her shop: if, in any way whatever, his aid had been indispensable. Lopoukhoff would have given it with pleasure. But why did he actually give almost no aid at all? He stood in the way of nothing; he approved what was done and rejoiced at it. But he had his own life as she had hers. Now it is not the same. Kirsanoff does not wait for his wife to ask him to participate in all that she does. He is as interested in everything that is dear to her as she is in everything that relates to him.

From this new life Véra Pavlovna derives new strength, and what formerly seemed to her as if it would never leave the realms of the ideal now appears entirely within reach.

As for her thoughts, this is the order in which they came to her:

X.

"Almost all the paths of civil life are formally closed to us, and those which are not closed by formal obstacles are by practical difficulties. Only the family is left us. What occupation can we engage in, outside of the family? That of a governess is almost the only one; perhaps we have one other resource,—that of giving lessons (such lessons as are left after the men have chosen). But we all rush into this single path and stifle there. We are too numerous to find independence in it. There are so many to choose from that no one needs us. Who would care to be a governess? When any one wants one, he is besieged by ten, a hundred, or even more applicants, each trying to get the place to the detriment of the others.

"No, until women launch out into a greater number of careers, they will not enjoy independence. It is difficult, to be sure, to open a new road. But I occupy an especially favorable position for doing it. I should be ashamed not to profit by it. We are not prepared for serious duties. For my part, I do not know how far a guide is indispensable to me in order to confront them. But I do know that every time I need him I shall find him, and that he will always take great pleasure in helping me.

"Public prejudice has closed to us such paths of independent activity as the law has not forbidden us to enter. But I can enter whichever of these paths I choose, provided I am willing to brave the usual gossip. Which shall I choose? My husband is a doctor; he devotes all his leisure time to me. With such a man it would be easy for me to attempt to follow the medical profession.

"Indeed, it is very important that there should be women-physicians. They would be very useful to persons of their own sex. It is much easier for a woman to talk to another woman than to a man. How much distress, suffering, and death would thus be averted! The experiment must be tried."

XI.

Véra Pavlovna finished the conversation with her husband by putting on her hat to follow him to the hospital, where she wished to try her nerves and see if she could stand the sight of blood and whether she would be capable of pursuing the study of anatomy. In view of Kirsanoff's position in the hospital, there certainly would be no obstacles in the way of this attempt.

I have already unconsciously compromised Véra Pavlovna several times from the poetical standpoint; I have not concealed the fact, for instance, that she dined every day, and generally with a good appetite, and that further she took tea twice a day. But I have now reached a point where, in spite of the depravity of my tastes, I am seized with scruples, and timidly I ask myself: Would it not be better to conceal this circumstance? What will be thought of a woman capable of studying medicine?

What coarse nerves, what a hard heart, she must have! She is not a woman, she is a butcher. Nevertheless, remembering that I do not set up my characters as ideal types, I calm myself: let them judge as they will of the coarseness of Véra Pavlovna's nature, how can that concern me? She is coarse? Well! be it so.

Consequently I say in the most cold-blooded way that she found it one thing to look at others do and quite another to do herself. And indeed whoever is at work has no time to be frightened and feel repugnance or disgust. So Véra Pavlovna studies medicine, and I number among my acquaintances one of those who introduced this novelty among us. She felt transformed by the study, and she said to herself: In a few years I shall get a foothold.

That is a great thought. There is no complete happiness without complete independence. Poor women that you are, how few of you enjoy this happiness!

XII.

One year, two years pass; yet another year will pass from the time of her marriage with Kirsanoff, and Véra Pavlovna's occupation will be the same as now; many years will pass, and her days will still be the same, unless something special happens. Who knows what the future will bring? Up to the time when I write these lines, nothing special has happened, and Véra Pavlovna's occupations have not changed. Now that the frank confession of Véra Pavlovna's bad taste in daring to study medicine and succeed in it has been made, it is easy for me to speak of anything; nothing else can harm her as much in the estimation of the public. So I will say that now, in the Rue Serguievskaïa, Véra Pavlovna's day is divided into three parts,—by her morning cup of tea, her dinner, and her evening tea; yes, she has kept up the unpoetic habit of dining every day and taking tea twice a day; she finds it pleasant; in general, she has kept up all her habits of that sort.

Many other things have remained the same as before in this new and peaceful life.

The rooms are divided into the neutral and the non-neutral; all the rules regarding entrance into the non-neutral rooms are still the same. However, there are a few notable changes.

For instance, they no longer take tea in the neutral room; they take their evening tea in Kirsanoff's study and their morning tea in Véra Pavlovna's chamber.

On awaking in the morning she dozes and tosses about as of old, now sleeping, now meditating. She now has two new subjects of reflection, which in the third year of her marriage were followed by a third, the little Mitia,* so named in honor of her friend Dmitry; the two others are, first, the sweet thought of the independence that she is to acquire, and, second, the thought of Sacha; the latter cannot even be called a special thought, being mingled with all her thoughts, for her dear husband participates in her whole life.

After having taken a bath, she takes tea, or rather cream, with Sacha, after which she lounges again, not on her bed this time, but on her little divan, until ten or eleven o'clock, the time when Sacha is to go to the hospital, or the *clinique*, or else the academical lecture-room. But her mornings were not on that account devoted to idleness; as soon as Sacha, after drinking his last cup, had lit his cigar, one of the two said to the other: "Let's go to work," or else: "Enough! enough! now for work!" What work? you ask. The private lesson. Sacha is her private tutor in medicine; she is aided by him still further in mathematics, and in Latin, which is perhaps even more tiresome than mathematics, but for that matter the Academy of Medicine requires but very little. I should be very careful about asserting that Véra Pavlovna will ever know enough Latin to translate even two lines of Cornelius Nepos, but she already knew enough to decipher the Latin phrases which she met in medical books, and that was what she needed. This is the finishing touch; I see that I am compromising Véra Pavlovna enormously: probably the reader with the pen". . . . .

XIII.

A DIGRESSION CONCERNING BLUE-STOCKINGS.

"*A blue-stocking!* The last degree of *blue-stocking!* I cannot abide a blue-stocking. A blue-stocking is stupid and tiresome!" exclaims angrily, but not without dignity, the reader with the penetrating eye.

The reader with the penetrating eye and myself are considerably attached to each other. He has insulted me once, I have put him out doors twice, and, in spite of all, we cannot help exchanging cordial words; a mysterious inclination of hearts, is it not?

---

* Mitia is the diminutive of Dmitry.

"O reader with the penetrating eye!" I say to him, "you are quite right: the blue-stocking is stupid and tiresome, and it is impossible to endure him. That you have seen correctly; but you have not seen who the blue-stocking is. You shall see him, as in a mirror. The blue-stocking is the man who speaks with importance and stupid affectation of literary and scientific matters, of which he does not know the a-b-c, and who speaks of them, not because he is interested in them, but to make a show of brains (of which nature has been very niggardly to him), of his lofty aspirations (of which he has as many as the chair on which he sits), and of his learning (he has as much as a parrot). Do you know this coarse face, this carefully-brushed head? It is you, my dear sir. Yes, however long you let your beard grow, or however carefully you shave it off, in any case you are indubitably and incontestably a blue-stocking of the most authentic stamp. That is why I have twice put you out doors, simply because I cannot endure blue-stockings. Among us men there are ten times as many as among women.

"But any person, of whatever sex, who, with any sensible object in view, engages in something useful, is simply a human being engaged in business, and nothing else."

XIV.

The Kirsanoffs were now the intellectual centre of a large number of families in a condition similar to their own and sharing their ideas; these associations took half of their leisure time. But there is one thing of which unfortunately it is necessary to speak at too great length to many individuals in order to be understood. Whoever has not felt himself must at least have read that there is a great difference between a simple evening party and one where the object of your love is present. That is well known. But what very few have felt is that the charm which love gives to everything should not be a passing phenomenon in man's life, that this intense gleam of life should not light simply the period of desire, of aspiration, the period called courting, or seeking in marriage; no, this period should be only the ravishing dawn of a day more ravishing yet. Light and heat increase during the greater part of the day; so during the course of life ought love and its delights to increase. Among people of the old society such is not the case; the poetry of love does not survive satisfaction. The contrary is the rule among the people of the new generation whose life I am describing. The longer they live together, the more they are lighted and warmed by the poetry of love, until the time when the care of their growing children absorbs them. Then this care, sweeter than personal enjoyment, becomes uppermost; but until then love grows incessantly. That which the men of former times enjoyed only for a few short months the new men keep for many years.

And why so? It is a secret which I will unveil to you, if you wish. It is a fine secret, one worth having, and it is not difficult. One need have but a pure heart, an upright soul, and that new and just conception of the human being which prompts respect for the liberty of one's life companion. Look upon your wife as you looked upon your sweetheart; remember that she at any moment has the right to say to you: "I am dissatisfied with you; leave me." Do this, and ten years after your marriage she will inspire in you the same enthusiasm that she did when she was your sweetheart, and she will have as much charm for you as then and even more. Recognize her liberty as openly, as explicitly, and with as little reserve, as you recognize the liberty of your friends to be your friends or not, and ten years, twenty years, after marriage you will be as dear to her as when you were her sweetheart. This is the way in which the people of our new generation live. Their condition in this respect is very enviable. Among them husbands and wives are loyal, sincere, and love each other always more and more.

After ten years of marriage they do not exchange false kisses or false words. "A lie was never on his lips; there was no deception in his heart," was said of some one in a certain book. In reading these things we say: The author, when he wrote this book, said to himself that this was a man whom all must admire as one to be celebrated. This author did not foresee that new men would arise, who would not admit among their acquaintances people who had not attained the height of his unparalleled hero, and the readers of the aforesaid book will have difficulty in understanding what I have just said, especially if I add that my heroes do not consider their numerous friends as exceptions, but simply as estimable, though very ordinary, individuals of the new generation.

What a pity that at the present hour there are still more than ten antediluvians for every new man! It is very natural, however. An antediluvian world can have only an antediluvian population.

XV.

"See, we have been living together for three years already [formerly it was one year, then two, next it will be four, and so on], and we are still like lovers who see each other rarely and secretly. Where did the idea come from, Sacha, that love grows weaker when there is nothing to disturb possession? People who believe that have not known true love. They have known only self-love or erotic fancies. True love really begins with life in common."

"Am I not the inspiration of this remark?"

"You? You will in a few years forget medicine, unlearn to read, and lose all your intellectual faculties, and you will end by seeing nothing but me."

Such conversations are neither long nor frequent, but they sometimes occur.

Conversations like these are more frequent.

"Sacha, how your love sustains me! It inspires in me the power of independence even against you. Does my love give nothing to you?"

"To me. No less than to you. This continuous, strong, healthy excitement of the nerves necessarily develops the nervous system [gross materialism, let us note with the reader with the penetrating eye]; consequently my intellectual and moral forces grow in proportion to your love."

"Yes, Sacha, I understand what they say (I should not dare to believe it if I were the only one to see it, not being a disinterested witness); others see, as I do, that your eyes are becoming clearer and your expression more intense and powerful."

"There is no reason to praise me for that, even in your behalf, Vérotchka. We are one and the same being. But it is sure that, my thought having become much more active, it must be reflected in my eyes. When I come to draw inferences from my observations, I now do in an hour what formerly required several hours. I can hold in my mind many more facts than before, and my deductions are larger and more complete. If I had had any germ of genius in me, Vérotchka, with this sentiment I should have become a great genius. If I had been given a little of the creative power, with the sentiment which dominates me I could have acquired the strength to revolutionize science. But I was born to be only a drudge, an ordinary and obscure laborer able to handle special questions only. That is what I was without you. Now, you know, I am something else: much more is expected of me; it is believed that I will revolutionize an entire branch of science, the whole theory of the functions of the nervous system. And I feel that I shall meet this expectation. At the age of twenty-four man has a broader and bolder intellectual view than at the age of twenty-nine, or thirty, or thirty-two, and so on. I am as strong as I was at twenty-four. And I feel that I am still growing, which would not be so were it not for you. I did not grow during the two or three years preceding our union. You have restored to me the freshness of early youth and the strength to go much farther than I could have gone without your love."

Conversations like these are very frequent also.

"My dear friend, I am reading Boccaccio now [what immorality! let us note with the reader with the penetrating eye. Only we men may read that; but for my part I am going to make this remark: a woman will hear the reader with the penetrating eye give utterance to more conventional filth in five minutes than she will find in all Boccaccio, and she will not hear from the reader with the penetrating eye a single one of those luminous, fresh, and pure words in which Boccaccio abounds]: you are right in saying that he has very great talent. Some of his tales deserve to be placed beside the best dramas of Shakspere for depth and delicacy of psychological analysis."

"How do his humorous stories, where Boccaccio is so broad, please you?"

"Some of them are funny, but generally they are tiresome, like every farce, from being too coarse."

"But he must be pardoned; he lived five hundred years before our time. What now seems to us too filthy and too much like Billingsgate was not considered improper then."

"It is the same with many of our manners and customs; they will seem coarse and unclean in much less than five hundred years. But I pay no attention to the license of Boccaccio; I speak of those novels of his in which he describes an elevated and passionate love so well. It is there that his great talent appears. I come back to what I was going to say: he paints very well and very vividly. But, judging from his writings, we may say that they did not know in those days that delicacy of love which we know now; love was not felt so deeply, although it is said to have been the epoch when they enjoyed it most completely. No, the people of that day did not enjoy love so well. Their sentiments were too superficial and their intoxication too mild and transient."

XVI.

A year had passed: the new shop, thoroughly organized, was doing well. The two shops coöperated: when one was overworked, it sent orders to the other. They kept a running account with each other. Their means were already so large that they were able to open a store on the Perspective Nevsky: but they had to coöperate more closely, which embarrassed Véra Pavlovna and Madame Mertzaloff not a little. Although the two associations were friendly, met frequently, and often took walks together in the suburbs, the idea of complete coöperation between the two enterprises was new, and a great deal had to be done. Nevertheless the advantage of having their own store on the Perspective Nevsky was evident, and, after experimenting for some months, Véra Pavlovna and Madame Mertzaloff finally succeeded. A new sign appeared on the Perspective Nevsky in French: *Au bon travail. Magasin de Nouveautés.** With the opening of the store business began to improve rapidly, and was done to better and better advantage. Madame Mertzaloff and Véra Pavlovna cherished the dream of seeing the number of shops rise from two to five, ten, twenty.

Three months after the opening of the store Kirsanoff received a visit from one of his colleagues with whom he was somewhat acquainted. The latter talked to him a great deal of various medical applications, and especially of the astonishing efficacy of his method, which consisted in placing on the breast and belly two

---

* Good work. Linen-draper's store.

small bags, narrow and long, filled with pounded ice and each wrapped in four napkins. In conclusion, he said that one of his friends wished to make Kirsanoff's acquaintance.

Kirsanoff complied with this desire. The acquaintance was an agreeable one, and the conversation turned on many things, — among others the store. Kirsanoff explained that it had been opened for an exclusively commercial purpose. They talked a long time about the sign; was it well to have the sign bear the word *travail?* Kirsanoff said that *Au bon travail* meant in Russian a house that filled its orders well; then they discussed the question whether it would not be better to substitute for this motto the name of the manager. Kirsanoff objected that his wife's Russian name would drive away much custom.* At last he said that his wife's name was Véra, which, translated into French, was *foi,* and that it would be sufficient to put on the sign, instead of *Au bon travail, A la bonne foi.* This would have a most innocent meaning, — simply a house that was conscientious, — and besides the name of the manager would appear. After some discussion they decided that this was feasible. Kirsanoff led the conversation on such subjects with especial zeal, and, as a general thing, carried his point, so that he returned home well satisfied.

Madame Mertzaloff and Véra Pavlovna, however, had to abate their fine hopes, and think only of preserving what had been already achieved.

The founders of the establishment considered themselves fortunate in the *statu quo.* Kirsanoff's new acquaintance continued his visits and proved very interesting. Two years went by, and nothing of especial note happened.

XVII.

LETTER OF KATÉRINA VASSILIEVNA POLOSOFF.

St. Petersburg, August 17, 1860.

My dear Polina, I wish to tell you of something new which I have just discovered, which has pleased me greatly, and which I am now zealously concerned in. I am sure that it will interest you. But the most important point is that you perhaps will engage in something similar. It is so agreeable, my friend.

It is about a sewing-women's shop, — two shops, to speak more accurately, both based on the same principle, both founded by one woman, whose acquaintance I made only a fortnight ago and whose friend I have already become. I am now helping her on condition that she will help me to organize a similar shop. This lady's name is Véra Pavlovna Kirsanoff, still young, kind, gay, quite to my fancy;

---

* The most famous and well-known dressmaking and millinery establishments in St. Petersburg are kept by Frenchwomen.

she resembles you, Polina, more than your Katia, who is so quiet. She is an energetic and fearless person. Hearing of her shop by chance,—they told me of but one,—I came directly to her without recommendation or pretext, and simply told her that I was much interested in her shop. We became friends at our first interview, and the more easily because in her husband, Kirsanoff, I found again that Doctor Kirsanoff who rendered me so great a service, you remember, five years ago.

After talking with me for half an hour and seeing that I was really in sympathy with these things, Véra Pavlovna took me to her shop, the one which she personally superintends (the other shop is now in charge of one of her friends, also a very excellent person). I wish now to give you an account of the impression made upon me by this first visit. This impression was so vivid and new that I hastened to write it in my journal, long since abandoned, but now resumed in consequence of a peculiar circumstance which I perhaps will tell you about some time. I am very glad that I thus fixed my thoughts; otherwise I should now forget to mention many things which struck me at the time. Today, after two weeks, what astonished me so much seems ordinary. And, curiously enough, the more ordinary I find it all, the more I become attached to it.

Having said thus much, dear Polina, I now copy my journal, adding to it some later observations.

We then went to the shop. On entering, I saw a large room, well furnished and containing a grand piano, as if the room belonged to the residence of a family spending four or five thousand roubles a year. It was the reception room; the sewing-women also spent their evenings there. Then we visited the twenty other rooms occupied by the working-women. They are all very well furnished, although the furniture is not alike in all of them, having been bought as occasion required.

After seeing the rooms where the working-women slept, we went into the rooms where they worked. There I found young girls very well dressed in inexpensive silk or muslin. It was evident from their gentle and tender faces that they lived comfortably. You cannot imagine how I was struck by all this. I made the acquaintance of several of these young girls on the spot. All had not reached the same degree of intellectual development: some already used the language of educated people, had some acquaintance with literature, like our young ladies, and knew a little about history and foreign countries; two of them had even read a great deal. Others, who had been in the shop but a short time, were less developed, but still one could talk with any of them as with a young girl who has received a certain amount of education. Generally speaking, the degree of their development is proportional to the time that they have been in the shop.

We stayed there to dinner. The dinner consists of three dishes; that day they had rice soup, baked fish with sauce, and veal; after dinner tea and coffee were served. The dinner was so good that I ate with great relish; I should not consider it a privation to eat so always, and yet you know that my father has always had a very good cook.

When we returned to Véra Pavlovna's, she and her husband explained to me that there was nothing astonishing in this. All that I saw, they said, was due to two causes.

On the one hand a greater profit for the sewing-women, and on the other a greater economy in their expenses.

Do you understand why they earn more? They work on their own account, they are their own employers, and consequently they get the part which would otherwise remain in their employer's pocket. But that is not all; in working for their own benefit and at their own cost, they save in provisions and time: their work goes on faster and with less expense.

It is evident that there is a great saving also in the cost of their maintenance. They buy everything at wholesale and for cash, and consequently get everything cheaper than if they bought on credit and at retail.

Besides this, many expenses are much diminished, and some become utterly useless.

According to the calculation made for me by Kirsanoff, the sewing-women, instead of the hundred roubles a year which they ordinarily earn, receive two hundred, but, by living in coöperation and buying everything at wholesale and in quantities not exceeding the wants of the association (for instance, the twenty-five working-women have only five umbrellas), they use these two hundred roubles twice as advantageously.

Such is the marvel that I have seen, dear Polina, the explanation of which is so simple. Now I am so accustomed to this marvel that it seems strange to me that I was ever astonished at it. Why did I not expect to find everything as I did find it?

Write me whether you can interest yourself in a shop of this sort. I am doing so, Polina, and find it very pleasant.   Yours,

K. POLOSOFF.

CHAPTER FIFTH.

New Characters and the Conclusion.

I.

Mademoiselle Polosoff said in her letter to her friend that she was under obligations to Véra Pavlovna's husband. To understand this it is necessary to know who her father was.

Polosoff had been a captain or lieutenant, but had resigned his office. Following the custom of the good old days, he had led a dissipated life and devoured a large inheritance. After having spent all he had, he reformed and sent in his resignation, in order to make a new fortune. Gathering up the *debris* of his old fortune, he had left about ten thousand roubles in the paper money of that time.* With this sum he started as a small dealer in wheat; he began by taking all sorts of little contracts, availing himself of every advantageous opportunity when his means permitted, and in ten years he amassed a considerable capital. With the reputation of so positive and shrewd a man, and with his rank and name well known in the vicinity, he could select a bride from the daughters of the merchants in the two provinces in which he did business. He reasonably chose one with a dowry of half a million (likewise in paper). He was then fifty years old; that was twenty years before the time when his daughter and Véra Pavlovna became friends, as we have seen. With this new fortune added to his own, he was able to do business on a large scale, and ten years later he found himself a millionaire in the money then in circulation. His wife, accustomed to country life, had kept him away from the capital; but she died, and then he went to St. Petersburg to live. His business took a still better turn, and in another ten years he was reputed to be worth three or four millions. Young girls and widows set their caps for him, but he did not wish to marry again, partly through fidelity to his wife's memory, and still more because he did not wish to impose a step-mother upon his daughter Katia, of whom he was very fond.

Polosoff's operations grew larger and larger; he might already have been the possessor, not of three or four millions, but of a good ten, had he taken the liquor privilege; but he felt a certain repugnance to that business, which he did not consider as respectable as contracts and supplies. His millionaire colleagues made great fun of this casuistry, and they were not wrong; but he, though wrong, held to his opinion. "I am a merchant," said he, "and I do not wish to get rich by ex-

---

* A silver rouble, in the money of today, is worth three and one-half times as much as a paper rouble.

tortion." Nevertheless, about a year before his daughter made Véra Pavlovna's acquaintance, he was furnished with only too glaring a proof that his business at bottom was scarcely distinguishable from the liquor monopoly, although in his opinion it differed much. He had an enormous contract for a supply of cloth, or provisions, or shoe leather, or something or other, — I don't know exactly what; age, his steady success, and the growing esteem in which he was held rendering him every year more and more haughty and obstinate, he quarreled with a man who was necessary to him, flew into a passion, insulted him, and his luck turned.

A week afterwards he was told to submit.

"I will not."

"You will be ruined."

"What do I care? I will not."

A month later the same thing was repeated to him, he gave the same reply, and in fact he did not submit; but he was utterly ruined. His merchandise lay upon his hands; further, some evidences of neglect or sharp practice were found; and his three or four millions vanished. Polosoff, at the age of seventy, became a beggar, — that is, a beggar in comparison with what he had been; but, comparisons aside, he was comfortably well off. He still had an interest in a stearine factory, and, not in the least humiliated, he became manager of this factory at a very fair salary. Besides this, some tens of thousands of roubles had been saved by I know not what chance. With this money, had he been ten or fifteen years younger, he could have begun again to make his fortune, but at his age this was not to be thought of. And Polosoff's only plan, after due reflection, was to sell the factory, which did not pay. This was a good idea, and he succeeded in making the other stockholders see that a prompt sale was the only way to save the money invested in the enterprise. He thought also of finding a husband for his daughter. But his first care was to sell the factory, invest all his capital in five per cent. bonds, — which were then beginning to be fashionable, — and live quietly out the remainder of his days, dwelling sometimes on his past grandeur, the loss of which he had borne bravely, losing with it neither his gayety nor his firmness.

II.

Polosoff loved Katia and did not let ultra-aristocratic governesses hold his daughter too severely in check. "These are stupidities," said he of all efforts to correct her attitudes, manners, and other similar things. When Katia was fifteen, he agreed with her that she could dispense with the English governess as well as with the French one. Then Katia, having fully secured her leisure, was at perfect liberty in the house. To her liberty then meant liberty to read and dream. Friends she had but few, being intimate with only two or three; but her suitors were innumerable: she was the only daughter of Polosoff, possessor — immense! —

of four millions! But Katia read and dreamed, and the suitors despaired. She was already seventeen, and she read and dreamed and did not fall in love. But suddenly she began to grow thin and pale, and at last fell seriously ill.

III.

Kirsanoff was not in active practice, but he did not consider that he had a right to refuse to attend consultations of physicians. And at about that time — a year after he had become a professor and a year before his marriage with Véra Pavlovna — the bigwigs of St. Petersburg practice began to invite him to their consultations often, — even oftener than he liked. These invitations had their motives. The first was that the existence of a certain Claude Bernard of Paris had been established; one of the aforesaid bigwigs, having — no one knows why — gone to Paris for a scientific purpose, had seen with his own eyes a real flesh-and-blood Claude Bernard; he had recommended himself to him by his rank, his profession, his decorations, and the high standing of his patients. After listening to him about half an hour, Claude Bernard had said to him: "It was quite useless for you to come to Paris to study medical progress; you did not need to leave St. Petersburg for that." The bigwig took that for an endorsement of his own labors, and, returning to St. Petersburg, pronounced the name of Claude Bernard at least ten times a day, adding at least five times, "my learned friend," or, "my illustrious companion in science." After that, then, how could they avoid inviting Kirsanoff to the consultations? It could not be otherwise. The other reason was still more important: all the bigwigs saw that Kirsanoff would not try to get away their practice, for he did not accept patients, even when begged to take them. It was well known that a great many of the bigwig practitioners followed this line of conduct: when the patient (in the bigwig's opinion) was approaching an inevitable death and ill-intentioned destiny had so arranged things that it was impossible to defeat it, either by sending the patient to the springs or by any other sort of exportation to foreign parts, it then became necessary to place him in the hands of another doctor, and in such cases the bigwig was even almost ready to pay money to have the patient taken off his hands. Kirsanoff rarely accepted offers of this sort, and to get rid of them generally recommended his friends in active practice, keeping for himself only such cases as were interesting from a scientific standpoint. Why should they not invite to consultations, then, a colleague known to Claude Bernard and not engaged in a race after patronage?

Polosoff, the millionaire, had one of these bigwigs for a doctor, and, when Katérina Vassilievna fell seriously ill, the medical consultations were always made up of bigwigs. Finally she became so weak that the bigwigs resolved to call in Kirsanoff. In fact, the problem was a very difficult one for them; the patient had no disease, and yet she was growing perceptibly weaker. But some disease must be found, and the doctor having her in charge invented *atrophia nervorum*, "suspension of nervous nutrition." Whether there is such a disease I do not know, but, if it exists, even I can see that it is incurable. But as nothing must be left undone to save the patient, however hopeless the case, the problem was one for Kirsanoff or some other bold young man.

So a new council was held, which Kirsanoff attended. They examined the patient and pressed her with questions; she answered willingly and very calmly; but Kirsanoff, after her first words, stood one side, doing nothing but watch the bigwigs examine and question; and when, after having worn themselves out and harassed her as much as the proprieties in such cases demand, they appealed to Kirsanoff with the question: "What do you think, Alexander Matvéitch?" he answered: "I have not examined the patient sufficiently. I will remain here. It is an interesting case. If there is need of another consultation, I will tell Carl Fœdorytch,"— that is, the patient's doctor, whom these words made radiant with happiness at thus escaping his *atrophia nervorum*. When they had gone, Kirsanoff sat down by the patient's bed. A mocking smile lighted up her face.

"It is a pity that we are not acquainted," he began; "a doctor needs confidence; perhaps I shall succeed in gaining yours. They do not understand your sickness; it requires a certain sagacity. To sound your chest and dose you with drugs would be quite useless. It is necessary to know but one thing,— your situation,— and then find some way to get you out of it. You will aid me."

The patient did not say a word.

"You do not wish to speak to me?"

The patient did not say a word.

"Probably you even want me to go away. I ask you only for ten minutes. If at the end of that time you consider my presence useless, as you do now, I will go away. You know that sorrow is the only thing that troubles you. You know that, if this mental state continues, in two or three weeks, perhaps even sooner, you will be past saving. Perhaps you have not even two weeks to live. Consumption has not yet set in, but it is near at hand, and in a person of your age and condition it would develop with extraordinary rapidity and might carry you off in a few days."

The patient did not say a word.

"You do not answer. You remain indifferent. That means that nothing that I have said is new to you. By your very silence you answer: 'Yes.' Do you know what any other doctor would do in my place? He would speak to your father. Perhaps, were I to have a talk with him, it would save you, but, if it would displease you to have me do so, I will not. And why? Because I make it a rule to undertake nothing in any one's behalf against his or her will; liberty is above everything, above life itself. Therefore, if you do not wish me to learn the cause of your very dangerous condition, I will not try to find it out. If you say that you wish to die, I will only ask you to give me your reasons for this desire; even if they should seem to me without foundation, I should still have no right to prevent you; if, on the contrary, they should seem to me well founded, it would be my duty to aid you in your purpose, and I am ready to do so. I am ready to give you poison. Under these circumstances I beg you to tell me the cause of your sickness."

The patient did not say a word.

"You do not deign to answer me? I have no right to question you further, but I may ask your permission to tell you something of myself, which may establish greater confidence between us. Yes? I thank you. You suffer. Well, I suffer too. I love a woman passionately, who does not even know that I love her and who must never find it out. Do you pity me?"

The patient did not say a word, but a sad smile appeared upon her face.

"You are silent, but yet you could not hide from me the fact that my last words impressed you more then any that preceded them. That is enough for me; I see that you suffer from the same cause as myself. You wish to die. That I clearly understand. But to die of consumption is too long, too painful a process. I can aid you to die, if you will not be aided to live; I say that I am ready to give you poison, poison that will kill instantly and painlessly. On this condition, will you furnish me with the means of finding out whether your situation is really as desperate as you believe it to be?"

"You will not deceive me?" said the patient.

"Look me steadily in the eyes, and you will see that I will not deceive you."

The patient hesitated a few moments: "No, I do not know you well enough."

"Anybody else in my place would have already told you that the feeling from which you suffer is a good one. I will not say so yet. Does your father know of it? I beg you not to forget that I shall say nothing to him without your permission."

"He knows nothing about it."

"Does he love you?"

"Yes."

"What shall I say to you now? What do you think yourself? You say that he loves you; I have heard that he is a man of good sense. Why, then, do you think that it would be useless to inform him of your feeling, and that he would refuse his consent? If the obstacle consisted only in the poverty of the man whom you love, that would not have prevented you from trying to induce your father to give his consent; at least, that is my opinion. So you believe that your father thinks ill of him; your silence towards your father cannot be otherwise explained. Am I not right?"

The patient did not say a word.

"I see that I am not mistaken. Do you know what I think now? Your father is an experienced man, who knows men well; you, on the contrary, are inexperienced; if any man should seem bad to him and good to you, in all probability you would be wrong, not he. You see that I am forced to think so. Do you want to know why I say so disagreeable a thing to you? I will tell you. Perhaps you will resent it, but nevertheless you will say to yourself: 'He says what he thinks; he does not dissimulate and does not wish to deceive me.' I shall gain your confidence. Do I not talk to you like an honest man?"

The patient answered, hesitating:

"You are a very strange man, doctor."

"Not at all; I am simply not like a hypocrite. I have spoken my thought frankly. But still it is only a supposition. I may be mistaken. Give me the means of finding out. Tell me the name of the man whom you love. Then — always with your permission — I will go and talk with your father."

"What will you say to him?"

"Does he know him well?"

"Yes."

"Then I will ask him to consent to your marriage on condition that the wedding shall take place, not tomorrow, but two or three months hence, in order that you may have time to reflect coolly and consider whether your father is not right."

"He will not consent."

"In all probability he will. If not, I will aid you, as I have already promised."

Kirsanoff talked a long time in this tone. And at last the patient told him the name of the man she loved, and gave him permission to speak to her father. Polosoff was greatly astonished to learn that the cause of his daughter's exhaustion was a desperate passion; he was still more astonished when he heard the name of the man whom she loved, and said firmly: "Let her die rather. Her death would be the lesser misfortune for her as well as for me."

The case was the more difficult from the fact that Kirsanoff, after hearing Polosoff's reasons, saw that the old man was right and not his daughter.

IV.

Suitors by hundreds paid court to the heiress of an immense fortune; but the society which thronged at Polosoff's dinners and parties was of that very doubtful sort and tone which ordinarily fills the parlors of the suddenly rich like Polosoff, who have neither relatives nor connections in the real aristocracy. Consequently these people ordinarily become the hosts of sharpers and coxcombs as destitute of external polish as of internal virtues. That is why Katérina Vassilievna was very much impressed when among her admirers appeared a real gallant of the best tone: his deportment was much more elegant, and his conversation much wiser and more interesting, than those of any of the others.

The father was quick to notice that she showed a preference for him, and, being a positive, resolute, and firm man, he instantly had an explanation with his daughter: "Dear Katia, Solovtzoff is paying you assiduous attention; look out for him; he is a very bad man, utterly heartless; you would be so unhappy with him that I would rather see you dead than married to him; it would not be so painful either for me or for you."

Katérina Vassilievna loved her father and was accustomed to heed his advice, for he never laid any restraint upon her, and she knew that he spoke solely from love of her; and, further, it was her nature to try rather to please those who loved her than to satisfy her own caprices; she was of those who love to say to their relatives: "You wish it; I will do it." She answered her father: "Solovtzoff pleases me, but, if you think it better that I should avoid his society, I will follow your advice." Certainly she would not have acted in this way, and, in conformity with her nature,—not to lie,—she would not have spoken in this way, if she had loved him; but at that time she had but a very slight attachment for Solovtzoff, almost none at all: he simply seemed to her a little more interesting than the others. She became cold towards him, and perhaps everything would have passed off quietly, had not her father in his ardor gone a little too far, just enough for the cunning Solovtzoff. He saw that he must play the *rôle* of a victim, but where should he find a pretext? One day Polosoff happened to indulge in a bitter jest at his expense. Solovtzoff, with an air of wounded dignity, took his leave and ceased his visits. A week later Katérina Vassilievna received from him a passionate, but extremely humble, letter. He had not hoped that she would love him; the happiness of sometimes seeing her, though even without speaking to her, had been enough for him. And yet he sacrificed this happiness to the peace of his divinity. After all, he was happy in loving her even hopelessly, and so on; but no prayers or desires. He did not even ask for a reply. Other letters of the same style arrived from time to time, and finally had an effect upon the young girl.

Not very quickly, however. After Solovtzoff's withdrawal Katérina Vassilievna was at first neither sad nor pensive, and before his withdrawal she had already become cold towards him; and, besides, she had accepted her father's counsel with the utmost calmness. Consequently, when, two months later, she grew sad, how could her father imagine that Solovtzoff, whom he had already forgotten, had anything to do with it?

"You seem sad, Katia."

"I? No, there is nothing the matter with me."

A week or two later the old man said to her:

"But are you not sick, Katia?"

"No, there is nothing the matter with me."

A fortnight later still:

"You must consult the doctor, Katia."

The doctor began to treat Katia, and the old man felt entirely easy again, for the doctor saw no danger, but only weakness and a little exhaustion. He pointed out, and correctly enough, that Katérina Vassilievna had led a very fatiguing life that winter,—every evening a party, which lasted till two, three, and often five o'clock in the morning. "This exhaustion will pass away." But, far from passing away, the exhaustion went on increasing.

Why, then, did not Katérina Vassilievna speak to her father? Because she was sure that it would have been in vain. He had signified his ideas in so firm a tone, and he never spoke lightly! Never would he consent to the marriage of his daughter to a man whom he considered wicked.

Katérina Vassilievna continued to dream, reading Solovtzoff's humble and despairing letters, and six months of such reading brought her within a step of consumption. And she did not drop a single word that could lead her father to think that he was responsible for her sickness. She was as tender with him as ever.

"You are discontented with something?"

"No, papa."

"Are you not in sorrow about something?"

"No, papa."

"It is easy to see that you are not; you are simply despondent, but that comes from weakness, from sickness. The doctor too said that it came from sickness."

But whence came the sickness? As long as the doctor considered the sickness trivial, he contented himself with attributing it to dancing and tight lacing; when he saw that it was growing dangerous, he discovered "the suspension of nervous nutrition," the *atrophia nervorum*.

V.

But, though the bigwig practitioners had agreed in the opinion that Mademoiselle Polosoff had *atrophia nervorum*, which had been developed by the fatiguing life that she led in spite of her natural inclinations towards reverie and melancholy, it did not take Kirsanoff long to see that the patient's weakness was due to some moral cause. Before the consultation of physicians the family doctor had explained to him all the relations of the patient: there were no family sorrows; the father and daughter were on very good terms. And yet the father did not know the cause of the sickness, for the family doctor did not know it; what did that mean? It was evident that the young girl had exercised her independence in concealing her illness so long even from her father, and in so acting through the whole of it that he could not divine its cause; the calmness of her replies at the medical consultation confirmed this opinion. She endured her lot with firmness and without any trace of exasperation. Kirsanoff saw that a person of such a character deserved attention and aid. His intervention seemed indispensable: to be sure, light some day might be thrown upon the matter in one way or another without him, but would it not then be too late? Consumption was about to set in, and soon all the care imaginable would be powerless. For two hours he had been striving to gain the patient's confidence; at last he had succeeded; now he had got down to the heart of the matter, and had obtained permission to speak to her father.

The old man was very much astonished when he learned from Kirsanoff that it was love for Solovtzoff that was at the bottom of his daughter's sickness. How could that be? Katia had formerly accepted so coolly his advice to avoid Solovtzoff's society, and had been so indifferent when his visits ceased! How could she have begun to die of love on his account? Does any one ever die of love? Such exaltation did not seem at all probable to so calculating and practical a man. But he was made very anxious by what Kirsanoff said, and kept saying in reply: "It is a child's fancy and will pass away." Kirsanoff explained again and again, and at last made him understand that it was precisely because she was a child that Katia would not forget, but would die. Polosoff was convinced, but, instead of yielding, he struck the table with his fist and said with inflexible resolution: "Well, let her die! let her die! better that than be unhappy. For her as well as for me it will be less painful!" The same words that he had said to his daughter six months before. Katérina Vassilievna was right, therefore, in believing that it was useless to speak to her father.

"But why are you so tenacious on this point? I am willing to admit that the lover is bad, but is he as bad as death?"

"Yes! He has no heart. She is sweet and delicate; he is a base libertine."

And Polosoff painted Solovtzoff so black that Kirsanoff could say nothing in reply. In fact, how could he help agreeing with Polosoff? Solovtzoff was no other than the Jean whom we formerly saw at supper with Storeshnikoff, Serge, and Julie. Hence it was evident that an honest young girl had better die than marry such a man. He would stifle and prey upon an honest woman. She had much better die.

Kirsanoff thought for a few minutes in silence, and then said:

"No, your arguments are not valid. There is no danger for the very reason that the individual is so bad. She will find it out, if you leave her to examine him coolly."

And Kirsanoff persisted in explaining his plan to Polosoff in more detail. Had he not himself said to his daughter that, if she should find out that the object of her love was unworthy, she would renounce him herself? Now he might be quite sure of such renunciation, the man loved being very unworthy.

"It will not do for me to tell you that marriage is not a thing of extreme importance if we view it without prejudice, though really, when a wife is unhappy, there is no reason why she should not separate from her husband. But you think that out of the question, and your daughter has been brought up with the same ideas; to you as well as to her marriage is an irrevocable contract, and, before she could get any other ideas into her head, life with such a man would kill her in much more painful fashion than consumption. Therefore we must consider the question from another standpoint. Why not rely on your daughter's good sense? She is not insane; far from it. Always rely on the good sense of any one whom you leave free. The fault in this matter is yours. You have put chains on your daughter's will; unchain her, and you will see her come to your view, if you are right. Passion is blind when it meets obstacles; remove the obstacles, and your daughter will become prudent. Give her the liberty to love or not to love, and she will see whether this man is worthy of love. Let him be her sweetheart, and in a short time she will dismiss him."

Such a way of viewing things was far too novel for Polosoff. He answered with some asperity that he did not believe in such twaddle, that he knew life too well, and that he saw too many instances of human folly to have any faith in humanity's good sense. Especially ridiculous would it be to trust to the good sense of a little girl of seventeen. In vain did Kirsanoff reply that follies are committed only in two cases,—either in a moment of impulse, or else when the individual is deprived of liberty and irritated by resistance. These ideas were Hebrew to Polosoff. "She is insane; it would be senseless to trust such a child with her own fate; rather let her die." He could not be swerved from his decision. But however firm an obstinate man may be in his ideas, if another man of more developed mind, knowing and understanding the circumstances better, labors constantly to free him of his error, the error will be overcome. Still, how long will the logical struggle last between the old father and the young doctor? Certainly today's conversation will not fail to have its effect on Polosoff, although it has not yet produced any; the old man will inevitably reflect upon Kirsanoff's words; and by renewing such conversations he may be recalled to his senses, although, proud of his experience, he deems himself infallible. In any case his conversion would be a long process, and delay was dangerous; a long delay would surely be fatal, and such delay was inevitable in view of all the circumstances. Therefore radical means must be resorted to. There was danger in so doing, it is true, but there was only danger, while any other course meant certain loss. The danger, though real, was not very grave: there was but one chance of loss against an infinity of chances of salvation. Kirsanoff saw in his patient a young girl of calm and silent firmness, and was sure of her. But had he a right to submit her to this danger? Yes, certainly.

"Very well," said Kirsanoff, "you will not cure her by the means within your power; I am going to treat her with my own. Tomorrow I will call another consultation."

Returning to his patient, he told her that her father was obstinate, more obstinate than he expected, and that it was necessary consequently to proceed energetically in opposition to him.

"No, nothing can be done," said the patient in a very sad tone.

"Are you sure?"
"Yes."
"Are you ready to die?"
"Yes."
"And if I decide to submit you to the risk of death? I have already spoken of this to you, but only to gain your confidence and show you that I would consent to anything in order to be useful to you: now I speak positively. Suppose I were to give you poison?"
"I have long known that my death is inevitable; I have but a few days more to live."
"And suppose it were tomorrow morning?"
"So much the better."
She spoke quite calmly.
When there is but one resource left, — to fall back on the resolve to die, — success is almost sure. When any one says to us: "Yield, or I die," we almost always yield; but such a resort cannot be played with without loss of dignity; if there is no yielding, then death must be faced.
He explained his plan to her, although it really needed no further elucidation.

VI.

Certainly Kirsanoff would never have made it a rule in such cases to resort to such a risk. It would have been much simpler to carry the young girl away and let her marry any one she might choose; but in this case the question was made very complex by the young girl's ideas and the character of the man whom she loved. With her ideas of the indissolubility of marriage she would continue to live with this base man, even though her life with him should prove a hell. To unite her to him was worse than to kill her. Consequently there was but one way left, — to cause her death or give her the opportunity of coming back to her right mind.

The next day the medical council reassembled. It consisted of half a dozen very grave and celebrated personages; else how could it have had any effect on Polosoff? It was necessary that he should regard its decree as final. Kirsanoff spoke; they listened gravely to what he said, and endorsed his opinion no less gravely; it could not be otherwise, for, as you remember, there was in the world a certain Claude Bernard, who lived in Paris and had a high opinion of Kirsanoff. Besides, Kirsanoff said things that — the devil take these urchins! — they did not understand at all; how, then, could they refuse their approval? Kirsanoff said that he had watched the patient very carefully, and that he entirely agreed with Carl Fedorytch that the disease was incurable; now, the agony being very painful, and each additional hour of the patient's life being but another hour of suffering, he believed it to be the duty of the council to decree, for the sake of humanity, that the patient's sufferings should be at once terminated by a dose of morphine, from the effects of which she would never awaken.

The council looked at the patient, sounded her chest once more to decide whether it ought to accept or reject this proposition, and, after a long examination, much blinking of the eyes, and stifled murmurs against Kirsanoff's unintelligible science, it came back to the room adjoining the sick chamber and pronounced this decree: The patient's sufferings must be terminated by a fatal dose of morphine. After this proclamation, Kirsanoff rang for the servant and asked her to call Polosoff into the council-chamber. Polosoff entered. The gravest of the sages, in a sad and solemn form and a majestic and sorrowful voice, announced to him the decree of the council.

Polosoff was thunderstruck. Between expecting an eventual death and hearing the words: "In half an hour your daughter will be no more," there is a difference. Kirsanoff looked at Polosoff with sustained attention; he was sure of the effect; nevertheless it was a matter calculated to excite the nerves; for two minutes the stupefied old man kept silent.

"It must not be! She is dying of my obstinacy! I consent to anything! Will she get well?"

"Certainly," said Kirsanoff.

The celebrities would have been seriously offended if they had had time to dart glances at each other signifying that all understood that this urchin had played with them as if they were puppets; but Kirsanoff did not leave them time enough for the development of these observations. He told the servant to take away the drooping Polosoff, and then congratulated them on the perspicacity with which they had divined his intention, understanding that the disease was due to moral suffering, and that it was necessary to frighten the opinionated old man, who else would really have caused his daughter's death. The celebrities separated each content at hearing his perspicacity and erudition thus attested before all the others.

After having given them this certificate, Kirsanoff went to tell the patient that the policy had succeeded. At his first words she seized his hand and tried to kiss it; he withdrew it with great difficulty.

"But I shall not let your father visit you immediately to make the same announcement to you: I have first to give him a lesson concerning the way in which he must conduct himself."

He told her what advice he was going to give her father, saying that he would not leave him until he should be completely prepared.

Disturbed by all that had happened, the old man was very much cast down; he no longer viewed Kirsanoff with the same eyes, but as Maria Alexevna had formerly viewed Lopoukhoff when, in a dream, she saw him in possession of the lucrative monopoly of the liquor business. But yesterday Polosoff naturally thought in this vein: "I am older and more experienced than you, and, besides, no one in the world can surpass me in brains; as for you, a beardless boy and a *sans-culotte*, I have the less reason to listen to you from the fact that I have amassed by my own wits two millions [there were really but two millions, and not four]; first amass as much yourself, and then we will talk." Now his thought took this turn: "What a bear! What a will he has shown in this affair! He understands how to make men bend." And the more he talked with Kirsanoff, the more and more vividly was painted upon his imagination this additional picture, an old and forgotten memory of hussar life: the horseman Zakhartchenko seated on the "Gromoboy"* (at that time Joukovsky's ballads were still fashionable among young ladies, and, through them, among civil and military cavaliers), the Gromoboy galloping fast under Zakhartchenko, with torn and bleeding lips.

Polosoff was seized with fright on hearing, in answer to his first question: "Would you really have given her a fatal dose?" this reply, given quite coldly by Kirsanoff: "Why, certainly."

"What a brigand!" said Polosoff to himself. "He talks like a cook wringing a hen's neck."

"And you would have had the courage?" continued he, aloud.

"Of course; do you take me for a wet rag?"

"You are a horrible man," said and repeated Polosoff.

"That only means that you have never seen horrible men," answered Kirsanoff, with an indulgent smile, at the same time saying to himself: "You ought to see Rakhmétoff."

"But how did you persuade all these physicians?"

"Is it, then, so difficult to persuade such people?" answered Kirsanoff, with a slight grimace.

Then Polosoff recalled Zakhartchenko saying to Lieutenant Volynoff: "Must I break in this long-eared jade, your highness? I am ashamed to sit upon her."

After having put a stop to Polosoff's interminable questions, Kirsanoff began his instructions.

"Do not forget that human beings reflect coolly only when not thwarted, that they get heated only when irritated, and that they set no value on their fantasies if no attempt is made to deprive them of them and they are left free to inquire whether they are good or bad. If Solovtzoff is as bad as you say,—and I fully believe you,—your daughter will see it for herself, but only when you stop thwarting her; a single word from you against him would set the matter back two weeks, several words forever; you must hold yourself quite aloof."

The instructions were spiced with arguments of this sort: "It is not easy to make yourself do what you do not wish to do. Still, I have succeeded in such at-

---

* The name of a ballad by Joukovsky, a romantic poet of the beginning of this century.

tempts, and so I know how to treat these matters; believe me, what I say must be done. I know what I say; you have only to listen."

With people like Polosoff one can act effectively only with a high hand. Polosoff was subdued, and promised to do as he was told. But while convinced that Kirsanoff was right and must be obeyed, he could not understand him at all.

"You are on my side and at the same time on my daughter's side; you order me to submit to my daughter and you wish her to change her mind. How are these two things to be reconciled?"

"It is simple enough; I only wish you not to prevent her from becoming reasonable."

Polosoff wrote a note to Solovtzoff, begging him to be good enough to call upon him concerning an important matter; that evening Solovtzoff appeared, came to an amicable but very dignified understanding with the old man, and was accepted as the daughter's intended, on the condition that the marriage should not take place inside of three months.

VII.

Kirsanoff could not abandon this affair: it was necessary to come to Katérina Vassilievna's aid to get her out of her blindness as quickly as possible, and more necessary still to watch her father and see that he adhered to the policy of non-intervention. Nevertheless, for the first few days after the crisis, he abstained from visiting the Polosoffs: it was certain that Katérina Vassilievna's state of exaltation still continued; if he should find (as he expected) her sweetheart unworthy, the very fact of betraying his dislike of him — to say nothing of directly mentioning it — would be injurious and heighten the exaltation. Ten days later Kirsanoff came, and came in the morning expressly that he might not seem to be seeking an opportunity of meeting the sweetheart, for he wished Katérina Vassilievna to consent with a good grace. Katérina Vassilievna was already well advanced on the road to recovery; she was still very pale and thin, but felt quite well, although a great deal of medicine had been given her by her illustrious physician, into whose hands Kirsanoff had resigned her, saying to the young girl: "Let him attend you; all his drugs cannot harm you now." Katérina Vassilievna welcomed Kirsanoff enthusiastically, but she looked at him in amazement when he told her why he had come.

"You have saved my life, and yet need my permission to visit us?"

"But my visit in his presence might seem to you an attempt at interference in your relations without your consent. You know my rule, — to do nothing without the consent of the person in behalf of whom I wish to act."

Coming in the evening two or three days afterwards, Kirsanoff found the sweetheart as Polosoff had painted him, and Polosoff himself — behaving satisfactorily:

the well-trained old man was placing no obstacles in his daughter's path. Kirsanoff spent the evening there, not showing in any way whatever his opinion of the sweetheart, and in taking leave of Katérina Vassilievna he made no allusion to him, one way or another.

This was just enough to excite her curiosity and doubt. The next day she said to herself repeatedly: "Kirsanoff did not say a word to me about him. If he had left a good impression on him, Kirsanoff would have told me so. Can it be that he does not please him? In what respect can he be displeasing to Kirsanoff?" When the sweetheart returned the following day, she examined his manners closely, and weighed his words. She asked herself why she did this: it was to prove to herself that Kirsanoff should not or could not have found any out about him. This was really her motive. But the necessity of proving to one's self that a person whom one loves has no outs puts one in the way to find some very soon.

A few days later Kirsanoff came again, and still said nothing of the sweetheart. This time she could not restrain herself, and towards the end of the evening she said to Kirsanoff:

"Your opinion? Why do you keep silence?"

"I do not know whether it would be agreeable to you to hear my opinion; I do not know whether you would think it impartial."

"He displeases you?"

Kirsanoff made no answer.

"He displeases you?"

"I have not said so."

"It is easy to see that he does. Why, then, does he displease you?"

"I will wait for others to see the why."

The next night Katérina Vassilievna examined Solovtzoff more attentively yet.

"Everything about him is all right; Kirsanoff is unjust; but why can I not see what it is in him that displeases Kirsanoff?"

Her pride was excited in a direction most dangerous to the sweetheart.

When Kirsanoff returned a few days afterwards, he saw that he was already in a position to act more positively. Hitherto he had avoided conversations with Solovtzoff in order not to alarm Katérina Vassilievna by premature intervention. Now he made one of the group surrounding the young girl and her sweetheart, and began to direct the conversation upon subjects calculated to unveil Solovtzoff's character by dragging him into the dialogue. The conversation turned upon wealth, and it seemed to Katérina Vassilievna that Solovtzoff was far too much occupied with thoughts about wealth; the conversation turned upon women, and it seemed to her that Solovtzoff spoke of them much too lightly; the conversation turned upon family life, and she tried in vain to drive away the impression that life with such a husband would be perhaps not very inspiring, but rather painful, to a woman.

The crisis had arrived. For a long time Katérina Vassilievna could not go to sleep; she wept in vexation with herself at having injured Solovtzoff by such thoughts regarding him. "No, he is not a heartless man; he does not despise women; he loves me, and not my money." If these replies had been in answer to another's words, she would have clung to them obstinately. But she was replying to herself; now, against a truth that you have discovered yourself it is impossible to struggle long; it is your own; there is no ground for suspicion of trickery. The next evening Katérina Vassilievna herself put Solovtzoff to the test, as Kirsanoff had done the evening before. She said to herself that she wished only to convince herself that she had injured him needlessly, but at the same time she felt that she had less confidence in him than before. And again she could not go to sleep, and this time it was with him that she was vexed: why had he spoken in such a way that, instead of quieting her doubts, he had strengthened them? She was vexed with herself too, and in this vexation could be seen clearly enough this motive: "How could I have been so blind?"

It is easy to understand that two days later she was completely absorbed by this thought: "It will soon be too late to repair my error, if I am mistaken."

When Kirsanoff returned for the first time after his conversation with Solovtzoff, he saw that he might speak to Katérina.

"Formerly you desired to know my opinion about him," said he: "it is not as important as yours. What do you think of him yourself?"

Now it was she who kept silent.

"I do not dare to press you for an answer," said he. He spoke of other things, and soon went away.

But half an hour afterwards she called on him herself.

"Give me your advice; you see that I am hesitating."

"Why, then, do you need the advice of another, when you know yourself what should be done in case of hesitation?"

"Wait till the hesitation is over?"

"You have said it."

"I could postpone the marriage."

"Why not do so, then, if you think it would be better?"

"But how would he take it?"

"When you see in what way he will take it, you can reflect further as to the better course to follow."

"But it would be painful to me to tell him."

"If that be the case, ask your father to do it for you; he will tell him."

"I do not wish to hide behind another. I will tell him myself."

"If you feel in a condition to tell him yourself, that is certainly much the better way."

It is evident that with other persons — with Véra Pavlovna, for instance — it would not have taken so long to bring the affair to a conclusion. But each temperament has its own particular requirements: if an ardent nature is irritated by delay, a gentle nature on the contrary rebels against abruptness.

The success of Katérina Vassilievna's explanation with her sweetheart surpassed the hopes of Kirsanoff, who believed that Solovtzoff would have wit enough to drag the matter along by his submission and soft beseechings. No; with all his reserve and tact Solovtzoff could not restrain himself at seeing an enormous fortune escape him, and he himself permitted the escape of the few chances that were left him. He launched out in bitter complaints against Polosoff, whom he called an intriguer, telling Katérina Vassilievna that she allowed her father to have too much power over her, that she feared him, and that in this matter she was acting in accordance with his orders. Now, Polosoff as yet knew nothing about this resolution of his daughter; she felt that she was entirely free. The reproaches heaped upon her father wounded her by their injustice, and outraged her in showing her that Solovtzoff considered her a being destitute of will and character.

"You seem to think me a plaything in the hands of others."

"Yes," he said, thoroughly irritated.

"I was ready to die without thinking of my father, and you do not understand it. From this moment all is over between us," said she, quickly leaving the room.

VIII.

For a long time Katérina Vassilievna was sad, but her sadness, which grew out of these events, soon turned to something else.

There are characters who feel but little interest in a special fact in itself and are only pushed by it in the direction of general ideas, which then act upon them with much greater intensity. If such people possess minds of remarkable vigor, they become reformers of general ideas, and in ancient times they became great philosophers: Kant, Fichte, Hegel, did not elaborate any single special question; such tasks they found wearisome. This refers only to men, be it understood; women, according to generally received opinion, never have strong minds; nature, you see, has denied them that, just as it has denied blacksmiths soft complexions, tailors fine figures, and shoemakers a pleasant odor. What do you expect? Nature is queer, and that is why there are so few great minds among women.

People of uncommonly small minds, with such a tendency of character, are generally phlegmatic and insusceptible; those having minds of ordinary calibre are prone to melancholy and reverie. Which does not mean that they let their imaginations run riot: many of them are deficient in imagination and very positive, only they love to plunge into quiet reverie.

Katérina Vassilievna's love of Solovtzoff had been inspired by his letters; she was dying of a love created by her imagination. It is evident from this that she had very romantic tendencies, although the noisy life of the commonplace society which filled the Polosoffs' house did not dispose her to exalted idealism. It was one of her traits, therefore. The stir and noise had long been a burden on her; she loved to read and dream. Now not only the stir, but the wealth itself, was a burden on her. It does not necessarily follow that she was an extraordinary person. This feeling is common to all rich women of gentle and modest natures. Only in her it had developed sooner than usual, the young girl having received a harsh lesson at an early age.

"In whom can I believe? In what can I believe?" she asked herself, after her rupture with Solovtzoff; and she was forced to conclude that she could believe in nobody and in nothing. Her father's fortune attracted avarice, strategy, and deception from all quarters of the city. She was surrounded by greedy, lying, flattering people; every word spoken to her was dictated by her father's millions.

Her inner thoughts became more and more serious. General questions—concerning wealth, which wearied her so much, and poverty, which tormented so many others—began to interest her. Her father allowed her a large amount of pin-money; she—in that respect like all charitable women—helped the poor. At the same time she read and reflected; she began to see that help of the kind which she lavished was much less efficacious than might have been expected. She was unworthily deceived by the base or pretended poor; and, besides, even those who were worthy of aid and knew how to profit by the money given them could not get out of their poverty with the alms which they received. That made her reflect. Why so much wealth in the hands of some to spoil them, why so much poverty for others? And why did she see so many poor people who were as unreasonable and wicked as the rich?

She was dreamy, but her dreams were mild, like her character, and had as little brilliancy as herself. Her favorite poet was Georges Sand; but she represented herself neither as a Lélia, or an Indiana, or a Cavalcanti, or even a Consuelo; in her dreams she was a Jeanne, and oftener still a Geneviève. Geneviève was her favorite heroine. She saw her walking in the fields and gathering flowers to serve as models for her work; she saw her meeting André,—what sweet rendezvous! Then they find out that they love each other; those were dreams, she knew. But she loved also to dream of the enviable lot of Miss Nightingale, that sweet and modest young girl, of whom no one knows anything, of whom there is nothing to know, except that she is the beloved of all England. Was she young? Poor or rich? Was she happy in her private life or not? No one speaks of that, no one thinks of it, but all bless the consoling angel of the English hospitals of the Crimea and Scutari. Returning to her country after the war was over, she had continued to care for the sick. This was the dream that Katérina Vassilievna would have liked to realize for herself. Her fancy did not carry her beyond these reveries about Geneviève and Miss Nightingale. Can it be said that she is given to fantasy? Can she be called a dreamer?

Had Geneviève been surrounded by the noisy and commonplace society of the lowest rank of sharpers and coxcombs, had Miss Nightingale been plunged into a life of idle luxury, might they not have been sad and sorrowful? Therefore Katérina Vassilievna was perhaps more rejoiced than afflicted when her father was ruined. It affected her to see him grow old and weak, he who was once so strong; it weighed upon her also to have less means with which to do good. The sudden disdain of the crowd which had formerly fawned upon her and her father offended her somewhat; but this too had its consoling side, — the being abandoned by the trivial, wearisome, and vile crowd, the being no more disgusted by its baseness and treachery, the being no more embarrassed by it. Yes, now she was tranquil. She recovered hope.

"Now, if any one loves me, it will be for myself, and not for my father's millions."

IX.

Polosoff desired to arrange the sale of the stearine factory of which he was a stockholder and director. After six months of assiduous search, he finally found a purchaser. The purchaser's cards read: *Charles Beaumont*, but they did not give this name the French pronunciation, as persons unacquainted with the individual might have done, but the English; and it was very natural that they should so pronounce it, for the purchaser was the agent of the London house of Hodgson, Loter & Co. The factory could not prosper; everything about it was in bad condition, — its finances and its administration; but in more experienced hands it probably would yield large returns; an investment of five or six hundred thousand roubles might give an annual profit of a hundred thousand. The agent was conscientious: he carefully inspected the factory, and examined its books with the utmost minuteness before advising his house to purchase. Then began the discussions as to the condition of the business and how much it was worth; these dragged along almost interminably, from the very nature of our stock companies, with which the patient Greeks themselves, who for ten years did not weary of besieging the city of Troy, would have lost patience. During all this time Polosoff, in accordance with an old custom, was very attentive to the agent and always invited him to dinner. The agent kept himself at a respectful distance from the old man, and for a long time declined his invitations, but one day, feeling tired and hungry after an unusually long discussion with the directors, he consented to go to dinner with Polosoff, who lived on the same floor.

X.

Charles Beaumont, like every Charles, John, James, or William, was not fond of personal intimacies and effusions; but, when asked, he told his story in a few words, but very clearly. His family, he said, was of Canadian origin; in fact, in Canada a good half of the population consists of descendants of French colonists; to these descendants belonged his family; hence his French name. In his features he certainly resembled a Frenchman more than an Englishman or a Yankee. But, he continued, his grandfather left the suburbs of Quebec and went to New York to live; such things happen. Therefore his father went to New York when still a child and grew up there. When he became an adult (exactly at that time), a rich and progressive proprietor, living in the southern part of the Crimea, conceived the idea of replacing his vineyards with cotton plantations. So he despatched an agent to find an overseer for him in North America. The agent found James Beaumont, of Canadian origin and a resident of New York,—that is, an individual who had no more seen a cotton plantation than you or I, reader, have seen Mount Ararat from our St. Petersburg or Kursk; progressive people are always having such experiences. It is true that the experiment was in no wise spoiled by the American overseer's complete ignorance of this branch of production, since it would have been quite as wise to try to grow grapes at St. Petersburg as cotton at the Crimea. Nevertheless this impossibility resulted in the overseer's discharge, and by chance he became a distiller of brandy in the government of Tambov, where he passed almost all the rest of his life; there his son Charles was born, and there, shortly afterwards, he buried his wife. When nearly sixty-five years old, having laid by a little money for his old age, he began to think of returning to America, and finally did return. Charles was then about twenty years old. After his father's death Charles desired to return to Russia, where he was born and where, in the fields of the government of Tambov, he had spent his childhood and youth; he felt himself a Russian. At New York he was a bookkeeper in a commercial house; he soon left this situation for one in the London house of Hodgson, Loter & Co.: ascertaining that this house did business with St. Petersburg, he took the first opportunity to express a desire of obtaining a place in Russia, explaining that he knew Russia as if it were his own country. To have such an employee in Russia would evidently be of great advantage to the house; so it sent him from the London establishment on trial, and here he is in St. Petersburg, having been here six months, on a salary of five hundred pounds. It was not at all astonishing, then, that Beaumont spoke Russian like a Russian and pronounced English with a certain foreign accent.

XI.

Beaumont found himself a third at dinner with the old gentleman and his daughter, a very pretty blonde with a somewhat melancholy cast of countenance.

"Could I ever have thought," said Polosoff at dinner, "that my stock in this factory would some day be a matter of importance to me? It is very painful at my age to fall from so high a point. Fortunately Katia has endured with much indifference the loss of her fortune sacrificed by me. Even during my life this fortune belonged more to her than to me. Her mother had capital; as for me, I brought but little; it is true that I earned a great deal and that my labor did more than all the rest! What shrewdness I have had to show!"

The old man talked a long time in this boasting tone; it was by sweat and blood, and above all by brains, that he had gained his fortune; and in conclusion he repeated his preface that it was painful to fall from so high a point, and that, if Katia had been consumed with sorrow because of it, he probably would have gone mad, but that Katia, far from complaining, still encouraged and sustained him.

In accordance with the American habit of seeing nothing extraordinary in rapid fortune or sudden ruin, and in accordance also with his individual character, Beaumont was not inclined either to be delighted at the greatness of mind which had succeeded in acquiring three or four millions, or to be afflicted at a ruin which still permitted the employment of a good cook. But, as it was necessary to say a word of sympathy in answer to this long discourse, he remarked:

"Yes, it is a great relief when one's family bears up so well under reverses."

"But you seem to doubt it, Karl Iakovlitch. You think that, because Katia is melancholy, she mourns the loss of wealth? No, Karl Iakovlitch, you wrong her. We have experienced another misfortune: we have lost confidence in everybody," said Polosoff, in the half-serious, half-jocose tone used by experienced old men in speaking of the good but naïve thoughts of children.

Katérina Vassilievna blushed. It was distasteful to her to have her father turn the conversation upon the subject of her feelings. Besides paternal love there was another circumstance that went far to excuse her father's fault. When one has nothing to say and is in a room where there is a cat or a dog, he speaks of it, and, if there is no cat or dog, he speaks of children; not until these two subjects are exhausted does he talk about the rain and the fine weather.

"No, papa, you are wrong in attributing my melancholy to so lofty a motive. It is not my nature to be gay, and, besides, I am suffering from *ennui*."

"One may be gay or not, according to circumstances," said Beaumont; "but to suffer from *ennui* is, in my opinion, unpardonable. *Ennui* is the fashion among our brothers, the English, but we Americans know nothing about it. We have no time for it: we are too busy. I consider . . . . . It seems to me," he resumed, correcting his Americanism, "that the same should be true of the Russian people also: in my opinion you have too much to do. But I notice in the Russians just the opposite characteristic: they are strongly disposed to spleen. Even the English are not to be compared with them in this respect. English society, looked upon by all Europe, including Russia, as the most tiresome in the world, is more talkative, lively, and gay than Russian society, just as it yields the palm to French society in this particular. Your travellers talk of English spleen ; I do not know where their eyes are when they are in their own country."

"And the Russians have reason to feel *ennui*," said Katérina Vassilievna; "what can they busy themselves about ? They have nothing to do. They must sit with folded arms. Name me an occupation, and my *ennui* probably will vanish."

"You wish to find an occupation ? Oh! that is not so difficult ; you see around you such ignorance, — pardon me for speaking in this way of your country, *of your native country*," he hastened to add in correction of his Anglicism; "but I was born here myself and grew up here, and I consider it as my own, and so I do not stand on ceremony, — you see here a Turkish ignorance, a Japanese indifference : I hate your native country, since I love it as my own country, may I say, in imitation of your poet. Why, there are many things to be done."

"Yes, but what can one man do, to say nothing of one woman ?"

"Why, you are doing already, Katia," said Polosoff; "I will unveil her secret for you, Karl Iakovlitch. To drive away *ennui* she teaches little girls. Every day she receives her scholars, and she devotes three hours to them and sometimes even more."

Beaumont looked at the young girl with esteem : "That is American. By America I mean only the free States of the North ; the Southern States are worse than all possible Mexicos, are almost as abominable as Brazil [Beaumont was a furious abolitionist]; it is like us to teach children ; but then, why do you suffer from *ennui ?*"

"Do you consider that a serious occupation, M. Beaumont ? It is but a distraction ; at least, so it seems to me ; perhaps I am mistaken, and you will call me materialistic ?"

"Do you expect such a reproach from a man belonging to a nation which everybody reproaches with having no other thought, no other ideal, than dollars?"

"You jest, but I am seriously afraid; I fear to state my opinions on this subject before you ; my views might seem to you like those preached by the obscurantists concerning the uselessness of instruction."

"Bravo!" said Beaumont to himself: "is it possible that she can have arrived at this idea ? This is getting interesting."

Then he continued aloud : "I am an obscurantist myself; I am for the unlettered blacks against their civilized proprietors in the Southern States. But pardon me; my American hatred has diverted me. It would be very agreable to me to hear your opinion."

"It is very prosaic, M. Beaumont, but I have been led to it by life. It seems to me that the matter with which I occupy myself is but one side of the whole, and, moreover, not the side upon which the attention of those who wish to serve the people should be first fixed. This is what I think: give people bread, and they will learn to read themselves. It is necessary to begin with the bread; otherwise it will be time wasted."

"Then why don't you commence at the necessary point?" said Beaumont, already a little animated. "It is possible; I know examples, with us in America," he added.

"I have already told you why. What can I undertake alone? I do not know how to go to work; and, even if I knew, could I do it? A young girl is so hampered in every direction. I am free in my own room. But what can I do there? Put a book on the table and teach people to read it. Where can I go? What can I do alone?"

"Are you trying to make me out a despot, Katia?" said the father: "but it is not my fault, you having given me so severe a lesson."

"I blush at the thought, papa; I was then a child. No, you are good, you do not thwart me. It is society that thwarts me. Is it true, M. Beaumont, that in America a young girl is much less hampered?"

"Yes, we may be proud of it, although we are far from where we ought to be; but what a comparison with Europeans! All that you hear about the liberty of woman in our country is really the truth."

"Papa, let us go to America, after M. Beaumont has bought the factory," said Katérina Vassilievna, jokingly: "there I will do something. Ah! how happy I should be!"

"One may find an occupation at St. Petersburg also," said Beaumont.

"How?"

Beaumont hesitated two or three seconds. "But why, then, did I come here? And who could better inform me?" said he to himself.

"Have you not heard of it? There is an attempt in progress to apply the principles lately deduced by economic science: are you familiar with them?"

"Yes, I have read a little about them; that must be very interesting and very useful. And could I take part in it? Where shall I find it?"

"The shop was founded by Madame Kirsanoff."

"Is she the doctor's wife?"

"You know him? And has he said nothing to you about this matter?"

"A long time ago. Then he was not married. I was sick; he came several times, and saved me. Ah! what a man! Does she resemble him?"

But how make Madame Kirsanoff's acquaintance? Could Beaumont give Katérina Vassilievna a letter of introduction to Madame Kirsanoff? What was the use? The Kirsanoffs had never even heard his name; but no introduction was necessary: Madame Kirsanoff surely would be very glad to find so much sympathy. As for her address, it would have to be ascertained at the hospital or the Academy of Medicine.

XII.

Such was the way in which Mademoiselle Polosoff came to know Véra Pavlovna; she called upon the latter the following morning; and Beaumont was so interested in the matter that he came in the evening to inquire about her visit.

Katérina Vassilievna was very animated. There was no trace of her sorrow left; ecstasy had replaced melancholy. She described to Beaumont, with enthusiasm, what she had seen and heard; she had already told the story to her father, but it was impossible for her to weary of it; her heart was so full: she had found an attractive occupation. Beaumont listened attentively; but does one listen like that? And she said to him, almost angrily: "M. Beaumont, I am beginning to be disenchanted with you: is it possible that you can be so little impressed? One would suppose that you felt almost no interest."

"Do not forget, Katérina Vassilievna, that I have seen all this in America; I am interested in a few of the details; but as a whole I know it only too well. It is only in the persons who have taken this initiative here that I can be much interested. For instance, what can you tell me of Madame Kirsanoff?"

"Ah, my God! she certainly pleased me much. She explained everything to me with so much ardor."

"You have already said so."

"What more do you want? What else could I tell you? Could you expect me, indeed, to be thinking of her, when I had such a sight before my eyes?"

"I understand that one entirely forgets persons when interested in things; but nevertheless what else can you tell me of Madame Kirsanoff?"

Katérina Vassilievna called up her recollections of Véra Pavlovna, but found in them only the first impression that Véra Pavlovna had made upon her; she described very vividly her external appearance, her manner of speech, all that one sees at a glance when first meeting a stranger; but beyond this there was almost nothing in her memory relating to Véra Pavlovna: the shop, the shop, the shop,— and Véra Pavlovna's explanations. These explanations she understood thoroughly, but Véra Pavlovna herself she understood but very little.

"For this once, then, you have disappointed my hopes; I should have been very glad to learn something from you as to Madame Kirsanoff; nevertheless I do not release you; in a few days I will question you again on this subject."

"But why not make her acquaintance, if she interests you so much?"

"I should like to do so; perhaps I shall some day. But first I must learn more about her."

Beaumont was silent for a few moments.

"I am considering whether I should ask a favor of you. Yes, it is better that I should. This is it: if my name happens to be mentioned in your conversations with them, do not say that I have questioned you about her, or that it is my intention to sometime make her acquaintance."

"But this is getting enigmatical, M. Beaumont," said Katérina Vassilievna, in a serious tone. "Through me as an intermediary you wish to obtain information about them, while you remain concealed yourself?"

"Yes, Katérina Vassilievna; how shall I explain it to you? I fear to make their acquaintance."

"All this is very strange, M. Beaumont."

"True. I will say more: I fear that it may be disagreeable to them. They have never heard my name. But I have had something to do with one of their relatives, and even with them. In short, I must first be sure that it would be agreeable to them to make my acquaintance."

"All this is strange, M. Beaumont."

"I am an honest man, Katérina Vassilievna; I venture to assure you that I shall never permit myself to compromise you; I see you now only for the second time, but already I esteem you."

"I see for myself, M. Beaumont, that you are an honest man; but" . . . . .

"If you think me an honest man, you will permit me to come to see you in order that, as soon as you shall feel entirely sure about me, I may ask you for details about the Kirsanoffs. Or rather, you shall break the silence yourself, whenever it may seem to you that you can satisfy the request which I have just made of you and which I shall not renew. Are you willing?"

"Certainly, M. Beaumont," said Katérina Vassilievna, slightly shrugging her shoulders. "But confess, then" . . . . .

This time she did not wish to finish.

"That I must now inspire you with some mistrust? True. But I will wait till that has disappeared."

XIII.

Beaumont visited the Polosoffs very often. "Why not?" thought the old man: "he is a good match. Certainly he is not such a husband as Katia might once have had. But then she was neither concerned nor ambitious. Now one could not ask a better."

In fact, Beaumont was a good match. He said that he thought of living in Russia for the rest of his days, as he regarded it as his native country. Here was a positive man; at thirty years, though born poor, he had a good position in life. If he had been a Russian, Polosoff would have liked it had he been a nobleman, but in the case of foreigners this is not an important consideration, especially when they are Frenchmen and still less when they are Americans. In America one may be today in the employ of a shoemaker or a farmer, tomorrow a general, the day after president, and then again a clerk or a lawyer. They are a people apart, judging individuals only by their wealth and their capacities. "And they are quite right," reflected Polosoff; "I am such a man myself. I began in commerce and married a merchant's daughter. Money is the most important thing; brains also, to be sure, for without brains one cannot get money; he has taken a good road. He will buy the factory and be its manager; then he will become a partner in the house. And their houses are not like ours. He, too, will control millions."

It was very probable that Polosoff's dreams concerning his future son-in-law were no more to be realized than the similar dreams of Maria Alexevna. But, however that may be, Beaumont was a good match for Katérina Vassilievna.

Was not Polosoff mistaken, nevertheless, in his prevision of a son-in-law in Beaumont? If the old man had had any doubts at first, these doubts would have disappeared when Beaumont, two weeks after he had begun to visit them, said that it was very probable that the purchase of the factory would be delayed a few days; at any rate he wished to defer the drawing-up of the contract, as he was waiting for Mr. Loter, who would soon arrive at St. Petersburg. "At first, when I was not personally acquainted with you," added Beaumont, "I wanted to conclude the matter myself. Now that we are so well acquainted, this would not be proper. And that later there may be no misunderstandings, I have written to my employers that, during the negotiations, I have made the acquaintance of the manager and principal stockholder, who has nearly his entire fortune invested in the factory, and have asked, in consequence, that the house should send some one to conclude the negotiations in my place; that is the reason, you see, why Mr. Loter is coming."

Prudence and wisdom,—these showed clearly an intention to marry Katia: a simple acquaintance would not have been enough to prompt such precaution.

XIV.

The next two or three visits of Beaumont were marked at first by a rather cold welcome on the part of Katérina Vassilievna. She began indeed to feel a little distrust of this comparative stranger, who had expressed an enigmatical desire for information concerning a family to whom, if he were to be believed, he was not known, and yet feared to make their acquaintance in the absence of knowledge that his acquaintance would be agreeable. But even during these first visits, though Katérina Vassilievna viewed him with distrust, she nevertheless was quickly drawn into lively conversation with him. In her past life, before making the acquaintance of Kirsanoff, she had never met such men. He sympathized so much with all that interested her, and understood her so well! Even with her dearest friends (for that matter, properly speaking, she had but a single friend, Polina, who had long been living at Moscow, after her marriage to a manufacturer of that city), even with Polina she did not converse so much at her ease as with him.

And he at first came, not, of course, to see her, but to inquire about the Kirsanoffs; nevertheless from the very first, from the moment when they began to talk of *ennui* and the means of escaping it, it was plain that he esteemed her and was in sympathy with her. At their second interview he was very much drawn to her by her enthusiasm at having found a useful occupation. Now at each new interview his good feeling toward her became more evident. Straightway a friendship of the simplest and most fervent sort was formed between them, so that a week later Katérina Vassilievna had already told him all that she knew about the Kirsanoffs: she was sure that this man was incapable of entertaining an evil design.

It is none the less true that, when she broached the subject of the Kirsanoffs, he stopped her.

"Why so soon? You know me too little."

"No, I know you enough, M. Beaumont; I see that your unwillingness to explain to me what seemed strange in your desire was probably due to the fact that you had no right to do so; there are secrets."

To which he answered:

"And, you see, I am no longer so impatient to know what I desired to learn about them."

XV.

Katérina Vassilievna's animation continued without weakening, but it changed into a perpetual playfulness full of luminous humor. It was precisely this animation which most drew Beaumont to her; that was very evident. After having listened two or three times to the stories that she told him regarding the Kirsanoffs, he said to her the fourth time: "Now I know all that I had to find out. I thank you."

"But what do you know, then? I have only told you so far that they love each other and are very happy."

"That is all that I had to find out; besides, I knew it."

And the subject of conversation changed.

The first thought of Katérina Vassilievna, on hearing Beaumont's first question about Madame Kirsanoff, had been that he was enamored of her. But now it was clear that such was not the case.

As well as Katérina Vassilievna now knew him, she even believed that Beaumont was not capable of becoming enamored. "Love he may. But if he loves anybody now, it is I," thought Katérina Vassilievna.

XVI.

But did they really love each other? Did she, for instance, love him? On one occasion she showed some feeling for Beaumont; but how it ended! Not at all as the beginning would have led one to expect.

Beaumont came to the Polosoffs' every day for longer or shorter calls, but every day; it was precisely on that fact that Polosoff based his assurance that Beaumont intended to ask for Katérina Vassilievna's hand; there were no other indications. One day the evening went by, and Beaumont did not come.

"You do not know what has become of him, papa?"

"I know nothing about it; probably he did not have time."

Another evening passed, and still Beaumont did not come. The next morning Katérina Vassilievna was getting ready to go out.

"Where are you going, Katia?"

"To attend to some affairs of mine."

She went to see Beaumont. He was sitting down, in an overcoat with large sleeves, and reading; he raised his eyes from his book when he saw the door open.

"Ah! it is you, Katérina Vassilievna? I am very glad, and I thank you very much."

This was said in the same tone in which he would have greeted her father, except that it was a little more affable.

"What is the matter with you, M. Beaumont? Why have you stayed away so long? You have made me anxious about you, and, besides, you have made time hang heavy on my hands."

"Nothing of importance, Katérina Vassilievna; I am well, as you see. Will you not take some tea? See, I am drinking some."

"Very well, but why is it so long since we have seen you?"

"Peter, bring a cup. You see, I am well; there is nothing the matter, then. Stop! I have been to the factory with Mr. Loter, and, in explaining it to him, I was careless and placed my arm on some gearing, which scratched it. And neither yesterday nor the day before could I put on my undercoat."

"Show me your arm; else I shall be anxious and believe that you are mutilated."

"Oh! no [Peter entered with a cup for Katérina Vassilievna]. I really have my two hands. But then, if you insist [he pulled his sleeve up to his elbow]. Peter, empty this ash-receiver and give me my cigar-case; it is on the table in the study. You see that it is nothing; it needed nothing but some court-plaster."

"Nothing? It is swollen and very red."

"Yesterday it was much worse, tomorrow it will be well. [After emptying the ash-receiver and bringing the cigar-case, Peter withdrew.] I did not want to appear before you as a wounded hero."

"But why did you not write a word?"

"Oh! at first I thought that I should be able to wear my undercoat the next day,—that is, day before yesterday,—day before yesterday I thought that I should be able to wear it yesterday, and yesterday today. I thought it not worth while to trouble you."

"And you have troubled me much more. Your conduct was not good, M. Beaumont. When will this matter of the sale be finished?"

"One of these days, probably, but, you know, this delay is not my fault, or Mr. Loter's, but that of the corporation itself."

"What are you reading?"

"Thackeray's new novel. To have such talent and repeat the same thing everlastingly! It is because his stock of ideas is small."

"I have already read it; in fact," etc.

They lamented the fall of Thackeray, and talked for half an hour about other similar matters.

"But it is time to go to Véra Pavlovna's; and, by the way, when will you make their acquaintance? They are excellent people."

"Some day or other I will ask you to take me there. I thank you very much for your visit. Is that your horse?"

"Yes, that is mine."

"That is why your father never uses it. It is a fine horse."

"It seems to me so, but I know nothing about it."

"It is a very good horse, Monsieur, worth about three hundred and fifty roubles," said the coachman.

"How old is it?"

"Six years, Monsieur."

"Go on, Zakhar, I am ready. *Au revoir*, M. Beaumont; will you come today?"

"I doubt it . . . . no; tomorrow, surely."

XVII.

Do young girls who are in love make such visits as these? In the first place, no well-bred young girl would ever permit herself to do anything of the kind; but, if she should permit herself, evidently something very different would result from it. If Katérina Vassilievna's act is contrary to morality, the content of this immoral act, so to speak, is still more contrary to all received ideas. Is it not clear that Katérina Vassilievna and Beaumont were not human beings, but fishes, or, if they were human beings, that they at least had fishes' blood in their veins? And when she saw him at her home, she treated him in a manner quite in conformity with this interview.

"I am tired of talking, M. Beaumont," said she, when he stayed too long; "stay with papa; I am going to my room."

And she went out. Sometimes he answered:

"Stay fifteen minutes longer, Katérina Vassilievna."

"Very well," she then replied.

But generally he answered:

"*Au revoir*, then, Katérina Vassilievna."

What sort of people are these, I should like to know; and I should like to know also if they are not simply honest people, whom no one prevents from seeing each other in their own fashion, whom no one will prevent from marrying whenever the idea occurs to them, and who, consequently, have no reason to bear up against obstacles. Yet I am embarrassed by the coolness of their association, not so much on their account as on my own. Am I condemned, in my capacity of novelist, to compromise all my heroes and heroines in the eyes of well-bred people? Some eat and drink, others do not get excited without reason; what an uninteresting set!

XVIII.

And yet, in the opinion of the aged Polosoff, the affair meant marriage. Considering the nature of the relations between the supposed lovers, how could he imagine such a thing? Had he not heard their conversations? Not always, it is true; sometimes they stayed with him, but oftener went to sit or promenade in other rooms. It is true that this did not change at all the character of their conversation. These conversations were such that a *connoisseur* in matters of the human heart (a *human heart* which men really do not have) would have lost all hope of ever seeing Katérina Vassilievna and Beaumont married. Not that they did not talk of sentiments to each other; they talked of those as they did of everything else, but only a little and in what a tone! In a tone that was revolting, so calm was it and so horrible in the eccentricity of the thoughts expressed. Here is an example. A week after the visit for which Beaumont had "very much thanked" Katérina Vassilievna, and two months after the beginning of their acquaintance, the sale of the factory was consummated; Mr. Loter was getting ready to start the next day (and he started; expect no catastrophe from his departure; after having completed the commercial transaction as a merchant should, he notified Beaumont that the house appointed him manager of the factory at a salary of a thousand pounds sterling; that is what need be expected, and that is all; what need he has of mingling in anything but commerce judge for yourself); the stockholders, including Polosoff, were to receive the very next day (and they did receive it; expect no catastrophe here either: the house of Hodgson, Loter & Co. is very solid) half of the sum in cash and half in bills of exchange payable in three months. Polosoff, perfectly satisfied, was seated at a table in the drawing-room, turning over his business papers, and half listening to his daughter's conversation with Beaumont as they passed through the drawing-room: they were promenading in the four apartments facing the street.

"If a woman, a young girl, is hampered by prejudices," said Beaumont, without further Anglicisms or Americanisms, "man too — I speak of honest men — suffers great annoyance thereby. How can one marry a young girl who has had no experience in the daily relations which will result from her consent to the proposition? She cannot judge whether daily life with a man of such a character as her sweetheart will please her or not."

"But, M. Beaumont, if her relations with this man have been daily, that surely gives her a certain guarantee of mutual happiness."

"A certain, — yes; nevertheless it would be much surer if the test were more thorough. The young girl, from the nature of the relations permitted her, does not know enough about marriage; consequently for her it is an enormous risk. It is the same with an honest man who marries. Only he can judge in a general way; he is well acquainted with women of various characters, and knows what character suits him best. She has no such experience."

"But she has had a chance to observe life and characters in her family and among her acquaintances; she has had excellent opportunities for reflection."

"All that is very fine, but it is not sufficient. There is no substitute for personal experience."

"You would have only widows marry," said Katérina Vassilievna, laughing.

"Your expression is a very happy one. Only widows. Young girls should be forbidden to marry."

"You are right," said Katérina Vassilievna, seriously.

At first it seemed very queer to Polosoff to hear such conversations or parts of conversations. But now he was somewhat accustomed to it, and said to himself: "I too am a man devoid of prejudices. I went into commerce and married a merchant's daughter."

The next day this part of the conversation,—the general conversation was usually devoted to other subjects,—this part of the conversation of the night before continued as follows:

"You have told me the story of your love for Solovtzoff. But what was this? It was" . . . . .

"We will sit down, if it is all the same to you. I am tired of walking."

"Very well. It was, I say, a childish sentiment, about which there was no security. It is a good subject for jest, when you look back to it, and also for grief, if you will, for it had a very sad side. You were saved only by a very unusual circumstance, because the matter fell into the hands of a man, like Alexander."

"Who?"

"Matvéitch Kirsanoff," he finished, as if he had not paused after the first name, Alexander; "but for Kirsanoff you would have died of consumption. You had an opportunity to deduce from this experience well-founded ideas as to the harmful character of the situation which you had occupied in society. And you deduced them. All that is very reasonable, but it by no means gave you the experience necessary to enable you to appreciate the character which it would be good for you to find in a husband. You do not want a rascal, but an honest man,—that is all that you have learned. Good. But should every honest woman be content, whatever the character of the man she may have chosen, provided he is honest? In such matters a better knowledge of characters and relationships is needed,—a wholly different experience. We decided yesterday that only widows should marry, to use your expression. What sort of a widow are you, then?"

Beaumont said all this with a sort of discontent, and in the last words there was almost a trace of spite.

"It is true," said Katérina Vassilievna, somewhat sadly, "but at any rate I have not deceived any one."

"And you would not have succeeded in doing so, for one cannot feign experience when one has it not."

"You are always talking of the insufficiency of the means afforded us, young girls, for making a well-grounded choice. As a general thing, that a choice may be well-grounded, no experience of this sort is necessary. If a young girl is not too young, she may know her own character very well. I, for instance, know mine, and it is evident that I shall not change. I am twenty-two years old. I know what I need in order to be happy: a tranquil life, with no one to disturb my peace, and that is all."

"Evidently you are right.

"Is it so difficult to tell whether these indispensable traits exist or not in the character of any given man? One can find it out from a few conversations."

"You are right. But you have said yourself that this is the exception and not the rule."

"Certainly it is not the rule, M. Beaumont; given our conditions of life, our ideas, and our customs, one cannot desire for a young girl this knowledge of everyday relations, this knowledge of which we say that, if it is lacking, the young girl runs a great risk of making a bad choice. Under her present conditions there is no way out of her situation. These conditions once given, whatever relations she may enter into, she cannot derive the necessary experience from them except in very rare cases; it would be useless to wait for it, and the danger is great. The young girl might, indeed, easily stoop and learn dissimulation. She would have to deceive her parents and the world, or hide herself from them, which is the next thing to deceit; and this would decidedly lower her character. It is very probable also that she would view life far too lightly. And if that did not happen, if she did not become bad, her heart would be broken. And yet she would gain almost no experience of actual life, because these relations, either so dangerous to her character or so painful to her heart, are never more than relations of appearance, not at all the relations of every-day life. You see that that would not be at all advisable, considering our present way of living."

"Certainly, Katérina Vassilievna; but that is just why our present way of living is bad."

"Surely; we are in accord on that point. What does it mean, in fact? Saying nothing of the confusion of general ideas, what is its significance in personal relations? The man says: 'I doubt whether you would make me a good wife.' And the young girl answers: 'No, I beg of you, make me a proposal.' Unheard-of insolence! Or perhaps that is not the way? Perhaps the man says: 'I have not so much as to consider whether I should be happy with you; but be prudent, even in choosing me. You have chosen me, but, I pray you, reflect, reflect again. It is much too serious a matter even in relation to me who love you much; do not give yourself up without a very rigid and systematic examination.' And perhaps the young girl answers: 'My friend, I see that you think, not of yourself, but of me. You are right in saying that we are pitiful beings; that men deceive us and lead us into error with bandaged eyes. But have no fear on my account: *I* am sure that *you* are not deceiving me. My happiness is sure. As tranquil as you are on your account, so tranquil am I on mine.'"

"I am astonished only at this," continued Beaumont the next day (they were again walking through the rooms, in one of which was Polosoff): "I am astonished only at this,—that under such conditions there are still some happy unions."

"You speak as if you were displeased that there are any," said Katérina Vassilievna, laughing. Now it became very evident that she laughed often, with a gay and gentle laugh.

"And indeed they may lead you to sad thoughts: if, with such inadequate means of judging of the needs and characteristics of men, young girls still know enough to make a tolerably happy choice, what lucidity and sagacity that argues in the feminine mind! With what clear, strong, and just mental vision woman is endowed by nature! And yet it remains useless to society, which rejects it, crushes it, stifles it; if this were not the case, if her mind were not compressed, if such a great quantity of moral power were not destroyed, humanity would progress ten times more rapidly."

"You are a panegyrist of women, M. Beaumont; may not all this be explained more simply by chance?"

"Chance! explain what you will by chance; when cases are numerous, they are the result of a general cause. No other explanation of this fact can be given than a well-weighed choice proportional in its wisdom to the mental intensity and perspicacity of the young girls."

"You reason on the question of women like Mrs. Beecher Stowe, M. Beaumont. She demonstrates that the negro race is endowed with greater intellect than the white race."

"You jest, but I am not jesting at all."

"You do not like it because I do not bow before woman? But consider at least as an extenuating circumstance the difficulty that there is in kneeling before one's self."

"You are jesting; it annoys me seriously."

"You are not annoyed with me, I hope? If women and young girls cannot do that which, in your opinion, is indispensable to them, it is not at all my fault. But I am going to give you my serious opinion, if you wish it, not, however, upon the woman question,—I do not care to be judge in my own cause,—but simply upon yourself, M. Beaumont. You, by nature, are a man of great self-control, and you get angry when you talk upon this question. What does this mean?

That you probably have had some personal experience in connection with it. Probably you have been the victim of what you consider an inexperienced young girl's erroneous choice."

"Perhaps myself, or perhaps some relative of mine. Nevertheless, think about this, Katérina Vassilievna. I will tell you, after I have received your reply. In three days I will ask you to give me a reply."

"To a question which is not formulated? Do I know you so little that I need to reflect for three days?"

Katérina Vassilievna stopped, placed her hand upon Beaumont's neck, bent the young man's head towards her, and kissed him on the forehead.

According to all precedents, and even according to the demands of common politeness, Beaumont ought to have embraced her and kissed her lips; but he did not; he only pressed the hand which had been thrown around him. "Very well, Katérina Vassilievna, but think about it, nevertheless." And they began to walk again.

"But who told you, Charlie, that I have not been thinking about it for much more than three days?" she answered, still holding his hand.

"Of course I saw it clearly. So I-will tell you all forthwith; it is a secret; let us go into the other room and sit down, that we may not be overheard."

They said these last words as they passed by the old man: he, seeing them walking arm in arm, which had never happened before, said to himself: "He has asked her hand, and she has given him her word. Good!"

"Tell your secret, Charlie; here papa will not hear us."

"It seems ridiculous, Katérina Vassilievna, to appear to have fears on your account; certainly there is nothing to fear. But you will understand why I put you on your guard in this matter when I tell you of the experience through which I have passed. Certainly we might both have lived together. But I pitied her. How much she suffered, and of how many years of the life that she needed was she deprived! It is very sad. It matters little where the thing occurred,—say New York, Boston, Philadelphia, or where you will. She was an excellent person and looked upon her husband as an excellent man. They were extremely attached to each other. And yet she must have suffered much. He was ready to give his head to procure for his wife the slightest additional happiness. And yet she could not be happy with him. Fortunately it ended as it did. But it was painful to her. You do not know this, and that is why I have not yet your final answer."

"Can I have heard this story from any one?"

"May be."

"From herself, perhaps?"

"May be."

"I have not yet given you an answer?"

"No."

"You know it."

"I know it," said Beaumont, and the ordinary scene that occurs between lovers began with ardent embraces.

XIX.

The next day at three o'clock Katérina Vassilievna called at Véra Pavlovna's.

"I am to marry day after tomorrow, Véra Pavlovna," said she, as she came in, "and tonight I will bring my sweetheart to see you."

"Undoubtedly it is Beaumont, over whom you have been mad so long."

"I? Mad? When all has happened so simply?"

"I am willing to believe that you have acted simply with him, but with me nothing of the sort."

"Really? That is curious. But here is something more curious still: he loves you much, both of you, but you, Véra Pavlovna, he loves even much more than Alexander Matvéitch."

"What is there curious about that? If you have spoken to him of me with a thousandth part of the enthusiasm with which you have spoken to me of him, it is needless to say" . . . .

"You think that he knows you through me? That's just the point; it is not through me, but through himself that he knows you, and much better than I do."

"That's news! How is that?"

"How? I will tell you at once. Since the first day of his arrival at St. Petersburg, he has wanted very much to see you, but it seemed to him that he would do better to postpone your acquaintance until he could come, not alone, but with his sweetheart or his wife. It seemed to him that it would be more agreeable to you to see him in this way. So you see that our marriage has arisen out of his desire to make your acquaintance."

"He marries you to make my acquaintance?"

"Marries me! Who said that he marries me for your sake? Oh, no, it is not for love of you that we are to marry. But when he came to St. Petersburg, did either of us know of the other's existence? And if he had not come, how could we have known each other? Now, he came to St. Petersburg on your account. Do you begin to see?"

"He speaks Russian better than English, you say?" asked Véra Pavlovna, with emotion.

"Russian as well as I do, and English as well as I do."

"Katennka, dear friend, how happy I am!"

Véra Pavlovna began to embrace her visitor.

"Sacha, come here! Quick! Quick!"

"What is the matter, Vérotchka? How do you do, Katérina Vass" . . . .

He had not time to pronounce her name before the visitor embraced him. "It is Easter today, Sacha; so say to Katenuka: 'He is risen indeed.'"* "But what is the matter with you?" "Sit down, and she will tell us; I myself know almost nothing as yet. It is enough to embrace you,—and in my presence, too! Say on, Katenuka."

XX.

In the evening the excitement was certainly still greater. But, when order was restored, Beaumont, on the demand of his new acquaintances, told them the story of his life, beginning with his arrival in the United States. "As soon as I arrived," said he, "I was careful to do everything necessary to enable me to speedily become a citizen. To that end I had to connect myself with some party. With which one? The abolitionists, of course. I wrote some articles for the 'Tribune' on the influence of serfdom on the entire social organization of Russia. This was a new argument, of considerable value to the abolitionists, against slavery in the Southern States, and in consequence I became a citizen of Massachusetts.† Soon after my arrival, still through the influence of the abolitionists, I obtained a place in one of their few business houses in New York." Then came the story that we already know. This part of Beaumont's biography, then, is beyond doubt.

XXI.

It was agreed that the two families should look for two suites of rooms next to each other. Until convenient suites could be found and prepared, the Beaumonts lived in the factory, in which, in accordance with the orders of the house, a suite had been arranged for the manager. This retreat into the suburbs might be looked upon as corresponding to the trip which newly-married couples make, in accordance with an excellent English custom, which is now spreading throughout Europe.

When, six weeks later, two convenient suites next to each other had been found, the Kirsanoffs went to live in one, the Beaumonts in the other, and the old Polosoff preferred to remain in the factory suite, the extent of which reminded him, if only feebly, of his past grandeur. It was agreeable to him to remain there for the

---

* During the Easter festivities the Orthodox, when they meet, embrace each other three times, one of them saying at the same time, "Christ is risen," whereupon the other responds, "He is risen indeed."

† Tchernychewsky's ideas of the method by which foreigners acquire citizenship in America are novel. His error, however, probably will not be considered a vital one except by the reader with the penetrating eye. — *Translator.*

additional reason that he was the most important personage for two or three miles around: innumerable marks of consideration were shown him, not only by his own clerks and commissioners, but by those of the neighborhood and by the rest of the suburban population, some of whom were beneath and some slightly above the former in social position. And it was with immense pleasure that he received, after the manner of a patriarch, these marks of respectful consideration. The son-in-law came to the factory every morning, and almost every day Katia with him. In summer they went (as they still do) to live entirely in the factory, which thus serves as a country-house. During the rest of the year the old man, besides receiving every morning his daughter and his son-in-law (who does not cease to be a North American), has the pleasure of receiving once a week and oftener visitors coming to spend the evening with Katérina Vassilievna and her husband, or the Kirsanoffs with some other young people, or an even more numerous company: the factory is made the objective point of frequent suburban excursions by the acquaintances of the Kirsanoffs and the Beaumonts. Polosoff is made very contented by all these visits, and how could it be otherwise? To him belongs the *rôle* of host, the patriarchal *rôle*.

XXII.

Each of the two families lives after its own fashion, according to its own fancy. On ordinary days in one there is more stir, in the other more tranquillity. They visit each other like relatives; one day more than ten times, but for one or two minutes at a time; another day one of the suites is empty almost all day, its inhabitants being in the other. There is no rule about this. Nor is there any rule when a number of visitors happen to come: now the door between the two suites remains closed (the door between the two parlors is generally closed, only the door between Véra Pavlovna's room and Katérina Vassilievna's being always open) — now, when the company is not numerous, the door connecting the reception rooms remains closed; at another time, when the number is greater, this door is open, and then the visitors do not realize where they are, whether at Véra Pavlovna's or at Katérina Vassilievna's, and the latter hardly know themselves. This might perhaps be affirmed: when the young people wish to sit down, it is almost always at Katérina Vassilievna's; when their inclination is to the contrary, they are almost always at Véra Pavlovna's. But the young people cannot be looked upon as visitors: they are at home, and Véra Pavlovna drives them away without ceremony to Katérina Vassilievna's.

"You tire me, gentlemen; go and see Katenuka; you never tire her. And why do you behave yourselves more quietly when with her than when with me? I am even a little the older."

"Do not worry yourself; we like her better than you."

"Katenuka, why do they like you better than me?"

"Katérina Vassilievna treats us like serious men, and that is why we are serious with her."

A device which was very effective was often made use of last winter in their narrow circle, when the young people and their most intimate friends came together: they placed the two pianos back to back: the young people, by drawing lots, divided themselves into two choruses, made their protectresses sit down one at each piano, opposite each other, and then each chorus placed itself behind its prima donna, and they sang at the same time, Véra Pavlovna and her forces *La donna è mobile* or some song from Béranger's *Lisette*, and Katérina Vassilievna and her forces *Depuis longtemps repoussé par toi* or *La chanson pour Iérœmouchka*.* But this winter another amusement was in fashion; the two women had reorganized in common, in conformity with their habits, "the discussion of the Greek philosophers concerning the beautiful"; it begins thus: Katérina Vassilievna, raising her eyes to heaven, says, with a languishing sigh: "Divine Schiller, intoxication of my soul!" Véra Pavlovna replies, with dignity: "But the prunella boots from Koroloff's store are beautiful also," and she advances her foot. Whichever of the young people laughs at this controversy is put in a corner. Towards the end of the controversy, of the ten or twelve individuals there remain but two or three who are not doing penance. But the gayety was at its height when they inveigled Beaumont into this play and sent him into a corner.

What else? The workshops continue to exist and to work in closer concert; now there are three of them; Katérina Vassilievna organized hers long ago, and now very often acts as a substitute for Véra Pavlovna in the latter's shop; soon she will take her place entirely, for in the course of this year Véra Pavlovna—forgive her for it—will pass her medical examination, and then she will have no more time to give to the shop. "It is a pity that the development of these shops is impossible; how they would grow!" sometimes said Véra Pavlovna. Katérina Vassilievna made no answer; only her eyes flashed with hatred.

"How headlong you are, Katia! You are worse than I am," said Véra Pavlovna. "It is fortunate that your father has something left."

"Yes, Vérotchka, one feels easier about her child." (Then she has a child.)

"But you have set me dreaming about I know not what. Our life will go on gently and tranquilly."

Katérina Vassilievna made no answer.

"Yes, why don't you say yes to me?"

Katérina Vassilievna smiled as she answered:

"It does not depend on my 'yes' or my 'no'; therefore to please you I will say: 'Yes, our life shall go on tranquilly.'"

---

* By Nekrassoff, the most famous Russian poet.

And indeed they do live tranquilly. They live in harmony and amicably, in a gentle yet active fashion, in a joyous and reasonable fashion. But it does not at all follow from this that my story about them is finished; by no means. All four are still young and active, and, though their life is ordered as above described, it has not ceased on that account to be interesting; far from it. I still have much to tell you about them, and I guarantee that the sequel to my story will be much more interesting than anything that I have yet told you.

XXIII.

They live gayly and as friends, working and resting, enjoying life and looking forward to the future, if not without anxiety, at least with the firm assurance that the farther we advance in life, the better it becomes. Thus they have spent the last two years. Towards the end of last winter Véra Pavlovna said to herself: "Will there be another cold day, so that we can have at least one more sleighing-party?" No one could answer her question; but the days went by one after another, and the thaw continued, and every day the chances for a sleighing-party diminished. But it came after they had lost all hope. There was a heavy fall of snow, followed, not by a thaw, but by slightly freezing weather; the sky was clear, and the evening could not have been more beautiful. "The sleighing-party! The sleighing-party!" In their haste they had not time to get many people together, — a small party collected without formal invitations.*

That night two sledges started. In one they chattered and joked, in the other all the proprieties were disregarded. Scarcely were they out of the city before they began to sing at the tops of their voices. What?

> Elle sortait la belle
> (The fair one went out)
> De la porte cochère neuve,
> (Of the new carriage gate)
> De la neuve porte cochère en bois d'érable,
> (Of the new carriage gate of maple wood)
> De la porte cochère à carreaux.
> (Of the tiled carriage gate)
> Mon père est bien sévère;
> (My father is very severe)
> Il m'est défavorable;
> (He is disinclined to favor me)

---

* The few pages which follow, in conclusion of this story, the translator does not pretend to understand. He cannot identify the new characters introduced or connect them with the story, nor can he fathom the purpose of their introduction. Whether they conceal some moral so revolutionary that the author from his prison cell did not dare avow it more openly, or whether the mystery is a device on his part to carry over the interest of the reader to the sequel which he undoubtedly intended to write, or whether the true explanation is something different from either of these, the reader must determine for himself. — *Translator.*

Il ne veut pas que je me promène trop tard
(He does not want me to be out too late)
Et que je joue avec les jeunes hommes.
(And to play with the young men)
Mais je n'écoute pas mon père;
(But I do not listen to my father)
Je veux satisfaire mon bien aimé . . . .
(I wish to please my beloved)

A song! But is that all? Now this sledge goes slowly and lags nearly a quarter of a mile in the rear; suddenly it glides rapidly ahead, its occupants give warlike shouts, and when they approach the well-behaved party, the snowballs fly furiously. The members of the well-behaved party, after two or three attacks of this sort, decide to defend themselves and lay in a stock of ammunition, but it is done so adroitly as to escape the notice of the noisy party. Now the noisy party goes slowly again, lagging behind, and the well-behaved party continues cunningly on its way. The noisy party again starts off at full speed, the warlike shouts begin once more, the members of the well-behaved party are prepared to make unexpected and vigorous resistance, but what? the noisy party turns to the right across the brook, and passes like a flash at a distance of a dozen yards.

"She saw us and has taken the reins herself," say some in the well-behaved party.

"Oh, no! oh, no! we will catch them! we will avenge ourselves!"

An infernal gallop. Will they catch them?

"We will catch them!"

No!

"We will catch them!" with fresh impetuosity.

"They will catch us!"

"They shall not catch us!"

Yes!

No!

In the well-behaved party were the Kirsanoffs and the Beaumonts; in the noisy party four young people and a lady, and the latter was the cause of all the mad conduct of the noisy party.

"Good evening, ladies and gentlemen, we are very glad to see you again," said she, from the top of the factory steps: "gentlemen, help the ladies out of the sledge," she added, addressing her companions.

Quickly, quickly, into the rooms! All of them were red with cold.

"Good evening, old gentleman. But he is not old at all! Katérina Vassilievna, why did you slander him by telling me that he was old? He will be courting me yet. You will court me, dear old man?" said the lady of the noisy party.

"Yes, I will court you," said Polosoff, already charmed by her affable caresses of his gray whiskers.

"Children, will you permit him to court me?"

New Characters and the Conclusion.

"We permit him," said one of the young people.

"No, no," said the three others.

But why was the lady of the noisy party in black? For mourning or out of caprice?

"But, after all, I am tired," said she, throwing herself upon a divan, in a corner of the reception room. "Children, some cushions! but not for me alone; the other ladies also are tired."

"Yes, you have harassed us," said Katérina Vassilievna.

"How this unbridled race in the ruts has tired me!" said Véra Pavlovna.

"Fortunately we had but a little over half a mile to go," said Katérina Vassilievna.

Unable to stand any longer, they fell on the divan stuffed with cushions.

"How unskilled you are! You should have risen up as I did, and then the ruts would not have tired you."

"We are tired ourselves," said Kirsanoff, speaking for himself and Beaumont. They sat down beside their wives. Kirsanoff embraced Véra Pavlovna; Beaumont took the hand of Katérina Vassilievna. An idyllic picture. It is pleasant to see happy unions. But over the face of the lady in black a sudden shadow passed, which no one noticed except one of her companions; he withdrew to the window and began to examine the arabesques which the frost had traced upon the panes.

"Ladies, your histories are very interesting, but I do not know them exactly; I only know that they are touching and pleasant and end happily; that is what I like. But where is the old gentleman?"

"He is busy about the house, getting us something to eat; he is fond of that sort of thing," said Katérina Vassilievna.

"Well, let him go on. Relate your histories, then, but let them be brief: I like short stories."

"I will be very brief," said Véra Pavlovna. "I begin: when the others' turns come, they will be brief also. But I warn you that at the end of my story there are secrets."

"Well, then we will drive these gentlemen away. Or, would it not be better to drive them away now?"

"Why? Now they may listen."

Véra Pavlovna began her story.

. . . .

"Ha, ha, ha! That dear Julie! I like her very much. And she throws herself upon her knees, says insulting things, and behaves most improperly, the dear Julie!"

. . . .

"Bravo, Véra Pavlovna! 'I will throw myself out of the window!' Bravo, gentlemen!" The lady in black began to applaud. At this command the young people imitated her in a deafening manner and cried "Bravo!" and "Hurrah!"

. . . .

"What's the matter with you? What's the matter with you?" cried Katérina Vassilievna, in fright, two or three minutes later.

"Nothing, it's nothing: give me some water, do not be troubled."

Mossoloff is already bringing some.

"Thank you, Mossoloff."

She takes the glass, brought by the young companion who had withdrawn to the window.

"See how I have taught him! He knows everything in advance. Now it has entirely passed. Keep on, I pray you, I am listening."

"No, I am fatigued," said she, five minutes later, rising calmly from the divan. I must rest, — sleep an hour or an hour and a half. See, I am going away without ceremony. Go and find the old gentleman, Mossoloff; let him prepare everything."

"Permit me, why should I not attend to it?" said Katérina Vassilievna.

"Is it worth while to trouble yourself?"

"You abandon us?" said a young man, assuming a tragic posture; "if we had foreseen that, we would have brought some daggers with us. Now we have nothing with which to stab ourselves."

"They will bring something to eat, and then we can stab ourselves with the forks!" said another, in a tone of exaltation.

"Oh, no, I do not wish the hope of the country to be cut off in its flower," said the lady in black, with like solemnity: "console yourselves, my children. Mossoloff, a cushion on the table!"

Mossoloff placed a cushion on the table. The lady in black assumed a majestic pose near the table and let her hand slowly fall upon the cushion.

The young people kissed her hand, and Katérina Vassilievna escorted the tired visitor to the bed.

"Poor woman!" said with one voice the three persons of the well-behaved party after they had gone out of the room.

"She is brave!" exclaimed the three young people.

"I believe you!" said Mossoloff, with satisfaction.

"Have you known her long?"

"Almost three years."

"And do you know him well?"

"Very well. Do not be troubled, I beg," he added, addressing the members of the well-behaved party: "it is only because she is tired."

Véra Pavlovna cast an interrogative glance at her husband and at Beaumont, and shook her head.

"Tired? You are telling us tales," said Kirsanoff.

"I assure you. She is tired, that's all. She will sleep, and it will all pass over," repeated Mossoloff in an indifferent and tranquil tone.

Ten minutes later Katérina Vassilievna returned.

"Well?" asked six voices. Mossoloff asked no question.

"She went to bed, began at once to doze, and probably is now fast asleep."

"Didn't I tell you so?" observed Mossoloff. "It is nothing."

"She is to be pitied, nevertheless," said Katérina Vassilievna. "Let us keep separate in her presence. You stay with me, Vérotchka, and Charlie with Sacha."

"But we need not trouble ourselves now," said Mossoloff, " we can sing, dance, shout; she is sleeping profoundly."

If she was asleep, if it was nothing, why should they trouble themselves? The impression made by the lady in black, which had disturbed their peace for a quarter of an hour, passed away, disappeared, was forgotten, not quite, but nearly. The evening gradually became what former similar evenings had been, and soon gayety reigned.

Gayety not unmixed, however; five or six times the ladies looked at each other with an expression of fear and sadness. Twice, perhaps, Véra Pavlovna said furtively in her husband's ear: "Sacha, if that should happen to me?" The first time Kirsanoff made no answer; the second he said: "No, Vérotchka, that cannot happen to you."

"Cannot? Are you sure?"

"Yes."

And Katérina Vassilievna also furtively said twice in her husband's ear:

"That cannot happen to me, Charlie, can it?"

The first time Beaumont only smiled in a half-hearted and not very reassuring manner; the second he answered:

"In all probability that cannot happen to you."

But these were only passing echoes, and were heard only at the beginning. But in general the evening went off joyously, and half an hour later quite gayly. They chattered and played and sang.

"She sleeps profoundly," Mossoloff assured them, and he set the example. In truth they could not trouble her sleep, because the room where she was lying down was a long distance from the drawing-room, three rooms away at the other end of the suite.

Therefore the evening's revelry was completely restored.

The young people, as usual, now joined the others, now separated from them; now in a body, now not; twice Beaumont had joined them; twice Véra Pavlovna had turned them away from Beaumont and from all serious conversation.

They babbled a great deal; a great deal too much; they also discussed things together, but much less.

All were together.

"Well, what is there of good or evil?" asked the young man who a little while before had assumed a tragic attitude.

"More evil than good," said Véra Pavlovna.

"Why so, Vérotchka?" said Katérina Vassilievna.

"At any rate life does not go on without it," said Beaumont.

"An inevitable thing," affirmed Kirsanoff.

"Altogether evil,—that is, very good," decided he who had started the question. His three companions nodded their heads, and said: "Bravo, Nikitine!"

The young people were by themselves.

"I never knew him, Nikitine; but you seem to have known him?" said Mossoloff, inquiringly.

"I was then a mere boy. I saw him."

"How do your memories seem to you? Do they tell the truth? Do they not exaggerate through friendship?"

"No."

"Has no one seen him since?"

"No. Beaumont was then in America."

"Indeed! Karl Iakovlitch, I beg your attention for a moment. Did you not meet in America this Russian of whom they have been talking?"

"No."

"What caprice has entered my head?" said Nikitine: "he and she would make a good pair."

"Gentlemen, come and sing with me," said Véra Pavlovna. "Two volunteers! So much the better."

Mossoloff and Nikitine remained by themselves.

"I can show you a curious thing, Nikitine," said Mossoloff. "Do you think she is asleep?"

"No."

"Only you must say nothing about it. Afterwards, when you know her better, you can tell her that you saw her. But no one else. She does not like that."

The windows of the room were raised a little.

"It certainly is the window where the light is."

Mossoloff glanced in that direction.

"Yes, do you see?"

The lady in black was sitting in an easy chair, near the table. With her left elbow she was leaning on the table; her hand lightly sustained her bowed head, covering her temple and a part of her hair. Her right hand was placed on the table, and her fingers rose and fell mechanically, as if playing some air. The lady's face wore an immovable expression of reverie, sad, but still severe. Her eyebrows came together and slightly parted again, and *vice versa*.

"Always this way, Mossoloff?"

"Do you see? But come; else we shall take cold. We have been here a quarter of an hour."

"How unfeeling you are!" said Nikitine, looking steadily at his companion, when they passed by the reflector in the ante-room.

"By constantly feeling one becomes unfeeling, my dear. To you it is a novelty."

The refreshments were brought in.

"The brandy must be very good," said Nikitine; "but how strong it is! It takes one's breath away!"

"What a little girl! Your eyes are red!" said Mossoloff.

Everybody began to make fun of Nikitine.

"Oh! that's only because I am choked up; were it not for that, I could drink," said he, in self-justification.

They took note of the time. It was only eleven o'clock; therefore they could chatter half an hour longer; there was time enough.

Half an hour later Katérina Vassilievna went to awaken the lady in black. The lady came to meet her on the threshold, stretching as if she had just been asleep.

"Did you sleep well?"

"Perfectly."

"How do you feel?"

"Marvellously well. I told you before that it was nothing. I was tired, because I had been acting so wildly. Now I shall be more prudent."

But no, she did not succeed in being prudent. Five minutes later she had already charmed Polosoff, was giving orders to the young people, and drumming a march or something of the sort with the handles of two forks on the table. At the same time she was urging a departure, while the others, whom her sauciness had already made quite gay, were not in such a hurry.

"Are the horses ready?" she asked, after having eaten.

"Not yet; the order to harness them has just been given."

"Unendurable! But if that is the case, sing us something, Véra Pavlovna: I have heard that you have a fine voice."

Véra Pavlovna sang.

"I shall ask you to sing often," said the lady in black.

"It is your turn, it is your turn," they cried on all sides.

The words were no sooner uttered than she was at the piano.

"All right! I do not know how to sing, but to me that is no obstacle! But, ladies and gentlemen, it is not at all for you that I sing; I sing only for my children. Children, do not laugh at your mother!"

She improvised a few strains on the piano by way of prelude.

"Children, do not laugh; I shall sing with expression."

And, with a squeaking voice, she began to sing:

>Un pigeon moiré . . . .
>(A watered dove)

The young people shouted in surprise and the rest of the company began to laugh, and the singer herself could not help laughing too; but, after stifling her laughter, she continued, in a voice that squeaked twice as much as before:

>. . . . Gémissait,
>(Wailed)
>Gémissait la nuit et le jour;
>(Wailed night and day)
>Il appelait son cher a——
>(He called his dear l——)

At this word her voice trembled and at once failed her.

"It does not come; so much the better, it ought not to come; something else will come to me; listen, my children, to the teaching of your mother: do not fall in love, and be sure that you do not marry."

She began to sing in a full, strong contralto:

>Il y a bien des beautés dans nos aoules;
>(There are many beauties in our Caucasian villages)
>Des astres brillent dans la profondeur de leurs yeux;
>(Stars shine in the depths of their eyes)
>Il est bien doux de les aimer, oui, c'est un grand bonheur;
>(It is very sweet to love them, yes, it is a great happiness)
>Mais . . . .
>(But)

this is a stupid "but," my children, —

>Mais la liberté de garçon est plus joyeuse.
>(But the bachelor's liberty is more joyous)

this is no reason, — this reason is stupid, — and you shall know why:

>Ne te marie pas, jeune homme,
>(Do not marry, young man)
>Ecoute-moi!
>(Listen to me)

"Farther on comes a piece of nonsense, my children; this too is nonsense, if you like: one may, my children, both fall in love and marry, but only by choice, and without deceit, without deceit, my children. I am going to sing to you of the way in which I was married; the romance is an old one, but I also am old. I am sitting on a balcony in our castle of Dalton; I am a fair-skinned Scotchwoman; the forest and the Bringale River are before me; some one stealthily approaches the balcony; it is certainly my sweetheart; he is poor, and I am rich, the daughter of a baron, a lord; but I love him much, and I sing to him:

> La raide côte de Bringale est belle,
> (The steep hill of Bringale is beautiful)
> Et verte est la forêt autour,
> (And green is the forest around)
> Où mon ami et moi trouvons notre asile du jour,
> (Where my friend and I find our retreat by day)

for I know that in the daytime he hides and changes his retreat every day,

> Asile plus chéri que la maison paternelle.
> (A retreat dearer than the paternal roof)

For that matter, the paternal roof was not indeed very dear. So I sing to him: I will go with you. How do you think he answers me?

> Tu veux, vierge, être mienne,
> (You wish, virgin, to be mine)
> Oublier ta naissance et ta dignité;
> (To forget your birth and your dignity)

for I am of high birth,—

> Mais d'abord devine
> (But first guess)
> Quel est mon sort.
> (What my lot is)

"You are a hunter?" I say. "No." "You are a poacher?" "You have almost guessed it," he says.

> Quand nous nous rassemblerons, enfants des ténèbres,
> (When we shall gather, children of darkness)

for we, ladies and gentlemen, are children of very bad subjects,—

> Il nous faudra, crois-moi,
> (It will be necessary for us, believe me)
> Oublier qui nous étions d'abord,
> (To forget who we were at first)
> Oublier qui nous sommes maintenant,
> (To forget who we are now)

he sings. "I guessed long ago," I say; "you are a brigand." And it is really the truth, he is a brigand, — yes, he is a brigand. What does he say then, gentlemen? "You see, I am a bad sweetheart for you."

> O vierge, je ne suis pas l'homme digne de tes vœux;
> (O virgin, I am not a man worthy of your vows)
> J'habite les forêts épaisses;
> (I dwell in the thick forests)

that is the absolute truth, — "thick forests"; so he tells me not to accompany him.

> Périlleuse sera ma vie,
> (Perilous will be my life)

for in the thick forests there are wild beasts, —

> Et ma fin sera bien triste.
> (And my end will be very sad)

That is not true, my children; it will not be sad; but then I believed it, and he believed it too; nevertheless I answer him in the same way:

> La raide côte de Bringale est belle,
> (The steep hill of Bringale is beautiful)
> Et verte est la forêt autour,
> (And green is the forest around)
> Où mon ami et moi trouvons notre asile du jour,
> (Where my friend and I find our retreat by day)
> Asile plus chéri que la maison paternelle.
> (A retreat dearer than the paternal roof)

Indeed, so it was. Therefore I could regret nothing: he had told me where I was to go. Thus one may marry, one may love, my children, — without deceit and knowing well how to choose.

> La lune se lève
> (The moon rises)
> Lente et tranquille,
> (Slowly and peacefully)
> Et le jeune guerrier
> (And the young warrior)
> Se prépare au combat.
> (Prepares for the combat)
> Il charge son fusil,
> (He loads his gun)
> Et la vierge lui dit:
> (And the virgin says to him)
> "Avec audace, mon amour,
> (Boldly, my love)
> Confie-toi à ta destinée."
> (Entrust yourself to your destiny)

With such women one may fall in love, and one may marry them."

("Forget what I said to you, Sacha; listen to her!" whispers one of the women, pressing his hand.—"Why did I not say that to you? Now I will speak of it to you," whispers the other.)

"I allow you to love such women, and I bless you, my children:

> Avec audace, cher amour,
> (Boldly, dear love)
> Confie-toi à ta destinée.
> (Entrust yourself to your destiny)

I have grown quite gay with you; now, wherever there is gayety, there should be drinking.

> Hé! ma cabaretière,
> (Ho! my hostess)
> Verse-moi de l'hydromel et du vin,
> (Pour me some mead and wine)

Mead, because the word cannot be thrown out of the song. Is there any champagne left? Yes? Perfect! Open it.

> Hé! ma cabaretière,
> (Ho! my hostess)
> Verse-moi de l'hydromel et du vin,
> (Pour me some mead and wine)
> Pour que ma tête
> (That my head)
> Soit gaie!
> (May be gay)

Who is the hostess? Me:

> Et la cabaretière a des sourcils noirs
> (And the hostess has black eyebrows)
> Et des talons ferrés!
> (And iron heels)

She rose suddenly, passed her hand over her eyebrows, and stamped with her heels.

"Poured! Ready! Ladies and gentlemen, you, old man, and you, my children, take it and drink it, that your heads may be gay!"

"To the hostess, to the hostess!"

"Thanks! to my health!"

She sits down again at the piano and sings:

> Que le chagrin vole en éclats!
> (Let sorrow fly away in shouts)

and it will fly away,—

> Et dans des cœurs rajeunis
> (And into rejuvenated hearts)
> Que l'inaltérable joie descende!
> (Let unalterable joy descend)

and so it will, probably.

La sombre peur fuit comme un ombre,
(Dark fear flees like a shadow)
Des rayons qui apportent le jour,
(Rays that bring the day)
La lumière, la chaleur, et les parfums printaniers
(Light, warmth, and the spring perfumes)
Chassent vite les ténèbres et le froid ;
(Quickly drive away the darkness and cold)
L'odeur de la pourriture diminue,
(The odor of decay diminishes)
L'odeur de la rose croît sans cesse.
(The odor of the rose ever increases)

CHAPTER SIXTH.

Change of Scene.

"*Au passage!*" said the lady in black to the coachman, though now she was no longer in black: a light dress, a pink hat, a white mantilla, and a bouquet in her hand. She was no longer with Mossoloff alone: Mossoloff and Nikitine were on the front seat of the barouche; on the coachman's seat was a youth; and beside the lady sat a man of about thirty. How old was the lady? Was she twenty-five, as she said, instead of twenty only? But if she chose to make herself old, that was a matter for her own conscience.

"Yes, my dear friend, I have been expecting this day for more than two years. At the time when I made his acquaintance (she indicated Nikitine with her eyes), I only had a presentiment; it could not then be said that I expected; then there was only hope, but soon came assurance."

"Permit me!" says the reader,—and not only the reader with the penetrating eye, but every reader,—becoming more stupefied the more he reflects: "more than two years after she had made Nikitine's acquaintance?"

"Yes."

"But she made Nikitine's acquaintance at the same time that she made that of the Kirsanoffs and the Beaumonts, at the sleighing-party which took place towards the end of last winter."

"You are perfectly right."

"What does this mean, then? You are talking of the beginning of the year 1865?"

"Yes."

"But how is that possible, pray?"

"Why not, if I know it?"

"Nonsense! who will listen to you?"

"You will not?"

"What do you take me for? Certainly not."

"If you will not listen to me now, it is needless to say that I must postpone the sequel of my story until you will deign to listen. I hope to see that day ere long."

April 4 (16), 1863.

THE END.

LIBERTY.

A FORTNIGHTLY ORGAN OF ANARCHISTIC SOCIALISM.

THE PIONEER OF ANARCHY IN AMERICA.

BENJ. R. TUCKER, ... Editor and Publisher.
A. P. KELLY, ... Associate Editor.

ONE DOLLAR A YEAR.

LIBERTY numbers among its contributors many of the ablest radical and revolutionary writers in America, including Henry Appleton, Lysander Spooner, Gertrude B. Kelly, "Phillip" (formerly of the "Irish World"), Dyer D. Lum, Sarah E. Holmes, M. E. Lazarus ("Edgeworth"), J. Wm. Lloyd, C. M. Hammond, Victor Yarros, and numerous others.

LIBERTY insists on the sovereignty of the individual and the just reward of labor; on the abolition of the State and the abolition of usury; on no more government of man by man, and no more exploitation of man by man; on Anarchy and Equity.

LIBERTY's war-cry is "Down with Authority," and its chief battle with the State,—the State, that debases man; the State, that prostitutes woman; the State, that corrupts children; the State, that trammels love; the State, that stifles thought; the State, that monopolizes land; the State, that limits credit; the State, that restricts exchange; the State, that gives idle capital the power of increase, and, through interest, rent, profit, and taxes, robs industrious labor of its products.

LIBERTY prints frequent translations from the foremost revolutionary authors and leaders in France, Germany, and Russia.

Address: Liberty, P. O. Box 3366, Boston, Mass.

WHAT IS PROPERTY?

—OR,—

AN INQUIRY INTO THE PRINCIPLE OF RIGHT AND OF GOVERNMENT.

BY

P. J. PROUDHON.

Prefaced by a sketch of PROUDHON'S Life and Works, by J. A. LANGLOIS, and containing as a Frontispiece a Fine Steel Engraving of the Author.

Translated from the French by Benj. R. Tucker.

A systematic, thorough, and radical discussion of the institution of Property, — its basis, its history, its present status, and its destiny, — together with a detailed and startling *exposé* of the crimes which it commits and the evils which it engenders.

AN ELEGANT OCTAVO VOLUME OF 500 PAGES.

PRICE IN CLOTH, BEVELLED EDGES $3.50
PRICE IN FULL CALF, BLUE, GILT EDGES . . . 6.50

Sent, post-paid, by the Publisher,

BENJ. R. TUCKER, P. O. Box 3366, Boston, Mass.

GOD AND THE STATE.

BY

MICHAEL BAKOUNINE,

FOUNDER OF NIHILISM AND APOSTLE OF ANARCHY.

Translated from the French by

BENJ. R. TUCKER.

One of the most eloquent pleas for liberty ever written. Paine's "Age of Reason" and "Rights of Man" consolidated and improved. It stirs the pulse like a trumpet call. — New York Truth Seeker.

52 PAGES. PRICE, 15 CENTS.

Address the Publisher,

BENJ. R. TUCKER, P. O. Box 3366, Boston, Mass.

TRUE CIVILIZATION.

A SUBJECT OF VITAL AND SERIOUS INTEREST TO ALL PEOPLE, BUT MOST IMMEDIATELY TO THE MEN AND WOMEN OF LABOR AND SORROW.

BY

JOSIAH WARREN.

A pamphlet of 117 pages, now passing through its fifth edition, explaining the basic principles of Labor Reform, — Liberty and Equity.

PRICE, 30 CENTS.

Address the Publisher,

BENJ. R. TUCKER, P. O. Box 3366, Boston, Mass.

"*In many respects the best Anarchistic work produced in America.*" — E. C. WALKER.

CO-OPERATION.

I.—ITS LAWS AND PRINCIPLES.
By C. T. FOWLER.

A PAMPHLET of 28 pages, with a fine portrait of HERBERT SPENCER as a frontispiece; showing logically, vividly, and eloquently Liberty and Equity as the only conditions of true coöperation, and exposing the violations of these conditions by Rent, Interest, Profit, and Majority Rule.

II.—THE REORGANIZATION OF BUSINESS.
By C. T. FOWLER.

A PAMPHLET of 28 pages, with a fine portrait of RALPH WALDO EMERSON as a frontispiece; showing how the principles of coöperation may be realized in the Store, the Bank, and the Factory.

PROHIBITION:
OR,
THE RELATION OF GOVERNMENT TO TEMPERANCE.
By C. T. FOWLER.

A PAMPHLET of 28 pages; showing that prohibition cannot prohibit, and would be unnecessary if it could; that it promotes intemperance; and that it is but a phase of that paternalism which leads to imbecility and crime, as opposed to that equal liberty which leads to virtue and self-reliance.

Six Cents per Copy; Two Copies, Ten Cents.

Address: BENJ. R. TUCKER, Box 3366, Boston, Mass.

SOCIAL WEALTH:

THE SOLE FACTORS AND EXACT RATIOS IN ITS ACQUIREMENT AND APPORTIONMENT.
By J. K. INGALLS.

This handsome octavo volume of 320 pages treats of the usurpations of Capitalism, showing that Land and Labor are the only natural capital, or source of wealth; exposing the trick of treating variable and invariable values as one, and explaining the true *mean* of Value in Exchange; showing that in the production of wealth coöperation always exists, and opposing the fraudulent methods by which equitable division is defeated; exploding the "Taxation" and other "Remedies" for the wrongs done Industry proposed by George, Wallace, and Clark, and demonstrating that the scientific is the only safe method of investigation for the employer or the employed who seeks salutary reform.

PRICE, ONE DOLLAR.

Address: BENJ. R. TUCKER, Box 3366, Boston, Mass.

A POLITICIAN IN SIGHT OF HAVEN:

BEING A PROTEST AGAINST THE GOVERNMENT OF MAN BY MAN.

By AUBERON HERBERT.

PRICE, 10 CENTS.

Address the Publisher, BENJ. R. TUCKER, P. O. Box 3366, Boston, Mass.

LIBERTY'S LIBRARY.

For any of the following Works, address, BENJ. R. TUCKER, Box 3366, Boston, Mass.

THE WIND AND THE WHIRLWIND. A poem worthy of a place in every man's library, and especially interesting to all victims of British tyranny and misrule. By Wilfrid Scawen Blunt. A red-line edition, printed beautifully, in large type, on fine paper, and bound in parchment covers. Elegant and cheap. 32 pages. Price, 25 cents.

THE RADICAL REVIEW: Vol. 1., handsomely bound in cloth, and containing over sixty Essays, Poems, Translations, and Reviews, by the most prominent radical writers, on industrial, financial, social, literary, scientific, philosophical, ethical, and religious subjects. 828 pages octavo. Price, $5.00. Single numbers, $1.15.

THE FALLACIES IN "PROGRESS AND POVERTY." A bold attack on the position of Henry George. Written for the people, and as revolutionary in sentiment, and even more radical than "Progress and Poverty" itself. By William Hanson. 191 pages, cloth. Price, $1.00.

NATURAL LAW: or, the Science of Justice. A Treatise on Natural Law, Natural Justice, Natural Rights, Natural Liberty, and Natural Society, showing that all legislation whatsoever is an absurdity, a usurpation, and a crime. By Lysander Spooner. Price, 10 cents.

AN ANARCHIST ON ANARCHY. An eloquent exposition of the beliefs of Anarchists by a man as eminent in science as in reform. By Elisée Reclus. Followed by a sketch of the criminal record of the author by E. Vaughan. Price, 10 cents.

SO THE RAILWAY KINGS ITCH FOR AN EMPIRE, DO THEY? By a "Red-Hot Striker," of Scranton, Pa. A reply to an article by William M. Grosvenor in the *International Review*. Price, 10 cents; per hundred, $4.00.

INTERNATIONAL ADDRESS: An elaborate, comprehensive, and very entertaining Exposition of the principles of The Working-people's International Association. By William B. Greene. Price, 15 cents.

THE WORKING WOMEN: A letter to the Rev. Henry W. Foote, Minister of King's Chapel, in Vindication of the Poorer Class of Boston Working-Women. By William B. Greene. Price, 15 cents.

ANARCHISM OR ANARCHY? A Discussion between William R. Tillinghast and Benj. R. Tucker. Prefaced by an Open Letter to Rev. William J. Potter. Sent on receipt of a postage stamp.

A FEMALE NIHILIST. A thrilling sketch of the character and adventures of a typical Nihilistic heroine. By Stepniak, author of "Underground Russia." Price, 10 cents.

MUTUAL BANKING: Showing the Radical Deficiency of the existing Circulating Medium, and how Interest on Money can be Abolished. By William B. Greene. Price, 25 cents.

CAPTAIN ROLAND'S PURSE: How it is Filled and how Emptied. By John Ruskin. The first of a projected series of Labor Tracts. Supplied at 37 cents per hundred.

SOCIALISTIC, COMMUNISTIC, MUTUALISTIC, AND FINANCIAL Fragments. By William B. Greene. Price, $1.25.

PROSTITUTION AND THE INTERNATIONAL WOMAN'S League. By Henry Edger. Price, 15 cents.

WHAT IS FREEDOM, AND WHEN AM I FREE? By Henry Appleton. Price, 15 cents; two copies, 25 cents.

www.ingramcontent.com/pod-product-compliance
Lightning Source LLC
Chambersburg PA
CBHW021200230426
43667CB00006B/478